ANTUAN VANCE
DAKOTA

Smoking Rose
Publishing

DAKOTA is a work of fiction. Names, characters, businesses, places, events and incidents are either the products of the author's imagination or used in a fictitious manner. Any resemblance to actual persons, living or dead, or actual events is purely coincidental.

Copyright © 2018 Antuan J. Vance
Published in 2019 by Smoking Rose Publishing

All rights reserved. Neither this book, nor any portion thereof, may be reproduced, distributed, or transmitted in any form or by any means, including photocopying, recording, or other electronic or mechanical methods, without the prior written permission of the author or publisher, except in the case of brief quotations embodied in critical reviews and certain other noncommercial uses permitted by copyright law. Contact publisher at contact@smokingrosepublishing.com

Scripture quotations are from the ESV® Bible (The Holy Bible, English Standard Version®), copyright © 2001 by Crossway, a publishing ministry of Good News Publishers. Used by permission. All rights reserved.

Cover Photo by Guilherme Stecanella on Unsplash

ISBN-13: 978-1-7340095-0-7 (paperback)
ISBN-13: 978-1-7340095-1-4 (hard cover)
ISBN-13: 978-1-7340095-2-1 (e-book)

www.AntuanVance.com

To my mother and sister, thank you for loving me.

DAKOTA

CHAPTER ONE

"Guess who just got invited to a Halloween party?" Val popped out of nowhere and asked.

Carissa flinched and dropped her breakfast bar. It sailed to the floor in slow-motion and bounced on the waxed floor.

Son of a—

She groaned and counted the seconds. *One Mississippi. Two Mississippi.* Sigh. The five-second rule was tacky. Once it hit the floor, especially this floor, it was a goner.

Aww! That was my last strawberry-flavored one!

Carissa eyeballed Val. "What did I tell you about sneaking up on me?" She grabbed the contaminated breakfast bar, tossed it in her locker, let out a hard sigh, and shoved an AP Psych book in her bag.

"Sorry, I'm excited," Val said, a smile still on her face. She wasn't *truly* sorry, was she?

I bet, if she were hungry, she'd be a little sorrier.

"Guess who got invited to a Halloween party."

"Elton John," Carissa said as she zipped her bag and pulled it on her shoulders. She said goodbye to her fallen snack and closed the locker.

Val scrunched her nose. "Jesse just practically *begged* me to come. He said to bring a friend." She wiggled her eyebrows. "It's at the Bradshaw house."

"Uh, you mean the Bradshaw *mansion*?" Carissa clarified. According to Richmond's Elite magazine, the "house" was three stories and had six master bedrooms, each with its own bathroom, three guestrooms, one full bath, two half baths, a library, study, dining room, entertainment room, and family room. That was a mansion. "How'd he manage that?"

"He's friends with Kent," Val said. "Apparently, Kent's going here now. Something happened at his private school. Jesse didn't elaborate. I'll get it out of him later."

Smile. "Yea. I'm sure that's not all you'll get out of him."

You and I both know your track record.

Val smiled back. "A girl's got needs. You'll figure that out soon enough."

"Yea," Carissa said. "Kinda need a boyfriend first, right?"

"That's why you're my plus one, bee-atch."

Carissa laughed.

"Parties are full of guys hoping to maybe, hopefully, possibly, get some action," Val continued. "You're a walking dream come true for them."

Says the fit, blonde cheerleader who looks like the progeny of Sarah Michelle Gellar and Britney Spears.

"Never heard someone put it that way before."

"We're hot," Val said. "I'm hot. You're hot. We both know it. Check out this guy."

Some shaggy-haired, pimple-faced kid stared at them as he walked by.

"He couldn't take his eyes off us if a bull was chasing after him," Val said. Carissa snorted. "If you put yourself out there, you'll have a boyfriend."

But I don't want just any random guy. It has to be special.

"Yea, you're right," Carissa agreed.

"You're damn right, I'm right," Val said. "Bait don't catch fish sitting in a cup. You have to take it out of the cup, put it on a hook, and toss it out into the water."

Wait, what? Carissa frowned. "Shouldn't I be the fisher, not the bait?"

Val blinked, considered that. "Hmm. Yea. Whatever. I don't fish. Point: you can get it girl; you just have to be out there to be had." She stopped at room one-oh-seven and pointed at Carissa. "Go to the party with me."

"Alright. I have to check with my mom, though," Carissa said. "See you at lunch."

DAKOTA

Val waved and disappeared into the classroom. The period bell sounded.

Dammit. Now I'm late.

2

The phone rang seven times before she answered. "Avery, Boisseau, Carter Consulting. This is Kate."

"Hey Mom," Carissa said while slipping a slice of vegetable pizza with white sauce on her yellow ceramic plate. The veggie rested on top of two pepperoni and meat-eater's pizza slices. *I think I've covered all the food groups.* "You got a minute?"

"For my kid, I'm allotted at least two," Mom said with a smile in her voice. "What's up?"

"Umm," Carissa started and stopped. She looked for a place to sit, saw Val wave a hand, and navigated through the crowd. "Val got invited to a Halloween party and was told she could bring a plus one." She pointed to herself and nearly dropped her pizza on the floor. *Dammit. That was close.* "It's tonight."

There was silence. *Hmm. Not a good start.*

"Sorry about the late notice," Carissa said. "I guess the guy that was invited by the host was invited today. So, he invited her after he was invited. She invited me after she was invited."

She heard Mom take in a deep breath and exhale. *Looks like this is going to take some convincing.*

"We were hoping to leave school, grab some of my things, shop for cute costumes, and then go. I'd sleep over at Val's place afterward. Tomorrow's Saturday, so, maybe we could hang out on Saturday and I could come home on Sunday. That would give you the whole weekend with Dad since it's your anniversary. And that way, you two can do what you two do, I won't have to be grossed out by it, and you don't have to get a hotel or anything."

"This last chapter needs some revision; but this cover art looks great, John," Mom said. "It's hard to make a book stand out these days without Grisham, Patterson, or King's name on it, but you killed it."

Seriously?

"Mom," Carissa sighed. She plopped next to Val, rested her plate, and raised her finger as Val was about to speak. Val leaned her head against the phone.

"I'm sorry, honey," Mom said. "You caught me in the middle of something. But I'm giving you two minutes." Pause. "You know how we feel about parties."

Val whispered in her ear, "It'll be talking, music, and dancing. That's it."

Mom sighed. "God, she must think I'm an idiot. I've been to high school Halloween parties before. I've seen what people do."

"But it's been a while, right?" *Shit. Probably shouldn't have said that. I've aged her.* "I mean, not that long of a while, you're still hip, but we're just going to show off our costumes, dance to music, and talk to boys. We're not going to do anything else."

There was another long sigh over the phone. Mom said, "It would be nice to have the place to ourselves for our anniversary, but you're putting me in a spot. If I make this decision unilaterally, without consulting your father, I don't want it to come back and bite me in the ass. You're not going dressed as some slutty looking 'sexy butterfly' with your ladies and hoo-hah barely covered, are you?"

"How'd she guess my costume?" Val giggled.

"No Mom, I'm not," Carissa managed before she put her hand over her mouth and stifled a laugh. She shushed Val and whispered, "You trying to get me in trouble? She'll say 'no'."

Mom didn't respond. Silence lingered for a whole minute.

This is the moment of truth. At this point, she'll say either 'yes' or 'no'. And once she's made her mind, there's no budging.

"Alright," Mom said, "if you promise to behave yourself, and don't do anything stupid, or reckless, like get drunk or hang out somewhere you know you're not supposed to be, you can go. But I want to know where the party is, who is hosting, and how long it's going to be. I want to know when you get there and when you leave. And I don't want you out past one."

"One?" Val whined.

"Let's try midnight," Mom answered.

"One's fine, Mom." Carissa nudged Val away from the phone. "One's perfect."

"You sure Val doesn't want to push it and go for eleven?" Mom pressured. The tone was serious, but she suspected her mom secretly enjoyed giving her a hard time. She could almost see the smirk on Mom's face having them twisting in their chairs.

"One, Mom," Carissa insisted. "We'll be home at one."

"Good, because you know what'll happen if you're not," Mom said.

Let's see, I'd get chewed out, told I couldn't go to any more parties or anywhere else, sent to my room, and my social life would consist of watching other people have fun over the internet while I'm stuck inside bored out of my mind.

"Yes, I know," Carissa said, "no more parties."

This is where she pats herself on the back for being a good mom, tells me she loves me, and goes back to work.

"Great," Mom said. "I'll let your father know he and I have the place to ourselves." There was typing in the background. "How's school, today?"

"Good." Carissa gave Val a thumbs up. Val punched the air and turned her attention to her pizza. "It's pizza day."

Mom sighed. "God, I'm hungry. I thought I could skip lunch but I'm this close to tackling our secretary and taking a bite out of her arm." Someone said something in the background. "I'm kidding, Shannon. I wouldn't do that." She paused. "I should probably finish this and head to lunch. I'll talk to you later, honey. I love you."

"Love you, too. Talk to you later," Carissa said quickly, her finger already headed to the 'end call' button. They both hung up. She put her phone down and grabbed the veggie slice. *Salad first. Come to mama.* She took a bite.

"Why does she always have to be such a hard-ass about you going out?" Val asked.

Carissa chewed and shrugged. *Sorry, can't answer. Too busy eating.*

"I don't know," she said between bites. She chewed and stared at Val while Val went on, not having an answer for her.

Why was Mom so up the ass about me going out and having a little fun?

The first time her parents rejected the idea of her going to a party; they said they knew what teens did at high school parties: drinking, soft drugs, hard drugs, and sex. A lot of them left the parties inebriated and drove home drunk. Her parents gave her a long lecture listing the risks of underage drinking and parties, which included unwanted pregnancies, STDs, car crashes, DUIs, and death.

Of course, they knew what happened at high school parties. They were there, at the parties, having fun and getting laid.

Now they were parents. They had to do the parental thing and walk around with a big stick preaching the same lessons their parents preached knowing damn well that, if they could do it all over again, they'd probably be at the parties they're harping about.

Wait. Why was she complaining? She was in. She was finally able to attend a party. And she wasn't going to let a one o'clock curfew stop it from being an epic night.

Maybe. Just maybe, I'll meet a boy.

CHAPTER TWO

The period bell sounded twice; they were free for the weekend.

Carissa went to her locker, collected the books she'd need for a slam homework session on Sunday night, and discarded the books she wouldn't. She grabbed her abandoned and defunct breakfast bar and headed for the bus. She tossed the bar in the trashcan at the exit and waited in line to get on the bus.

She always sat in the back of the bus. She didn't know why exactly. It just felt right, private, safe. She felt pulled to keep on going. The rear exit sign sang its siren song that escape was possible and instant if she ever really needed it. It made perfect sense to sit in the back. She didn't like people pushing and bumping her with their books as they passed. And while she didn't want to step over people when it was her time to get off, she was one of the last stops. Conveniently, the back was her best chance at peace after a day of school.

She didn't like to admit it, and rarely did, but she wasn't a fan of people. *People are exhausting.* The back of the bus was her safe haven. She was going to reach in her bag, pull out her iPod, plug her ear buds into her ears, turn on a band she recently discovered called *Band of Horses*, and zone out.

When she got home, the plan was to take a hot shower and quick nap before Val arrived. Then, she'd pack for the weekend and set out Mom and Dad's anniversary present she didn't tell them she was getting. With everything packed, she'd get the hell out of dodge before they got home and the fireworks sounded.

She appreciated the fact that they were still in love, even

after Dad lost his job in the recession, fell off the wagon, and they had to relocate to Richmond. Whenever their anniversary came around, those two were like rabbits in heat. And that was gross. People having sex wasn't gross. No, not at all. She was hoping she'd have herself some "good ole toe curling sex" as Val called it. But her parents? No. Hell no. Hells to the no. She didn't want to hear about it. She didn't want to think about it. And she certainly didn't want to smell the aftermath of it lingering out of their open door like a mist monster from planet Mind Fuck.

No, thank you. Goodbye.

She reached into her book bag to pull out her purse when she smelled peaches and someone asked her, "Hey, mind if I sit here? Looks like a full house today."

Do I mind? Of course, I mind. I'm trying to enjoy some peace and quiet over here!

Carissa looked up at a black girl with long straight hair, greenish brown eyes (*Her eyes are like mine*), and a wide button nose. She was short, slim, and wore a light blue sundress and matching open-toed flats. "Sure. Yea. Take a seat."

The black girl smiled, "Thanks," and sat. Her bulging book bag banged as she dropped it.

God. Are you taking all your books home? I hope your laptop isn't in that bag considering the way you just dropped it.

The smell of peaches filled Carissa's nostrils as the black girl adjusted herself and the bag, and then let out a sigh of relief. *She smells nice.*

"Hey, aren't you in the same English class as me?" the black girl asked.

Carissa took a closer look. The black girl wasn't wearing any makeup but had perfect skin. *Must be her complexion. No need to fix what ain't broken, right?* Her eyelashes were long and full. *Okay, those can't be real.*

"Oh, yeah." *I don't know how I didn't recognize you first. You're the one that makes my writing look like Swiss cheese.* "You're Gabrielle, right?"

Gabby brightened at the sound of her own name. *Are you used to people not remembering who you are?* "Yep. Though, I prefer to be called Gabby. You're Carissa, the poet."

Well, I wouldn't go that far. "I write what I'm assigned."

"Well, I liked your poem about conversation being like an ocean," Gabby said. "You said you needed a life-preserver to keep you from drowning in the redundant details." She smiled. "I was impressed."

"Thanks."

Gabby pointed at Carissa's earbuds. "What are you about to listen to?"

Here we go. "Band of Horses."

Gabby's mouth hung open for two seconds; then she smiled. "That's funny. I was just introduced to that band last Sunday. Someone from my church was driving into the parking lot with it playing. It sounded nice so my sisters and I asked him what he was playing. He said, 'Band of Horses'. They must be getting around. Is that a new band?"

One of the members of her church? Oh great... "Nah. They've been around for years. I guess, with anything, it takes time for them to get around. I'm not sure if you watch the Grammy's, but they were nominated for this album."

"Oh," Gabby said. "I don't watch the Grammy's. Not really my thing. Plus, I'm usually at church on Sunday nights—" *Of course you are.* "—or doing homework."

Carissa pointed to her iPod and slid her finger across the screen until she found the right album. "*Infinite Arms* is the name of the album if you're interested."

"Thanks," Gabby said. She whipped her phone out of her purse and quickly made a note of the suggestion. Both her phone jacket and purse were white with multi-colored polka dots.

Where'd she find that cute phone jacket? Okay. I like her a little bit more now.

"Where'd you get that phone jacket?" Carissa asked.

"Birthday gift." Gabby beamed and handed over her smartphone. "My sister is a last-minute shopper. Last-minute anything, really. But I guess she knew my mom was getting me the purse. So, when she saw the phone jacket, she bought it for me. It's perfect because I have a dress in every one of these colors."

That's convenient. Carissa handed her the phone. "Must be nice having a sister."

"Yea. I have two, actually. It's great, most of the time.

Sometimes they borrow my clothes or purses without asking. Sometimes I go into the bathroom and my makeup isn't where it should be, and I have to look around for it." She shrugged. "You know. Stuff like that. Otherwise, we get along pretty well."

"Cool." Carissa returned her attention to her iPod.

I think we've reached the point in the conversation where things gradually fade as we run out of things to talk about and drift into the mundane.

"Do you have any siblings?" Gabby asked.

Carissa nodded, ready to put the earbuds in her ears. "Yea. I have a younger brother."

"What's his name? How old is he?"

This is getting personal. "Sean. Fourteen."

"Really? My younger sister, Rebecca, is fourteen." Gabby smiled. "Sean. I like that."

"Cool."

I am drowning. Remember the poem you mentioned earlier. I am drowning here. Cut me loose. Check your Facebook status. Check your Twitter feed or something. Find something else to do. This conversation has run its course. You're kind. You have good taste in clothing and music. I like you just enough to consider a future conversation. Now, let me sit quietly, in peace.

"You have any plans for tonight, it being Halloween and all?" Gabby asked. "My youth group is having a get together. You're welcome to come. We'll be playing music and dancing. They're going to set up a karaoke station and have plenty of snacks. Dressing up is optional. Oh, and you can bring your brother. It's thirteen and up."

So, no peace, then. Carissa pressed play on her iPod. "I've already been invited to a party, but thanks." She smiled and plugged in her earbuds.

Gabby sighed and wrinkled her nose. Her lower lip stuck out and slipped back in. "Okay. Well, pass on my invitation to your brother. Perhaps, if he's not doing anything tonight, he might be interested. There'll be plenty of young people there. He can make some new friends."

Carissa shrugged. *He has friends.*

"It's at Kingdom First Trinitan Church," Gabby continued.

This girl doesn't quit. "Sure, I'll pass it on."

"Great," Gabby said. "I look forward to meeting him."

That's assuming he wants to come. That's a giant assumption. Carissa closed her eyes.

"Can I listen?" Gabby pointed at the iPod.

If by listen, you mean shut the hell up, by all means, please do.

"Sure," Carissa said. She took the earbud from her right ear and passed it to Gabby. *I hope you have clean ears.* She changed the audio settings on her iPod so it didn't split the sound into two channels. She didn't want one to hear the music, while the other heard the vocals.

Gabby stuck it in her ear and nodded. Carissa restarted the song *On My Way Back Home* by Band of Horses and closed her eyes. "This is really nice."

Gabby is such an accurate name for you. Carissa put her finger to her lips, quietly shushed, and whispered, "Let's just enjoy the song, shall we?"

Gabby nodded and shut her eyes as well. Both sat quietly, heads leaned back.

Finally. Maybe there is a God.

2

"Bye. I hope you have a great day and enjoy your party," Gabby said and waved as Carissa headed down the empty aisle. They were the last two. *Where does she live anyway?* "Don't forget to invite your brother to the youth gathering. It starts at six."

Oh, I won't forget. Carissa smiled and waved back. "Thanks. I'll let him know." *Probably won't.*

She stepped off the bus and headed for her house. It was pale green with white framework and a light blue door. It was three houses from the end of the block. She peered back to see Gabby watching from the back window as the bus drove off. She wasn't sure if that was weird or normal. *But her eyes.* As the bus drove away, all Carissa could see was Gabby's eyes locked on her. They were deeper than the girl that possessed them like some greater force had taken control to watch history unfolded from front row seats.

You've been reading too much sci-fi. Next time Mom suggests a book, just put it down and walk away, slowly.

Carissa walked up the empty driveway and noticed the grass was a little longer than Dad wanted it. She hopped the three whitewood porch steps expecting to see a note on the screen door addressed to her brother *suggesting* that he cut it. Dad loved to make suggestions. It was easier for everyone if those suggestions were taken seriously. She wasn't disappointed when she saw it.

Regrettably, Dad believed in equal work and punishment. If he left a note for Sean, he usually left a note for Carissa as well. There was a note for both:

One: Akio, look at the grass. See how high it is? What else needs to be said?

Two: Asami, while you're getting your snack, and we all know you will, notice there are dishes in the sink.

Three: I don't expect to see either of you by the time I get home tonight. So be safe and have fun.

I repeat. Be safe.

- Dad

Dad called them by their middle names. Names *suggested* by grandma to preserve their heritage.

Val once said Carissa looked as Japanese as a hamburger.

Carissa grinned, collected her keys, and unlocked the door. The alarm system beeped. She closed the door and keyed in the security code. It stopped beeping and gave her a green light.

She slipped out of her sandals and carried them barefooted down the white hall, past the family room on the left and the kitchen and dining room on the right, to the stairwell. *These floors are freezing. Why is the air so high? No one's here!* She climbed the carpeted stairs, passed Sean's room, and turned left to her room. A yellow 'Do Not Disturb' sign welcomed every visitor that came to knock on her door. *If only people followed its instructions.* She entered, closed the door behind her, and walked straight to her cherry-wood sleigh bed. She dropped her sandals, climbed under the rose-colored sheets, and stretched out. *Oh, baby! I missed you, love.*

She yawned, took a deep breath, and closed her eyes.

There was a curse and banging sound from the window.

DAKOTA

Then, a burring engine came to life. Carissa's eyes shot open.

Shit! Crap! Sean's home? No no no no! How long did I sleep? I don't even remember going to sleep.

She looked at the clock. It was three-forty. She frowned. *What's he doing home so early? Doesn't he have practice?*

Carissa climb out of bed, slipped into her sandals, and trotted downstairs. She stepped out the front door and waved at Sean.

Sean, in his khaki cargo shorts and faded green t-shirt, pushed the lawnmower and grumbled. He stopped, kicked a stone away with his old grass-stained sneakers, and continued. He ignored Carissa's waves. She frowned and stormed forward, waving her hands. He stopped.

"What are you doing here so early?" Carissa yelled over the lawnmower.

"What?" Sean yelled back.

Oh no. I am not yelling over this stupid lawnmower. Carissa pointed at the lawnmower and shook her head. He turned it off.

"I thought you might have been home," Sean said. "You didn't reactivate the alarm system. Were you taking a nap?"

"Kinda," Carissa said. "I dozed off for a few minutes, apparently." She glanced at the front door and noticed the note was missing. "I didn't hear you come in. What are you doing home so early? I thought Mister Brown insisted on practice. You have your first game in almost two weeks, right?"

Sean shrugged. "Yea, well, we were supposed to have practice; but his wife went into labor an hour before class was over. I guess he must have contacted everyone else but me because when I made it to the locker room, it was empty all except for two."

Carissa smirked. "See, obviously he didn't contact everyone else but you or those other two wouldn't have been there. Don't take it so personally."

Sean teared up and turned away. "Oh. They knew practice was cancelled. That's why they were there."

He's about to cry. God, what happened?

"Who was there? What's going on?" she asked and rested her hand on his back.

"Kelsea was there," he said and let out a deep breath, "with Brandon."

Oh. She frowned. *That's not good.*

"What exactly was Kelsea doing in the locker room with Brandon?" Carissa asked. *Why did I ask that question? The answer is written all over his face.*

Sean wiped his face with the back of his hand and breathed deeply, again. "Wha do you think? Her shirt was off. His shorts were down. And they were kissing."

So, I'm going to make her life a living hell. Kelsea! I'm going to make your life a living hell!

"Which Brandon?" Carissa asked already confident of the answer but hoping it was someone else. "Liverwood, Bramby, Thompson?"

You know which Brandon it is, Carissa. But I suppose this is wishful thinking.

"Oakley," Sean said and sat on the grass.

Son of a—dammit! It had to be his best friend. Why did it have to be his best friend? Of all the people in the world to cheat on him with, why did she have to choose his best friend? There's low. And then there's this. She knew what she was doing. God, I hate girls like that. He was so nice to her. Too nice, if you ask me. He wasted his birthday money from Grandma on a gold necklace for her. That cunt.

"I'm sorry," she rubbed his hair and immediately regretted it. His head was sweaty.

I'd sit down next to you, but there is no way on God's green earth I'm going to stain my skirt. Do you know how hard it is to get grass stains out and maintain the integrity of the fabric?

"She didn't deserve you, and Brandon's shit," she said. "You don't need friends like that."

"Yea," Sean sighed. "I suppose."

Hmm. "So, I guess you're not dressing up and hanging out with Kelsea and her family tonight, are you? What are you going to do?"

"I don't know." Sean shrugged and looked at the house. "If I'm not with her, I'm usually with Brandon."

Brandon, you slimy piece of—

"I mean, I have other friends," Sean continued. "But I really don't feel like going out now. I just want to stay home and watch a movie. There's a Harry Potter marathon on tonight."

DAKOTA

There's always a Harry Potter marathon on! Not that I'm complaining. I can watch that for days. I love Hermione.

"That's lame, Sean," Carissa said. "You can see that anytime. We have to get you out. Mom and Dad are supposed to, you know, enjoy their anniversary at home. They're going to have sex."

"Again?"

"I know, right?" Carissa complained.

Sean sighed. "Well, what should I do? What are you doing tonight?"

I love you, but I'm not going to a house party with my little brother.

"I'm going out with Val," Carissa said and patted him on the back. "She was invited to a thing, and I'm her plus one. It's not something I can invite you to." *Wait a second.* "But you know what, I did get invited to something else while I was on the bus. I said I couldn't come, but you were invited."

Sean's eyebrows rose. "I was invited? Is it someone I know?"

This'll be rich. "No. At least, not that I'm aware of. Someone from class sat next to me on the bus. We got to talking and mentioned each other's siblings in passing. Anyway, she said that she's part of a youth group at a church—"

"A church?" he groaned and scrunched his nose. "Seriously?"

"Yes, a church," Carissa said with a smile, "and they're having a big gathering. There are supposed to be a lot of young people there around our age. So, maybe you might make a new friend." *Which you desperately need.* "Someone to replace Brandon."

Sean stood and checked his gold watch, a family heirloom made in Japan. "You don't just replace people."

Tell that to Kelsea. The little skank. "Yes," Carissa said and put her hands on her hips. "Yes, you do. Yes, you can. And yes, you will."

Sean snorted and reached down to turn on the lawnmower. "You're not the boss of me."

"Yes, I am," Carissa said. "I'm the older sibling."

"Yea, so was Esau," Sean said.

Carissa blinked.

"See," he said. "You're the one who needs to go to church, not me. You don't even know who Esau is."

Why would I care? Carissa shrugged. "How the hell do you know who Esau is?"

"This girl from my math class," he said. "We all had to share something about ourselves. She chose to talk about her family, which led to a bible lesson on Jacob and Esau."

And you remembered? Carissa narrowed her eyes. "You thought she was cute, didn't you?"

He grinned. "Oh, yea."

"Well, what was her name?"

"No." Sean pushed the start button. The lawnmower came to life.

"Come on, Sean!" she yelled. He pushed the lawnmower forward. "Sean! You're a free agent, now! Why not make a move?" He shook his head. "What are you, a chicken?"

Sean paused and looked back at her. He turned off the lawnmower. "You did not just Marty McFly me."

"Yea, I did," Carissa said. "What does it hurt to give me her name?"

"It doesn't hurt. I'm just not going to roll over and give you her name because you called me a chicken."

Stop being so stubborn. "You are being a chicken," she said before deepening her voice. "I have the hots for this cute girl, but my feelings are hurt and I'm too afraid to pursue something else."

"Rebecca," Sean said. "Her name is Rebecca."

Wait what? "What did you say?"

"Ruh-beh-kuh," he said slowly, clearly.

You're kidding me, right? That's Gabby's sister's name. And, she's the same age as Sean. Probably the same math class. What are the chances?

"Wait," Carissa said with a finger raised. "Is she black?"

Sean frowned. "Are you becoming Dad?"

"No." Carissa laughed. "I'm not racist. I just—is her big sister's name, Gabrielle?"

Sean narrowed his eyes. "How'd you know that?"

"Because she's the one that's inviting you to the church party." She poked Sean's sweaty shoulder. "She's in my English class."

Sean's mouth hung open. "Really? Hot Gabby Cole invited me

to a party?"

"Yep," Carissa smiled. "Though, I probably shouldn't say party. It's a church gathering. Dress-up optional."

"Did she say she was dressing up?" he asked. "What is she going as?"

Aww man. "Umm, no," Carissa shrugged. "I didn't ask. I was trying to listen to my music. She was asking me too many questions."

Sean nodded and looked back at his lawnmower. "Oh yea, right. I forgot. She invited us to a party, and you wanted to listen to your music. Your social skills are spot on as always."

"Hey!" Carissa complained. "If you're going to insult me, I can cancel your invitation."

His eyebrows rose again. "You have her phone number?"

Hmm. He has a good point. I can't cancel shit.

"No. And if I did, I wouldn't give it to you." She gave him a light pop on the head. "Are you into Rebecca or Gabby?"

Sean smiled. "I'm into whichever one is into me."

"Really? Gabby is a senior. You're a freshman. Ask Rebecca out and save yourself the embarrassment."

Sean glared and grabbed the handles of the lawnmower. "Which church?"

"Don't go after Gabby, Sean," Carissa insisted. "It'll ruin your chances with Rebecca."

"Dammit!" Sean complained. "Just tell me the church. You don't see me giving you advice on what guys you should be with, as if anyone's asked you out."

Oh no you didn't! Her eyes narrowed. "You know what. Nevermind." She turned around.

"Asami." He grabbed her shoulder. Beads of sweat glistened on his slick hands. "I'm sorry. I didn't mean that."

Ugh. Great. Now I need to take a shower, reapply my makeup, do my hair, pack, ugh, and do those stupid dishes before Val gets here. Hmm. Unless I can convince Val to do the dishes while I'm getting ready.

"I have to get going." She swatted his hand.

"Where is the party?"

She sighed. "It's at the, umm, umm, church."

Sean stared at her back. "Which one? You know how many

churches there are in this area? Like fifty."

Crap. I can't believe I forgot the name of the church. I said I'd tell him. Though, I didn't genuinely intend on him getting the invitation or taking it seriously. I was going to joke about it. Aww.

Carissa turned around. "I, I don't remember the name of the church."

Sean threw his hands up. "Great. I'm cheated on by my girlfriend and best friend, get invited to a party, but hey, can't remember where. That's the most important part of the invitation!"

Really? "Don't guilt trip me," she said.

Wait! Wasn't there something about a king on first? No. King's not on first. Who's on first. That's what I'm trying to figure out. Who's on first? Exactly. Who's on first. What's on second. I Don't Know's on third. Hahahaha. Grandpa's Abbott and Costello joke...

"What are you smiling for?" Sean asked. "Are you messing with me?"

Oh! I remember now.

"It's Kingdom First," Carissa said. "That's what it is. Kingdom First Trinitan Church."

"You sure?" Sean asked. "I don't want to show up dressed as Ensign Kim and interrupt a church service."

Really, Sean? Carissa smirked. "That's your costume? You're going as a *Star Trek* geek? You're going there to see a girl. If you're going to be a geek, why not dress as something masculine like Goku from Dragon Ball or Ryo from Street Fighter or Danny Rand? You're not even Asian enough to pull off Ensign Kim."

Sean sighed. "Did she give you a time or did you forget that too?"

"Yea, six," Carissa said.

I think I hurt his feelings. But seriously, what guy goes to pick up a cute girl at church dressed as a Star Trek geek?

Wait. Didn't coffee shop guy mention loving Star Trek?

"Thanks." Sean turned on the lawnmower. "Have fun at your party."

"Okay," Carissa said. "You have fun, too, okay? Try not to think about Brandon or Kelsea. Make some new friends. Get a few numbers." She thought about it. "And hey, who knows, maybe you can win over Gabby. Get her talking. She lives up to

her name."
　　Sean smiled and pushed the lawnmower forward.
　　Carissa returned to the house. *Better get ready for Val.*

CHAPTER THREE

"Val's here!" Sean yelled up the stairwell.

Crap. Carissa turned from her Wonder O's and glanced out the window. She saw a blue convertible pull into their driveway. She turned to her pink clock. *Dammit.* It was half past four. *Why is it that the only time she arrives on time is when I'm running behind?*

"Thanks!" Carissa yelled back. Mom and Dad hated when they yelled back and forth. But they weren't there, were they?

She ran down the stairs and opened the door.

"Yes, thank you," Val said on her smartphone. "Thank you. Please hold them for an hour. I'll be there as soon as I can to purchase them. Great." She waved at Carissa and walked past her to the family room. "That's wonderful. Thanks. Bye." She sat on the couch. "We have costumes."

Carissa pumped her fist. "Yes! Fairy princesses!"

"No. They didn't have any more Tinkerbell costumes." *Aww! You would have looked great in it.* "I refuse to be anything other than *Tinkerbell*. But I got the next best thing."

I'm afraid to ask. "What?"

Val smiled. "It's a surprise. But you're going to love it."

I suddenly have the feeling I won't. Carissa frowned. "Well, what about me? Did they have mine?"

"Well, they didn't have *Silvermist*, but they have *Rosetta*," Val said, her eyes on her phone. "You ready to go?"

Umm... "No, not yet."

"Well, get a move on," Val said. "The store is twenty minutes away and we have less than an hour to get there."

Crap. "I have to wash the dishes. I haven't finished my hair and makeup."

"We're not doing that now, anyway, remember?" Val said. "We'll get the costumes, grab some dinner, and doll each other up before we go to the party. It doesn't start until nine."

"Okay."

"You packed?" Val asked.

Not even close. "For the most part. I have to toss a few more things in my bag and I'll be good to go." *I'll toss a few things in my tote and sort it all out later. Glad I didn't unpack my makeup bag.*

"Okay," Val said. She typed a text message. *Who is she texting?* "Let me know when you're ready to go."

Well, maybe she'll help me out with the dishes. "Hey, come help me with the dishes."

Val sighed. "I don't get it. Why are you and your mom the only ones that know how to rinse off the dishes and put them in the dishwasher? It takes seconds. You rinse, turn on the garbage disposal unit, turn it off, and put the dish in. It's annoying. And they leave a pile of crap on the counter and ask you to clean? Really?"

You're preaching to the choir. Carissa shrugged and walked to the kitchen. Val followed. "Mom makes breakfast and dinner. I do the kitchen and dishes. Sean takes care of the trash, lawn, and outdoor stuff. Dad does maintenance and other outdoor stuff. We rotate on bathrooms and family room. It's a system."

"I know all about your system," Val said. "I just think they're stupid. You'd have less work if they rinsed for a couple seconds and put it in the dishwasher."

"I'm not—," Carissa began before looking at the sink. *What the hell? There's nothing there.*

"Had I known you were going to call me stupid," Sean said from behind. Val jumped. "I would have left the dishes right there for you. But I knew you were dragging ass and thought I'd do you a favor. Now we're even."

Thank God. Carissa turned around. "Try not to say 'dragging ass' when you're at church." She examined him. He was in his white workout shorts and tank top. "You're not wearing your geek outfit. Does that mean you've come to your senses?"

Sean stared at her straight-faced. He rubbed his hand through his wet hair. "No. I thought I'd take a shower and relax first."

"Mmm, you smell nice," Val said and rubbed his left shoulder. Sean tensed, his eyes wide. *Hahaha! Don't do that, Val. He's going to ruin his shorts.* "Since when did you become bible thumpers? And who puts on cologne for church? Are you meeting a girl?"

"I, uh, as a matter of fact, I am, or will, yes, possibly," Sean said. He breathed in deep. "Mashed potatoes."

Mashed potatoes?

Val snickered. "Okay then." She patted Sean's head, "You have fun with that," and turned to Carissa. "We should get going. Those costumes aren't going to buy themselves."

"Yea," Carissa said. "I'll grab my things."

"What are you going as?" Sean asked.

Oh, brother. "Have fun, Ensign," she said. "Don't choose the wrong sister like Kim."

Sean stuck his tongue out.

2

Val parked and checked the time. "Look at that. Only five minutes late. Not bad, eh?"

Carissa patted herself. "I'm still in one piece. Shocker." She smiled as Val shot her a glare.

"Next time, I'll let you drive," Val said and got out of the car. "We might make it before Christmas."

But we'd make it there alive... and at the most wonderful time of the year. Carissa smiled, grabbed her red Coach purse, and opened the passenger door. "I'm kidding, Val."

"Sure you are," Val said. She entered *For Every Occasion*. Carissa followed.

For Every Occasion was a department store that sold apparel, accessories, decorations, cards, gift bags, and party planning services for every occasion. And they meant every occasion. There were arrangements for weddings, baby showers, engagements, birthdays, funerals, new jobs, promotions, retirements, lost jobs, vasectomies, housewarming, all major holidays, and then themed events, like period parties with eighties outfits to renaissance wear. Most holiday apparel, accessories, and decorations were in stock on a seasonal basis. But they kept the basics year-round.

This month, they decorated the store with cobwebs and fake spiders along the doors and shelves, pumpkins with candy at each cashier station, lanterns at the entrance, ghouls at the entrance to the dressing rooms, decapitated heads were idly scattered on the floor along the aisles for someone to kick, and more. Carissa was sure the male cashier was dressed as a zombie. The female cashier wore a white tank top covered with fake blood and had patches of peeled flesh and brain stuck in her hair.

That girl is showing way too much cleavage or has breast so big that they can't be contained. Looks like a bit of both. Lucky. I have 'B' cups that wanna be 'C' cups when they grow up. I bet he loves playing zombie with her.

Val nudged her and pointed.

The costumes department was on the right. As was the custom order station. Upon advanced request, they had tailors available to custom design and make costumes and outfits. The concept was genius, the prospect heavenly, until she saw the price tag. As much as she wanted a custom dress made exclusively for her, she didn't have hundreds or, in some cases, thousands of dollars to drop for a single outfit. She wished she did.

Carissa had a vision of a sleeveless and strapless white dress that fell just above her knees. The dress would be tight and layered with sparkly fringe. She would carry a small, white, sparkly-fringed purse and wear short, white, heeled boots with sparkly fringe on the sides. Lately, she loved anything with fringe, and suspected living in the south had something to do with it.

"Stop daydreaming," Val hissed from the custom order counter.

I wasn't daydreaming. I was fantasizing about my perfect dress. There's a difference.

Carissa strode over to Val and the dark-haired man behind the counter. His face was muscular and pale. His cleft chin was like perfectly sculpted marble. The black polo shirt was tight against his muscles. His silver, embroidered nametag read: Bastian. General Manager.

Oh, God. He's hot. She felt a warm, tingling sensation rise to her stomach.

Bastian smiled. "Hi."

Carissa stared. Her heart raced as her mind went blank. She blinked.

Val glared and whispered, "Say hi back."

"Uh, yeah," Carissa said. "Hi." *Oh man. I'm smiling like an idiot.*

Val smirked and returned her attention to Bastian. "So, we're here. Do you have the items?"

Bastian pointed at two dresses behind the counter. One was a short and strapless pink dress with fairy wings attached at the back. *That would be my Rosetta costume!* The other dress was—no, it couldn't be. *Oh hell.*

"Val! You can't be serious," Carissa complained. "You can't wear that. That's the one specific outfit my mom said not to wear."

Val laughed. "Yea, well, she gave you that restriction. Not me. The moment I saw that in their online inventory, I had to get it just to spite her."

"Now we can't post any pictures," Carissa said. She aggressively pointed at a low v-cut, short-skirted dress with a butterfly design and wings. The dress was blue, sea green, purple, and black. "My mom's going to want to see pictures, see what you wore, and I won't be able to show her this. She can't see you wearing this."

"It doesn't fit her description," Val said with a calm and reassuring tone. "It won't show off my 'hoo-hah'. I'll do that all by myself." She laughed and glanced at Bastian. *Val is such a hoe. But I love her.* "So, we buying these or what?"

"Yea," Carissa resigned and dug into her purse for her debit card.

Bastian scanned and charged each of their dresses. "Was there anything else you ladies needed?"

"Yea," Val said. She checked the business cards on the counter, grabbed one, and said, "I need you to let me put this in your pocket." She wrote her phone number on it.

Bastian pointed at the gold band on his ring finger. *Party's over girls. He's spoken for.* "I'm flattered but very married."

Val looked him in the eye. "I don't care, and neither do your eyes. You've been checking me out for months. So, just do us both a favor and undress me with more than your eyes." *Val is so bold.* She stretched across the counter and put the business card in his shirt pocket. *Bold, italics, underlined, and full caps.* "You're going to call me. Don't worry. I'll be discreet."

Bastian stared at her long and hard. He pulled the business card out of his pocket, examined it, and then said, "Your name is Val?"

"Yep."

"Aren't you two in high school?"

Right you are, sir.

"No, we're in college," Val lied. *Oh no.* "Freshmen. Going to our first Halloween sorority party."

What are you doing, Val?

"Right, okay, where?" Bastian grilled.

"VCU," Val lied again. *Stop while you're ahead, Val.*

"Studying what?" Bastian tested.

Theatre. Can't you tell?

"Gender, sexuality, and women's studies, with a minor in psychology," Val lied once more with a big smile on her face. She leaned against the counter. "I'm going to be a sexologist."

I can't believe my eyes and ears. It's like you came prepared.

Bastian swallowed hard. "I don't believe you."

Val studied him. "You don't have to. All you have to do is call me. No strings attached." She pointed at his left hand. "And little miss sunshine will never be the wiser."

Val really shouldn't be doing this. I don't feel right about this. I need to leave.

"Let's go," Carissa whispered and slowly stepped away.

Val winked. "I'll talk to you soon, Bastian," and walked with Carissa. She whispered, "I'm not going to look back. But I want you to watch him watch us walk away."

Aww. I don't want to. Can't we walk away and pretend that never happened?

Carissa looked back. Bastian watched them leave and glanced at the business card in his hand. *Throw it away. Put it in the trash. Never call Val. Though, I honestly can't blame her for trying. You do look yummy.* He put the business card in his pocket. *Oh, Val. You made that guy a cheater. He's not done it, yet. But he's already contemplating it.*

"He was watching us," Carissa whispered as they exited the store and walked to Val's car. "He put the business card in his pocket. Why'd you say you were a college student? And why'd you seduce a married man, anyway? Don't you know that's trouble?" *We don't even know his wife. What if she's unstable or something? She might start slashing tires and boiling pet rabbits.*

Val shrugged. "I did it because I can." She unlocked the car, put her dress in the back, and got in. "You don't realize how much power we have, Carissa. What did I tell you earlier? We're hot." *God, I wish I was as confident as her.* "Guys see us and they can't help themselves. They can't help but to look at us and want us. A look becomes a lingering eye. A lingering eye becomes a split, momentary fantasy. And, if it suits me, I can make that fantasy come true." She started the car.

I don't know what to say to that.

"Come on, Cari," Val said. "I saw how you responded to him. You got all flush and silly. You clearly had the hots for him."

Yes. I literally felt hot for him.

"If you want, when he calls, I can setup a rendezvous for you and him, or all three of us," Val said. "Why not get that cherry popped by a pro, instead of an amateur?"

That, no, no, that, no. That's not me. I don't sleep with married men. I don't sleep with anyone. I'm definitely not going to start with a married man. No matter how muscular he is. No matter how great his hair is. No matter how flawless and sharp his jawline and chin are. "No. I couldn't."

"Suit yourself." Val pulled out of the parking lot.

Carissa always wondered what it was like to be like Val. Val had this sexual confidence and knowledge. Despite some of her questionable choices, her humor was rich. Her wit was sharp. Her vigor for life was unmatched. She sparkled with self-esteem and charisma. Carissa wanted that. She wanted to feel strong and sure of herself.

There was more of course. Confidence and sex appeal weren't all that Carissa wanted. She felt a deep yearning burning inside of her. It was deep and low. She wanted sex. And, though she resolved to herself that she wouldn't just give it away as Val suggested, she secretly wished that something casual would lead to something serious. She hoped that tonight was the beginning of a fulfilling relationship. She wanted to hold hands while walking in public, soft kisses whenever and wherever, romantic candle-lit dinners, films at the theater, cuddling on the couch while watching television, long conversations full of deep emotional intimacy, and sex.

She would find a guy tonight at the party. She knew it. She felt it. Tonight was her night to find a boyfriend.

Speaking of boyfriends...

"What about Jesse?" Carissa asked. "Aren't you going to hang with Jesse tonight?"

"Ha!" Val laughed. "What about Jesse? If I'm pantless with Jesse and Bastian calls, I will put those pants on, walk right out the door without saying a damn thing, and get in bed with a real man. Jesse is a high school boy. Bastian is a man." She inhaled and exhaled deeply. "A big, strong, handsome man."

My girl is a homewrecker. I need to make better friends.

"I'm hungry," Val said. "Let's get something quick and get ready."

Fine by me.

CHAPTER FOUR

It was nine o'clock when Carissa and Val made it to the Bradshaw Mansion. After dinner, they bought makeup and accessories for their costumes and went to Val's house to shower, dress, and beautify. Carissa clocked fifty minutes for hair and makeup and then took pictures with Val's younger sister Samantha, who was going trick-or-treating with her first boyfriend, Thomas.

They look amazing.

"I look stupid," Thomas complained. He stared in the mirror and studied his pale complexion and yellow eyes. Samantha and Thomas were going to a sophomore lock-in as Rosalie and Emmett from the Twilight Saga. Thomas didn't care much for the franchise or the idea, but Samantha, the romantic, insisted that if Thomas wanted to go out with her, he had to look the part. Neither of them was old enough to drive, so they would begrudgingly leave with Thomas's parents as their chaperones.

Val's mom, Katherine, a makeup artist and actress, led Val out of the bathroom and said, "Ta-da!" Val looked as authentic as a mystical butterfly fairy could without CGI. Katherine knew her stuff. She helped with everyone's outfit and makeup, but more so with Val's. Despite how Val felt about her mother, it was as clear as daylight that Val was the favorite. Carissa assumed it was because Katherine saw so much of herself in Val—*they're damn near clones*—and hoped Val would follow in her footsteps.

"Wow," Carissa said. She pulled out her smartphone and took a couple pictures. Val posed with her hands on her arched hips and lips pouting. She posed with her left arm raised and a winking eye. She posed again with both arms out wide as though she was flying. The last shot, the best shot, she blew pixie dust from her cupped hands.

Katherine smiled. "Don't make too much of a mess with that pixie dust. You want to be invited back."

Yea. We won't get invited back. Carissa and Val exchanged a look and laughed.

They drove fifteen minutes to the Bradshaw Mansion. Val parked on the street in a line with other cars and hopped out.

"I'm leaving my purse in the car," Carissa said and pulled a small, ruby red rhinestone purse out of her strawberry purse. "I don't want anyone rummaging through it." She grabbed her phone, locked the doors, and followed Val.

"Yea, I'm not bringing mine either," Val said. She held a key purse in her hand, but that was it. "I had that happen to me a couple weeks ago at a house party. Someone took a hundred and forty dollars."

A hundred and forty dollars? That sucks! "What did you do? Did you find out who did it?"

"No, and there wasn't much I could do," Val said as they walked through the gate leading to the Bradshaw Mansion. "Too many people were there. It could have been anybody. I was pissed. I mean, that was some of my Christmas money. I saved it for that purpose. But yea. People don't give a shit. They just go through people's stuff."

And that's why I left my purse in your car. My phone is locked. My phone has a tracking app on it so I can remotely turn it on and track it if someone took it. But why am I thinking about this? I'm here to have fun, not to worry about having my purse and phone stolen. But, if it was stolen, I wouldn't be able to call Mom at one. If she doesn't get the call, she'll employ the family tracker app. If she sees me somewhere other than where I'm supposed to be, I'd get in trouble. Then again, she'd know later that my phone was stolen. But she'd get mad and reconsider letting me go to other parties.

No. At one, Val would call. And if I lost it sooner than one, we'd just call her and tell her my phone is missing so she at least knows that I'm calling and not trying to sneak past the one o'clock deadline. Pssh. We probably won't be here at one.

They approached the mansion. She heard Moby's *Extreme Ways* and the thumping sound of bass through the front door.

Wow. I have never been in a house this big. How much does something like this cost? How loaded is this family? And what do they do?

"Nice, right?" Val nudged Carissa with her elbow. "Wouldn't you love to live in a house like this?"

"Yea," Carissa said. "I would."

I wouldn't know what to do with a house this big. But it's nice to think about. I'd turn into my Aunt Carrie and spend half my free time watching HGTV and flipping through Better Homes magazines.

At the front of the line, next to the door, was a crowd of people. Towering over them was a black guy with dreads named DeQuan Jacobs, a dominating center expected to take their basketball team to the national championship. College scouts already knew his name.

DeQuan pointed at Carissa. "Hey, I know you. You're Sean's sister." He snapped his fingers several times. "Carissa, right?"

Umm. Carissa stared at his large biceps. They were larger than her head. She was sure of it.

"I heard his girl hooked up with Brandon. That's messed up, man. Where's mah boy at?"

Wow. News gets around quick. "He's at church."

DeQuan blinked. "Church? Really? Damn. Dude so upset, he's about to make a vow of celibacy and shit." His groupies laughed. As did Val.

Carissa glared. *Nope. That's not it at all.*

"I was hoping he'd be here," DeQuan said. "I've got pussy lined up and waiting for him."

Ugh. I am so glad he didn't come to this party. The last thing I want to think about is my little brother having sex. And I definitely don't want to see a line of hos trying to get with him.

"Yea, I'm sure he would have appreciated that," Carissa said. *Lying through my teeth.* "I'll let him know the next time I see him." *This will never come up in conversation, ever.*

"Yea, please do," DeQuan said. "I'll hook him up."

"No doubt." Carissa smiled and gave him two thumbs up. *No*

doubt that it's never going to happen. I don't want my little brother anywhere near your hos. Gonorrhea cha-cha-cha. She followed Val into the Bradshaw Mansion.

2

The entrance hall was large, dimly lit, and crowded with people standing around and talking with red plastic cups in hand. JJ Sweet Spot's newest release, 'Booty Pop', thumped and blared. Carissa didn't know how they arranged a party in their parents' absence, but she didn't care. The party felt like something out of the movies. Their house was incredible.

The wide entry hall had white marble pillars and floors. To the right, an arched doorway led to a family room with chairs and couches. To the left, another arched doorway led to a dining room with a long table. One wide set of stairs with red carpeting in the middle stood straight ahead. Her eyes traced the stairs to the painted and framed family portrait that rested at the top.

In the portrait, a dark-haired man stood in a tuxedo behind a thin, blond-haired woman with his hand on her shoulder. The woman wore a sleeveless, navy blue evening dress and sat on a white chair. One dark-haired boy in a tuxedo stood to her left, his father's hand on his shoulder. A smaller dark-haired boy in a tuxedo sat on her lap. She assumed the man was Robert Bradshaw, owner of the family real estate and landscaping business. The woman would then be Janice Bradshaw, his wife and operator of the interior decorating side of their business. The older boy she didn't know but assumed it was Kent's older brother. The boy on the lap was Kent.

"Can you believe this place?" Val asked.

Shh. You'll ruin the moment, Carissa thought, having somehow blocked the other people and loud music from her mind.

Music: *"...so girl just let me see that booty pop. Oh yea-yea, booty pop. Make that booty pop..."*

Carissa closed her eyes, shut out the music, and imagined herself walking down the carpeted stairs in a red nightgown, lounging in the family room with her toes out, eating a sandwich at the dinner table in her pajamas. She was sure they kept a fully stocked fridge and had one of those oversized bathtubs with jets. Those were the necessities of life. That was the dream.

Oh, and they have a pool. A full-sized pool. I could do laps! Oh my...

"Hey, there's Jesse," Val said. She waved, grabbed Carissa's arm, and tugged her over to the family room.

Carissa followed, slipping past the idle talkers crowding the entry hall. They moved around the few pairs of drunk teens dancing to the atrocious song blasting from the speakers. They had to be drunk. Watching them dance was like watching two people being electrocuted in slow motion. Their dance moves, in no way, corresponded with the music. It wasn't humanly possible for anyone's rhythm, physical intelligence, or musical awareness to be that poor without liquid or drug influence.

Music: *"...I gotta tell ya, girl. That body don't stop. I'd drop a thousand dollars just to see that booty pop..."*

Carissa rolled her eyes. *I'd drop an anvil on your head just to make your career stop.*

"Hey, Jesse." Val beamed.

"Woah," Jesse said, eyes on her costume. "You look amazing."

Doesn't she?

Val posed in her sexy butterfly costume and then hugged and kissed him. He was a head taller than Val and wore a tattered t-shirt covered in fake blood and blue jeans. Fake, bloody guts sagged from his stomach. Random bruises and cuts stretched his lean and defined arms. His face was pale. A knife stuck out of his head.

They did not coordinate their costumes at all.

"Doesn't my girl look amazing?" Jesse said and turned to the person to his left.

It was Kent, dressed in a black tuxedo with a bowtie. His dark brown hair slicked back. He carried a half-full martini glass. *Damn. He cleans up nice. What is he supposed to be?*

"She'd make a dead man rise," Kent said.

"That's the plan." Val poked the fake knife stuck out of Jesse's head. *That's Val. Straight to the point.*

Jesse laughed.

"Hi Kent." Carissa grinned. "Great place. Thanks for inviting us."

Kent walked forward, collected and kissed the back of

Carissa's hand. "The pleasure's all mine."

What? Carissa stared at her hand. Is this real? No one has ever kissed my hand like that before. Kudos to you. Very suave. She admired Kent. His eyes locked on hers. *This is going to be interesting.*

"You look amazing," Kent complimented. "Totally, and absolutely extraordinary."

"Thanks." Carissa blushed. "You're pretty extraordinary yourself."

That kind of sucked. I just repeated what he said. How about: that tux looks so good on you? Or, wow, your house is giant, and you look like a movie star. How soon before I wake up in your arms with my hair in my eyes and drool running down my face?

Can I pretend I never thought that last question?

"Would you like a drink?" Kent asked.

"Sure," Carissa said. *Just be cool. Remember what Val said. We're dreams come true.*

"Okay. What would you like?" Kent pointed towards a red cooler full of an assortment of bottled beers. "Beer or," he pointed towards a large glass bowl full of a red, murky liquid and an assortment of chopped and sliced fruit, "jungle juice?"

Hmm. Difficult choice. The only alcoholic drinks I've had were wine coolers, wine, or a few mixed drinks. Hmm. I tried beer once. Just once. It tasted terrible. I imagine, if you mixed hatred, sweat, and watered-down piss into a bottle, it would taste like beer. If I had to name it, I'd call it Liquid Revenge. Ugh. Don't remember the taste, Carissa. Don't remember the taste. What kind was that? If I could remember the name of that beer. Nope. Not taking any chances.

"Anything but beer," Carissa said. "What's in the jungle juice?"

Kent walked to the glass bowl. Carissa followed. He said, "Vodka, rum, peach schnapps, gin, orange juice with sliced oranges, lemonade with sliced lemons, limeade with sliced lemons, chopped strawberries, strawberry puree, sliced bits of pineapples, strawberry soda, and a secret ingredient. It's a good blend. You'll love it." He pointed out the fruit ingredients. There were no liquor bottles.

Vodka? Rum? Peach schnapps, whatever that is. Gin? Aren't

those kind of strong? I can't get too drunk. Buzzed, totally fine. A little drunk, that'll pass. Drunk, well, I might get my ass chapped a little bit. But hard liquor drunk, Mom would kill me. And, I don't want to get sick. I've seen what sick and drunk looks like from Dad. Not looking to repeat that. But, one cup won't hurt. I mean, I can just sip on it for a while.

"Try some." Kent grabbed a red plastic cup. "I made it for the girls in the party that don't like beer. You can barely taste the alcohol in it. It's fruity and sweet, kind of like juice."

"Really?" Carissa asked.

"I went heavy on the strawberries," Kent continued.

Really? Carissa blinked. "Why?"

"Val said you like strawberries."

Val's been talking to you about me? Oh! Oh, God. This is a setup. Val! She set me up with Kent. That doesn't make any sense. Why would she set me up with one of the most sought-after guys in school and stick with Jesse, who is about fifteen to twenty names down if there was a list? If, pssh, there's a list.

"Yea, I do," Carissa said. She turned around to give Val a glare, or maybe a thank you, or maybe a wink and smile, or maybe two thumbs up. *I'm not sure how I feel about this setup.* But Val was nowhere in sight. She wasn't in the family room. She wasn't in the entryway. Carissa looked to the back room, lit only by the flashing multi-colored lights that flashed in sequence with the music. JJ Sweet Spot's next worse number "In My Face" boomed. *Maybe they're dancing?*

"Where are Val and Jesse, anyway?" Carissa asked. *They ditched us. This was totally a setup.*

Music: *"...I'm gonna move (move, move) you into place (you into place). So you can shake it shake it shake it shake it shake it in my face. In my face. In my face. Come on shake it in my face..."*

A very classy setup.

What I don't get is how you can go from playing Moby to JJ Sweet Spot. That right there is the truest form of blasphemy. A lightning bolt should crash down from the sky and kill the DJ right now. He should die.

"Oh, who knows?" Kent said. "They probably went to the kitchen. There's a keg." He filled the cup with jungle juice and handed it to Carissa. "Try it."

DAKOTA

She sipped it. *Mmm. Yes. Sweet. Fruity. Odd texture. A little tart. Oh! Oh, a lot of tart. Might have gone too heavy on the lemon and lime, but it overpowers the yucky alcohol taste. I can handle this. He's right about the strawberry. There's that strong hint of strawberry. Is that the strawberry puree?*

"It's good." Carissa smiled. "Thanks."

Well, he's handsome, rich, and seems nice. Charming. Not a bad setup, Val. I'm surprised you didn't snag him for yourself. Which begs the question: why didn't she snag him?

Something's missing. She's my friend, but she's not that good of a friend. No. Girls don't pass over opportunities like this with guys like this. I wonder if there's something wrong with him. Something she knows that I don't. It has to be something that's not too bad. She's not a bad friend. She wouldn't pass me off to a weirdo or psychopath. But it would have to be some giant pet peeve of hers. A real deal breaker.

"Are you a Cowboy's fan?" Carissa asked. *That's so random. I shouldn't have asked him that. That doesn't make any sense, considering our conversation.*

"Yes." Kent laughed, then sipped his martini. "They said you're from the New York area. I guess that makes you a Giants fan, and us mortal rivals."

I don't give a damn about football, but yes, I was right. The universe is making sense again. Val's a huge Skins fan. Her family has season tickets safely tucked into their Skins shrine with all the cups, shirts, jerseys, hats, wristbands, keychains, playing cards, and well, good lord, any other unnecessary but somehow cute memorabilia. The feud is real. If she saw Kent in a Cowboys jersey, she'd probably beat him over the head, drag him into a ditch, and set him on fire. But because I couldn't give a rat's ass about football, she knew it wouldn't matter to me.

"If you consider Connecticut the New York area, then yea," Carissa said. "I just, uh, was curious."

"Are you a big football fan?"

Ha. Definitely not. Complete waste of time. She shrugged. "I wouldn't say *big* football fan. But I've watched it with friends and family. Hard to go through a Sunday night without enjoying a good football game."

Why are these words coming out of my mouth? What am I

talking about? Mom reads. Dad catches up on his shows on DVR. Sean plays video games. No one is watching football.

"I got half of that." Kent pointed at his right ear. "How about we go somewhere a bit quieter so we can talk?"

"Sure." Carissa grinned and took a sip of her tart jungle juice.

Some place quieter. And probably private, right? I see where this is going. Or do I? Is he going to try to kiss me? Do I want him to kiss me? I'm not sure, yet. I mean, he's cute, but I didn't put lipgloss in this purse. Alcohol dries skin, right? The last thing I want is for it to go around that Carissa has dry lips. Not that I want it to go around that I'm kissing. I don't think Kent would kiss and tell, would he? Dammit. He better not.

Kent took a heavy gulp of his martini and put it down. He placed his hand on Carissa's lower back and guided her through the crowd, into the library. There were two couples on the chairs and one on the couch, all making out. He nodded; they backed out; and he led her to the back, past the dancers and blinking lights, out the back door to the patio.

It was overcast and cool, like most of the day. Only an hour ago, there was a light rain. But that didn't stop a crowd of teens from stripping down to their shorts and bras and taking a dip in the pool.

Oh my God.

"It's freezing out here," Carissa said. "Please tell me that pool's heated." She was a seasoned swimmer and part-time lifeguard in the summer, but it didn't take either to know that swimming in frosty water was a risky idea, especially after consuming alcohol.

"It's not that cold." Kent smirked. "But yes, it's heated. Trust me. If it was too cold, I wouldn't let them swim."

"Great," Carissa said. *I hope I didn't just insult his intelligence, or his family's. I just don't want to have to dive in and save somebody, tonight. I spent an hour on this hair and makeup and might want to return this costume.*

"We keep it open until the leaves become a pain in the ass or right after Halloween," Kent explained and turned the corner to the far end of the patio. "It's usually my parents who host a Halloween party inside, while Brian, some friends, and I have a Halloween pool party."

It's okay. You don't have to keep talking about it. I was just making sure no one was going to die.

"Where are we going?" Carissa asked.

Kent rubbed her lower back. "The hot tub."

Yep. He's looking for a make out spot. How funny would it be if he lives here but all of his make out spots are taken?

Carissa grinned, then frowned. *Wait. No. That would not be funny. That would mean we wouldn't make out. Still. Do I want to make out with him? That has yet to be determined. I mean, he's cute; but we haven't spoken more than a few sentences to each other. I barely know him.*

No. Rephrase that. I don't know him. I know a few things about him. I know he has a strong jaw line, blue eyes, great hair, played varsity basketball at his previous high school, and his family is filthy rich. That and he's charming, confident. Wait. We're going to the hot tub? I'm not dressed for the hot tub.

At the far end of the patio, four people in bathing suits laughed in the hot tub. Bottles of beer were in hand and circled the hot tub.

Good God. This is why my mom doesn't want me to go to high school parties. They're all idiots. Okay. Maybe that's harsh. Maybe they're not all idiots. But, they clearly didn't pay attention in health class. Drinking or getting drunk before getting into or while in a hot tub can cause either heat exhaustion or extreme dehydration. I'm about to save someone's life.

"Kent, I don't want to be that person, but they shouldn't be drinking while in the hot tub," Carissa said.

"Why not?"

"Alcohol dehydrates the body. So does sweating in the hot tub. They could suffer extreme dehydration. And, alcohol warms the body. So does the hot tub. They could suffer heat exhaustion. Hell, they could suffer both and pass out." *I think I said suffer too many times.*

"Is that so, doctor?" Kent smiled.

If you're mocking me, I will cut you. This is not a joke. I'm being serious here. They're at risk right now.

"Yes, it is so," Carissa said. "They're in danger."

Kent smirked and yelled, "Ha! Wow! Great suggestion, Carissa!" He said it loud enough for the four in the hot tub to look at them.

What the hell? What just happened? What are you talking about?

"Hi Kent!" One of the girls with long black hair yelled and flagged him over. The blond guy with his arm around her rolled his eyes.

Across from the couple was a guy with a shaved head, bodybuilder build, and large three-headed dragon tattoo that wrapped around his torso. He said, "Why don't you two come in? Things were just about to heat up." He looked like a heavier version of Kent.

This must be his brother. Brian, is it? I'm sure Val said Brian.

"Umm," Carissa hesitated.

Kent stepped forward. "Our co-host, Carissa, has some legitimate safety concerns about the pool and drinking in the hot tub. So, we're going to start a beer pong tournament in twenty minutes."

What? Co-host? When did I become a co-host? I guess the moment I opened my mouth. Sigh. I suppose that's one way to get them out of the pool. At least no one's gonna die tonight. Well, no, people will die today. People die every day, but not on my wat—

Brian laughed. "Co-host? Oh, that's rich. Real rich. But sure, man. Sure. Whatever you need to do to get the deed done." He climbed out of the hot tub. He didn't have any shorts on.

"Oh." Carissa gasped, wide-eyed, and turned around. *Oh my God. I just saw his penis. I just saw his penis.* She put her hand over her mouth to stifle a laugh. The unveiling played again and again in her head as she concluded what and how much she saw.

"Ugh, Brian," Kent complained. Everyone else in the hot tub laughed. "Come on, man. We talked about this. Can't you at least wait until everyone else is obliterated before you go full Dad on us? I don't want to see your dick."

And neither do I. Well, if we're being honest...

"Apple doesn't fall far from the tree," Brian said. He stepped over the beer bottles and put his red shorts on one leg at a time. "Especially tonight, right?"

Kent shot a glance at Carissa. "Dude, stop foreshadowing. I'll see you four inside. We'll get everyone else from the pool."

He ushered Carissa back inside.

CHAPTER FIVE

Twenty minutes later, the dining room was crowded with enthusiastic teens dressed in costumes varying from bananas and tacos to Batman and Robin to the bumblebee from the Cheerios commercial. Others with wet hair, bathing suits, towels, and flip flops.

Kent and Brian converted their hand-carved, solid oak dining table into a beer pong table. Kent cleared the table. Brian placed ten red plastic cups on each end in a bowling pin formation. Each cup was to be filled halfway by a drink of the team members' choosing. To the right of the table was an easel and easel pad with names and brackets. Carissa wrote the names of the teams in capital letters. After which, she went back and drew small strawberries slash hearts over the I's.

The first teams to compete would be Carissa and Kent, under the team name, Goldeneye, Kent's choice, and Super Mario, a couple named Terrance and Amanda. Terrance was dressed as Mario and Amanda as Luigi from the video game. They gave each other a smooch as Brian introduced them. After which, Amanda had to adjust her fake mustache. When complimented, Terrance said he started growing his mustache three months in advance and applied plenty of wax to keep it curled.

Some guy in the back said, "This is the first time I've ever wanted to pork Luigi." His friends laughed and gave him a high five.

So much class, Carissa thought, but agreed. Amanda wore the costume well. Her green shirt was a size too small and pressed tight against her pointy nipples.

"So, how does this game go again?" Carissa asked.

"It's simple," Kent said. "Each team gets a turn per person. I throw the ball. If it gets in the cup, one of them drinks. I throw until I miss. Then, you throw. If it goes in, they drink from that cup. If you miss, it's their turn. The game goes until one team has no more cups. The team that has no cups loses. The goal is to sink cups and drink less. Whoever loses has to drink the other team's remaining cups."

Ugh. Carissa frowned. She and Kent filled their cups halfway with jungle juice and rum and coke. The other team filled theirs from the keg. "They're drinking beer."

"Yea, I noticed." Kent grinned. "That's incentive to sink as many as possible."

"I'll try my best," Carissa said. *If not, I nominate you to drink their beer cups.*

"Let's get this party started!" Brian yelled over the crowd. He was shirtless with a whistle around his neck. There was a fake patch of hair on his chest. Someone whispered something about him being a *Street Fighter* character. Carissa couldn't remember the name of the guy but knew he had a mohawk. "We'll flip a coin to see who shoots first. Home team chooses."

"Heads," Kent called.

Brian flipped the coin, caught it, and smiled. "It's your lucky night. Tails."

Sibling sarcasm at its finest.

Kent glared at Brian.

Brian shrugged. "Get ready to drink your panties off. Mario's good at throwing more than turtles."

Terrance laughed. "You know I'm not Mario, right?"

"What? You're not?" Brian put his hand on his chest. His eyes widened and mouth opened, aghast. "Get out."

Terrance laughed again and shot. It hit the tip of the first cup and bounced away.

"The first shot of the night is a tragic miss," Brian announced. "Need a mushroom?" Everyone in the room laughed. "Next up, Miss Amanda Henshaw. The hottest Luigi any of us has ever seen. But is she all good looks? Does she shoot worth a damn?"

Amanda gave Brian a hard look and grabbed the ping pong

ball. She aimed and shot. The ball flew straight for the middle cup in the third row. It circled around the rim and plopped into the strawberry-powered jungle juice. The crowd cheered.

Dammit. 0-1.

"Luigi strikes first blood," Brian announced. "And it looks like the first drinker of the night will be," he inched forward and looked at the jungle juice cup, "our newcomer, Carissa!"

Hesitantly, Carissa grabbed the cup, took out the ping pong ball, and handed it to Kent. *Great. This is a good start.* She downed the contents of the cup. *This jungle juice is growing on me.*

Amanda took another shot. That one went into the second cup in the last row. The crowd roared again. *0-2.*

"Another great shot for Luigi!" Brian cheered.

Shut up, Brian. Carissa groaned. *Another jungle juice cup.* She picked it up, passed the ping pong ball, and finished the cup. *Whatever, this is all in good fun. I can make this fun. Even if we lose, we're all having a good time.*

Amanda shot again. It went into the first cup in the last row. Another jungle juice cup. *0-3. Son of a bitch. Are we going to get a shot off?*

"This girl is on fire!" Brian laughed. "This could be over before they get a shot."

Carissa looked at Kent. He shrugged and put his hand on her shoulder. He whispered in her ear. "Don't worry. We got this. I'm a great shot. And, the fewer the cups, the harder it is to hit them."

I hope you're right.

Amanda's next shot spun around the rim of the third cup in the back and then spun out to the table.

"See?" Kent nudged Carissa. "Our luck is changing."

Carissa smiled. *He's kind of sweet, trying to reassure me like that. I kind of want to kiss him right now.*

Kent collected the ping pong balls, wiped them, and aimed for his next shot. "It's showtime." He shot. It bounced on the tips of two adjacent cups and on to the floor. "Crap."

Well, there went that.

"And the home field advantage is not quite panning out for Double 'O' Seven," Brian announced. "It looks like all of the hope on this team is in the hands of our, uh, fairy princess here, who is shooting for her first time. If you have fairy dust, now is the time to use it on yourself."

From behind, as if on cue, Val appeared with Jesse in tow. She reached in a little brown pouch on her hip and collected small bits of glitter in her hand. She sprinkled it on Carissa's shoulder and whispered, "Time to show the boys how it's done."

Yea. Fat chance of that happening. We're doomed.

"Just aim and shoot," Kent said. "I'll get 'em next round."

My confidence in you is staggeringly low. Come through, and then we'll talk.

Carissa collected one of the two ping pong balls in Kent's hand. She held it in her hand, got a feel for it. It was light, almost too light to get any real control over it. But, if it was any heavier, it would probably knock over the cups. Though she'd rather see the beers knocked over than drank; that would be a poor way to play the game.

This isn't golf. But hey, I'm putting a ball in a hole, right? She sighed, breathed, targeted the middle cup in the third row, and fired off her first shot. After the ball left her hand, on instinct, she shut her eyes. She wanted to know the outcome, but not to see herself miss.

The crowd roared. She opened her eyes.

1-3.

"Yea!" Val cheered in her ear.

"And the fairy sinks it!" Brian announced, then said in a lower voice, "That's the first time I've said that when not talking about a gay dude or that guy from Miami Heat." His friends laughed.

Pssh. You would say that.

"Way to go, Carissa!" Kent hugged her. It was an awkward side hug because she wasn't prepared for it.

Aww. Come on. I want a better hug from you than that. She smiled. "Thanks, Kent."

"Now let's see if you can do that again," Kent said.

Carissa did. She hit four more before she finally missed. The room was in a buzz and so was she. She finally felt the effects of the jungle juice. There was a subtle vibration throughout her body. She felt warm and fuzzy. She smiled.

5-3. Unbelievable.

"I'm going to have to commandeer that fairy dust," Brian said to Val and Carissa. They laughed. "You know, for science."

Val put her hand over the brown pouch, gave him a big toothy smile, and shook her blond head. "Over my dead body."

Brian grinned. "That can be arranged."

"Speaking of bodies," Jesse said and collected Val's hand. "There's one I have to give a thorough examination. We'll see you guys later." Val raised her two eyebrows, smiled, and they disappeared into the crowd. *Great. There she goes again.*

Terrance missed. The crowd gave him an "aww".

"Oh! Another missed shot for the legendary plumber," Brian announced. "Keep this up and Luigi might not let you clean her pipes."

The dining room filled with laughter.

Amanda kissed Terrance on the cheek and grabbed the ping pong ball. She shot. It landed in Kent's rum and coke cup.

5-4.

"Well, look at that," Brian said. "The ladies are carrying the teams tonight. So far, it's four for Super Mario and five for Goldeneye." He walked towards Kent. "Which, by the way, didn't have any fairies in it." Kent frowned. "Maybe you should have gone with 'You Only Live Twice'." A devilish smirk appeared.

"Dude. She's like, a quarter, maybe. Doesn't even look—that doesn't work."

"Still works," Brian dismissed.

What are they talking about? Dammit. I should have asked more questions about his costume. I know he's supposed to be some kind of spy. I've heard of the movies. Sat through a few that Dad and Sean watched.

"Have you seen that movie?" Kent asked Carissa. He grabbed his cup and passed the ping pong.

Why? What does that mean? She shook her head no.

"Thank God," Kent said under his breath.

Amanda sunk another one. This time, a jungle juice cup.

5-5. It's a tie.

"We're going to lose," Carissa said as she grabbed her cup. She took a sip and passed the ping pong ball. "It's tied. And, last time she shot, she got three in a row. My five in a row was a totally fluke. There's no way I'm getting that again."

Wait. Did I just say totally fluke*? The buzz is real.*

Kent rubbed her bare shoulder. His hands felt warm and tingly against her skin. She blushed. "Not with that attitude, you're not. Come on. It's a tie. I've come back from worse odds than this."

Yea. Well, I'll feel more secure if you sink something on your next round. But maybe losing wouldn't be so bad. I bet one of those make-out spots are free right now. It's been so long since I kissed a boy. And, you're nice enough. Dreamy. Oh, wait. Yes. Yes, he does look like McDreamy! A very young McDreamy. This is so on. Maybe I can convince him to, I don't know, find someone with a lab coat as part of their costume and take off his tux. That would totally do it for me.

Amanda missed. *Or that.*

"Yes!" Kent cheered. "And now, it's time for me to... to not jinx myself again." He stretched his arms and twisted his neck from left to right. "Okay. Okay. I can do this."

Brian watched and smiled. "It looks like our favorite spy is ramping himself up for a shot. Will he be able to fire a sharp shot like the assassin he is? Or, is it time to turn in his license to kill?"

Kent fired a shot. It coasted to the back and landed in the corner cup. *6-5.* The crowd erupted with cheers. People gave each other high fives. Kent winked at Carissa. She gave him a hug.

"Great shot, Kent!" Carissa said. *We might actually win this.*

"Thanks," Kent said. He held her close. Real close.

"If you two want to go pound it out, we can pause the game," Brian said. The crowd laughed.

Carissa and Kent separated. *You really know how to spoil the moment. Don't you Brian?*

Kent shot Brian the evil eye.

"Don't worry, Bro," Brian said with what sounded like some sincerity. "The night is young."

Not for me. I have to be gone by one o'clock.

"Throw the ball," Amanda called after finishing her cup. "We're getting thirsty over here."

"Help her out, Bro," Brian chimed in.

Kent shrugged and shot. It went in. *7-5.* The crowd cheered again.

"And the home field advantage is once again in effect for our favorite special agent," Brian said. "There are only three cups left for the Mario squad. And five cups left for the fairy and," he grinned, "the spy who loved her."

The spy who loved her? What? Kent doesn't love me. Wait. Wait a second. I think that might have been one of the movies Dad was watching. Oh. I see what you did there.

Kent shook his head. "How long have you been waiting to use that one?"

"Since you put on that tux," Brian said. "By the end of the night, I'll have gone through the rest of the movies. Shoot."

Kent shot. It bounced off the tip and on to the table. "Dammit. So close."

"It's fine," Carissa said. "You got two. That's more than last time. We just have to get three more between the two of us."

Brian said, "Don't worry about it, man. Live and let die."

"That," Kent smirked. "I'll be looking forward to seeing how you can squeeze *Octopussy* into a quip."

Squeeze what? What?

"Dude," Brian laughed. "Oh damn, man. That's rich. I could say so much right now. You made it too easy for me, right there. I'm going to let that one fly. Just pass her the thunderball."

"Oh, another one," Kent said. He handed Carissa the ping pong ball.

Alright, while they joke around, I'm going to finish this game.

Carissa shot for the cup. It spun around the tip and flew out. *Dang it. Put too much muscle in it.* She frowned.

"We're still in the lead," Kent said.

Terrance smiled, aimed, and shot. It went in. *7-6.* It was the last jungle juice cup. "There ya go!"

Dang it. I had to miss. Now we're going to lose.

"Finally, after two failed attempts, the king of jump, hop, and stomp has finally landed a shot," Brian announced. "He needs one more shot to make this a tie again."

Amanda rubbed his back. "You can do this baby."

Apparently, he couldn't. Terrance shot over the cup.

Yes! Now, we need Amanda's hot streak to come to an end.

"Well, we won't be calling him the man with the golden gun tonight." Brian smiled at Kent. Kent rolled his eyes. "But hey, it's

Amanda's turn. She's had a real gold finger this whole time."

"That one didn't even make sense," Kent complained.

None of this is making sense to me. Boys.

"Stop being jealous, Kent." Brian smirked and took a swig of his beer. "Of course, it did."

Amanda shot. It spun around the rim of the cup and fell in. 7-7. The crowd roared. Amanda and Terrance hugged.

Carissa covered her eyes. *Well, it's not so bad. I'd only have to drink one cup of beer compared to five or six. We did pretty good.*

"And we have ourselves a game, people!" Brian shouted. "It's a tie. A true seven-seven matchup. With three cups left on either side, this is when things get interesting. The game can end at any moment if someone has a hot streak."

Kent whispered, "But she hasn't hit more than three in a row. So, we still have a shot."

Amanda missed. "Dammit."

Thank God. We still have a shot. Whatever you do, don't miss, Kent. Don't miss.

Kent looked at the ball, pointed, aimed, pointed, aimed, and breathed. *Oh no. He's putting too much thought into it.* And then, he fired. It bounced off the back tip of the cup and on to the floor.

Son of a bitch.

"Ooo, and a miss," Brian announced. "Too bad. So sad. Looks like her majesty's secret service needs to hire better agents."

That's mean. I know siblings make fun of each other. But I'm never that mean to Sean. Err. Well, umm, not usually. Rarely. I don't know. Okay. Yes, I am. That's still mean.

Kent frowned and passed the ping pong ball. "Looks like it's all on you."

Great. His sex appeal just decreased by eighty percent. Wasn't he the one who suggested this game?

Carissa aimed and shot at the front cup. It sunk. The crowd cheered. *8-7.* Carissa narrowed her eyes and gave Amanda a hard stare. *Take that, Amanda.*

Amanda glared back and drank from her cup.

"Well, this is quite a showdown," Brian announced. "With only two cups left on the opposing team, it looks like Carissa has a view to a kill." He smiled at Kent.

Kent ignored Brian. "Are you sure you haven't played beer

pong before? You're a natural."

"No," Carissa said. "Never played it before in my life." *But don't jinx me! One of us has to win this.*

"You could have fooled me," Kent said. He was close. The crowd pressed in to see the last shots of the game and they were elbow to elbow. But that was okay.

Carissa breathed, aimed, and shot. It hit the front of the cup and bounced away. *Dammit! Ugh. Come on, Carissa! You had that. There's no way they're both going to miss. Oh man, we're done.*

"Oh!" Brian shouted. "So close. So unfortunate. This is it, people. This is the clutch round. It could all end right here, which means all bets are closing."

Bets? What? I don't understand. Carissa looked around. To her surprise, people pulled cash out of their pockets. Brian's dark-haired girl from the hot tub collected the money and took notes. *I-I'm blown. I can't believe this. They are gambling. This is new. I just hope no one's betting on my team. We stink.*

Terrance snapped the straps of his overalls, aimed, said, "It's suh me, ah Mario," and shot. The crowd cheered as it landed in the cup and splashed the rum and coke on to the table.

Oh. I get it. That's why they've been getting excited this whole time. They have money riding on it. I feel bad for anyone that bet on me. I had some good shots. I'm sure some did. They'll be so disappointed. Carissa frowned. *Then again, who bets on a stupid drinking game at a high school Halloween party? Is this normal?*

Brian yelled, "Clean up in aisle one!" Laughter followed. Someone fetched napkins. "And with that, the game's tied once more. Can the adventuring plumber finish the level?"

Carissa put her hand to Kent's ear and asked, "Is he always like this? Your brother?"

"No," Kent said. "We're hosting a party, remember? He's more of a showman and host. I'm better at the other stuff."

The other stuff? Carissa shrugged. "What other stuff?"

Kent smiled. "Everything else."

Carissa laughed. *Yep. They're brothers, alright.*

Terrance fired and missed. *Thank God.*

"Maybe next time, we'll use turtle shells instead of ping pong balls," Brian said.

Terrance gave him the finger.

"Sorry," Brian said. "I've already got two lovely ladies lined up tonight. But I'll check my calendar."

Ugh. Two girls? That's. Ugh. Do they know you have them lined up after each other like meat? Or are they at the same time? Nope. Don't wanna know. Probably the second one. Nevermind. I'm sorry I asked.

Amanda winked at Carissa and fired. It sunk. *8-9.* The crowd cheered again. A couple high fives were exchanged.

That's it. We're done for. Stick a fork in us.

"Boom!" Brian yelled. "Oh, they are knocking the living daylights out of you. One more shot and the game is over!"

"We get it, Brian," Kent said. He finished his cup of rum and coke and gave out a satisfying "ahh". He smiled, "Thanks, Luigi. I was getting thirsty."

Really, Kent? You're talking trash? We're about to lose!

"Oh, getting thirsty, huh?" Amanda said. "Here's another." She shot. It bounced next to the cup and into Kent's hand. He smiled.

Brian laughed. "So close! So close. Maybe you'll die another day." Kent facepalmed.

Get your head in the game, Kent. We have one more chance to hit something before we lose.

"Kent," Carissa said. "We only have one cup left."

"I know. I know. I got this."

You haven't had it so far.

He held two balls in his right hand. He pointed at the first cup. Shot. It went in. *9-9.* A few cheered. He pointed at the second cup. The last cup. Shot. It went in. The room erupted in cheers and complaints.

"Game, set, match," Kent gloated and smiled. Amanda and Terrance glared at him, collected their cups, and drank.

Carissa stared with her mouth wide open. *What the heck? He just pointed and shot like a pro. Why wasn't he doing that the whole game? And game, set, match. That's a tennis thing. How did he know I played tennis? Or, does he play tennis? Who am I kidding? He's a country club kid. Of course, he plays tennis. They probably have a tennis court in the backyard.*

"Well-played, man," Brian said. "Well-played. I thought you were going to give this one up."

"Can't win them all." Kent grinned. "That'd look suspicious." He winked. "But I had to win this one. I didn't want to disappoint Carissa."

"You were holding back?" Carissa frowned. "You mean, you were intentionally losing?"

Kent shrugged. "I had to make it interesting, especially after how you were shooting. You're telling me that was the first time you've played beer pong."

"Yes," Carissa said. "I've never played beer pong before."

"I'm calling bullshit," Brian said and wrote Goldeneye on the second-round bracket. "Where's my phone? I'm calling bullshit right now."

"I haven't," Carissa said with a smile. Her face felt warm and tingly. "Really."

Kent pointed. "Oh. She's cracking. She's totally lying to us. See. We aren't the only ones who are running a game here." He stepped close and put his arms around her.

Is he about to kiss me? Am I about to be kissed? Carissa lifted her chin. "When we're bored, my brother and I will sometimes throw coins into cups. We've played since we were tiny. It was never with liquid or ping pong balls. Just a game to pass the time."

"Ah, see," Kent leaned in. "I sure know how to pick 'em." His soft lips met hers. *I'm being kissed! He's kissing me!* She smiled as he pressed himself against her. *Hmm. And a very take charge kisser.* She reached up and rested her arms around his neck.

Brian nodded. "Looks like things are moving on nicely. I'm going to grab some drinks. Get the night started."

Started? It hasn't started, yet? Carissa unclasped her lips from Kent's. "I have to leave by one. My mom said I have to get out of here by one."

"Is that so?" Brian asked with a smirk.

"Well, can't you just tell her you left and stay?" Kent asked.

Ha. You don't know my mom. She will track me on her GPS. Carissa smirked. "No. I can't do that."

Kent frowned. "But, don't you want to stay the night?" His hand rubbed her lower back. *Oh, that feels good.* "You know. Stay with me?"

"I'll stay as long as I can," Carissa said. "There's just no way I can stay past one." She looked into his eyes. They were intense. He was intent on her staying.

It's nice to be wanted and to be wanted by someone I want. I really like him right now. It helps that he's a good kisser.

Kent smiled and collected her hand. "Well, in that case, let's you and me go somewhere a bit more private. You know. So we can enjoy the time we have left."

You mean, your bedroom, right? You want me in your bedroom so we can kiss. And probably more than kiss. Well, definitely more than kiss. I mean, he wants to have sex with me. Of course, he does. Am I ready for that? I want it. If it's as good as Val says it is, if it's as good as it feels to have someone touching you, better than how it feels when I've touched myself, I want it. But I don't think I'm ready yet. Not tonight. Not with him. Not yet.

"How about that drink?" Carissa asked. "Let's have some drinks. We still have a few more games to win, remember?"

"Yea, we do," Kent said. He looked at Brian. "Drinks?"

Brian watched the two. "Alright. I'll be back with drinks. What are we having?"

"Carissa doesn't like beer," Kent said. "So, mixed drinks. Mix something for her." He smiled. "Something special."

"Special drink, for a special girl, right?" Brian said and flagged the dark-haired girl from the hot tub. They moved through the crowd.

Carissa kissed Kent and smiled. "You're such a nice guy. Good kisser, too. Let's leave it at that tonight, okay? See where things go later?"

Kent kissed her forehead. "Yea. Sure."

CHAPTER SIX

The room was a blur. The world was spinning. And her insides were ready to become her outsides. Carissa staggered.

Oh, I think I'm going to be sick.

It was three hours, three beer pong games, and fourteen drinks into the party that she stood in the bathroom looking at herself in the mirror. When she said she felt sick, Kent helped her to his personal bathroom. Her head hung over the toilet as she surrendered the bits of fine Italian cuisine that remained in her stomach from dinner. Kent held her hair and rubbed her back.

Ugh. I feel so terrible. Oh my God. How did I drink so much? It was supposed to be a few drinks. Sigh. I'm so glad Kent's here to take care of me. He's such a good guy.

After she felt a little better, she asked Kent to go outside while she cleaned herself. He gave her a towel and soup, guest toothpaste and toothbrush, mouthwash, and left. She spent the next fifteen minutes cleaning herself to be more presentable. But honestly, she was ready to leave. It was time to go home. She was exhausted. She could barely stand and was using all of her will to avoid collapse.

Kent knocked. "You okay in there? It's been a while."

"Y-yes," Carissa forced out. She could barely speak.

"Can I come in?" Kent asked.

"Y-yes," Carissa said again. "Please do."

Kent opened the door. There was an expression she hadn't seen before. A suspicious smirk. But then again, he was kind of fuzzy. Her vision shifted in and out of focus. "You look tired. Do you want to lie down?"

God yes. I could sleep for days. She nodded.

"Okay," Kent said. "Let me help you to bed."

Yea. Sure. Help me to bed. I need to rest. I'm so tired. I can barely keep my eyes open. My legs are so weak. I could topple over at any moment. Carissa barely lifted her arm and whispered, "Help."

Kent stepped in, knelt behind her, put her arm around his neck, and helped her step-by-step out of his bathroom to his bed. She faded in and out, staggered. One of her legs gave out on her, but he caught her. "Woah, woah. I got you. I got you. We're almost there."

Sleep. I just want to sleep. I can't go any further. She teared up and sniffled.

"It's okay," Kent reassured her with a soft voice. "It's okay. I'm right here. And the bed's right here." He guided her on to the bed and let her lay down. He took off her shoes and pulled the fairy wings off her back. Then, he guided her legs and feet on to the bed. "See. You're on the bed."

"Thank you, Kents." Carissa smiled. There were three Kents. Each one of them: very helpful. Now, if only they could stop the room from spinning. She closed her eyes. "I'm going to sleep."

Kent rubbed her face with the tip of his fingers and whispered, "You do that." He kissed her forehead. "Sleep well."

"Mm, kay," Carissa said and gave in to sleep.

2

She heard whispers. And though she couldn't open her eyes yet, because those eyes refused to open, because those eyelids felt like anvils, she listened.

"I must say," a familiar voice said. "I'm impressed. I mean, she's a fucking tank. She should have been unconscious an hour ago. It's like you drugged Wolverine and shit."

Drugged? I don't understand.

"Well, if at first you don't succeed, try and try and try and try again," the second voice said. *Kent?*

They were in the same room but sounded as though they were down the hall. Someone sat on the bed. She could feel a hand rest on her stomach. It moved to her chest and then down between her legs.

What are you doing? Why are you touching me? You're not supposed to be touching me. Especially there.

Carissa fought her eyes opened and blinked them clear. She saw Brian sitting on the bed next to her and Kent standing over the bed, watching. Her eyes fought against her and slammed shut.

"She's nice," Brian said. "Where was she when I was in high school?"

"A freshman," Kent said. "Hands off. She's mine. You already have two."

I am not yours. I am definitely not yours.

"Shit, her body's incredible," Brian said. His hand moved to her chest and squeezed. "She's fit as fuck. Has great tits. I'll trade you. Two for one. This might be your best find, yet."

Trade? What the hell? You don't trade people.

"Yea, finders' keepers," Kent said. "This is why I keep an eye out for the athletic girls. Swim team. Soccer team. Or in her case, the tennis team. Hard bodies, bro."

Brian's hand left her body. "The student has become the master. But if you're going to do something, you might want to do it now. I'm sure Val's gonna wanna know where her girl is."

Val? Val. Where's Val?

"Nah, Val knows she's in here with me," Kent said. "She said I should help her girl lose her virginity."

Wha-what?

"Well, do it then," Brian said. "I'm hard as a motherfucker. Initiation or not, if you don't do her, I will."

Someone got off the bed. And a minute later, a smaller set of hands replaced the first, exploring her body. *No. No. This is not happening. Please no. Don't allow this to happen. Someone stop this.*

Carissa fought with all her will to move but couldn't. Her body was useless to her. She started to cry. She wanted to scream but couldn't. Kent rolled her over and unzipped. He pulled the strapless costume off her and to the floor. She could feel the air on her skin. She was reduced to her bra and panties.

This can't happen. Someone has to come in and stop this.

Anybody. Somebody. Val. Where are you Val? Where did you go?

Kent rolled her on her back and massaged the inside of her thighs.

"Black laced panties," Brian said. "They've always been my favorite."

The hands stopped. "Listen, if you're going to record this, shut the fuck up. You don't hear Spielberg narrating shit."

"Yea, well," Brian said. "That's actually pretty good. I don't have a comeback for that one."

Kent's hands removed her bra and settled on her breasts. *Get your hands off me. Get your hands off of me!* Get your hands off me!!

"Oh, yea, they're nice," Kent said. "So soft. Shit. I'm about to cum just touching them."

She could feel her adrenaline increase, some of the fog in her head faded. But it wasn't enough. Whatever they gave her, it was stronger. *I'm not strong enough. I can't, I'm too tired. Why are they doing this? If I could just scream.* No. The music was too loud. *But I'll try. I still have to try. Someone has to hear me. Someone has to stop this.* Someone, please stop this!

Kent's hands moved from her chest to her panties and slowly pulled them down past her knees to her ankles. With a tug, they were gone and cast who knows where. He spread her legs open.

Anytime now, Val! Any time now! *Please stop this.* Please! Don't do this!

Carissa's eyes opened and connected with his. Somehow, she managed to say, "Nuh-no. D-don't. S-s-stop. S-s-stop."

Kent hovered over her and leaned in close. "You have the prettiest pussy I've ever seen, Carissa. You're so perfect." He kissed her.

You are a piece of shit! Go to Hell!

"For the fraternity."

And that's when it happened. Kent reached down and pushed himself inside of her, slowly, until all of him was inside of her. It was over. Kent stole her virginity.

3

Kent only lasted two minutes, but it was the worst two minutes of her life. She laid there, slowly regaining control of her body from whatever they gave her.

After Kent was done with her, he wiped himself on the sheets, pulled up his boxer briefs and tuxedo pants, and walked out.

Brian, with one hand holding his camera, started to unzip his pants. He crouched down to Carissa and said, "Time for round two." He dropped his shorts.

No. Not again.

"Wait a minute," Brian said. He leaned down and stared at her vagina. He yelled, "Kent, you fucker! You didn't use a condom."

"No sloppy seconds, Brian!" Kent called back into the room. "Unless you want your dick swimming in my jizz."

Brian scowled and pulled up his shorts. "That's a dick move, man!" He stormed out and left the door wide open.

Carissa laid in the bed, helpless and exposed. *I want to die.*

A few passer-byers looked in, whispered, and laughed. "Check this out." They pulled out their cellphones and took snaps. After five more minutes, more people gathered, and someone yelled, "Damn! The dick was so good she's just layin there." The group laughed hysterically.

Another guy said, "Get out the way. She ain't seen nothin till she seen this." Someone else said something she couldn't understand. More pictures were taken. "I'm about to go in her."

Val pushed past the group, her face flushed. "Hey! What do you think you're doing?" Her mouth went slack when she saw Carissa lying naked on the bed with wide eyes and tears streaming down her face. "Shit." Val looked at the group, yelled, "Show's over!" and expelled them from the room. She slammed the door, locked it, and ran to Carissa.

Val? Val? Where have you been?

"Did Kent do this to you?" Val asked. "Did he just screw you and leave you here like this? Drunk and naked?" She grabbed the covers and flung them over Carissa. Then, she raised Carissa head on the pillows.

Yes. Carissa forced a nod, sobbing. Her arms were weak and numb with not enough strength in them to cover herself.

"I'm so sorry, Carissa," Val said. Her eyes searched for the fairy costume and panties cast on the floor. "I'm getting you out of here."

Where were you?

"Val? Where... were... you?" Carissa struggled to ask before a world's worth of tears poured out of her. She sobbed while Val dressed her, until she could stand, and on and off again all the way to the car.

4

Val said she wasn't sure she was in the right state of mind to drive but would have to be. Carissa was a mess of tears and snot and couldn't give a damn how buzzed Val was.

You can drive us into a tree for all I care. Then it can all be over, and I won't feel so dirty and pathetic anymore. I won't feel their hands all over me, anymore. I won't feel him inside me anymore. Feel and smell his breath in my face as he hovered over me and pushed himself into me again, and again, and again. Just kill us both, Val.

Getting no response from Carissa, Val pushed the car from idle to forty-five in three seconds. She made it to the end of the block, made a sharp right, and pushed it.

Go faster, Val. Go faster. I want to die. Just kill me now. Carissa sobbed, unsure if she'd ever stop.

Val stole glances between her friend, the road, and the clock. Her face was still and red. Her blue eyes were dark and distant.

"It's one fifteen, Carissa," Val said with a soft, low voice. "We have to call your mom. We're already late."

I, I can't talk to her right now. I'm a total mess, and she'll want to know why. What am I going to tell her? Hey Mom, guess who just got raped? You were right. I went and got myself drunk, which you said not to do. They put something in my drink. I got stupid drunk and fell around and puked my guts out like an idiot. And they had their hands all over me. And he put himself inside of me, and pushed, and pushed, and laughed, and came inside of me.

Ugh. Carissa wretched.

Val shot a glance at her with wide eyes. "You're not about to puke, are you?"

Carissa shook her head. *No Val. I'm not about to puke in your precious car! But if I did, I'd aim right for your seat!*

"Okay," Val said. "If you need to, just wave at me and I'll pull over. Do you have your phone? I gave you your phone. You still have it, right?"

"Yea," Carissa whined.

"Okay," Val said. "You have to call your mom. It's after one. Call her before she calls us."

What does it matter? If I don't call her, she'll call me. She'll be upset, pissed. She might even say I can't go to another party. Fine! *Why would I* ever *want to go to another party? I* don't! *I hate parties! I hate people! Kent raped me. Brian wanted to. And the others, they just stood and laughed at me. Naked and alone! Helpless. For all I know, they knew this was going to happen. Someone even said he was next. What the hell is wrong with these boys? They go to these parties to have sex with sick, drunk, drugged girls.* You disgust me!

Val stopped at a red light and met Carissa's eyes, then looked back at the road. Carissa looked at herself in the mirror. She'd washed away some of her makeup after getting sick, but what remained streaked down her face. Her hair was blown in every direction by the car ride. The air was thick, cool, and refreshing. But there was no doubt that the humidity would make her hair frizzy. As if that was anything to be concerned about at a time like this.

Who needs hair, anyway? Maybe I'll cut it all off. How many guys out there drug and have sex with drunk bald girls?

"Okay." Val reached for her purse. "I'll call her."

"No, no," Carissa said. "I have to do it. Just give me a minute."

And by a minute, I really mean, give me a year. I just can't. I don't know what to say. And the moment I hear her voice, I know I'm going to cry. She'll answer the phone, say my name with her mom voice, and I'll break down into tears. She'll ask me what's wrong because that's what moms do. They ask the hard questions. The right questions. The questions that hit emotional buttons and send you spiraling into mother and daughter mode, be it supporter and comforted, or mortal enemies.

Sigh. I really want to talk to her. I need my mom. I wish I could be with her right now and tell her everything. Cry in her arms while she lies and tells me everything is going to be okay. But I just, I couldn't bear to look at her. See the look on her face when she realizes that her daughter isn't clean anymore. She isn't innocent anymore. She's filthy. She's just some drunk, used up ho now.

"It's been a minute," Val said.

Shut up, Val. You weren't counting the minutes when you were off with Jesse doing God knows what while I was in that room with Kent and Brian getting raped. Where was your sensitivity to time then? You left me alone with them almost the whole night. We arrived. You slipped away. We were playing beer pong. You slipped in and out occasionally. You had a few drinks with us before Jesse took your hand and pulled you off somewhere. And there I was, sandwiched between Kent, Brian, and some strange girls. All insisting on shots, after I already took in too much from the beer pong games. At least we won the tournament. I can wear that badge, for what it's worth. Nothing...

Kent was a shyster. Apparently, he and his brother practice playing on that table all the time, giving them an incredible advantage. He was pretending to be bad to get people to bet against him. What can I expect from a cheat other than for him to be a rotten cheating raping scumbag? Mom warned me about boys like him, too.

God, I hate that she's right. Oh, and she's going to rub it in my face, too. "See, Carissa. I was right. You should have listened to me. You never should have gone to that party. You'll get drunk and raped like all those girls I knew in college that got involved with the wrong guys."

Was she raped? Was Mom one of those girls? Is that why she was so hell bent on me not going? Was she raped and wanted to spare me the horror? I wish you told me, Mom! I wish you said something.

"She's far gone," Val whispered to herself. "Oh, what a night."

When I have a daughter, if I have a daughter, assuming any other guy will want to have anything to do with me after being raped, and if I even want to be near or touched by a guy again, would I tell her I was raped? Would I tell her that I was stupid enough to go to a party with Val and accept drinks from a rich guy I barely knew anything about, who put God knows what in that stupid jungle juice?

No. I wouldn't want to embarrass myself and look like an idiot. I wouldn't want to say, "Hey kid, your mom was a giant idiot. Don't be such a stupid idiot like I was and get yourself raped. Now go to

DAKOTA

your room and cradle your innocence while you still have it. And lock that vagina up tight. Lock it behind a chastity belt if you even think about sneaking to a party without my approval."

Shit! And Mom gave me her approval without Dad's consent. She gave me the okay. Now, if she finds out, or if he finds out, she'll be in trouble, too, for letting her stupid daughter go out and get raped. It's not like I wanted to. It's not like I went there, bent over, and said, "Stick me, boys! I'm drunk and ready to be taken advantage of." Okay. So what? I had drinks. It doesn't entitle them to anything. It's not my fault. I just wanted a boyfriend. I wanted someone to fall in love with me like in the movies.

We were supposed to make each other laugh, walk under the moonlight. Our hands were supposed to casually touch each other, giving each of us a shock. Then, we'd peer into each other's eyes and know we're meant to be with each other forever.

Whatever. I know that's total bullshit. The movies are a lie. But it's not supposed to be like this. I didn't want this. I never asked for this. I don't deserve this!

"Hey, Misses Boisseau," Val said into her phone. "It's Val calling to check-in with you."

Carissa's head spun around quickly. Her eyes wide. She reached for the phone, but Val batted her hand away. This, while she drove down the street at forty-five miles per hour.

"Val, why are you calling me instead of Carissa?" Mom asked. Her tired and annoyed voice boomed from the car speakers.

Oh no. Not that voice. That's not her disgustingly cheerful after-sex voice. Nope. It's her "things haven't gone according to plan and everyone else will suffer for it" voice. Dammit! Not tonight, of all nights! What did you do Dad?

"Where's Carissa?"

And now she wants to talk to me.

"I'm here, Mom," Carissa whined. She tried to control her voice. Tried not to cry. Tried to sound chipper, and not at all how she actually felt. How did she feel? *I feel like a flaming pile of shit that's been smashed by a steam roller.*

"It's past one o'clock," Mom said. "Are you at Val's place?"

"We're literally two minutes away," Val said. "It's right around the corner."

"That question was for Carissa, Val," Mom said and let out a loud sigh. "Why is Val calling me and not you?"

That's it. I'm losing it. Carissa burst into tears.

"What? Are you crying?" Mom asked. Her tone changed from ready to chastise to concerned parent. "Is that Carissa crying? What happened? Tell me what happened, now."

Val parked the car. "It was a rough night. Some of the boys at the party were really mean and embarrassed her in front of a lot of people."

Carissa shot Val a glare. *Calling them "really mean" is the understatement of the century. They ruined me! Embarrassed? I was naked, unable to move, and covered in semen! They were ready to run a train on me! Mean and embarrassed doesn't cover it.*

Mom grumbled something under her voice that didn't translate over the phone. "Val, what happened? Be straight with me."

Val gave Carissa a side glance and said, "These two guys pulled the wings off her costume and made inappropriate comments." She paused and thought about it. "And one of them grabbed at her." Carissa's eyes widened. Val pressed mute on the phone. "I don't know what else to say unless you want to tell her the truth."

Carissa put her hands over her face. *Oh, I should have gone trick or treating with Lizzie. Or maybe accepted the invitation from that talkative church girl on the bus. It's kind of hard to get drunk, drugged, or raped at a church party. Well, unless you're an altar boy.*

"Carissa, don't let those boys get to you," Mom said in her soothing mom voice that compelled Carissa to cry even more and confess everything. Spill all the unpleasant, gruesome and graphic details. She fought the urge.

Will this woman get off the phone before I seriously lose my shit?

Val took the phone off mute. "We're home, now. My home, that is. I'll get her to bed."

"Were you two drinking?" Mom asked.

I see our bag, but where's the cat?

"No," Val spit out quickly and shrugged her shoulders at Carissa. "Definitely not."

You are such an idiot.

"Val, I'm going to give you a chance to rethink your answer," Mom said. Her tone had enough bite to chew through the telephone cord. "Were you and Carissa drinking at the party?"

Carissa put her hand to her face. *The woman is a lie detector. She can smell lies coming from a mile away. I don't know why she's wasting her time in a publishing agency when she could work law enforcement.*

"Okay," Val said. "We had a few. Only because they didn't have any alternatives and we didn't want to be the only squares at the party that didn't have a drink. That kind of stuff carries itself around the halls."

Val...

"You know, Val," Mom started. *Oh no. When she starts a sentence with "you know", she usually rips you to pieces.* "It's late. I'm tired. I'm sure you are, too. So, I'm going to take it easy on you tonight. But if you lie or give me some lame excuse like that again, you'll be the one in tears."

You got off easy, Val. Oh wow, you got off easy.

Val shrank in her seat. "Okay."

"You two go to bed," Mom said. "Cari, you feel better, okay? I love you."

"Okay, Mom," Carissa whimpered. "Love you, too."

"Night, Misses Boisseau," Val said.

It was too late. Mom hung up.

5

At Val's place, Carissa sat in the bathtub, arms wrapped around her legs, hair in her face, as hot water poured down on her. It would take a world of water to make her clean, she suspected, as tears poured out of her eyes.

I'm going to cry so much that I die. Is that a thing? Can you die from crying too much? It'll be me. I'll be the first.

Val sat on the other side of the curtain, quiet, until the sobs came to rest. Carissa stood, turned off the water, and sighed a long sigh.

Maybe it's my fault. I wanted to kiss him. I wanted to have sex with him, later, in a romantic setting, as a couple. I did hug him, flirt with him, and after some drinks, many drinks, and after we won the games, I did kiss him. Just a few innocent kisses. Maybe I led him on. Maybe, if I hadn't kissed him, none of this would have happened.

Val held out a white robe as Carissa stepped out of the bathtub. She grabbed a towel and wrapped her hair in it. They strode to bed, climbed under the covers, and lay silently until Val asked, "Cari, what happened before I found you?"

What do you mean what happened before you found me? Kent had his way with me and left me naked and exposed.

"You know, Val," Carissa said, her tears welled up again.

"I don't, actually," Val said. "When I got there, you were naked and crying, in the bed, alone, with those pervs staring at you, and one about to come in on you. What happened before that? I mean, I'm assuming you and Kent had sex. But you seem to be a lot more upset and Kent was nowhere in sight on our way out."

Carissa sighed and took deep breaths to keep her tears at bay. "*We* didn't have sex, Val. He just, he just used my body."

Val blinked. "I don't understand."

"I was out of it, exhausted," Carissa said and took another deep breath. "I couldn't move. I could barely open my eyes. And, he, he and Brian came in the room. They, they said they drugged me."

Val froze. Her face lost all its color. She whispered, "They drugged you?"

"That's what they said," Carissa said. "And then they undressed me. I couldn't move. I couldn't speak. I tried so hard. I wanted to protest, yell, say something." Tears leaked and streamed down her face.

Val grabbed a box of tissues from her nightstand and handed it to Carissa. She wiped her face and blew her nose.

"They, they took my clothes off and had their hands all over me. And, Brian said he wanted to have sex with me, and, and, umm, umm," she wrestled with her fatigued mind, "he said he'd trade his girls for me. He'd trade them with Kent for me."

Val stared at her.

"Kent rejected his offer, pushed his thing inside of me, and kept pushing until he was done," Carissa said. "I was raped." The word "raped" clung to the air, lingered. It was the heaviest word she'd ever spoken.

"Shit," Val cussed. It was all she could say, apparently.

"I wanted to scream," Carissa said. "I wanted to fight and yell, and resist, but I couldn't. I couldn't do anything." Her face was red and nose raw. She batted her tears with tissues. "I've never felt so helpless in my life."

"I'm so sorry," Val said in a low voice. She stared off in the distance. Where was she now? Where was she then? Why did she feel a hundred miles away?

"I can't believe this," Carissa said. "They, they took my virginity. They stole it from me. That was it. I don't—" She paused. "I won't ever have another first time. That's how I'll remember the first time. Lying, half sick and drunk, while he pushed himself into me. And, I didn't even enjoy it. It, it hurt."

"It does for some," Val said. Her eyes locked on Carissa's. "The first time. It hurts for some. And then it doesn't. It feels good. Really good. You'll see."

"Sex is the last thing I want right now, Val!" Carissa snapped. "I don't want to be anywhere near boys. They're disgusting."

Val didn't say anything. *Of course, she won't. Sex is all she can talk about, lately.*

"Where were you?" Carissa asked. She could feel her blood start to boil. "We went to the party together, but I barely saw you."

"I was with Jesse," Val said. Her face reddened. "We danced and drank, made out, danced more. We watched you play beer pong, had drinks with you. But I saw you and Kent connecting and wanted to give you two space. You seemed to be into each other. So, I was like, cool. My girl's going to hook up with Kent. That's why you were invited." She put her hand to her face. "So you and Kent could connect and potentially hook up."

"What?" Carissa spit out and sat up.

Val sighed. "Apparently, Kent saw you playing tennis at a home game. He watched the whole game and was fascinated by you. So, he asked around about you. A few people knew that you and I are close. And, it was going around that Jesse and I were talking. And, Kent was friends with DeQuan's brother, the football player, umm..."

Oh, that figures. Mister, I got hoes set aside for your little brother. What a piece of work.

"Nathan, that's his name," Val continued. "He's in our AP math class. The tallest one who got a tattoo of a bull on his right shoulder. He's the one they call the bull because he can rush through just about any defensive line and has a temper. Remember?"

Carissa nodded. *Yes. I also remember you saying you wanted to ride the bull.*

"Anyway, Nathan asked Jesse about you and me. Jesse spilled the beans that you were Sean's big sister. So, Nathan got DeQuan to ask what you and he were doing for Halloween. Sean said he was hanging out with his girlfriend's family. He mentioned you didn't have plans but might go trick or treating with a younger cousin or something. DeQuan told Nathan. Nathan told Kent. And, Nathan and Kent talked to Jesse. They told Jesse that if he and I could convince you to come to Kent's Halloween party, then he and I were invited."

Carissa sighed. *I hate people.*

"I'm sorry, Cari," Val apologized. "I had no idea, no idea, that this was his intention. I mean, he was really into you. And, he was excited about a chance to spend Halloween with you. He asked all these questions about your interests and likes and people you knew. How popular you were. It was like he had a cute crush on you. Plus, his family is rich. It seemed like a win-win for you. A win-win for all of us, really."

Of course. You get invited to a party at a mansion. Your near and dear friend could potentially be with a rich guy. There's no way you wouldn't benefit from it. And, I'd probably have done the same. Not realizing his intentions, I might have done the same.

"I'm sorry, really," Val said. "I can't believe he, he would do that." She paused. "I can't believe he drugged you and—" She bit her lip and chewed on the thought. Then, she froze. "What are you going to do?"

What am I going to do? That's a good question. What should I do? Call the police? I have to do something about it.

"I don't know," Carissa said. "I've been so upset. I haven't even thought about it. I should go to the police, shouldn't I?"

Val didn't say anything. She sat silently; her eyes locked on Carissa.

"I mean, he raped me," Carissa said. "Kent's a rapist. Him and Brian. And they were so, so casual about it." Her mind flashed to a visual of Kent leaning over her. She wanted to vomit. "They've probably done it before to other girls. Or, they'll do it again if they haven't already. Shouldn't I tell the police? I've been raped. They should suffer. They should go to jail. And, I don't know, get raped by some big muscled guys named Bubba and Meat. They should go to prison. They're monsters."

Val whispered. "Yea. But, if we go to the police, you'll have to tell your parents what happened."

Shit. She's right. But if they locked me in my room until I go to college, I honestly wouldn't mind it.

"And, well, it's possible that everyone else at school will hear about the rape, too," Val said.

Ugh. That's terrible! I suppose it's a good thing I'm a nobody. People don't follow the ladies' tennis team or golf team. Or amateur sports leagues. They probably don't even know we have those teams. Maybe I'll be safe? They won't know me enough to make a big deal out of it, right? The last thing I want is everyone talking about me.

"You'll be called rape girl, like, umm, what's her name," Val snapped her fingers, "Lizzie Malone." But the guys called her, Moaning Malone.

Carissa slumped. *Oh my God! Would that really be my nickname? No one knew who Lizzie was and then that was all she was known for. She was so embarrassed; she left school. If this gets out, people will stare at me and whisper about me wherever I go. I hate him! I hate him so much! He's ruined everything.*

Val continued, "And, well, I'm concerned."

You're concerned! You're concerned? Concerned about what? Your reputation isn't going to be ruined. People aren't going to be looking at you as rape girl. The girl that had too much to drink and got screwed and left naked for all to see and laugh at. Oh no. And people took pictures of me. That's a thing to be concerned about. People have naked pictures of me on their phones. There are pictures of me out there for anyone to see and share. Dirty boys looking at naked pictures of me, jerking off and sharing them with friends who will do the same. Ugh. I feel sick.

"Why?" Carissa asked.

"Well, did anyone else see Kent or Brian in the room with you?" Val said. "Or did they see them leave?"

"I-I don't know." Carissa frowned. "I didn't see anyone. I was in a bad place at the moment. You know, after being raped."

Val, what are you getting at? You're making me feel worse and worse!

"I'm worried, when it comes down to it, it'll be a he said, she said, you know? Your word against theirs."

No. No. Someone had to see them leave. Someone had to be outside the room, in the hall, somewhere in that area.

"I mean, you two looked really close," Val went on. "I pretty much figured you two were going to hook up. A couple people thought you two were already. It sure looked like you two were headed in that direction. It might be hard to convince people, after everything seen in the party, that it wasn't, umm, you know, consensual."

So, what you're saying is, "Carissa, you shouldn't go to the police. You'll become a social pariah. Everyone will look down at or pity you. And, no one's going to believe you anyway, because you two looked like you were a couple. You looked like you were into him." I hate people. I hate Kent. I hate Brian. And Val, I'm really starting to hate you, too. God. Why did I go to this party? I-I'm going to cry again. If, if I cry one more time...

"Let's just sleep," Carissa barely whispered while holding back more tears. She could feel a lump in her throat. "I'm so tired. Let's just, let's go to sleep."

"Okay," Val said. She settled under the blankets. "Good idea. I'm exhausted."

I bet you are.

A half hour later, Carissa laid beside Val, drained and sleepless. Every time she closed her eyes, she could hear Brian and Kent talking about her as though she were a piece of meat. She could hear, smell, and feel Kent's alcohol breath. She could feel his hands against her. She could feel his tongue gliding along her cheek. She cringed and squirmed. She could feel the pressure of him inside of her.

Please. God. If you're really out there, make it all go away. I don't want to think about it anymore.

And then, she fell asleep.

CHAPTER SEVEN

Saturday, Carissa was not interested in having a girl's day with Val, which included shopping, eating at *Nom Nom Nom*, and watching *Zombieland* in the theater. She wanted to go home, take a bath, and sleep all day. Val, however, insisted on salvaging the weekend. She suggested staying in bed, eating crème sticks, pizza rolls, cheese bites, and watching movies on demand.

Well, I was going to lay around, anyway. It's hard to resist cheese bites. Are those strawberry and cherry crème sticks? Okay. I guess I'll stay a little while longer. I'll probably sleep through the movies, anyway.

"Or, instead of movies on demand, we can watch these." Val revealed her secret weapon, a Julia Roberts movie collection.

Carissa's eyes shot open. *Ugh. There went sleeping. She's the only person I know, besides myself, that owns a collection of Julia Roberts movies. The mentioning of it, and our mutual enthusiasm, is what made us close friends. Our first sleepover was a Julia movie marathon. I suppose it's only fitting for our last.*

Val's eyes locked with Carissa's. The expression on her face was both sad and angry. It lasted for seconds, and then faded as she took out the first disk, titled *Mystic Pizza*, and placed it in the player. Her hands trembled as she pressed the close button. She knew. Somehow, she sensed Carissa was counting down the hours and then their friendship would sputter to a halt.

It pained Carissa, sitting there for the next two hours, watching a movie without either of them saying a word. Without exchange, they passed the box of crème sticks between each other as it was needed. The crinkling of the packaging as they retrieved the processed pastries filled the silence.

I honestly don't have anything to say to her right now.

When the movie was over, Val went to the bathroom. She sat in there for twenty minutes. Carissa thought she heard crying, sniffles. She wanted to say something. She wanted to speak some words of kindness or reassurance about their friendship. But honestly, yesterday was the worst day of her life. And she wanted to blame Val for it.

Part of Carissa told her it was her own fault. No one forced her to go to the party. No one forced her into the costume. No one forced her to drink jungle juice or play a drinking game. No one forced her into having a drink in-between the games. The only thing she was forced into was sex. And well, in her state, she wasn't capable of resisting as much as she wanted to.

The real bad guys were Kent and Brian. *But they aren't here.* And Carissa wasn't sure what she could or would do about them. That left the blame in the hands of Val, Jesse, and herself. Maybe Mom for letting her go the one time she should have stuck to her guns.

But Val was here, now. She was the easy target. She used Carissa to get invited to a party, ditched her to dance, make out, and most likely have sex with Jesse, and made it pretty clear that telling anyone about the rape would be a bad idea. *I feel total helplessness.* If Carissa would blame anyone, Val was the obvious choice.

If you were there, I wouldn't have been raped.

Val stepped out of the bathroom, her face freshly washed of any sign of tears and plopped on the couch next to Carissa. She sighed and pulled her blanket to her shoulders. "Cari, I'm sorry I wasn't there for you. We went there to have fun. We were having fun. It just never occurred to me that anything like that would happen, could happen. I didn't know they were capable of that kind of thing."

They were definitely capable.

"I never would have left you with them had I suspected they were, that they'd do that," Val said. "I can't believe it." She sighed.

Well, believe it. It happened.

"Yesterday, I was in shock and kind of wasted," Val said. "All

I could think was how we were going to get in trouble if you told anyone about the rape. You know, because we were drinking at that party. My parents didn't know there was drinking at the party. And, if they knew I drove us home buzzed, I'd be in deep shit. They'd probably take my keys."

They probably would. Though, you got us home safely. That's something.

"But, what they did, what they did to you, it's unforgivable," Val said. "If you want to go to the police, tell them everything, I understand. Just, please don't be mad at me. I wanted us all to have fun at a party. And, I didn't want us to get in trouble."

I don't know what to say. I feel like shit. But Val's apologized. I get her reasoning. We went there to have fun. We had a lot of fun, up until I got sick. And if this gets out, if I go to the police, I don't know what will happen next. I don't even know if they'll believe me. If they do believe me, we're all in trouble. This makes me sick.

"Okay, Val," Carissa said. "Okay." She teared up. "I'm really tired and," she sniffled, "I feel so helpless. They took so much from me and it feels like there's nothing I can do about it. I can't go back and stop it. And, I can't report them without getting in trouble. And I just feel off. In addition to all of this, I feel like something's wrong. I just don't know what."

Carissa studied her body with conflicted eyes. "And, it feels, it feels different down there. It feels empty and a little sore. It feels like I was full, and now I'm empty, and I don't want to feel that way, but I do. It's like he pushed a hole inside of me and now I need to fill it."

That doesn't make any sense does it? I don't make any sense. I wish I could stop feeling for a while. I just want to be numb.

"I know how you feel," Val said. "I felt something similar after my first time. The soreness goes away. I can't say the desire to fill that hole will, though. In fact, the more I fill it, the more I have sex, the more that hole demands to be filled. It's this pulsing, aching need." She sighed. "You understand now, don't you?"

Unfortunately, yes.

"Yea, Val," Carissa said. "I finally do."

2

It was Sunday when Carissa made it home. Mom was in the

kitchen hovering over a book and sipping a cup of coffee while something smelling of chicken and garlic cooked in the oven. Her head perked up when she heard Carissa rolling her suitcase down the hallway. She set her bookmark, rested her client's latest proof copy on the counter, and ushered Carissa to join her.

"How's my baby?" Mom opened her arms for a hug.

Mom, your baby is not your baby, anymore. Carissa hugged her. "I'm pretty sure Sean's your baby."

I am not going to cry. I am not going to cry. I don't think I have any tears left, anyway.

"You're both my babies," Mom said. She held Carissa several seconds longer before letting go. "Always have been. Always will be. From birth and diapers, to seventies and diapers."

Carissa snorted. "I hope neither of us are changing either of our diapers at that sad old age."

She must have been on pins and needles most of Saturday, waiting to hear and talk about what happened.

Carissa insisted on not talking about what happened when her mom called Saturday. She would continue to insist they not talk about it. She didn't want to think about it. She didn't know what to do about it. But mentioning anything to her mom would certainly send things spiraling out of control. If she opened her mouth, she was in for a long, rough ride and wasn't ready for it.

"Considering the things and smells that came out of you," Mom said before pinching her nose with her fingers, "the least you can do is change my diapers, so I can return the favor."

Carissa gave her a hard stare.

Mom smiled, "How much did you eat this morning?"

Clearly, you know me well enough to know not to ask if I ate, but how much. That's comforting. Now I feel like a fat ass that eats all the time.

"We had eggs and toast with grape jam," Carissa said. "Not a lot. Just enough to hold us through. Her parents wanted to go out for lunch. How much did you make?"

"Enough for the two of us," Mom said. "I'm making chicken with steamed broccoli and rice. Oh, and you're going to love this light gravy packed with garlic and mushrooms."

Carissa inhaled and agreed. "Mmm, yea. Smells good." *Wait a minute.* Her eyes narrowed. "Why just the two of us? Where's

Sean and Dad?"

"Sean, well," Mom smirked, "Sean was invited back to church by a girl from that church party. Her name's Rebecca."

"Really?" Carissa asked. *I guess he took my advice and didn't go after Gabby after all. At least one good thing came out of that night.*

"She's pretty, too," Mom said. She walked over, grabbed her smartphone, and fetched an image on her app. "I looked her up. They're already friends. This is her profile picture." She presented her phone.

"Good for him," Carissa said as she looked at the first picture. She felt lighter, as though she carried a burden without realizing it and now it was gone. *Rebecca's prettier than her sisters. And few are.* Carissa gripped the phone and flipped through the pictures. "Holy crap. Her whole family's beautiful."

"Yea," Mom said. "No kidding. I'm tempted to invite them over just to get a closer look at them. I honestly think we're the prettiest ones in our family. Thank God my parents are beautiful. You got our genes."

Classic Mom humility. Definitely got that *from grandpa. Then again, he was a male model and actor, grandma an actress. A classic romance of two co-stars falling in love and making babies. I suppose if psychology doesn't agree with me, I could get into the family business and be an actress or model. Grandma's been nudging me to consider it.* "You have the perfect face for a role that's opened." *She offered to walk me through the lines. I have to hide this family from her purview, or she might try to cast the whole damn family in a reimagining of the Cosby's or something.*

"Did you just say, 'Thank God'?" Carissa asked teasingly and poked her. "Who thought looks alone could lead to conversion?"

Mom laughed. "Your brother said it five times this morning. Apparently, it's contagious."

Yea, contagious. Okay. She flipped through more pictures.

"So, Dad's okay with her being black?" Carissa asked. She'd worried about Dad's response if romance materialized between her and a cute coffee shop guy she met a week ago. At least, before she lost the guy's number. "With Sean potentially dating a black girl, I'm surprised Dad's head didn't explode."

"He's in the doghouse," Mom said in a tone that settled that conversation. "He doesn't have ground to protest anything right now."

Okay, then.

Carissa handed back the phone after one more glance at the pretty black girls. "Did Sean tell you what happened with Kelsea?"

"Yes," Mom frowned. "Thanks for reminding me. It pisses, me, off." She huffed. "It was only two weeks ago that she said she loved our family and thought of you as a sister and me as a second mom. A *second* mom! I mean, what is that?"

Girl likes her seconds. Second mom. Second boyfriend. Second foot up her—

"She really said that?" Carissa asked.

"I kid you not," Mom said. "She said she looked up to me. I showed her pictures of my wedding dress. Not that I would let her try it on before you. I know you said it's not your style. But you still get first dibs."

It's not my style because I didn't inherit your boobs. You're a cup size plus larger than me. And Kelsea and I are the same bust size. So, it wouldn't have fit her anyway. Wait a second! She borrowed one of my bras when she slept over that one time. I guess I'm not getting it back.

"It's fine, Mom," Carissa said. "Neither of us have the boobs to fit that dress, anyway."

Smile. "It can be adjusted."

Carissa pointed at her chest. "Might as well toss it in the washing machine and shrink it."

Mom laughed. "Fair. But if there's any consolation, I was breastfeeding. You weren't complaining at the time."

Carissa shrugged.

"Speaking of complaining," Mom asked, "I know you didn't want to talk about it yesterday when I called, but what happened at that party?"

Ugh. Again?

"Mom," Carissa whined. She crossed her arms. "No. I don't want to talk about it, okay?" *I really don't want to talk about it, ever.* "You were right. I shouldn't have gone to that party. And I'm not going to any others. They're terrible."

"Hmm." Mom frowned and examined Carissa. "Did they try

anything with you, Cari?"

Dammit. The lie detector is now clairvoyant. I'm going to have to tell her something. I can't tell her everything. I certainly can't tell her what happened. I don't know what she'll do or say. And she'd have to tell Dad. And, he'll be pissed that I went to a party and got raped. He'll be mad at Mom and me. And the police will get involved and I can't... No. I have to tell her enough truth to appease her curiosity. That's it.

"Yea," Carissa mumbled and looked down. "Two of the boys from the party were aggressive. They wanted to, you know, but I didn't want to."

"So, they ripped the wings off your costume," Mom said, filling in the blanks from the story Val told her very early Saturday morning.

"Yea." Carissa avoided eye contact.

Mom hugged her. "It's nothing to be ashamed about, Carissa." She gave her a squeeze. "It wasn't you. It wasn't anything you did. There are guys out there who have one thing on their mind, have no respect for women, see us only as sexual objects, and that's how they treat us. They treat us like we owe them sex just because they're attracted to us. It's stupid, ridiculous, perverse. But it's not our fault. It's not your fault, okay?" She released the hug to initiate eye contact.

It's not my fault. It wasn't. It wasn't my fault. Carissa looked into Mom's intense, honest eyes. "Okay."

"Let me hear you say it," Mom said. "I need you to believe it. I beat myself up so many times when guys tried things with me. I need you to say it and truly believe it."

Carissa teared up. "It's, it's not my fault."

Mom teared up, too. "I don't know about you, but it's too early for tears. So, let's not cry about this. It's them, not us." She glanced at the clock on the stove. "Plus, you got home just in time. It should be finished by now."

"Great," Carissa said. "I can feel myself getting hungry."

Mom opened the stove.

"Mom," Carissa said. "Where's Dad? You never told me."

"He relapsed. So, I sent him to church with Sean." Mom smirked. "Who knows, maybe they'll have an impact on him. A conversion wouldn't be the worst thing for him."

Carissa blinked away her tears and chuckled. "Dad at church. It's like seeing a zebra wearing a bowtie reading in a library."

"Oh, we have those at our library."

I love it when she entertains my random analogies.

3

After lunch, Carissa dragged her luggage to her room, closed the door, and plopped on the bed. She sighed and stretched out. *Finally.*

And then she cried, quietly, secretly, until she fell asleep.

Mom woke her for dinner. Carissa opted to stay in her room and finish the homework her killjoy English teacher assigned her. She had to write a short story with a Halloween theme. She had one in mind.

"Girl is invited to a Halloween party and goes hoping to have fun and meet a cute guy. She's set-up with a cute guy. Only, cute guy gets her drunk playing drinking games, drugs her, and takes advantage of her. He then leaves her lying there, helpless and humiliated. And she leaves violated, humiliated, and helpless, feeling shameful, dirty, and pathetic."

The teacher never said it had to have a happy ending. In fact, Carissa didn't have an ending in mind. She didn't know the ending. Perhaps some stories don't have endings, just an ellipsis.

So, dot dot dot...

Obviously, I can't write that. That would raise flags with the teacher. Fine. What if, what if I replaced the rapist with a vampire. And instead of getting raped, my blood is sucked out, not enough to kill me, but just enough so he can feed, turn me, and I live the rest of eternity as a member of the miserable undead. Yes. Yes, that sounds accurate enough.

"Girl is invited to a Halloween party by a friend and goes hoping to have fun and meet a cute guy. Little did she know, it was a setup. The cute guy arranged her invitation. Only, cute guy did so to get her drunk playing drinking games. He brings the staggering and helpless girl to his large bedroom, has her lay down and take a nap, and then sucks her blood until she's barely alive, so she can turn. She lies there helpless. He smiles, wipes his mouth, and leaves her there. And people at the party gawk at her, lying there, drained. She eventually stands and stumbles out with the help of her friend, but now she has a taste for blood. Plot twist! Her friend was a vampire all along. And when she realizes that they're both sisters in blood thirst, she shows her teeth. The End."

Yea. That works.

Carissa wrote her story while eating salad and spaghetti. When she finished, she crawled into bed in her strawberry print pajamas, shut off the lamp next to her bed, and closed her eyes.

That night, she had a dream. The dream matched her story with frightening detail, except with the addition of Brian who transformed into a dragon. He watched her with bright red eyes as Kent drained the blood out of her. Brian looked on, licking his long fangs. She could feel a thick, heavy, invisible fog radiating off him, suffocating her. She couldn't breathe. She tried to scream but couldn't at first. When she finally could scream, no one came. All she could see was the vampire, Kent, wiping his mouth and walking away. And the dragon smiled.

CHAPTER EIGHT

The following weeks, Carissa had one plan: maintain a low profile. She wore every hoodie she owned and borrowed her brother's. She sat by herself at lunch, ate as quickly as possible, and avoided conversation as much as possible. Fortunately, for her, there was enough drama daily that she wasn't a topic of discussion, much.

Guys who previously paid her little attention, the wrong guys, started to kiss at her and make suggestive comments. She wasn't sure how they got her number, but a few guys sent her pictures of their penis. One guy had the nerve to say, "Hey girl, I hear you're open for business now. I've got a nice car with a lot of room in the back seat. I'll make it worth your while."

You hear that I'm open for business? What the hell does that mean? Are you calling me a prostitute? I will kill you! I will put you in a body bag! Is there someone out there saying I'm taking money for sex? Make it worth my while? Is this guy serious?

Plenty of guys had come on to her before, but no one ever implied she was open for business. She gave the guy a dirty look and walked away as quickly as possible. If there was one thing her mom told her, it was not to give these guys any attention or allow herself to get upset or emotional about these things, which was her forte. The best thing to do was ignore them. Don't give them any control or power by acknowledging their words.

Nevertheless, Carissa clenched her fists and held back her tears until she got to the bathroom. There, she let it all out. She cried until she heard the period bell. Then she wiped her face and told herself she'd finish where she left off once she got home. She hoped no one noticed how frequently she cried. She didn't wear makeup and kept to herself, outside of sports.

Someone she least expected approached her: her English teacher. Perhaps the Halloween short story was too close to the truth.

One day after class, Misses Braun pulled her to the side and asked Carissa if she was okay. Of course, she lied and said she was fine. She avoided Braun's eyes as much as possible throughout the conversation. She looked down and away as the woman said, "If there is anything you feel the need to talk about, even if it's expressing your feelings, I'm here for you. And, if you don't want to talk about it, write it. Get it all out on paper. I'm here for you. I'm always here for you."

Carissa said thanks and went about her way. She registered the worry in Braun's eyes and felt those eyes follow her as she rushed out of the classroom and into the hallway.

Okay. Perhaps I don't have it all together. But there's no point in staring at me, Carissa thought as she looked herself over in the bathroom. Her clothes were wrinkled. Without makeup, she looked pale, plain. Makeup didn't do her complexion justice while she had her crying fits, which was an everyday thing. She'd spend thirty to forty minutes on makeup only to ball her eyes out in the bathroom and ruin it in five minutes. Nope. Not happening. Then she'd have to wash her face before anyone noticed.

If they noticed, not only would she be known as the girl that puts out at parties, but she'd be the girl that cried every day in the bathroom.

It wasn't as though a lot of people knew her. She maintained a low profile. She slid in the bathroom in-between classes to avoid conversation with some of her friends, especially Val. She hadn't spoken to Val since the sleepover three Sundays ago. Phone calls and texts were dodged. Excuses were made. If there was one thing that caught the attention of a few, it was that she wasn't making any more friends. She was a ghost. And girls didn't like being ghosted. In fact, they hated it.

There were two friends who were genuine and patient. Charlotte and Alana from her tennis team. Both texted concern and said they were there for her if she needed anyone to talk to. They called her mom and asked if something happened. Asked if she knew why Carissa didn't spend time with the team after practice anymore. Mom was floored and asked her the same question. Carissa said she didn't feel like talking to anyone.

Mom, the lie detector, looked concerned. But she didn't say anything.

It was the truth, sort of. Carissa didn't feel like talking to anyone. She couldn't share what happened or express how she felt with anyone. Part of her wanted to get it all out. Another part of her couldn't talk about it. It was real. It happened. She got raped. She wished it didn't happen. She wished she could blot it out of her life. She wished she didn't think or dream about it. But she did. It haunted her. Talking about it would bring it all the pain and memories to the surface again. She wanted to avoid that.

Focus on school. Focus on sports and scholarships. Focus on college acceptance. Focus on anything but people and that. All people want to do is talk. Talking turned on the water works.

And of course, days later, after Carissa finally convinced everyone that she didn't want to talk, and would rather be alone, the talkative black girl decided she wanted to sit down and have a conversation about her little sister and Sean.

"Hi Carissa, how are you today?" Gabby asked as she plopped down in the desk next to Carissa's. As always, her hair and makeup were flawless. Her perfect skin glistened. She smelled of peaches. Her knee length skirt was pressed, white, and covered with pink flowers.

That dress is stupid pretty. Dammit. I wonder where she got that.

"I'm fine," Carissa said. It seemed to be the only thing she said these days.

"Cool." Gabby set her book bag down. "Great news about Sean and Rebecca, right? As I said before, I'm so glad you told him about our Halloween party. They're having such a fun time together. I've never seen her smile so much. In a few years, she might need cheek transplants." She laughed at her joke. Carissa glared at her.

"She thinks he'll be her first boyfriend," Gabby continued.

DAKOTA

"My question is, what does your brother think? I mean, he looks happy with her. It's only been a month but they're inseparable. He texts her. She texts him back. They send each other these cute good morning and good night texts. It seems legitimate. But, she can't ask him to be her boyfriend. You know how it works. He must ask her. So, umm," she scooted her desk closer and leaned over, "when do you think he'll ask her to be his girlfriend? Has he said anything to you about it?"

"No," Carissa said. "We haven't talked much, lately. Sorry."

Gabby frowned. It was only the second time Carissa saw that expression on Gabby's face. The first was when she got a *B* on a group project. Group projects were the bane of intellectual individualists' existence.

"But hey, like you said, it's been a month." Carissa shrugged. *He was dating Kelsea for as long as he's been in Richmond. That's a little over a year. It's only been a month since he met your sister.*

"Yes, precisely." Gabby smiled. "It's been a whole month. He's likely to make it official any time now."

Good grief. It's hard to believe it's only been a month. It feels like time is dragging on and on. I want this fall and winter to go by, please! I need spring and summer weather. I need outdoor swimming pools, sunbathing at the beach, sand between my toes, and sipping iced tea with a slice of lemon on the porch with my shoes off. Yes, please.

Wait. It's been a month. Why don't I feel like shit? Why aren't my insides trying to drill their way out of my vagina?

"So, I hear your grandma's coming for Thanksgiving," Gabby reminded her. *Crap. I forgot she was coming.* "She's from, umm, umm, Manchester, right?"

"Well, technically, she's from Miura, Japan," Carissa said while glancing towards the front of the class. *At some point, Misses Braun is supposed to start class.*

Gabby frowned. "Why did your brother say she was from Manchester?"

Great. Now I have to tell her the whole story or she'll think my brother's lying.

Carissa sighed. "Her father was a banker that traveled to London frequently, trying to pick up the pieces of international banking after World War Two. His wife died, and with no other living relatives, his daughter, Katsuko, my grandmother, was stuck traveling with him for a couple years. Eventually, she met Tristan Boisseau, my granddad. She was this young pretty exotic girl from Japan that was getting comfortable with her English, and he was this confident twenty something banker with a well-established life."

Carissa paused to visualize it. "He was part of the boy's club. You know the type. Guys in suits smoking cigars and talking about numbers over cocktails. He was invited to join a small circle of men who wanted to establish a network of private and elite banks from Japan and Hong Kong to Spain, France, and London, all the way to America. Something big. Anyway, my grandpa was early," *something I obviously didn't inherit*, "and he met her in the lobby. He said it was love at first sight. She says it was definitely lust at first sight. But after they were married, there wasn't much to be done about it. She was stuck with him."

Gabby laughed. It was infectious. Carissa smiled for the first time in days.

Grandma is too damned honest for her own good. If her honesty doesn't drive grandpa to the grave, her driving will.

"Anyway, after they married, she lived in London and Manchester until they moved to America. They bounced around between Manchester, New York, and Connecticut for several decades. Most of their summers were spent in Manchester. They eventually moved back permanently."

Gabby smiled. "I see. That's so cool." She beamed. "Have you been there? I'd love to spend a summer in another country. Nice thing about England: no language barrier."

"You'd be surprised about the language barrier," Carissa said. "I was over there about five years ago and couldn't understand half of what they were saying. They speak fast and use slang. I love the accents, but that combined with everything else, I needed captions. But I won't generalize. It's not all conversations, and just at the start. After a little bit of time, you start to pick up on the lingo and you're solid. The British folk I met were very polite, funny, incredible people. They're diverse, too. Some parts are like New York and others are small towns with hills and farms. If I decided to move somewhere, I think I'd move to the UK. Probably live in a small city a short train ride from the big cities. And maybe a short ride from the hill country when I needed to get away from it all. Which is always these days."

Maybe I can convince grandma to let me spend spring and summer in Manchester, before college starts. Or, maybe I can take classes overseas. I hadn't considered that before.

"Well, with your grandma coming to town, maybe you can convince her to let you spend some time over there."

"You read my mind," Carissa responded, then frowned. "I hope you're not."

"Oh, if I could do that," Gabby said, "I wouldn't tell anyone and probably wouldn't have a lot of friends. I think we're better off not knowing what others are thinking. I can barely handle my own thoughts." She laughed.

Dammit. Your laugh is so cute. But that's okay. I'm surprised to say this, but I don't mind talking to you as much as I used to. In fact, I want to talk to you more for some reason. Hmm. If we keep this up, I might want to be friends—

Without explanation, nausea overwhelmed Carissa. "Ugh," she grimaced.

Gabby leaned forward. "You okay?"

"I-uh-no," Carissa said. She felt lightheaded, dizzy. "I-uh-I feel—"

Two boys sat behind her. The smell of feet and armpit stormed her nostrils and opened fire. Did they run a marathon, stop to change into sweatier, mustier clothes, and then run another half?

"I'm going to be sick," Carissa croaked. She covered her mouth with one hand, clutched her stomach with the other, and bolted out the classroom as Misses Braun closed the door. She heard footsteps and Gabby call out, "I think she's sick," behind her as she charged down the hall to the bathroom.

I'll make it to the bathroom. I'll make it to the bathroom. There's no way I'm going to puke in a trashcan in our class. There's no way I'm going to puke in the hallway. No, I'm not going to be puke girl. That'll be what everyone talks about for the rest of the week. "Did you hear? Carissa got sick in the hall." "Why'd she come to school? Is she trying to get everyone sick?" "Oh, gross. That stinks. Thanks, Carissa."

Carissa found her comfort stall, her safe place, unoccupied. She wretched, expecting something terrible to come out. Nothing did. But the nausea remained. She wretched more. Still nothing. She was okay with that. She wasn't in the mood to puke today. That wasn't on her task list, in between eat shit and die. If she could get by with dry heaving and slipping outside to get some fresh air, that was fine.

Crap. She left her purse and backpack in class. How could she fix her face and breath without her essentials?

The bathroom door opened.

"She and I were talking," Gabby said. "She was fine. Then, suddenly, she wasn't."

"It could have been something she had for breakfast," Braun said. "I've had some bad eggs sneak up on me before."

Who's going to start class? Are they going to wait out there for me until I stop? Are we all going to walk into class together with everyone's eyes on me? I would much rather hide in here and maybe take a nap until the next class. Maybe I can call Mom, get picked up, and go home. Climb into bed and sleep the rest of the day.

"Carissa," Braun said. "Are you okay in there? Do you need anything?"

No, I'm not okay. I feel like crap and have no idea why. Wait. No. She's right. Mom made me an omelet for breakfast. Maybe it was the omelet. What if I had bad eggs?

Honestly, this doesn't feel like stomach sickness. I've never felt dizzy. I've felt weak. I've felt like sending my lunch on a permanent vacation. Never, never have I felt dizzy. Not like this. Or have I? Maybe I have? I can't remember! I don't take notes on how I feel when I'm sick. I don't journal symptoms. For all I know, I could be dizzy every single time I've had a food illness.

"I, I left my purse," Carissa groaned. Someone stepped forward and slid something into the stall. She turned from the toilet and saw her purse. *Holy cow.*

"I figured you'd want that," Gabby said. *You've earned some major points today, Gabby.*

"Thanks." Carissa collected it. The nausea slowly faded away. "I'm feeling a little bit better."

Great. All of that and I didn't puke. It probably would have been better if I did puke. Now I get all this attention I don't want, and it was some come and go weird crap.*

Carissa flushed the toilet. *Subterfuge. Subterfuge! Now, they'll never know that nothing came out. Maybe I'll wash my face and gargle. Otherwise, they'll think I'm nasty. I mean, if they think I puked, and I don't gargle or brush my teeth, they'll think some stuff is still in there. I mean, who doesn't gargle mouthwash after a quick terror spit?*

"Take your time, Carissa," Braun said. "Gabby, do you want to stay with her while I start class?"

"Sure."

"Okay," Braun said. "Carissa, if you need anything, let me know. And, if you don't feel well and want to go home, I can get the paperwork started. Just call your mom and let me know."

"I'm fine, Misses Braun," Carissa said. "I can come to class. I just have to fix myself up."

"Umm, yea," Braun reluctantly said. "Okay. I'll see you in class." She stepped out.

"Are you sure you don't want to wait it out for a bit?" Gabby asked. "I'd hate for us to walk to class and then you have to run all the way back here again. You might not make it next time."

Girl has a good point. Nothing came out the first time around. Next time, I might not be so lucky. I'm not even sure what caused the dizziness and nausea in the first place, but those smelly boys didn't help. I mean, good grief. They've come in from morning practice without showering before, but that was ridiculous. It shouldn't even be allowed. I'm surprised that funk didn't set off alarms.

"Okay," Carissa said. "I'll wait it out a bit." She opened the stall. Gabby stood out of the stall, fidgeting with her hands.

Yea. I never really know what to do with my hands when I'm wearing a skirt or dress. There's no pockets. I'm not one of those "I always have to talk with my hands" gesticulating girls. Nope. Glad I wore jeans today.

Let's not talk about the fact that I've gained five pounds and had resistance putting on my jeans this morning. Oh God! I can't afford to gain weight. I wear tight clothes. I have a great body I've worked hard to maintain. Please, don't let them take that away, too.

"Come." Carissa motioned to the floor next to her. "Have a seat. The janitor was just in here. So, no worries."

And that lady loves bleach. Good grief. She's probably inhaled it so often that it's killed half of her brain cells. It smells like she spilled the whole container of bleach and ran the mop around the floor.

Gabby smiled and sat. "Thanks."

Oh no. We're becoming friends.

2

On an early December morning, Carissa stumbled to the bathroom, dropped to her knees, and surrendered her midnight snack. *Oh, my beloved crème sticks, why do you hate me so?* She shut her eyes and rested her head on the toilet seat. When she opened them, she looked down at the wastebasket and saw a used tampon in the trashcan.

Nothing new here. Nothing to see, kids. Mom's bleeding again. It's that time of the... oh shit.

Her head popped up. She looked at the small calendar on the wall and looked at the date. *Oh no, oh no, oh no. I'm late. I should have had it by now. I'm like, umm, hmm, let's see. I started on the nineteenth and ended on the twenty-third. Naturally, my period had to ruin my whole week during midterms. So, about four weeks later, that would mean... Oh, I'm three weeks late?*

She looked at the toilet. *Oh. No. No, No, it's not. No. It's the morning. I'm sick in the morning. I was sick last morning. Oh, this can't be happening. This is not happening.* She stood and looked in the mirror. *You do not have morning sickness. You do not have morning sickness. There's a logical reason for this that does not involve even the slightest possibility of that—*

"What's that?" you may ask. Nope. I'm not going to say it.

Say it.

I am not going to say it.

Pregnancy.

Son of a—I said not to say it! Dammit. I am not pregnant. I am not, no way, no how. I can't be. Well, I mean, technically I'm capable of being pregnant, but I can't be. This would ruin everything. This is terrible!

Oh, oh no. Kent got me pregnant. Ugh. That means it's his.

DAKOTA

No. Not necessarily.

What do you mean not necessarily? I am not the Virgin Mary! It's Kent's. He's the only person that's ever been down there outside of Amy. There's no way she got me pregnant. Oh. I think I'm going to faint and die. I'm, I'm just going to fall over, hit my head, and die.

That might be okay. That might just have to work. How can I possibly be the mother of a child? I-I'm not ready to be a mother.

Hold your horses, Carissa. Pull yourself together. Let's at least get tested first. I mean, it could be the depression. It's been known to happen. Lizzie Georgioni was super depressed and didn't menstruate for like two months. Lucky girl. After a few pills and couple weeks, she was right as rain and felt her uterus punching its way out of her vagina just like the rest of us.

Anyway, I'll have to get a pregnancy test.

How? How am I going to get a pregnancy test? The closest pharmacy is miles from here and I don't have a car! I'd have to get someone with a car to take me. If I asked Mom to take me to the grocery store or pharmacy, she'll want to know what I'm getting. She'll snoop through my bag. And, if I'm secretive about it, she'll be all the more persistent about knowing what I got.

Wait. Christmas is right around the corner. I could say I'm getting her another Christmas gift. No. She would snoop even more. She's notorious for ruining Christmas gifts. Grandpa had stories about her sneaking downstairs at night and taking a glimpse. She was smart enough to bring tape to replace the tape she cut. Little six-year-old evil genius. She's grown worse, cleverer with age.

Okay. So, no gift. No Mom. I could ask Dad if he'd take me to get lady stuff; but he always shrinks away and tells me that's not his department. In fact, if I ask him to go anywhere near a store, he points me to Mom. Goodness. My dad is sexist. What? Only women should go to the store? What's that about? If he asks me to make him a sandwich, I swear to God... I would probably make him a sandwich. I love my dad.

Okay. Who else has a car?

Val.

No. I can't ask Val. I haven't spoken to her in weeks. It would be strange asking her for help. Though, clearly, she owes me. I mean, I wouldn't be pregnant or possibly pregnant if I never went to that stupid party with her.

There was a knock at the door. "Carissa?"

I zoned out. How long have I been in the bathroom? "Yes, Mom?"

"Are you okay?" Mom asked. "I heard you. Do you want some water? Are you sick?"

"I'm fine," Carissa lied. *Oh God. She's gonna figure it out. I mean, she's obviously been pregnant before. At least twice. I don't know what I'll do if she finds out. What will I say? Oh my God!*

There was another knock. "Okay, Carissa," Mom said. She used her stern voice. "I'm going to need you to open the door."

It's over! She knows. I'm blown. Carissa hesitantly opened the door.

"You are not fine," Mom said. She pressed her hand against Carissa's head. "Hmm." Carissa held still while Mom looked her over and frowned. "I don't feel a fever. Could be a stomach bug, but it might be time to see Amy."

Shit, no! She'll know I'm pregnant the moment I step in there. Well, okay. Maybe not that quickly. That's not how science works. You can't just look at someone and tell they're pregnant. I haven't put on that much weight. Have I?

Carissa looked down at herself.

Nope. I definitely haven't put on that much weight. But still, I can't go see Amy. She'll ask questions and run tests. I mean, even if it comes down to peeing in a cup or asking me questions like hormones or menstruation. If she asks me when I had my last period, I would have to lie. And the lie detector would know. I have to get out of this somehow.

"Really, Mom," Carissa said. "I don't have to see Amy. I'm good. I think maybe it's just that box of crème sticks. Maybe we can throw those out and get another one."

"Or not eat them so late in the first place," Mom suggested.

Carissa frowned. *I hope she doesn't start restricting my crème stick intake. Why couldn't I think of a different, less satisfying snack to use as a scapegoat?*

Mom sighed. "I've tried to give you space, Carissa. I've tried to be this comforting, take it easy mom that lets you handle this on your own. I mean. You'll be a grown woman off to college soon. I was testing myself as much as I was testing you. And, well, I'm done testing. You need to fill me in on what's bothering you."

"Mom," Carissa whined.

"No," Mom said. "Don't mom me. You've been distant and depressed, and I've heard you in your room crying. This all happened after that party." Carissa opened her mouth to speak. Mom shook her head. "Yes. You've said it a bunch of times. You don't want to talk about it. But we have to talk about it. I haven't seen Val over here in almost two months. That's a relief to me, but you two were bosom buddies."

That's okay, assuming I'm Tom Hanks.

"Now, you're strangers. Not a text. Not a phone call. And, the worst part out of this is that we've stopped communicating. You haven't opened up about why you and Val are split or why you've kept to yourself. It must stop, Carissa. Whatever it is, we need to talk about it, fix it."

Oh, Mom. This can't be fixed. Everything's ruined. If I'm pregnant, my life is over. I'll be humiliated even more at school. I'll be like one of those stupid teen moms on television. What about my future? I mean, I could have got an academic, tennis and golf scholarship. How can I if I'm pregnant? I mean, can I go to college with a kid? They're a lot of work. All my hopes and dreams are crashing down right at this very moment.

"See," Mom said. "Right now. You're somewhere else. Have you been taking your meds?"

Oh my God! My meds. I won't be able to take them while pregnant, can I? I won't be able to focus on my classwork. My grades will suffer. So, in addition to being fat and nauseated and not able to play tennis or golf, now my grades will slide. I might not be able to go to my choice school if my grades start to slide. I'm glad I finished most of my college applications early. Maybe I can get accepted before it all falls apart.

My meds are the only things that kept me together.

"No, I'm fine," Carissa said. "I'm taking them. I just haven't taken it this morning, yet." *Okay self. We need a convenient lie.* "I was just thinking about college applications and my scholarships."

Mom blinked at her. "Is that what you've been stressing

about?"

Carissa nodded. *Sure, why not?*

Mom inspected her face, determined the honesty of her answers. "I was impressed by how quickly you filled out all your applications." She paused. "Is Val going to a different school? Is that what your split is about? You two want to go to different schools and you won't have any friends there?"

Hmm. That's a better excuse than what I can come up with. I'm going to run with that, at least until I get tested. Oh God of Gabby, if you're really out there, let me not be pregnant. Let me get all negatives on the tests and suffer the period of all periods. A super period with a big freaking blood-smeared cape flapping in the wind. I have never wanted anything as much as I want to bleed out of my vagina right now.

Carissa frowned.

That, that sounds terrible. Why am I asking for that? But seriously, as much as I hate it, I need it. I don't care if it ruins all my outfits or sheets or where it happens at this point. I could be in the middle of a golf match and bleed a river. I don't care. Let me bleed.

"She wants to go to California," Carissa said. "That's way on the other side of the country. I'm surprised she didn't say Hawaii. She might still. And, well, I know we can't afford out of state tuition at this point, considering everything that happened with Dad's investments, even if I got scholarships from golf and tennis and grades. I mean, the chances of either tennis or golf paying for half of my tuition is slim, and it's still super expensive. I don't want to have to take out loans. All so she can pal around Los Angeles, stumble across Brad Pitt, and have a tabloid affair."

That was a pretty good lie, but also the truth. Val wants to go to California, but not for school. And she said if she ever saw him, she'd tackle Brad Pitt, rip her shirt off, and grind him. She said she'd grind him in the middle of the airport if she found him. She'd get arrested. She might even get jail time. She doesn't care. I don't know. Brad's an impressive specimen, but I'm more of a Zac Efron or Ryan Reynolds kind of girl.

Mom pressed her lips together. "Sadly, that sounds like Val."
I know that look. She's not buying it.

"But I was thinking about reaching out to her," Carissa

blurted out. *Really, Carissa? Sorry.*

Mom's eyebrow raised. "Really?"

"Yea. I'm tired of looking at my walls. I was thinking, maybe we'd go to the mall or something. Buy some new socks and sports bras. My panties are starting to feel a little tight." *I could seriously be pregnant.* "We'll have some bonding time before we go our separate ways, assuming either of us goes to the school we intended."

"Okay." Mom continued to study Carissa's face. "And you're certain there's nothing else? I know you're not being honest with me. It's only a matter of time before I figure out what's going on, if there is something else."

Sigh. "Can we just, like, drop this?" She huffed. "I know I've been to myself for the past couple of weeks." Almost two months. *Shut up.* "Let's do something soon. Just the two of us. Then, maybe then, you can stop bugging me?" She forced a smile.

"No," Mom said, still suspicious. "But I'll come up with a game plan for us." She looked in the toilet and frowned. "And you're not sick?"

"Nothing more than my usual face stuffing," Carissa said. "I just had to get it out of my system. I'll clean up and get some shut eye. I'm sure I'll feel right as rain now that I've emptied my stomach."

"Alright. Get some sleep." Mom backed out. There was an expression on her face Carissa never saw before. Remorse.

I think she knows, or at least suspects. I have to get this figured out. She's going to come at me again. I need some assurances that I'm not pregnant before the next conversation. God. I wish I didn't need to hide anything. I wish I could tell her what happened. I have no idea what I'm doing. If I am pregnant, I don't know what I'll do. I'd have to tell her. I'm not looking forward to that conversation.

Carissa flushed the toilet, rinsed her mouth, and brushed her teeth.

Now I have to talk to Val. Ugh. How am I going to approach this? Should I get straight to the point and tell her I'm three weeks late? Or will I suggest hanging out and find a way to buy a pregnancy test on the sly? I suppose it'll depend on the call.

She cleaned up and walked to her room.

I'll take a nap and then call Val. If she answers, we'll figure it out from there.

CHAPTER NINE

The phone rang five times for the fifth time, before Carissa hung up and stuck out her lower lip. Val wasn't answering her phone. No doubt, she was ignoring Carissa's call. Val never pressed the ignore button. She either silenced her phone or danced to her ringtone until the person she was ignoring went to voicemail.

Well, you can ignore calls. But if there's one thing you always do, it's read texts. You may not respond to them, but you do read them.

Carissa: "I'm sorry I haven't spoken to you in a month, plus. But after what happened, I needed space. Please call me back."

Ten minutes passed. No reply.

Carissa: "It's urgent. We need to talk."

Twenty more minutes passed. *Dammit. I'm going to have to tell her.*

Carissa: "I'm late. And Kent didn't use a condom."

A minute later, the phone rang. *You're such a, ugh.* Carissa glared at the phone as Val's name and picture appeared, but answered, "Val?"

"Were you saying that to get me on the phone, or are you really late?" Val asked. Her voice was tense, laced with bitterness.

"Right," Carissa said. "I'm so anxious to talk to you that I'd fake missing my period. That makes total sense, Val." She felt the dagger eyes peering through from the other side of the phone. It was like needle marks digging into her spine. "I'm at least three weeks late. My mom's already bled twice. That's how I knew something was wrong. That and, I've been feeling nauseous. I woke up the last three days and had to rush to the bathroom. I'm in trouble."

"Shit," Val said. Silence hung on the line for ten long seconds. "What are you going to do? Did you tell your mom?"

"Hell no," Carissa said. "I have to be sure before I drop a nuclear bomb." *Not powerful enough.* "Hydrogen bomb?"

"What do you mean?" Val asked.

"I need to get a pregnancy test," Carissa said. "I should at least pee on a stick or two or twenty and wait for confirmation before I make any other moves."

"And, that's why you called me?" Val asked. "You think I have pregnancy tests?"

You do get around. Carissa slapped herself on the forehead. *I hadn't thought of that.*

"No, I don't think that," she said with a smirk. "But I have to go buy several. I can't possibly buy them with my mom. If I sneak off to buy it, she'll see the bag and wonder what's in there. I can't go with my dad. He doesn't go shopping, period, except for Christmas. He leaves all of that to Mom."

"So, you want me to pick you up?" Val asked. "You want a ride to the grocery store."

Carissa closed her eyes and braced herself for rejection. "If you don't mind."

There was another lingering silence. This time, only eight seconds.

"Sure," Val said. "I suppose, in a way, I got you into this mess. Might as well help you figure it out. I have Claire, Alexis, and Fiona coming over for a girls' movie night. And I was going out to grab some snacks and movies anyway. I can pick you up after school. We can grab some tests. But I have to rush home and do some cleaning. There won't be time to drop you back off. So, you'll be stuck with us until late tonight."

Aww! I miss girls' movie night. Those girls are always so much fun.

"I think I can manage," Carissa said. She bit her lower lip. "I miss you all."

Val whispered something unintelligible and followed that with, "I'll see you later." She hung up.

DAKOTA

Carissa looked at her phone and frowned. *I should get dressed for school.*

2

Mom wasn't a fan of Val. She said Val reminded her of an old friend she'd rather not remember. Yet, she perked up when she saw Val's convertible park on the curb. Carissa rushed past with a quick, "Later, Mom," and sped out the door.

"Have fun," Mom said and waved.

Carissa waved back, opened the car door, and climbed in. It was cold enough outside that Val had the top of the convertible on and heat blasting from the vents.

Funny, lately it was either too hot or too cold for Carissa. She usually loved the heat. But right now, she felt like the leftovers of a breakfast burrito in the microwave.

Goodness she has the heat on maximum blast. And she hates it when someone gets in her car and changes the heat or AC settings or radio station or mp3 playlists. I'm glad I brought some water.

"Hey Val," Carissa said. "Thanks for grabbing me." She reached in her handbag and pulled out a bottled water. She chugged it.

Val examined Carissa. "You don't look pregnant."

Are you saying I don't look like I've gained weight? Do you think I'm pretending that I might be pregnant? What does that mean?

Carissa shrugged. "Uh, thanks?"

"Don't take it the wrong way. I just mean, you look the same. I expected you to have shown signs or something. I don't know any pregnant women. When I did, they were already far enough along to where you can see at least a bump or something. But I suppose between tennis, golf, and swimming, you probably don't gain weight."

"I've gained," Carissa said. "I was on a scale. I've gained ten pounds. I just think it's all going to my ass."

Val snickered.

"No," Carissa said. "I'm serious." She adjusted herself to reveal her butt. "I don't know if it's all the exercises Coach Maddie has us doing or what. I've grown one of those black girl asses. Maybe it's the mix of the pregnancy and exercises, like a hormone thing."

Val inspected Carissa's butt. "Well, we should get that test and figure it out. If it's not the pregnancy, I need to join your tennis team. I would rob, steal, murder, and kill for a butt like that."

Carissa laughed. She missed laughing with Val. There was a time when she loved that crazy blonde.

3

It was a quick run to the grocery store. They grabbed healthy snacks, popcorn, and drinks before sifting through home pregnancy tests. Neither knew what *mIU/L* meant on the packaging.

"I don't understand," Carissa whined. "There are too many choices. Should I just stick with a name brand and cross fingers hoping it'll give me the right results?"

Val picked up a box, read the back, and frowned. "How late are you again?"

"Three weeks-ish."

She put down the box, whipped out her phone, and tapped madly. After a few minutes, she put the phone back in her bag and grabbed two name brand boxes. "Online, it says you should take a test a week after your first missed period. You're almost a month late. At this point, it's a sure bet you'll get the correct result. If you're really pregnant, it'll show up right away."

"Those are fifteen dollars each!" Carissa pointed at the price tag. "If it's a sure thing, shouldn't we get cheaper ones?"

"No. It also says the more expensive pregnancy tests are usually more sensitive and accurate. Now, let's go home and test that vagina."

4

On the way to Val's place, Carissa slowly sipped at another bottle of water. *Fuel for the fire. Fuel for the fire. I need a good pee for these sticks. They better show up negative. Be negative! Be negative!*

Upon arrival, Carissa hopped out of the car with bags in tow and rushed to the door. She didn't have to pee but hoped there was just enough juice in her to squeeze out some results. When she made it to the bathroom, pulled out a test, stuck it under her, and pressed her muscles, nothing happened. *You have got to be kidding me.*

She leaned over and pressed herself even more. Nothing. Not a single drop. It was dry city in the wetlands. There was no chance of precipitation.

What the—? I usually come out with something. If I force it, really put my back into it, I should at least have a drop or two. I mean, I just drank two bottles of water. Something going in means something should be coming out. It's science, right?

"How's it going in there?" Val called out.

Carissa frowned and yelled back, "It's like the freaking Sahara Desert down there! I'm getting nothing!"

Val cackled as she walked away from the door. *Shut up, Val. It's not funny. I need to pee. I need to know.*

Carissa sat on the toilet for ten minutes before giving up. She put the stick back in its packaging and placed the small boxes in the cabinet below the sink. She didn't want anyone to enter the bathroom, see the package, and jump to any conclusions.

Wait. What if someone looks in the cabinet? Ugh.

She stuffed all the tests in her purse, crushed the boxes, and carried them to the family room. "Where can I put these where no one will find them? Do your parents ever check the trash?"

Val's nose wrinkled. "Why would they check the trash? Do your parents check the trash?"

Carissa nibbled her lower lip. "On occasion, my mom searches for small liquor bottles, in case Dad relapses."

"Oh right, that."

"Yea, that. Though, she skips my brother's trash. She found a magazine once."

"Oh my God," Val leaned forward. "Really? I wish I could have seen the expression on her face. Priceless."

"It was."

"I'm sure. But to answer your question, we're not looking deep into it. You could put a body in the trash and we'd drag it out without a second thought." She pointed behind her. "The one in the kitchen was recently replaced. Toss those boxes in there."

The doorbell rang. Val's eyes shot to the door. "Get them out of here!" She shooed Carissa away.

Carissa rushed the boxes to the kitchen and slammed them in the trash. The last thing she wanted was for it to get around that one of them was using a pregnancy test.

"Carissa's here?" Fiona's cheery voice raised from down the hall. She raced to the kitchen with grocery bags in hand and smiled. "I can't believe my eyes. You're back." She tossed her bags on the table and gave Carissa a tight hug. "We thought you were, well, we thought there was no way you'd hang out with us again." Her voice lowered to a whisper. "You know, after the Kent situation."

Oh no! She knows. Carissa froze, wide-eyed.

"I don't blame you, honestly," Fiona continued. "I'd die of embarrassment after being left naked like that. I mean, he took your virginity. I hope the sex was good, at least."

Carissa looked away and teared up. *It wasn't sex. It was rape.*

Fiona gave her a hug.

Claire and Alexis showed five minutes after Fiona and girl's movie night was in full swing. They ordered Chinese food and filled each other in on their activities during the wait. Carissa was debriefed on the latest gossip swimming through the halls, which included rumors about Sean's ex, Kelsea, who Carissa vehemently despised. The movie selections of the night: *I Love You Beth Cooper* and *Four Christmases*.

Val relaxed in her dad's recliner. By his rules, hosting guests was the only time she could sit in it. To her left, Claire and Alexis snuggled up together under a blanket on one end of the couch. To their left, Carissa sat in a heavy, oversized sweater Grandma Cowden knitted for her. She called it her movie sweater. To her left, Fiona sat on a fluffy chair, feet stretched out on an ottoman.

"So, is Beth Cooper supposed to be Val?" Fiona asked. The girls burst into laughter.

She is so Val.

Val smiled. "Say what you will, but I have had moments where I considered giving nerdy Roger Malone a pity kiss. I mean, he's eyeballed me for four years. That's dedication."

Fiona chuckled. "Well, if you do, you might want to watch your back. Melinda has a thing for him. She's never said anything to him about it but might ask him out to the Winter Dance. She's pretty territorial."

Winter Dance. Ugh. Why not just call it the Sadie Hawkins dance? That's what it is.

"Great," Val said and raised her hands, "Now I *have* to give Malone some tongue action. I hate Melinda."

"Why?" Fiona asked.

"She's so annoying," Val complained. "Her laugh is stupid. Her voice is too high. And the way she breathes, girl. She breathes so fucking hard. It's distracting. It's like, shut up, I'm trying to read here. Suffocate and die already so I can finish my exam in peace. Shit."

Claire and Alexis laughed.

Val really has a thing about other people's breathing. If you snore, she will smother you in your sleep. Oh, oh, I have to pee. This is it.

Carissa stood. "I'll be back."

"Okay, Arnold," Alexis said and made a smooching sound.

Claire kissed Alexis's cheek. "Hey! Those kisses are mine, and mine alone."

Alexis scrunched her nose and gave Claire a peck on the lips. "There, honey bunny."

Val picked up the remote. "Should we pause it?"

"No, you're fine," Carissa said. "I'm just going to the bathroom." She eyed Val. "I'll be quick."

Nod. "Gotcha."

Carissa grabbed her purse and walked to the bathroom. Her feet filled with lead. Her heart pounded into her eyes. This was it. She'd unwrap the test, pee, and whatever was on the test would determine the direction of her life. If it was positive, she could probably kiss college goodbye, right? They don't allow babies in freshman dorm rooms, do they? If it was negative, well, that would be the biggest relief since the great constipation of 2007.

Breath, Carissa. Breath. You don't want to get too anxious about it. That's what blocked you up the first time. Let's just pee and get it over with. It'll be negative. It has to be.

Four tests were pulled out of her purse and lined up like contestants in an elimination round. She took deep breaths, looked up and sought out a God she narrowly believed existed, then grabbed the first test. *Here goes nothing.*

She peed moderate streams on each of the four tests, then let herself go. *And now, we wait.* She distracted herself by looking at her friends' pictures on social media. When there was nothing new left to like, she checked the results.

Be negative. Be negative. Please, please be negative.

The first test showed a plus. *Positive? No. Maybe a false positive. Next...*

The second test showed a plus. *Positive again. Two false positives? Dammit. It must be this brand. Let's try...*

The third test showed two lines. *You have got to be kidding me. You have got to be kidding me. No! No!*

The fourth test showed two lines. *They're all positive. I'm, I'm pregnant. Dear God, no! It can't be! Please don't let this be. Please don't let this be. I don't want to be pregnant!*

She cried.

My life is over.

5

Ten minutes later, Carissa sat on the floor of the bathroom, lost in the dismal loop of it can't be.

Someone knocked. "Carissa? You okay in there?" It sounded like Val.

Carissa sniffed and grabbed a tissue. "Yea."

"Are you constipated?" Claire asked. There was a hush and whisper on the other side of the door. "Sorry."

"I'm not constipated."

"I thought your period was next week," Alexis chimed in. "You're supposed to be on the same schedule as me and Val. Are you breaking our period pact in there?'

Carissa couldn't help but smirk at the accusation. "No. I'm definitely not having my period, Lexis."

I wish I was. I hate it, but I wish I was. I would kill for a period right now. I never, ever thought I would wish that on myself.

She flushed the toilet, shoved the tests in her purse, and washed her hands. When she opened the door, the four stood in wait. Their curious eyes examined her. Except Val's eyes. Her face still and pale. Their eyes connected. The verdict was in. She was guilty of pregnancy.

"Was it the Chinese food?" Claire asked. "Should we call them and get our money back?"

I would love to blame it on them. It would make for an easy excuse. But, I can't. I won't.

"No. That's not it. I'm fine." She walked past them to the family room. "Let's just watch the movie."

Just within earshot, Claire whispered, "She's been hanging out in the bathroom a lot at school. I've seen her go in there. She goes in there to cry."

Ugh. I guess I'm not as discreet as I thought I was.

The girls returned to their spots and pretended to watch the remainder of the movie. Not a lot was said. All eyes shifted to and from Carissa.

Great. Just great.

CHAPTER TEN

After the first movie, Claire went to the bathroom while Alexis and Val tackled the remaining Chinese food. Fiona sat on the couch and wrapped her arms around Carissa. She was warm, soft, and smelled of lilacs.

This feels nice. I miss Fiona.

Carissa felt her body relax and hadn't realized how much she needed a hug. She comfortably leaned back and rested her head on Fiona's shoulder.

"Cari," Fiona whispered in her ear. "What's going on? Please tell me."

I wish I could say. I really do. But I can't. I can't tell anyone. I hate it.

"I, I can't say," Carissa whispered back. "Things are getting worse. I don't know what to do. I'm in so much trouble, Fi."

I'm pregnant. I'm going to be a mother. Technically, I am a mother? I mean, it's inside of me, growing. It's a baby inside of me. So, I guess, I am a mother. I'm a mom. And I don't know where to begin with that. We had a dog, Frankie, but lost him right before the move to Richmond. That's the closest I've ever come to being a parent. He chased after a squirrel and got hit by a car. What if that happens to my kid? What if I'm not paying attention and my kid runs into the street? What if my baby kid chases a squirrel across the street and gets careened by some douchebag in a sedan with his music too loud?

Fiona squeezed tightly and kissed her on the cheek. "I want to help, Cari. You know what I do when I need advice? I meditate.

DAKOTA

Sometimes the answers just come to me."

Meditation is not going to make me any less pregnant.

"Ooo." Claire sat on the couch to Carissa's right. "I saw that peck. Please, please, please tell me you two are about to hook up."

Carissa snorted. "No, we're not."

Fiona glared at Claire. "I'm just comforting her. I'm not trying to get in her pants."

"Too bad," Claire said. "You'd make an excellent couple. Cari's usually the quiet, serious, but funny one. You're the talkative free spirit. It would work."

"Claire!" Alexis called from down the hall and startled everyone. She and Val walked around the corner with a small plate of sweet and sour chicken in each of their hands. "Are you recruiting lesbians again?"

Again?

Claire and Fiona laughed. "You know I love to try," Claire said.

"I know cookie," Alexis said. She put her plate down and pulled out her phone. "I know." She kissed at Claire. Claire kissed back at her. "But instead of converting our friends to team 'V', how about I share some juicy gossip with you?"

Claire's eyebrows rose. "You had me at juicy."

Oh get a room, you two. Carissa rolled her eyes.

Alexis bit her lower lip. "I know I did, you bad girl." She waved her phone before typing in her password. She swiped a few times before reading out loud, "This is why I always told Sam to strap it up. The loser just got me pregnant."

Carissa and Val's eyes locked. *Who? Who's pregnant?* You are. *No, Carissa! Besides me!*

"O-M-G! Who?" Claire launched off the couch to the phone. "Who's pregnant?"

Alexis turned her phone towards Claire. "Chelsea's pregnant."

Val's eyes popped out of her sockets. "Get out of here!" She leaned over Alexis and read her phone. "Chelsea's pregnant? Dammit. She's on my squad. She's one of the best on my team. We're going to competition next month."

Well, how pregnant is she? If she just got pregnant, she can still compete. I mean, I've been playing golf and tennis. I've been pregnant for like, uh, seven weeks, apparently.

"No," Alexis said. "Not that Chelsea. Not Chelsea Granders. She doesn't even have a boyfriend. I'm talking about Chelsea Theron. She's Julia Theron's sister."

Oh, I know that Julia.

Fiona asked, "Which Julia is that again?"

Val pointed at her head. "Blonde."

Fiona frowned. "There are like fifteen blondes named Julia in our graduating class alone that I know of. I can't remember the last name."

Claire said, "She's the short one with the annoyingly perfect teeth and curly hair. Is obsessed with Taylor Swift."

"Oh," Fiona snapped her fingers. "Yea. She's in my sociology class."

"Our sociology class," Alexis corrected. "But yea. Her sister is pregnant and just broke up with her ex because he cheated on her."

Val twisted in her chair and scratched the back of her head. "How'd she find out?"

Oh Val, you have that guilty face on. Please tell me you're not one of the girls he was cheating with.

"Well, my dears," Alexis put her phone back on the table, "he got the other girl pregnant. Some girl named Melinda Bowers. She called him out on it. Said he needed to learn how to properly apply a condom. Then, she contacted Chelsea when he denied being the one that got her pregnant."

Right. Well, maybe she shouldn't have been screwing around with someone else's boyfriend. And then she has the audacity to contact Chelsea after the fact? I would punch her lights out. Maybe a roundhouse kick to the face. Follow that with a flowing sweep. And when she's down, one good final shot to her diaphragm. Bam! She's down.

"Wow," Fiona said. "Chelsea must be livid."

"I'd burn his house down," Claire announced. "I'm so glad I'm not into guys. No mistaken pregnancy for this girl." She kissed Alexis's cheek.

Unless, of course, you come across some sorry creep that decides he wants to drug and rape you. In which case, you're stuck.

"So," Claire said, "what's she going to do about it? Is she going to keep it?"

Wait. What? What do you mean?

"Hold on," Fiona said. "What do you mean is she going to keep it? It's a baby."

"Well, not yet, technically," Claire said. "It's early enough. She could still have an abortion."

An abortion? Oh my God. The idea never entered my mind. Is that even an option for me? I mean. Would I do that? Could I do that? Should I do that?

Fiona frowned. "I hope she keeps the child."

Alexis shrugged, "I don't know. I could ask her. But that's a weird question to ask someone on social media."

"About as weird as saying, 'I told him to strap it up' and announcing a pregnancy for anyone to see," Claire said.

"Text her," Val said.

"But you're right," Claire continued. "No way her parents would go for that conversation. They're probably losing their minds over this whole thing, anyway. They're very conservative."

"So are my parents," Fiona said. "It took them forever to let me go on a date last week. My dad was a little too enthusiastic to hear it was a dud."

"You think she would do that?" Carissa chimed in, hoping to reignite what seemed like a passing issue. "You think she would get an, umm, you know, abortion?" The word felt weird coming off her tongue. She'd rarely uttered the word.

Val's eyes shifted and locked on Carissa like a missile targeting system. She smirked. *I mean. I just found out I'm pregnant, Val. And, the idea that I might not have to carry it and can go on with my life had never crossed my mind.*

Alexis shrugged, grabbed her phone, and typed for a minute before putting it down. "I just asked her what she's going to do about it. I didn't drop the 'A' bomb on her. But, I think it's pretty clear what I'm asking."

What did you say exactly? I'd like to know. If someone asked me some vague question about whether I intended to keep my child, I'd tell that person to mind their business and press mute on their account. I wouldn't ever want to talk about it, especially if I was considering not having the child. Hmm. Now that I think about it, I wouldn't announce being pregnant at all if I planned on not having it. Otherwise, I'd be inviting scrutiny.

"Do you know her well enough to ask her that question?" Carissa asked.

Does anyone know anyone well enough to ask that question? That's a very private question.

"Yea." Fiona forked sweet and sour chicken from Alexis's plate. "That's a weighted question."

Alexis smiled. "Well, she walked in on me and her sister in our skivvies. So, I think she knows me well enough to feel comfortable sharing something intimate."

"You and Julia?" Val put her hand over her mouth.

Alexis shrugged. "We were experimenting. She realized she wasn't into it. I realized I was."

Claire wrapped her arms around Alexis's waist and put her chin on her shoulder. "And that's when I swooped in to pick up the pieces. The very sexy, tasty pieces."

We're getting off topic again. How is it we rarely talk about your lesbianism and suddenly, that's all we're talking about tonight? Let's get back to the pregnancy stuff. This is important.

Alexis's phone buzzed and vibrated on the table. She picked it up, typed in her code, and read. The light from the phone gave her skin a ghostly blue haze. She laughed. "This girl is crazy."

Everyone in the room watched her with intense eyes. *What did she say? Tell us what she said!*

"Oh wow," Alexis laughed again as her phone beeped three more times. "Yea. She's got that right."

I will beat you over the head and take that phone from you, girl! What is she saying?

Claire read over her shoulder. "I've considered not keeping it. Who wants to carry the bastard child of a sorry, cheating bastard who lasts long enough to get you pregnant, but not long enough to accomplish anything else? I mean, half of the time after he was done, I'd spend the next twenty minutes in the bathroom taking care of myself. If I have a boy, what if he grew up just as pathetic as his father? I can't do that to the next generation of women. I need to shut this down right now. But then, the more I think about it. He's got two kids on the way. Two kids he has to pay for. I'd be making it easy on him if I didn't keep the child. It's better if I maintain custody and he pays child support for two children. That'll be his punishment. I own him for the next nine months and eighteen years of his life. And I intend on making his life a living hell the entire time."

Wow. Chelsea is mad. And kind of an evil genius. But mostly mad. Hmm. I hadn't thought about the child support thing. I mean, I'd have to prove that Kent was the father. However, after I did, he would have to pay for childcare, medical expenses, stuff like that right? He's rich. So, maybe he could also pay for childcare while I'm taking classes. Maybe I can still go to school?

"I guess that answers that," Val said.

Fiona crossed her arms. "I hate that she intends to use the child as leverage over the father. I have an older cousin who's dealing with that. His ex-wife has made it difficult for him to see his child but insists on him paying for all of these crazy expenses. His daughter wants to see him, but the woman won't let her."

I couldn't be that person. I wouldn't. I'm too nice. Though, I certainly wouldn't be nice to Kent. I mean. He's a rapist. He deserves to suffer. I can't speak much for Fiona's cousin, but Kent is a total scumbag. He needs to pay, in more ways than one. But I don't want it to be about money. Whatever this is inside of me, boy or girl, I can't treat it like some tool for revenge, can I?

"I'd burn his house down," Claire said, fist clenched like a comic book villain. "Secretly, of course. Make it look like an accident. And then I'd demand he buy me a house with his insurance money, so I have some place to take care of my child."

Alexis laughed. "The guys really lucked out on you being a lez, huh babe?"

Yea. No kidding. I would never burn someone's house down. Well, no. I can't say never. I shouldn't say never, right? I mean, the moment you say never the universe starts to ponder situations. "Oh really? Never, huh? Under no circumstances can you see yourself burning someone's house down? We'll see. We'll see." I don't want to be the person that burns a house down. So, universe, I didn't mean never. I'm sure there's got to be some scenario where I would be willing, able, and likely to burn a house down. There's got to be some circumstance where I'm holding that match and matchbox in hand and have that crazy look in my eye. Please,

please, don't let that circumstance come my way. I don't wanna be that girl... unless I'm standing inside Kent's house.

"So," Val looked directly at Carissa, a mischievous sparkle in her eyes. "Do you think she should have an abortion? It sure would make things easy for her. She could get rid of it and wouldn't have to see her ex again." She held her hands parallel to one another, then raised and lowered them like scales. "Think about it: custody battles, arguing, pregnancy and labor. She'd lose her figure and ruin her vagina. She'd be a single mom. I mean, it seems like her best bet is to cut her losses."

Oh Val, I just told myself I wasn't going to burn a house down and then you start tugging the strings of my sanity. Don't make me start pondering this!

"I, uh, umm, I wouldn't even know where to begin," Carissa said. She felt weak and hot. "I don't know anything about abortion outside of that you go in pregnant and leave not pregnant."

Fiona studied Val and Carissa with a frown. Then, her eyes went wide. "I think she should keep the baby," she chimed in. "Not to get back at the guy or anything. I think she should keep the baby because you know, things happen for a reason." Carissa frowned. "Maybe it was destiny for her to have a kid. Who knows, what if something happens during the surgery or later and she can't have a kid. You know, like an accident. She'll at least have this one kid. Plus, kids are so amazing. I can't wait to have kids. It might be the best thing to ever happen to her, assuming it's a girl. Boys are too much to handle, I think. Always running around and wrestling each other. Plus, I wouldn't know what to say to a horny teenage boy. Keep it in your pants... or in your hands?"

Claire laughed. Alexis facepalmed.

This is why Fiona and I get along so well. We both start an idea and fly completely off course. I do it in my head. She does it out loud.

"But," Val raised her index finger. "What about relationships? I mean, any time she meets a guy, she'll have to tell him she has a kid. That's baggage. Most guys aren't into women with kids, especially young guys. Being a single mom sucks for a dating life." She raised another finger. "Plus, you won't have much of a life. Think about it. You can't have as much fun hanging out with the girls because you're watching your kid all the time. You'd have to find babysitters and rely on family members to watch your kid. If you can't find anyone, you're stuck. At least, with an abortion, you have control over your situation and can enjoy freedom."

You're laying this on pretty thick, Val. There's no question what you want me to do. Is that your solution for my situation? Kill the, uh, fetus, baby, thing, and act like it all never happened?

Claire said, "I'm going to have to agree with Val on this one. If I somehow got preggo, as if that would ever happen," she rubbed Alexis's back, "I'd probably go that route. I have college, travel, and life to experience. I don't have time for babies. Nope, nope, nope."

Fiona frowned, "But I mean, those are awfully selfish reasons. It's a baby. You'd be killing a baby. I've taken enough biology classes to know that it's a life. A human life. Small, not complete by any measure, but it is a life. It's alive in there. You wouldn't want someone to just pop up and kill you when you were a baby, right? If my mom had a choice between having me and not having me, I'm glad she had me. Don't you agree?" She looked at Carissa.

Carissa shrugged. *She makes a good point. I was an accident. I mean, that sounds terrible when I put it that way, but my parents were pretty frank with me by mistake. Mom got pregnant by her college boyfriend, my dad, after a party. They had a bit too much to drink and didn't use protection. Bam. Here comes Carissa. And now we have round two. I get drunk. Kent drugs and takes advantage of me. He doesn't use a condom. And now we have future baby. Oh, oh man. I don't have a name for the baby. What will I name the baby? Will it be a girl or boy? How long before I'll be able to tell the baby's sex?*

"I was, kind of, an accident," Carissa mumbled. "So, I suppose, if my parents went the whole freedom option, I wouldn't exist right now."

Am I actually considering keeping this child? I hadn't really thought about not keeping the child until they mentioned abortion. Now I have another option. I don't know. If I got one, that would kind of mean I wouldn't have to tell Mom about the pregnancy. I could totally scoot past them strangling me or freaking out. And, eventually, maybe, some day, I won't feel so terrible about being raped. So, there's hope. I mean, if I keep the baby, everyone will know I am pregnant. It'll be all over the school. Pregnant girl. It'll get around that Kent's the father. And, well, I just don't know what'll happen. At least, if I got an abortion, I wouldn't have to worry about the public ramifications of being raped.

But this is a life. A little life like I was a life.

"Well," Alexis said while looking at her screen. "I think I forgot to mention that Chelsea looks like a supermodel, and her family is really Catholic. She has like five uncles and six aunts. So, while she's in trouble with them for getting pregnant with her boyfriend, she'll have plenty of support. And, she won't have to worry about guys either. Some guy on here just asked her out and said he'd happily be the father of her baby. These guys get bold behind a keyboard."

But I'm not a supermodel.

"I love her chin," Claire said while looking at Alexis's phone. "How do you think I would look with that chin?"

Alexis looked at her closely. "Not like you." She pressed the power button on her phone.

Okay, then.

"So, are we watching that other movie or what?" Carissa asked. "The longer we wait, the longer it'll take for me to get back and prep for finals. I have grades to maintain if I'm going to get those scholarships."

"Yea, sure," Val said. "This is kind of a dead subject, anyway. It's not like one of us is pregnant." She smirked again and caught Carissa's eyes before loading the next DVD.

Really?

Alexis and Claire sat on their half of the couch. Fiona and Carissa squeezed closer together. Val settled in her dad's chair.

"Where do you want to go?" Fiona asked in a whisper as the DVD menu appeared on the screen.

Carissa shrugged. "Anywhere with a good psychology program. Most of the local Virginia universities like William and Mary, George Mason, James Madison, VCU, UVA, Old Dominion, and some out of state ones: Duke, Vanderbilt, University of

Pennsylvania, Rutgers." She rubbed her eyebrow. "I applied for Harvard, Princeton, and Yale just for kicks. I mean, there's no way I'm getting in there or can afford it. A girl has to try, though."

"Cool. I'm considering a medical program. Expensive as hell. So, I'm definitely staying local. Probably VCU, MCV program. We should talk afterward."

"Yea." Carissa grinned. "We should."

The movie started.

2

After the movie, Val said she was exhausted and needed to take Carissa home. Fiona waved and said she'd call. Carissa waved back. Claire and Alexis gave each of them a hug. Once everyone was gone, Val grabbed her keys and headed to her car.

"So," Val said as she started the engine, "what are you going to do?" She cranked the heat to maximum.

So, we're having that conversation. It's honestly too early to say. I don't know what I want to do.

"I don't know." Carissa buckled her seatbelt as the car reversed abruptly. *Val seriously needs to get a hold on that lead foot. You shouldn't back out that fast. You might hit somebody.*

"Well, you got the results, right? You're pregnant. I can tell from how you were acting."

"Yea," Carissa said. "Four out of four say I'm pregnant." Val whispered a stream of cuss words under her breath. "But I haven't the slightest idea how to proceed from here. I mean, I guess I'll go to the doctor and umm, have them run tests and stuff. Maybe, maybe, I can get some of that doctor-patient confidentiality from Amy. But at this point, I have to tell my mom. I can't hide this pregnancy from her. It's stupid to think I can."

"Not necessarily. Like I was saying at home, it's still early. You can get rid of it. Then, you don't have to worry about telling anyone. It'll be over. Things can go back to the way they were before any of this happened."

If there's one thing that's not going to happen, it's that. Things will never be the way they were before. Why are you pushing this so hard? Do you miss me that much? Maybe that's what it is. Maybe she thinks, if we get rid of it, we can somehow be what we were again. Maybe she thinks we can be best friends again.

"As I said," Carissa said. "I don't know. And, I'm not, I'm not just going to get rid of it like it's nothing. It's a baby. He or she. I suppose I'll have to find out which."

Val rolled her eyes. "It's too early for it to have a sex."

"Really? Are you sure?"

"Yea," Val said. Her eyes were locked on the road. "You'd have to be pregnant for like, three months before you know what the sex is. You've been pregnant for what, six weeks?" *Seven.* "It's just a tadpole at this point. It hasn't really developed any organs or anything. It doesn't even have a brain."

That doesn't sound right, Val. I'm taking AP biology. Please tell me you're not trying to feed me a bunch of bull.

"Val, its brain starts developing in its third week. The heart starts to beat after, like, the fifth week."

Holy cow! I wonder, if I sat quiet and still, would I hear the heartbeat? I'll have to get one of those stethoscopes. I wonder where I can find one and how much they cost. I might be able to find one on the internet. You can find anything on the internet. Anything.

Val swatted the comment out of the air. "But it's tiny. I mean, really. You're going to let something so small completely take over your whole life? Why even talk about what college you're going to with Fiona if you're not going to college? How do you think you'll manage a baby and college?"

I don't know. Mom could help. I know she would. I'd have to go to school locally. Maybe I can go to VCU. They're one of my choices. They have a good psychology program.

"I'm still figuring that out," Carissa said. She rubbed the sweat off her forehead. *Feels like I'm being interrogated in a sweat lodge.* She was hot before Val cranked the heat in the car. "I, I just got the news. I need time to process it."

"Don't. Don't process it. Just get rid of it. I mean, you have tennis, golf, school, a future to think about. Everything you've worked for could be gone."

Carissa closed her eyes. *Dammit, Val. Can't you just let me think about it? Why are you pushing this so hard? Jeez.*

"Can we talk about something else?"

"No. We have to figure this out. I mean, you're about to go

home with four pregnancy tests in your purse. I need to know you're not about to go blabbing to your mom."

Why? Carissa frowned. "What does it matter if I talk to my mom? It's my problem, not yours. You're not the one that's pregnant! You're not the one that was raped!" She balled her fists. "You're off the hook! I'm the one that's been lying to my mom about what happened. I'm the one that will have to either have an abortion or keep this baby for the rest of my life. It'll be on me. All of it is on me! What do you care?"

The rest of my life. I hadn't even thought about that. If I keep this kid, I'm stuck with it for the rest of my life.

Val swallowed hard and locked her eyes on the road. She didn't have an answer.

You're the reason I'm in this mess, Val. I can't believe you're acting like this affects you somehow. It won't affect you getting into college. It won't affect your career, your body. My having to tell my mom will only mean I probably won't be able to talk to you anymore. That's a big boohoo, right? This doesn't affect you at all.

If it affects anyone, it affects Kent. Mom's gonna wanna know who the father is. I'll have to tell her it's Kent's. I'll have to explain the circumstances of the pregnancy. I don't know how she'll react to finding out Kent raped me. And, well, Mom might get the police involved. She'll get Kent's parents involved. It's going to be a total nightmare. But again, this doesn't affect you, Val. You're off the hook. You get off scot-free.

3

Nothing else was said until Val parked in front of Carissa's house. That's when Val gave Carissa a cold stare. "Be smart, Carissa. Just think about this and don't say anything until we can get things figured out. The best thing for everybody is if you don't say anything to anyone and get that thing out of you."

"Bye, Val," Carissa got out of the car, head down, and walked to her house. A set of eyes bore into her soul. Those eyes were angry. Hate pressed into her back like a thousand tingly little daggers. It stung. It burned. She rushed inside and closed the door behind her. It slowly faded away. She exhaled.

"Cari," Mom called out from the family room. "Is that you?"

"Yea," Carissa called back, her voice wavered. She wanted to cry. She wanted to burst into tears. She needed to get out before she spilled everything to her mom. It was imperative she ran before the whole world knew she was pregnant.

"How was Val?" Mom called out. The floor squeaked as she stood. Footsteps lead to the hallway. "Did you have fun at girl's movie night?"

"Yea, I did," Carissa said before rushing forward. "But those girls really know how to wear you out. I'm going to take a shower and get started on homework." She made it to the stairs and hopped up the stairs before Mom made it to the hallway. She rushed to her room and closed the door.

The footsteps continued up the stairwell and stopped at the door. She could feel Mom on the other side of the door. Why Mom didn't knock, she didn't know. The footsteps moved away from the door.

Sigh. *Is this my life now? Is this my life?*

4

Carissa stepped out of the shower and grabbed her robe. She put it on and snatched a folded towel from the shelf for her hair. She stole a glance at the foggy mirror to get a glimpse of herself, to confirm she was still herself. She didn't feel herself.

Who am I now? I feel like I've become someone else. I don't know how long I can do this. I don't know if I can go on like this.

Her eyes shifted to the razor on the counter. They found and settled on the blade. There was a passing, foreign thought of the blade and her wrist.

What am I thinking? Of course, not. I'd never do that. It would never come to that. Would it? No. That's not me. I'm not one of those suicidal girls. I mean, it's not that bad is it? Is it?

What if it was? What if things were only going to get worse? If she decided to keep the baby and told her parents about the pregnancy, about the rape, everything would change. Certainly, it wouldn't be for the better, right?

Last year, Linda Mars got pregnant. Half of her friends left her. A quarter stuck around just to gossip about her behind her back. The few that didn't were also isolated. Linda and her loyalists were the social pariahs of the school.

Whatever. People sucked anyway. Carissa was more

concerned with her future.

How many colleges, especially scouts, would consider recruiting a pregnant athlete? She had a very low handicap for her age and already won first, second, and fourth in three established women's amateur golf tournaments in the last year. She won third and fourth in women's tennis. That wouldn't do much for her when she was pregnant. A single mother in college would have too much on her plate to meet the demands necessary to be a star athlete, right?

What was her future going to look like?

I hate to say it, but maybe Val's right. Maybe I should just get rid of it.

Her phone buzzed. Caller ID said Fiona Rogers.

Your timing is impeccable, Fi.

"Hey, what's up?" Carissa answered. She hadn't realized she was crying until she heard the tone of her voice. She wiped the few tears from her eyes with the sleeve of her robe.

"Hey, Cari." There was a hesitation. "Is this a bad time?"

Carissa sat on the toilet and shrugged, knowing Fiona couldn't see her, "Yea and no. You know what Mister Northrop says, 'Time is time.'"

"Okay," Fiona said. Another pause. "I'm calling because I, umm, I know what's going on with you now. I know why you've been so upset."

Wait, what? You know what? How do you know? Are you sure you know? How could you possibly know? I never said anything. Did Val say something? Did Val share with you that I'm pregnant after she dropped me off? Did she tell you all why I was there?

"What do you mean?" She wasn't sure what else to ask. "I don't understand."

Fiona whispered, "You're pregnant."

Carissa held her breath. *Oh no. Oh no, no, no. It's started already. It's begun. Dammit! Val told you, didn't she?*

"Why would you?" Carissa paused. "Who said I was pregnant?"

"Don't deny it, Cari. I watched you tonight. The way you and Val were talking about pregnancy and abortion. Val was asking you questions and directing everything towards you. Before you went to the bathroom, you were at least laughing. You stayed in there until we knocked on the door. And after you came out, you were overwhelmed. Did you just find out tonight?"

"Fiona," Carissa started. What would she say? What could she say? Fiona was clearly on her side tonight. Was she ready to share the secret, the truth, with another person?

I've wanted someone to talk to for a while now. I can't talk to Mom. I don't want to talk to Val. I've isolated myself from all my friends. Even Gabby, my new friend, sort of, hasn't been clued in. It's for the best. I can't imagine telling her the truth and breaking her Christian heart. She'd probably think I was a giant hoe-bag or something. I don't know. Maybe telling Fiona won't be so bad. She's figured it out anyway.

"Eh, hello?" Fiona called out. "You still there?"

"I'm here," Carissa said. That was all she could say.

"Listen," Fiona said. "I'm not trying to get in your business or anything, but we're friends, right? I'm here for you." She paused. "I'm not going to blab to anyone, not Alexis or Claire, or any of the other girls. It's you and me, okay?"

Carissa teared up. *Oh, Fiona. I'm so tired of dealing with this on my own. I just can't do it anymore. I need help. I need someone to tackle this with me. I, I don't know what I'm doing.*

"Fiona," Carissa said with a heavy voice. Her lips trembled. "I, I don't know what to do." She sobbed. "It's, it's all too much. I can't take it."

"It's okay, Cari. We'll figure this out."

"You don't understand, Fi," Carissa said. "It's not just, it's not just that I'm pregnant." She took in a deep breath and exhaled. "I was raped."

"Wha-what?" Fiona sputtered. "Who? When?"

"It was, it was, it was," Carissa stammered before blowing her nose. "It was Kent, at the Halloween party."

Fiona didn't respond. Silence lingered for fifteen unbearable seconds.

"Hello?" Carissa called out before checking her phone. The timer was still running. The call hadn't disconnected. "Hello? Fi?"

"I'm sorry," Fiona said in a hushed tone. "I, it's a lot to process."

"I know!" Carissa exclaimed before putting her hand over her mouth. She realized how loud she was and stood. *I need to take this conversation to my bedroom.* "Can you hold on a minute? I have to go to my room."

There was a creak on the other side of the bathroom door, followed by light footsteps. She couldn't tell which direction they went. *Oh no! Oh my God! Oh, I'm in trouble. Was someone listening? Did whoever it was hear me say that I was raped, that I was pregnant? Was it Mom? Dad? Sean?*

"I think someone just overheard our conversation," Carissa whispered. She opened the door and peeked her head out into the hallway. There was no one out there. Whoever it was, if there was someone, was in his or her room. Surely, if it was Mom or Dad, one of them would have said something, right? He or she would have knocked on the door and insisted on having all the details, right?

"Who?" Fiona asked.

"I don't know," Carissa whispered into the phone as she scurried across the hall to her room. "I don't see anyone."

"Are you sure you heard someone?" Fiona whispered back. *Why is Fiona whispering? Where is she?*

"Yea," Carissa closed the door behind her, slipped out of her robe, and tossed it on her computer chair. "I did. The floor creaked. It's a bad spot. You can always tell when someone's waiting for you in the bathroom. It's like a 'get off the toilet' alarm that always lets you know when you're taking too long to pee."

"Okay then," Fiona said. "So, umm, about the pregnancy, what are you going to do? I'm sure you and Val talked about the abortion option more on the ride home. Have you made a decision?"

I don't even want to think about it! Oh, it seems like the best way out of this situation. But, I mean, it's a baby, isn't it? I'm six- or seven-weeks in. I know it's more than goo now.

"No," Carissa said. "I haven't. It's an unbelievable decision to have to make. I need time to figure it out and, well, I don't know what to do. The longer I wait, the further along the baby is, the harder it'll be to decide. I wish I could just, just, just freeze time."

Fiona sighed. "Well, you know where I stand on this. He or she is a life, a tiny human sprout, just like we all once were. But

I'm not going to push you my way. Don't let Val push you hers. It's your decision. I'll support you either way. Whether I agree or not, I'm with you all the way."

You have no idea how much I needed to hear that. It's a lot better than Val's pressure to end the pregnancy. It's not that simple. I can't base a life or death situation on selfish reasons. Then again, this affects my life, too.

"Thanks," Carissa said. She yawned and looked at her bed. She could feel an invisible weight bearing down on her again. The strength in her legs waned. "I'm tired. I feel like I haven't slept in a week. Can we talk tomorrow?"

"Sure."

"Okay, let's. Later, Fi."

"Later, Cari."

Carissa hung up and sighed. *I'm not alone in this anymore.*

CHAPTER ELEVEN

Carissa nibbled at her apple-flavored breakfast bar and wished it was strawberry or blueberry. *Stupid Sean. Always dipping into my stockpile.* She closed her locker to Val's face.

What the—?

Startled, Carissa's hand released the breakfast bar, which, again, sailed to the floor in slow-motion. Both reached for it and, wham, banged heads. Their hands knocked the bar into the path of a heavyset boy who always wore shorts, no matter how cold it got. Charles was his name? *Yes. That's right. Charles.* He crushed it.

"Son of a—," Carissa grumbled. Both massaged their noggins.

"That wasn't my fault," Val said. "You startle easily."

"Yea, well," Carissa collected the smashed breakfast bar quickly before someone decided to make a mess of it or crush her hand. "You're the one popping up out of nowhere like a psychopath."

Val's hands shot to her hips. "Please. If I announced myself from down the hallway, you'd still drop the damned thing. You've lost like five or six being too damned jumpy. Maybe you should tape them to your hand."

"Whatever," Carissa said. She slammed the mushed bar in the trash. *Wasn't my favorite flavor anyway.* "Maybe I will." She headed to class. "Have you come to convince me to kill the baby again?"

Eye roll from Val. "It's not a baby, Cari. It's barely a tadpole. It's like the size of a pea." She stared at Carissa. "But your breasts are developing nicely. I can't believe I didn't notice it the other day."

Oh, yea. I've been gaining weight. Thanks for reminding me. "None of my bras fit anymore. My mom had to buy me some new ones two days ago. I lied and said I incidentally shrunk my other bras. Kinda hinted that it might be a late breast growth like she and her sister had at my age. She just, she just gave me this weird look, kinda sad. I can't imagine what she's—umm."

"Wow," Val cupped Carissa's breasts. "You've upgraded half a cup. Maybe I should get knocked up."

Ow! Carissa grimaced and slapped Val's hand. "Stop. They're sensitive."

"When aren't they?" Val asked. *She makes a good point.*

Carissa waved away the question. "Class is about to start. What's up?"

Blink. "What do you mean?"

"You have something you want to say. So just say it."

Val bit the corner of her lower lip. "I'm thinking we can use this pregnancy to your advantage."

Carissa's eyes narrowed. "What does that mean?"

"Kent's family is sick rich." *Yea, no kidding.* "Like, seriously, loaded up the ass in money, rich." *That sounds uncomfortable.* "Loaded. And you might be carrying his baby." *Might? Like I slept with someone else before or after he raped me?* "I mean, this couldn't get any better for you. We can leverage him into, ya know, paying you off."

Paying me off? Pay me off for what? To keep it quiet that he raped me? It's not something I want to advertise. I don't want to think about. Why would I put myself in the public eye? Unless that's not what she meant. Perhaps she meant his family is rich and he'd owe me child support if I kept the child. Technically, it is his child. He would owe me child support for eighteen years.

"So, what you're saying is, you think I should keep the child and demand child support?" Carissa asked.

"Hell no." Val clutched Carissa's arm. "No, no, no. Not at all. Take that thought out of your mind." She leaned in close and whispered in Carissa's ear. "I'm suggesting you threaten to keep the child unless they pay you off."

Ah. I see. You've lost your mind. Good grief, Val. What

happened to you? You weren't always like this, were you?

"No."

"Listen," Val whispered. *No.* "Just listen. You want to go to college. You want to have a life and career. You want to play golf and tennis in college. You want to travel to the UK, France, Germany, and Japan. You can do all of that if you don't have that baby. They can finance it all for you. And, well, think about this, they have a lot more to lose than you do. And, if you put this out there, you won't need a scholarship. You're totally clear and free."

"No scholarship?" Carissa asked, enticed by the thought of not needing to beg people for money or commit herself to a team or agency for the next four years.

I can't believe I'm considering this. But if they can pay for my school, it doesn't matter if I get accepted by one of the teams. Either way, I'd be golden. I can focus on winning, classes, having fun, and won't have to work a part-time job to pay off my tuition. I won't have to take out a loan to pay for classes. If, if they can pay for everything: school, room, board, travel...

"They have *deep* pockets," Val said. The overhead lighting gave her blue eyes an alluring sparkle. "All you have to do is threaten to have the child unless they pay you off. They'll cut you a nice, juicy check."

Juicy?

"You can cash it and tuck the cash under your pillow." *Worst hiding place, ever.* "College comes around. You can go anywhere you want. If you want to, you can take classes abroad in London or Paris and meet some sexy guy that goes down on you every night."

Take classes abroad? They'd have to pay me in the hundred thousand range for classes, travel, room, and board. Would they really drop that much just so I don't have a kid? If they offered that much, could I resist? Should I resist?

Tempted, and hard-pressed to agree, Carissa considered the possibilities. She loved Europe, at a glance. Her family visited the tourist attractions and had the luxury of staying in distant relatives' homes in London, Paris, and Munich. She slept in the house where her Parisian great grandfather was raised. Family still owned the Boisseau land. But why just Europe? She had family in Japan. She'd never been to Japan.

"And you'll be doing your family a favor," Val sweetened the deal. "I mean, your parents won't have to pay for anything and can focus on Sean. With you, they can relax and take a huge load off. Be a couple again. You popping out a kid would burden them with being grandparents too soon or having to take care of you and the kid when they're ready to be to empty-nesters. You know Sean's trying to go to New York. Go through with this plan and everything works out for all of you." She paused and smiled. "Oh, and of course, you'd have money to buy a car."

A car? Carissa's eyes widened. *That would be the very first thing I bought with that money. I need a car. I'm tired of depending on everyone for a ride. Oh, I would get a nice cute car like a Volkswagen Beetle, Toyota Prius, MINI Cooper, or something. I'd get a cute red or pink one and name it Princess Veronica... and nickname it The Strawberry.* Hmm. *But of course, I'd keep that to myself.*

"So, what do you think?" Val asked. She put her arm around Carissa's shoulder as the bell rang.

Is it just now ringing? It feels like we've been talking forever. It's like time slowed down just so we can have this conversation.

"Umm," Carissa hesitated. "I'll have to think about it."

Val stopped in front of her class. Mister Friedman stood at the door in wait. He cleared his throat and pointed inside the class. She said, "Don't think yourself out of this. This is an opportunity for you. This is your future we're talking about. This idea, this plan, it works out for everyone."

It works out for everyone? What does that mean? Who's everyone? Okay, Mom, Dad, Sean, and me. That's us. But that's not everyone. Certainly doesn't work out for the baby. Does everyone include you? What do you get out of it? I guess, I suppose, in the end, you expect to get some money out of them or me for coming up with this plan. Is that what this is about? It works out for everyone? I don't know. How would it work out for Kent and his family? They're the ones that would be shelling out cash. I don't see how it would work out for them. Who's everyone?

"It's time to get to class, ladies!" Mister Friedman barked. It jarred her out of her train of thought. She flinched. *Gosh. I am jumpy. But dude seriously shouldn't talk at us like that. I want to give him the finger so much right now!*

Val rolled her eyes, huffed, and walked into class. Carissa rushed away to class while Friedman was distracted.

That's one way to get her off my back. Now I have to figure out what I'm going to do, whether or not I should do it, and if this would really work.

Should I talk to Fiona about this? Who else am I going to talk to?

2

"It's a bad idea," Fiona said as they left sociology. "Not to mention, criminal."

Carissa ground her teeth. "Rape is criminal." A girl from their class *(Lacy, is it?)* turned her head. Carissa lowered her voice. "I mean, there's no question or doubt about it. Kent raped me. And his brother encouraged him on about it. I have nightmares. That's as criminal as it gets. Why not make them pay for it?"

Fiona pulled her aside and whispered harshly, "You should have gone to the police, Cari. You should have told someone official about it, like my dad. He's a police captain for God's sake. They could have run a blood or urine test and used a rape kit. Kent would have been behind bars with his butt cheeks taped shut to keep the neighbors out."

Don't you think I know that? Carissa frowned. "I couldn't. I was so far gone and crying. And, Val was driving drunk. We would have been in terrible trouble."

Fiona put her hand on her forehead and closed her eyes. "At this point, what can you do? What can you prove? You can prove that you're pregnant. With his DNA, you can prove that he's the father. But you can't force him to give you his DNA nor prove that he raped you. So, now you have a girl that's blackmailing or extorting a prominent, rich family. All you look like is an opportunistic girl that intentionally got pregnant to get money out of him."

"I know!" Carissa shot back. "This doesn't bode well for me either way. Either I keep it and all my life plans go to Hell. Or, I don't keep it and, what, it was all for nothing. I got raped and humiliated and he gets away with it."

Fiona threw her hands up. "This is insane. This is totally

insane. I'm really hating Val right now for even suggesting this."

"I know," Carissa said. "I, I hate her too." She paused and thought about it. Did she really mean that? Did she hate Val? "I can't prove it was rape. But with Val's plan, I can at least, maybe, I don't know, get something out of this." Globs of tears formed in her eyes and slowly trickled down her face. "He's ruined my life." She sat on the cold tile floor. "He still is."

Fiona sat beside her. The hallway cleared as the other students went to class. *I'm going to be late again. I don't care.*

"He took a lot away from you," Fiona whispered. "Don't let him take away who you are. Don't let him make you a blackmailer or extortionist or murderer."

Carissa wiped her face with the sleeve of her red cardigan. "I don't even know who I am anymore. Maybe this is who I am now. Maybe this is who I have to be."

"No, it's not." Fiona rubbed Carissa's back. "You're better than this. You don't have to do this. This is something that Val would do. It's something that Val conjured up. But isn't she the one that got you in this mess in the first place? Won't taking their money be an easy out for them? You taking their money lets them off the hook. It's like paid services. I refuse to believe this is the result that's right for you."

"But," Carissa said, "I need the money. If I don't take their money but still get rid of the baby, then that's it. It's over. He raped me. There's no baby. There's nothing tying him to what he's done. And, if I keep the baby, it's all over. No college. No sports. I just, I'm stuck maybe going to community college and working a part-time job at a gas station making minimum wage while everyone I know leaves town. What is my life then? Everything I've worked for, gone. And, my family will be so ashamed."

"You can still play golf and tennis. Join the LPGA or WTA and have someone watch the baby during competitions. That's what babysitters are for." Fiona frowned. "You keep seeing this baby in a terrible light. But maybe, just maybe, he or she is the best thing to ever happen to you."

Please. That's the line Mom fed me about me. She said I was the best thing that ever happened to her. What she's not saying is that she would have traveled more. She wanted to backpack across Europe and write books about her adventures. Instead, she's invested her life in promoting other people's literature. The best thing to ever happen to her? Pssh. Having me stunted her career.

"Sure, right, okay. Let's hear it. How will having this baby improve my life?"

"Umm, well," Fiona started. She froze and formulated.

"Exactly."

"Give me a moment," Fiona said. Her brow furrowed as she processed her thoughts.

"I'll give you time to think about that one," Carissa said. "Fill me in at lunch. Okay?"

"Sure." Fiona crossed her arms and headed to her class.

I know you're on my side. You have the right intentions. I don't like the idea of an abortion, either. It's a life. But, what choice do I have? What life will I have? What life will it have?

The tardy bell rang. *That's three times late today.*

3

Carissa sniffed the air of the cafeteria. *It's Taco Tuesday! I totally forgot.* She got in line and eyeballed the selections. Would she get soft or hard shells? *Hard shell. Yes. Okay. Wait. No. Maybe soft shell after all.* Alright. Softshell. Chicken or beef? *That's a hard one. I'm probably going to have to do one chicken, one beef.* Okay. Toppings. *Cheese under the meat. Cheese over the meat. Salsa. Lettuce. Tomatoes.*

The phone vibrated in her purse. *Who could this be?* She reached in, riffled past her lipstick, comb, mascara case, lip gloss, tissue packet, lollypops, and random papers she assumed were receipts. *Why do I hold on to these? It's not like I pay taxes.* She found her phone. *How does it always manage to sink to the very bottom and tuck itself under the impossible secret nooks of my purse? This purse doesn't even have nooks.*

Carissa slid her finger across the screen. "Hey Mom, what's up?"

"I just wanted to give you a reminder," Mom said. "We're due for our annual checkup with Amy. I've scheduled it for Monday."

Wait. Wait, what? No. Oh no!

"Monday?" Carissa's heart skipped a beat, then raced. Her

head felt light. Everything began to blur. "What? Why? I don't need a checkup. I'm fine."

Five seconds of silence. "You do know, the purpose of an annual exam is to ensure that statement is accurate, right? You've been off emotionally and physically lately. You're sick in the mornings. We need to make sure everything is okay with you."

"Mom," Carissa started. *This is it. She's going to find out I'm pregnant. Everything goes downhill from here.*

"Nope," Mom said. "The appointment is set. We're going right after you get out of class. You don't have any practices that day. I've already confirmed it with both your golf and tennis coaches. Now, how's Taco Tuesday?"

Ruined. Carissa teared up and crafted her tacos. "It's, it's okay."

"What's wrong, Carissa?" Mom insisted. She sounded upset, concerned. "Please, just tell me. Tell me what's going on with you."

Carissa couldn't say a thing. Certainly not now, not in line. The lunch lady stared at her. *Seriously? Staring is rude.* Some of the boys in line watched her. *Take a picture. It lasts longer.* Well, they already had pictures of her. *Oh great.*

"I'm just, I'm just tired," Carissa mumbled and blinked back her tears. That wasn't a lie. She was exhausted.

She swiped her lunch card, waited for the green light, and walked with her tray to a far table. She sat alone these days, if at all possible.

"Carissa," Mom started before her office phone rang. *Saved by the bell.* She sighed. "We'll talk about this later, okay?"

"Yea."

"I love you."

"I love you, too," Carissa said. She meant it this time. She knew how much her mom cared. She felt terrible that she lied and kept her mom in the dark. It honestly made it worse. The more she lied, the more she felt she had to keep up the lie. Otherwise, all of her lies would be exposed. One day, all of those lies would come crashing down on top of her. That day, Carissa feared, was Monday.

Mom hung up.

Fiona sat in front of her and huffed, "Boys are pigs."

In the next table over, a bunch of boys overheard her, turned around, and oinked while lifting their nostrils with their fingers. Then they flashed her a friendly set of middle fingers and returned to their plates.

"You were saying?" Carissa said while wiping away her tears.

Fiona shook her head. "Some guys are exchanging pictures of naked girls on their phones. Girls that go here, apparently. It's been circulating. It's so gross." Hard sigh. "But, forget that. What's wrong?"

I'm so upset, I've lost my appetite. Yet, my body is craving food. I'm compelled to eat. I feel sick. Carissa stuffed a taco in her face with one hand and dabbed her eyes with a napkin with the other. After chewing and swallowing, she sighed. "My mom scheduled an annual check-up for me on Monday."

"Oh, wow," Fiona said. She watched Carissa stuff her mouth with tacos and wondered if this was pregnancy cravings or stress eating. "I'm sorry, Cari. I guess that's that. I mean, what are you going to do? You're going to tell your mom, right? I mean, they're going to find out you're pregnant. There's no way around that now, right?"

Carissa took another bite of her taco and chewed quietly.

"You're going to tell your mom, right?" Fiona repeated. "I mean, you have to. Surely, you don't want to wait until the check-up and act oblivious."

You know, technically, I could act oblivious. It's not like I've been pregnant before. The questions that would hit me are who, where, and when. Who's the guy? Where and when did it happen? I'm not ready to answer those questions. I honestly don't think I ever will be. But at this point, what are my options?

"I have to get rid of it," Carissa said with wide eyes. She pushed her plate forward. "And fast. I mean like, immediately. I can't postpone this. There's no other way out of it."

"Hold on a minute," Fiona urged. "That's not the only way." She walked over to Carissa's side of the table, sat, and put her arm around Carissa's shoulder. "You can keep the child."

"No," Carissa said. "My mom, she would lose it. I, I don't know why I even hesitated. Me being pregnant, that would, I mean, my mom would lose it. My dad? Oh man! I honestly, I honestly can't imagine what he would say or do. Seriously. Like, I'm beyond clueless how he would respond. I mean, okay, it'll be negative. Very negative. I just don't know how bad it would get with him. He might lose his mind. He'd definitely relapse again."

"Don't worry about them," Fiona said with an eerie calm. "Your parents are like, crazy in love with you." *Wanna bet?* "They'll be upset, but you'll be fine."

No. Carissa pouted. *No, I won't be fine.*

"You will," Fiona reassured. "And, I mean, it's not like you were out whoring around or anything. You went to have fun at a party and you were," she lowered her voice, "taken advantage of. I mean, it's not your fault. It's not. And, they can't be mad at you about this. They'll be mortified that this happened to you. But they'll be on your side. It's okay."

"I can't be a mother," Carissa whined and gasped, struggled to breathe. She clamped her eyes closed and used all her strength to hold back tears. "I just. I just can't be. I'm not ready. It's too much." She got up and rushed out of the cafeteria to the bathroom. She found her usual stall, sat on the toilet seat, and sobbed.

CHAPTER TWELVE

The period bell rang. Carissa collected her book bag and hurried out of class. Her bladder screamed at her.

It's like I live in the bathroom now. I should have a designated stall with my name on a plaque. Sigh. *I don't understand why I have to pee so bad suddenly. I had one bottled water during breakfast. One between first and second period. One at lunch.*

In the hallway, Val waited with a small, tan envelope in her hand. "Good news," she said, a big smile on her face. She wagged the envelope. "You wouldn't believe how quick the turnover can be for something like this."

"I have to pee." Carissa pointed towards the bathroom and rushed past the other girls hoping to beat any attempts at a line. She glanced back at Val.

"Umm." Val followed.

Carissa dashed to her stall, grabbed three toilet seat covers, mashed them against the seat, and squatted.

Aahhhh! Yes. That really snuck up on me. Oh, oh crap. This would get a lot worse if I was pregnant-pregnant. That's another reason to get rid of it. If I went through with this kid, I'd get fat! Oh man. And the baby would press up against my bladder. I don't want to have to pee every other hour. Already do. *Yea, yea, yeah. So, I don't want to have to pee every hour.*

"Aren't you curious what's in the envelope?" Val asked outside the stall.

What else could it possibly be besides what we talked about while I was in the bathroom balling my eyes out *because I am several days away from an exam that reveals my pregnancy? I just don't know what to do.*

"I know what it is, Val," Carissa snapped. A jumble of excited conversations entered the bathroom preventing Carissa from hearing Val's response. She heard her say something, but it was muffled. "Hold on! Let me finish and we can talk somewhere private and quieter."

Eight minutes later, Carissa balled up her paper towel and followed Val to her car. "I can't believe I'm about to do this."

Val shrugged. "I can't believe Kent's mom was able to get you into a clinic so quickly. She wrote that check so fast; I thought she was gonna get a papercut."

"Yeah," Carissa mumbled. She was having second thoughts. Third thoughts. Fourth thoughts. Her mind bounced back and forth between whether she should or could go through with an abortion. Her mind was a warzone of conflicting arguments.

It's a life. It's a human being. If I kill it, I'm a murderer. But it's an incomplete life, right? It's not even thinking yet. And what about my life? I didn't have a choice! I didn't choose this. I like my life. And if I don't go through with this, nothing will ever be the same again. My happy life will become a hardship. I'll be a single mother. I can't be one of those. I can't even take care of myself. I haven't had to.

"How convenient."

"Seriously, the timing is perfect," Val gushed. "I'm glad you called yesterday. Apparently, there's a bible-thumper protest scheduled outside the clinic today. There's been a flood of cancellations because people don't want to be harassed on their way to, uh, you know." She unlocked her car and got in.

Carissa stood at the car door, frozen, hesitant.

"It's unlocked." Val pressed the unlock button again just to make sure.

Carissa felt weak. Her heart beat hard and fast in her chest. She reached forward and held on to the door handle. *I hate that I have to do this. I don't want to do this.* She teared up and opened the door.

"It'll be over soon," Val said. "Think of it this way. You can buy a car now. She couldn't cut you the check we were hoping for, but I mean, we're talkin ten-grand. Ten G's, Carissa! That's a lot. I mean." She beamed. "You can buy a nice used car just like that, right off the lot. If you want, we can make Jared's Car Bazaar our next stop, after going to the clinic and bank."

"Bank first. Then the clinic."

"Of course," Val agreed. "Smart move. Last thing we want is for you to go through with it only to have the check bounce."

Sigh. "Exactly. I can't afford to get screwed by this family twice."

"You want to grab something to eat first?"

No. Honestly, after this is done, I never want to see your face again. I just want to go home and sleep.

"Let's just get this over with," Carissa breathed and clamped her eyes shut. The tears had started again. It was a good thing she'd stopped wearing makeup. She'd look like a clown. *This, this feels oddly like déjà vu.*

Val rolled her eyes, started the car, and put it in reverse. Forty minutes, and a thick stack of hundreds later, they drove to the clinic.

2

Val turned the corner and brought the car to a stop. Ahead, a group of people with signs stood in front of a brick building. There were only a few cars in the parking lot. One of them was a news van. She turned to Carissa. "Well, this is where I stop."

Wait. What? Carissa frowned. "You're not coming in with me?"

"Nope." Val bit her upper lip.

"But you, you, you can't expect me to do this alone."

"Oh, come on." Val rolled her eyes. "It's not that big of a deal, Cari. It's a very quick procedure. It's like a vacuum. They plug in, suck it out, and boom, no more baby. You'll be back in ten minutes. Besides, you won't be alone. You have ten-grand right there. That's a lot of company."

How were we ever friends? I just, I just can't believe this. I hate you so much right now, Val. I seriously hate you.

Carissa pointed ahead. "Well, can't you at least park in the parking lot so I don't have to walk all the way over there and back? It's cold."

"Well." Val shifted in her seat. "If I did that, someone might recognize me or the car. I mean. That's a news van. My car would be on the news."

Really, Val? Really? But you have no problem with me trapesing up there for everyone to see. If there's even one person up there that knows me—well, actually. Ha! What am I worried about? No one up there knows me. I'm a nobody. I've only been in this city for a year and change. I only know a handful of people at school. I should be good.

Wrong.

It's almost as though I've forgotten I'm a local golf celebrity after taking second in that last amateur golf tournament. Would a low-status celebrity be worthwhile news? "Is local amateur golf sensation Carissa Boisseau getting an illegal abortion; or is she a pro-life protestor? We'll tell you at eleven."

"You're wearing a hoodie," Val continued. "So, put your hood on, keep your head down, and be discreet about it. It's only about a hundred yards. You might even be able to slip past the news people without being in the shot for the six o'clock news."

Thanks for confirming my fears, Val. The last thing I want, after going through all of this, is to be outed. My parents would be royally pissed that I got pregnant, hid it from them, got an abortion of all things, and then was caught on the local news while doing it. It would embarrass the entire family. Even Grandma would disown me.

Though, I mean, I could always lie and say I went in to get information. I'm going to college to study psychology. Maybe, maybe I could spin this into going inside to volunteer to talk to the women that come in. I could say I'm considering an internship as a before or after abortion counselor. Besides, they do more than abortions at this clinic. Yes. That's right. That, that would most certainly fly. I mean, I'm sure that's an option on the table. I'm sure someone's already got that job. And, volunteer work would look great on college applications. Even though I completed and mailed most of them before early admission deadlines, I can still add it to new ones.

What am I talking about? It's not like I'm actually going to do that. I'm going over a lie like it's something I plan on doing. Hmm. If I can convince myself, surely, I can convince the lie detector. Isn't that how you fool lie detectors? You believe the lie?

"Well?" Val said. Her eyes narrowed. "Are you going or what? Get moving."

I could slap a bitch right now, Val. Don't make me!

Carissa grabbed her purse, got out the car, slammed the door closed, and stomped towards the clinic with her fists balled. A cold gust of wind blew in her face and down her slate hoodie, sending a chill all over her body. Goosebumps sprouted. She hastily flipped her hood on, crossed her arms, and rushed at a steady pace to get to the clinic.

As she approached, she could hear the crowd more clearly. Some casually talked amongst themselves. Their voices played as background noise. The louder voices yelled different chants.

One woman yelled, "A life is a life, no matter the size!"

Another woman chanted, "A fetus is all of us. We were all a fetus!"

One man yelled, "Abortion is death. And we are pro-life!"

A father and daughter held up poster board signs. The father's said, "Give me years" while the daughter's continued, "not just weeks." The daughter looked no older than seven with her yellow ducky dress and blond hair in pigtails. *Aww. She's so cute.*

Two twins held up one large sign that said, "Don't do it. There's not just one of us in there!"

If I was pregnant with twins, I would kill myself.

One man communicated his disagreement with abortion through an "I Love Fetus" t-shirt and the art of interpretive dance. His girlfriend wore a shirt with a fetus inside of a heart-shaped womb. She danced alongside him. The cameraman trained his camera on those two.

Thank God. That means no one will see me.

One sign looked professionally done with thick white posterboard, printed letters, and a glossed finished. It said, "I'm PRO-CHOICE and PRO-LIFE. It's the baby's CHOICE to LIVE."

That's fair, Carissa thought before looking at the person holding the sign. *Oh shit.*

They caught each other's eyes. Gabby stared at her. Her mouth agape. She mouthed the word *Carissa.*

Oh no! Oh no! Oh no! I've been spotted!

Carissa turned her head and sprinted past the news van to

the clinic. Feet kicked grass and dust into a cloud. She skidded to a stop, face inches from the door, and yanked the door handle hard. The door resisted. *Why is the door locked?* She yanked the second door and almost hit herself in the face. *Good grief!* She glanced back, just to confirm her own doom, to see Gabby and her sisters Rebecca and Hannah.

Oh, she yacht!

Gabby passed the sign to her identical twin, Hannah. Or, Hannah passed the sign to her identical twin, Gabby. Carissa stared longer than she should have trying to tell the two apart. *They're identical twins, you idiot! Aren't we trying to escape detection?* Gabby walked forward.

Shit. I was this close! This close *to this all being over. Now, I'm done for.*

Carissa rushed into the clinic.

3

Is it worth it to hide?

Carissa looked around the clinic. There was a service window with three women on headsets typing at their computers. In the waiting area straight ahead, two women in their late twenties sat on blue fabric chairs with wooden armrests. To the right were the bathrooms. To the left was a swinging door that led to the doctors' offices. There was no place to hide, besides the bathroom, the obvious place to look.

Why hide? I mean. She saw me. No doubt about it. But, she doesn't know why I'm here. I can go with the lie I considered earlier. Only, how would that explain the running away? I'm weird? Well, yes. That's not enough. Though, maybe I could say I was worried they wouldn't agree with me working here.

That's legit. That's a legit excuse. But what about the blue, zippered envelope full of money? Hmm. *I mean, it's not your average eight by eleven envelope. It's for things like money, receipts, and such. I don't think this falls into the category of application, research notes, and general paperwork. It's too big for my purse. I could slip the envelope into the pouch of my hoodie. She won't see it.* Carissa slipped the envelope into her pouch. *Okay. That's legit. Too legit to quit.*

Wait. I do have paperwork in here. It's the payment and

appointment documentation Misses Bradshaw provided. It's folded up. Duh! What am I thinking? I'm losing it. She doesn't have to know about the envelope. I mean, but even if she did, I could say, "Ignore the thick bulge. It has questions about an internship and stuff for the administrator to go over." She doesn't need to know if I get over there pronto and give them this documentation. I'm glad we filled out all the necessary forms online before my getting here. It'll look far less suspect.

Carissa approached the service window and pulled out her envelope. "Carissa Boisseau." She glanced at the entryway, expecting three peeved black girls to come through that door at any moment to pull her out by her wrists and ankles.

"Right on time," said the black woman at the counter. "Doctor Green was just calling about you. Unfortunately, he had to step out. Protest and all. Doctor Sanders will be performing the procedure instead." She studied Carissa with a long and critical gaze before pointing at the envelope. "Is that what I think it is?"

"Oh yes," Carissa checked the woman's name tag. Sharice. "The documentation required for my meeting with the doctor." She lowered the envelope, opened it conspicuously, pulled out the folded documentation, and then resealed the envelope.

"Are you sure you should be carrying that around?" Sharice asked. She pointed her stylized and bedazzled nails at the blue envelope. "That looks like a lot of money."

"It looks like more than it is," Carissa lied before cramming the envelope in the pouch of her hoodie. "It's all ones. Stripper life, ya know." *On what planet are you a stripper, Carissa?* "Are we good to go?"

Sharice gave her a long stare before looking over the documentation. "Yea. We are." She paused. "I'm not going to pretend I don't know what's going on here. But it's none of my business." *Phew.* "I do have one question for you."

I hate when people do that. Just ask the question! Don't tell me you have a question. Just ask the question. I don't need an introduction to the question. You don't need to announce the question like it's some high-collared dignitary. "Ladies and Gentlemen, it is with great humility and honor that I present to you, Her Majesty's latest question."

"What's that?" Carissa asked.

"Is that your friend?" Sharice asked and pointed at the door. "The protestor?"

Carissa glanced at the door again and nearly jumped out of her skin. Gabby watched her through the glass entry door. Her face was so close to the door that her breath fogged the glass. *Gabby, that's creepy as hell.*

"Kind of." She smiled nervously at Sharice. "She didn't know I was going to be here."

"Okay." Sharice silently communicated her annoyance with her eyes. She gripped the paperwork under her armpit, said, "Please take a seat and we'll be right with you," and walked away.

Gabby walked in and marched straight towards Carissa. "Carissa," she said in a hushed voice. She glanced at the two women in the room before pointing at Carissa's abdomen. "The sickness. Nausea. The wooziness. I suspected but didn't want to believe it. And, then there were the rumors." *Wait. What rumors?* "And your crying in the bathroom. Why didn't you tell me you were pregnant?"

Alright. How am I going to play this? Denial? Yea. Sure. I can deny. Deny, deny, deny. It depends on how you define "is".

"I can't believe you're about to have an abortion," Gabby whispered. The word *abortion* was spat out like a forkful of bad fish. She opened her arms and gave Carissa a hug.

O...K. I did not expect a hug. Why is she giving me a hug? Why is she being so nice to me? Doesn't she hate abortions? Shouldn't she be dragging me outside and setting the clinic on fire to save my baby?

"What rumors?" Carissa asked. There was no point in denying it anymore. It was all about to be over anyway. Yet, she needed to know what was being said about her. She'd enjoyed the juicy details of gossip when she was plugged into Val's wide circle of friends. She rarely contributed. But she did enjoy a good story. The tales of high school hookups, breakups, and melodrama were tantalizing. Now, she wanted everyone to shut the hell up.

"Let's talk about what you're doing here," Gabby said.

"What...rumors?" Carissa insisted through her teeth.

Gabby sighed and mulled it over. "You were at a Halloween

party, drank too much, seduced some guy, and was found naked in one of the upstairs bedrooms," Gabby said.

Wait! Wait a minute! No way did she just say I seduced a guy. I...seduced a guy?! That's what you heard? I, as in me, Carissa Asami Boisseau, seduced a guy? I can't believe it. I cannot believe it. Who said this? Who is saying this? I will kill somebody!

"Now, let's talk about your pregnancy," Gabby said. "How long have you known? Have you told anyone else? Sean doesn't know. That's obvious. But what about your parents? Do they know? Did they sign off on this?"

Too many questions. Too many questions.

"No," Carissa said and stepped towards the bathroom and out of the earshot of the two women who watched them with interest. She whispered, "No one knows. And no one needs to know."

"You're here by yourself?" Gabby frowned and glared in the direction of the service window. "How's that even legal?" She pondered it and rebutted. "It's not. You can't do this without a parent. It's the law."

"It's doable, okay?" Carissa said. "Talk to the right people and they can make it happen."

"Why?" Gabby asked. Her big brown eyes searched for answers.

Carissa sighed and led her back towards the chairs. They sat as far away from the other two women as possible. "Because I can't have this baby. I just can't. I'm only seventeen. I'm not ready to be a mother. I shouldn't be a mother. And, I definitely don't want to be like one of those stupid teen moms on that television show. I just, I want to go to college, play golf and tennis, graduate, have a career. None of that is possible if I have this baby."

"And my mom and dad will kill me if they find out I'm pregnant," Carissa continued. "I can't bear to see the look of disappointment in their faces. Especially when they find out how. And, I've been lying to them all this time. It just, it's all going to blow up and fall apart if I don't get this done right now."

Gabby considered Carissa's words. "What if you could?"

What? Carissa shrugged. "What if I could what?"

"What if I told you that you could be a mother, an athlete, and go to college," Gabby said. "You can do school, be a star and mom."

Carissa wanted to ask how but hesitated.

"My sister and I are taking classes locally and getting an apartment near campus," Gabby said. "It'll be cheaper for all of us if we got a three-bedroom instead of a two-bedroom. We can split everything three ways. Plus, my mom is crazy about scholarships. She's been searching the web for the last three years looking for stuff for us. You could use some of those resources. She'd be happy to help you out." She paused and thought about it. "And, I mean, aren't you a star golf and tennis player expected to go pro? I'm sure you can get recruited through that, pregnant or not. Most of the professionals are parents."

"I can't take classes, do homework, work, and sports and be a mom," Carissa returned. "There aren't enough hours in the day. I'd be exhausted."

Gabby nodded. "But you won't be a mom alone. Your mom and dad will be a grandma and grandpa." *I can imagine Mom pulling her hair out being called grandma just as she hits her forties.* "Your brother an uncle. And you'll have me and my sisters."

I'm not sure your sister would agree with you recruiting her for this task. Babies cry and need to be cleaned and fed. I mean. I would be the college roommate from Hell.

"Plus," Gabby said and continued. "I'm sure the father and his family will want to have some involvement with the child."

Carissa's face twisted. "I don't want them involved, and they don't want anything to do with it. Who do you think funded the abortion?"

"Wait." Gabby frowned and glared at the service window again. "This is wrong, Carissa. You're having a secret abortion funded by the parents of the father without your parent's knowledge or consent? This, this shouldn't even be possible. How old are you, again?"

"Seventeen, of course," Carissa muttered. "We already went over this."

"Yea, my age," Gabby said. "You're a minor." Her wheels were spinning. It was clear. Carissa only wished those wheels spun her out the door. Any minute, the doctor was going to come to do what he was paid rather handsomely to do.

"Obviously," Carissa said. "Aren't your sisters outside—"

"This is completely illegal," Gabby repeated. "In the state of Virginia, a minor can't get an abortion without the consent of a parent or legal guardian and must be fully informed of the procedure and what it entails, including risks, before it's allowed to occur. I should call the police."

What the? You're going to call the police on me? That's the last thing I need right now.

"This is exactly why we're out there protesting to shut this place down," Gabby argued. "This place, the parents of the father, they're taking advantage of you. You shouldn't be doing this without your parents. You shouldn't be doing this at all."

Carissa's face went a bright red. Her eyes widened. "Listen. This is none of your business."

"When there's a life at stake, it sure as hell is," Gabby said before her eyes popped open wide and her hands flew to her mouth. "Oh wow. I'm sorry. I don't usually cuss."

Seriously? We're arguing about abortion and you're worried about cussing? We are from two different worlds, girl.

"I'm going to do this," Carissa said. "I have no choice. It's out of my hands now."

"Yes, it is," Gabby said. "All you have to do is walk out of that door with me and we can find a way to make this work. There's a way. I know it. We will find it. And I will personally work with you to make it happen. And, Carissa, I have God on my side. His will is at work. There is nothing that can stand between Him and what needs to be done to make this right. God will make this right for you. God is going to come through for you. Just give Him a chance."

For ten seconds, there was complete silence. What felt like a cool breeze blew straight through Carissa's chest, rested in her core, and exited out of her back, leaving a fuzzy chill. With it, all her anxieties were swept away. Her muscles relaxed. Her mind grew quiet. What remained was nothingness and contentment.

What just happened?

Carissa looked intently at Gabby, her mouth agape. Stunned to silence, she reconsidered her position.

Alright. What if I kept the child? I have ten thousand dollars, blood money, really, that was paid in exchange for my abortion. What do I do? Give it back? Nuh-uh! Nope! After all, I was raped. I suppose we could consider this payback. Besides, what am I going to say? Hey, here's the money for the illegal abortion you orchestrated for the girl raped by your son. Thanks, but no thanks. No. I actually need that money. I'm going to need that money. But it's not about the money.

It's about a life. There's a little baby inside of me. I wonder if it's a girl or boy. Honestly, I don't even know which one I want. Do I want a little girl? Do I want a baby boy?

Oh, if I go through with this, I'm going to be in so much trouble. I can't begin to imagine how my parents are going to respond to all of this. My dad's head is going to literally explode off his neck.

"I don't know how to tell my parents. I don't know if I can look them in the eye and tell them I'm pregnant. It'll destroy them."

Gabby put her arm around Carissa. "I'll be there for you if you'd like. I'd be happy to support you as you tell them the truth. I'll hold your hand through the entire thing."

Carissa breathed. "And school. What about school? Everyone will be looking at me. I'll be pregnant girl. I mean. I'll be the gossip of the whole school." *Already am.*

Gabby smiled with pleasant, deep, loving eyes. "There are ten other girls in our school that are pregnant. Did you know that?"

Wait, what? "No. I've only heard of one." *Wait. No. Can't forget Chelsea Theron and Melinda Bowers.* "Three."

"Discretion," Gabby said. "The school has policies about discretion and a support system. You can stay in class until you start to show. After which, you have the option of taking the remainder of your classes at home."

"Really?" Carissa asked with a smile. That was a load off, assuming she had a home to come back to after her parents lost their minds. She wouldn't have to waddle around the school and get made fun of.

"Yep," Gabby said. "You'd have to meet the teachers at least once every two weeks to go over what they gave you. They closely monitor your grades and have the option of pulling you back into class if you slip. But that shouldn't be a problem for a student of your aptitude. You're near the top of our class. I'm confident you'll be able to keep up with the schoolwork and keep your grade point average." She stopped. "If you don't mind me asking, how far are you along?"

Carissa sighed. "Seven weeks now."

"Okay," Gabby said and counted on her fingers. "So, we're looking at, umm, something along the lines of, umm, hmm, a summer baby." She smiled and snapped her fingers. "You know, there's a really good chance you won't even have to worry about it. I mean, you may find yourself showing in May. Then again, we're seniors. That last month is a jiff for us. We'll be doing gowns and everything else. You don't have to worry about a thing. Keep wearing hoodies and other baggy clothes."

This could work. This could actually work.

"Oh!" Gabby exclaimed with wide eyes and a smile. "We can go shopping for maternity outfits."

I'm pregnant and you're thinking about shopping. Is there such a thing as a wrong time to think about shopping? *Okay. You make a valid point.*

This girl really has turned this around in my head. But, there's the matter of the money. Are they going to be pissed at me because I have ten thousand dollars of their cash? Of course. But again. Screw'em. They're getting off light. They should be glad their son isn't behind bars where he belongs.

"Okay." Carissa took a deep breath. "Let's say I did keep it. That's a big if. I won't have any more friends, except Fiona. All my friends are Val's friends. She brought me up here. She put herself on the line to get me here. There's money involved." Gabby frowned. "Shit's gonna hit the fan when I get in that car with a fetus still inside of me. So, I don't know if you're just saying this because you hate abortion or something, but I'm going to need a lot of help. A lot of support. You're not just doing this as part of some Christian anti-abortion crusade, are you?"

"No." Gabby scrunched-up her nose. "I'm doing this because I care about you and it's the right thing to do. And yes, I'll be there for you. But umm, what do you mean there's money involved?"

Sigh. "They're paying me."

"To have an abortion?" Gabby asked. She looked horrified.

Slow nod. "Yea."

"How much?" Gabby pressed.

Do I really want to tell you how much? Do I want anyone to know how much? Carissa hesitated.

"How much?" she insisted.

Fine. Carissa leaned over and whispered, "Ten thousand."

"Holy cow!" Gabby exclaimed. She looked around the clinic. The two other women had at some point stepped away. It was just them. She lowered her voice. "That's a lot of money. Who's the father?"

"Kent," Carissa said and breathed deeply. She felt her throat tighten. She hated saying his name. "Kent Bradshaw."

"Oh," Gabby said. "Kent Bradshaw of the Bradshaw family. One of the most well-to-do families in the city." She looked down. "I see."

"What?" Carissa hadn't expected that response.

Gabby remained silent. *Oh, now you decide to be quiet. That's a first.*

"What?" Carissa insisted. "Tell me what you're thinking."

"Well, the rumor going around doesn't work in your favor, Carissa," Gabby said. "It sounds like you seduced him while you two were drinking. Then you're pregnant. And, now they give you money in exchange for an abortion." She breathed. "I hate to ask but, did you sleep with him with the intention of getting money?"

Are you kidding me right now? After all this, you ask me that question?

Carissa stared at Gabby for an uncomfortable length of time before saying, "I didn't have a choice, Gabby." She could feel herself getting hot. "He got me drunk and put something in my drink. I was half unconscious as I was brought to his room. I puked my guts out, washed my mouth and face, and then went to bed. Next thing I know, Kent and his brother come in the room. I'm half out of it. But I'm awake enough to hear them gloating about drugging me. And then, they touched me, took my clothes off, and Kent raped me." There was a sudden wave of nausea. Carissa tilted over, ready to lose her lunch, but didn't. She breathed in and out, ready to burst into tears for what felt like the thousandth time since that terrible night.

This will never be over, will it? I'm going to have to relive that night over and over again for the rest of my life.

"Oh," Gabby said and put her hand over her mouth. "I'm so sorry. I shouldn't have insinuated anything. I'm so sorry." She lowered herself to Carissa who was ready to keel over in her chair. "Are you okay? Do you need water? Do you want to go to the bathroom?"

"Ugh," was all Carissa could muster. Nausea swooshed through her in waves. Her heart pounded in her ears.

A blond woman behind the service window rushed around the corner. "She okay?"

"I'm not sure," Gabby said. "We were talking and, she said she was umm, well, she said something private and then, this."

The blond older woman, Barbara, according to her name tag, knelt in front of Carissa and asked, "Do you need to move?"

Yes. Out of this city. Out of this state. Maybe out of the country? How far would ten thousand get me? How long could I survive on it in the Caribbean?

Carissa breathed deeply. "I need to leave."

"But," Barbara started. "What about your procedure?"

"It's," Carissa said. "It's been cancelled."

Barbara looked back at the service window and then said, "You've already paid for the procedure. A, umm," she glanced at Gabby, "a significant amount. If you cancel it, you'll lose your deposit."

Thank God, it's not my money.

Gabby frowned at the woman. "She said it's been cancelled. You can keep your blood money."

Woah.

Barbara shot Gabby the evil eye and opened her mouth to speak. "You," she started, but then bit her lip, stood straight, and stormed off.

Carissa felt her nausea pass. "You had to say blood money."

"Sorry," Gabby shrugged. "It just kind of came out."

"Alright." Carissa stood. "I just canceled my appointment. I can't believe I'm going through with this."

"You mean, keeping the baby," Gabby confirmed.

"Yea."

"Did you really want to have the abortion?" Gabby asked. "Or was it just, all those reasons that pushed you into that direction?"

"I." Carissa put her hand on her abdomen. "No. I didn't, don't want to have the abortion. It just, I don't know how I'm going to live my life. I don't know what's going to happen next. My whole life is about to change now. Not going through with it, not having that procedure, it means everything I planned out and thought my life would be is gone. Whatever happens next, that's my life." She inhaled and exhaled slowly. "I don't want to get rid of the baby. I'm just so scared of keeping it."

Gabby rubbed Carissa's shoulder. "I think I understand."

"I already feel connected to it, to the baby," Carissa said. "I already care about it. It would have broken my heart if I went through with it." She looked back at the service window. Barbara and Sharice watched them. Their eyes were strange. Deeper. Collective. *What the?* It felt like the whole world was watching her through their eyes. *This is strange. I'm getting outta hear before their heads start spinning and vomit starts shooting out of their mouths.*

"Well." Gabby pointed towards the door. "Are you ready to go?"

"Yea," Carissa lied. She wasn't ready to go. She wasn't ready for whatever was ahead of her. She'd have to tell Val that she didn't go through with the abortion, but was keeping the money, which would not go over well. She had to go home and tell her parents the truth, the whole truth, and nothing but the truth, so help her God.

Honestly. Gabby's God, wherever and whoever you are, I need all the help I can get with my parents. I really don't want to get yelled at, punished, and grounded. I know I lied. But, I just, felt so ashamed and scared about everything.

What about Val? She did somehow arrange for me to get ten thousand dollars cash out of Kent's mom. I don't even know how she was able to accomplish that. But they're going to feel a certain way about me not going through with the abortion. Will they lash out at her? Will she lash out at me?

"What if Val gets super pissed that I didn't go through with it?" Carissa asked. "I mean, she arranged all of this, including the payoff. What if she gets pissed and drives off?"

"I have a better idea." Gabby stretched out her hand. "How about we give you a ride home?"

So, I don't go through with the procedure and *ditch her? That would be awfully cold of me. I can't do that to her, no matter how I feel about her.*

"If she doesn't want to drive me, I'll come with you, okay?"

"Deal," Gabby said and wiggled her fingers.

Carissa took Gabby's hand. They walked out of the clinic together.

CHAPTER THIRTEEN

"You what?" Val said shooting spittle from her mouth. Her face went red and twisted into a snarl. "What do you mean you didn't go through with it?"

Wow. She's pissed. A lot more upset than I thought she would be. But why? I mean, I know she got this going but, she shouldn't be this mad at me. It's my choice. It's my life.

"I couldn't go through with it," Carissa said, more confident with her decision. "It wasn't the right thing to do."

The more she thought about it, the more it felt right. The moment she stepped through the clinic doors and into the light of day, she was hit by a wave of confidence about her future. Despite the troubles that were ahead for her, she knew, absolutely knew, that her life was going to be better than it ever could have been had she gone through with the abortion. Her absolute confidence in her future felt foreign and unsettling. It didn't make sense but was tangible, real.

Now, sitting next to a fuming Val, Carissa felt at peace with her decision. There was more going on here than she originally thought. How she knew that she didn't understand. But it was revealed to her that Val was playing a part in it and was mad that things hadn't gone according to her plan.

"Right!" Val threw her hands in the air. "Right. So, I guess you're giving the money back then, too, right? Since you're suddenly so interested in doing the right thing."

Carissa shook her head. "No. I'm keeping the money. You seem to be forgetting the part where I was *raped*." The word launched out of her mouth like a missile and left a bitter taste in her mouth. "They got me drunk, put something in my drink, and proceeded to rape me. They're lucky as hell that ten thousand dollars is the only thing they're losing here."

Val's jaw tensed. She brooded for a few seconds, calculated, then smirked. "Fine, Carissa. You keep your dirty money. But that's the last bit of help you get from me. I'm done." She looked ahead at the road and unlocked the doors. "Get out."

You have got to be kidding me! Carissa looked at Val wordlessly. *You're such a pouty, rotten little—whatever.*

Relieved that Gabby and her sisters offered to give her a ride, Carissa opened the door, grabbed her purse and backpack, got out, and walked away.

Her final words for her friend, which Val would smell in thirteen seconds, was a silent fart.

2

"You did the right thing," Gabby said for the fifth time and flashed a smile back at Carissa from the front passenger seat. "I'm proud of you."

Carissa shrugged. It was all she could do. Her confidence in her decision waned the more she thought about what was coming up next. So, she disagreed with Val. So that friendship met its end. Big deal. She hadn't spoken to Val for a month after the attack. It was completely different telling her parents she was seven weeks pregnant.

"It'll be okay," Rebecca said and rubbed Carissa's shoulder. "The worse thing they can do is ground you. And honestly, that might be the best thing for you right now."

If there's such a thing as a good time to be grounded, it would be during the winter season. It's getting cold. Not a lot of fun outdoor activities that I can think of in Virginia for a pregnant person. Can't ski, sled, snowboard, or snowshoe. Besides, I have to find as many scholarships as possible and write a bunch of pointless but required essays. "Dear scholarship fund, I desperately need to go to college. So, show me the money!" I would probably lounge around in tees and pajamas and watch television, anyway. I've grounded myself for the last seven weeks. If I get television privileges, things pretty much won't change for me, especially since girl's tennis season is over and golf practices are suspended for two months. I'll still go to the indoor facilities but can't think of much else to do. I can catch up on my reading.

"The best thing for you," Hannah chimed in from the driver's seat, "would be to come to church with us and your brother. You can make some new friends. Some better friends."

Eh. I don't know about that. I'm feeling rather shaky about making new friends. I've had enough with friends for now. I'm still reeling from Val. And honestly, I can't imagine what I'll have in common with church girls. You'll be talking about God and Jesus all the time. Singing your cutesy, happy religious music with your hands up. I mean, more power to you. That's you. You do you. But I don't think that's for me.

Plus, some of those Christians are judgy. I mean, you do you. I'll do me. That's that. No need for me to criticize what you do, who you are. Live and let live. I can't imagine how they'll respond to a pregnant teen. Oh God, I'm a pregnant teen. They'll probably call me a whore or something.

"Yea," Rebecca agreed. "You should come. Sean really likes it there."

Sean did say he likes it there. He said the people are nice and fun. But, then again, you're a pretty girl, Rebecca. Correction. You're all freaking gorgeous. Of course, Sean's going to like it there. He'll say anything and everything to be around you three. He thinks you're amazing. You've got him firmly wrapped around your fingers. You're all he talks about. You could have daily human sacrifices and he'd sing your praises. I've never seen a prettier set of girls in my life.

"I know," Carissa said. "He's got nothing but nice things to say about all of you. He's changed. I've never seen him so happy. It's annoying."

Rebecca chuckled and placed her hand on her chest. "He's such a sweetheart."

"Yea, yea, yea." Carissa waved her hand. "I suppose he has his rare moments."

She's good for him. That's for sure. Kelsea was demanding, difficult, and played games. Rebecca's laid back. When she comes over, they spend most of their time laughing. Sean's not that funny. It must be her.

"Please come for a while," Gabby pleaded. "Once or twice at least, just to try it out. Hang out with us." She stuck out her lip, pouted, and fluttered her eyes. It was a strange gesture, but somehow it worked.

You're so freaking nice! Ugh. It almost makes me sick. Hmm. She's been nothing but sweet towards me since we met. And, I need a new friend. Val certainly won't be my friend anymore, ever again, no matter what. Ever. After everything that's happened, why would I want her to be my friend? Nope. Not happening.

Carissa sighed. "Fine. I'll go with you if my parents haven't killed me or locked me in the basement or grounded me until I'm fifty."

"That's silly." Hannah glanced back. "They can't legally do that. They'd go to jail if you stopped showing up to class. There are safety measures put in place now to prevent that kind of stuff in abusive homes."

Are you serious?

"I," Carissa started and glanced at Rebecca who shrugged. "I wasn't serious. They wouldn't actually confine me for years. They wouldn't confine me for months. It's too much work." Gabby laughed. "They're trying to get rid of us as soon as possible so they can start traveling. They've already planned their trips and Sean's still a freshman. I can't imagine what being grandparents will do to their plans."

Rebecca and Gabby exchanged prolonged eye contact. Then, Rebecca collected Carissa's hand and held it. "It'll be fine."

"Yea," Gabby said. "I'm sure they'll be upset at first. But, the further along you are in the pregnancy, the better it'll get. Once that baby comes, they'll be so in love with it, err, him or her, they won't care about the trivial stuff."

Let's hope. We can only hope.

"I'm starving," Hannah said. "Hey, before we drop her off, you want to grab something to eat?"

"Yes!" Carissa, Rebecca, and Gabby exclaimed in unison.

They looked at each other and laughed.

3

They parked in front of Carissa's house. She stared at both cars in the driveway and felt her heart race. She gripped the door handle and took deep breaths. Gabby offered to be there for moral support as Carissa gave her parents the news. She declined. It was a conversation she had to have with her parents alone, even if she didn't want to.

Sean opened the front door and waved. *Of course, he's going to invite them in.* He rushed forward as Rebecca hopped out of the car.

"Hey, Sean!" Rebecca called before they met and hugged.

I'm jealous of my little brother. That was cute, dammit. Now, I'm seriously jealous of my little brother.

"What's she doing with you three?" Sean asked. He pointed his thumb at Carissa as she got out of the car.

"Well," Rebecca smiled, "I have to get all the dirt I can on you from somewhere. Is it true you wore diapers until you were five?"

Wait. What?

Sean turned bright red, opened his mouth, and turned to Carissa with an expression she hadn't seen on him before. He looked mortified and genuinely hurt.

Oh my God, Rebecca! I never said that! Carissa rose both of her palms and backed off.

"I'm kidding, love," Rebecca said. She poked Sean in the ribs and gave him a peck on the lips. "We were talking about how sweet and wonderful you are."

Sean's previous expression evaporated and was replaced by a goofy smile. "Really?"

Hmm.

Gabby got out of the car and gave Carissa a hug. She whispered, "Are you going to tell them tonight?"

The longer I wait, the harder it'll be to tell them. "Yea."

"Okay," Gabby said. "Call me afterward, please?"

"Assuming they don't take my phone," Carissa mumbled. One of the rules of being grounded was no cellphone privileges. Of all the punishments they dealt, being away from social media was torture.

Gabby squeezed tight and whispered, "It won't be that bad, Carissa. You're the victim here, okay? You didn't ask for this. Yet, you chose to do the right thing. It'll be okay."

It'll be okay? I'm terrified. I don't know what it will be but okay seems like the furthest thing from reality. I have no clue how they're going to react to this news.

Sean watched them and frowned. "What happened?"

Gabs, I'd ask you to "let go, you're making a scene." But honestly, at this point, it's going to come out anywhere so why hide it?

"Umm." Rebecca shrugged and rubbed the back of her neck. "It's not my business to tell. But don't ask, okay? Not yet. Trust me."

Gabby hugged a little bit harder and then released the hug. "It'll be okay."

"Hey, uh," Hannah called out. "We have to go. Mom just called wondering where we are. She said, 'It's time to scoot and bring our butts home.'"

"Just the butts?" Gabby responded with a smile.

Hannah laughed. "I said the exact same thing. She said to bring whatever we intend to keep."

Rebecca said, "In that case, I'm bringing Sean with us."

Sean beamed.

"Please do." Carissa smirked. "We've had enough."

Sean put his hand on his chest and stuck out his lower lip. "Oh, your words cut deep."

"Uh-huh, that's great," Hannah said. Her expression said the opposite. "Let's go before she calls back."

Gabby agreed. "Yea. It's a school night. We can't be out past eight." *It just turned seven.* "Plus, I've got to finish a paper." She gave Carissa one more hug before getting in the car. "Call me."

"I will if I can."

"Bye," Rebecca said before giving Sean a hug and kiss on the cheek. He rubbed her back and gave her a peck of his own.

Oh. They're getting handsy. Better keep an eye on these two.

"Becca!" Hannah called from the front seat.

"I'm coming," Rebecca whined before getting in the car. She waved back at Sean before closing the car door. They drove away.

Carissa waved goodbye. *She's good for him.*

Sean watched the sedan drive down the block and turn left. Then, he looked at Carissa. "So, you're hanging out with the Coles now?"

Hanging out with the Coles. That sounds like a reality show. With these girls, it would probably be a hit.

"Something like that," Carissa said and walked across the lawn. Her legs felt ten times heavier with each step. "You and Rebecca look like you're getting pretty serious."

"Yea," Sean smiled. "It looks that way, doesn't it?"

Carissa took each step one at a time and stopped at the front door. She could hear Mom and Dad through the screen door and weighed what was to come.

"You going in or what?" Sean asked.

"Yea," Carissa said trying to keep her cool. Her heart raced. Beads of sweat burst from her forehead. "Just thinking."

"Think and move," Sean pressed. "It's almost dinner time."

Hmm. Should I tell them before, during, or after dinner?

Carissa stepped inside as butterflies filled her stomach. She was ready to pass out as she peeked around the corner for her parents.

"What's up with you?" Sean asked as he passed her. He flicked her ear and then headed up the stairs before she could retaliate.

You booger.

"Sean! Slow down up those stairs!" Mom called from the kitchen. "Carissa?" Carissa's heart pounded through her ears. She could feel her body tighten and throat closeup as she tried to call back. Mom's soft footsteps approached the hallway. "I thought you were spending the day with Val. Why'd the Cole sisters drop you off?"

"Umm," Carissa started. Her lips trembled. She couldn't finish. The moment Mom appeared around the corner with her hair in a bun and Super Mom apron, Carissa burst into tears. It was time to reveal everything.

4

"I'm pregnant," Carissa admitted to her mother as they sat on her bed.

After she broke down, it took her ten minutes to settle down. Both Sean and Dad looked on in confusion and pestered Carissa with questions until finally, Mom insisted they go somewhere quiet and talk, at least until Carissa calmed down. In her room, with the door locked and windows closed, effectively shutting out the world, Carissa would finally share the truths she hadn't been able to tell for the last seven weeks.

"I suspected you were," Mom said and rubbed Carissa's back. Carissa looked up, shocked. "I've been pregnant before, ya know." Mom smirked, despite the seriousness of the situation. That was her gift. "I saw the signs. The slight changes in your body and mood. Your morning sickness. But I wasn't completely sold until I overheard your conversation the other night."

It was her! She was the one outside the bathroom.

"Why, why didn't you say anything?" Carissa asked. She looked up at her mother, scared but relieved. She expected yelling and anger and lecture. She didn't expect that her mother knew, or suspected it, but hadn't said anything. But why not? Why didn't she say something?

"At first, I wasn't sure what to say," Mom said. "No matter how much I pressed you, you didn't want to talk about it. And I didn't want to force that kind of conversation with you. I mean, if it was what I thought it was, I knew you had to tell me eventually. It's a pregnancy. It was just a matter of time before you showed." She looked out the window, at the darkness of night, and sighed. "I heard you on the phone in the bathroom. I was curious what you were talking about, so I listened. And, I heard what you said." She froze. Her face tightened.

"That I was, I was," Carissa tried. She'd told Val, Fiona, and Gabby. Yet, it felt impossible to say the word to her mother. Why? Why was it so hard to tell Mom she was raped? She teared up again.

"Raped," Mom finished. Her jaw clenched. She blinked away tears and breathed deeply. She bit her lip and lowered her head. "I didn't know what to say to you. Part of me hoped that, that I misheard what you said. But then it all made sense. The way you've been acting. How you've been so closed off, even more so than before. You've always been an introvert, but not like this."

This is strange. I thought I'd be doing most of the talking. Is this my confession or hers? But it's better. I'm not afraid anymore. Not of her. Not of punishment. What was I so afraid of?

"I talked to your coaches," Mom said. Carissa frowned. *What? When?* "They agreed with me. You went to practice. You played.

You had your meets and won. But you were cold and distant. We all thought you were just going through senior year stress. Senioritis or something. Yet, I suspected deep down that there was something more. Something worse. It felt familiar."

What do you mean it felt familiar?

"Were you?" Carissa asked. Mom nodded. Tears streamed down her face. They both hugged each other and cried.

It never even occurred to me. All the warnings. All the insistence on not going to parties. You were so overly protective of me all the time. Always wanted to know where I went, who I was with, why I was going, how long I was going to be there. You insisted that I not be anywhere near alcohol ever. I thought it was because of Dad's drinking. It never occurred to me that it was because you went through the same thing.

After a few minutes and blown noses, they both held each other's hands and looked each other in the eyes.

"Tell me what happened," Mom said. "I know it was at the party. It's the only thing that makes sense." She breathed. "Tell me everything."

5

As best as she could, Carissa recounted the last seven weeks, starting with Val inviting her to the party. She highlighted meeting Kent and Brian and summarized the beer pong games. She cried her way through the events leading to and including the assault. It was grueling. They had to take a break.

Mom went downstairs to fill their plates. Through the open door, Carissa could hear Dad pelting Mom with questions, seeking an explanation, but all he got were assurances that they would talk about all of it later. It didn't please him. He was gruff and demanding, but "later" was all he got.

"We'll talk about it later, end of discussion," Mom commanded at the foot of the stairs before coming up with plates and glasses on two circular wooden serving trays. She waitressed part-time while in college. Her balance and knack with serving trays hadn't faltered in twenty years.

When Mom returned, they ate, and Carissa detailed everything that happened after the assault. The drive home with Val. Showering and sleeping off the effects of the alcohol and drug they gave her. She recounted the seven weeks up to the discovery that she was pregnant. Mom didn't interrupt, but listened intently, patiently.

After Carissa accounted for the last seven weeks, she stopped and sighed. How could she tell Mom she planned to have an abortion and accepted money from Kent's mother?

"What? What is it?" Mom asked. She measured Carissa's expressions with keen eyes.

Of course, the lie detector would know I'm withholding. Do I really want to tell her this? Sigh. *We've told her everything else.*

"Today, after school, Val took me to an abortion clinic," Carissa confessed.

"What?" Mom shrieked. This was the first time she'd raised her voice that evening. Her brow was furrowed. Her nose flared.

"Obviously, I didn't go through with it," Carissa rushed. "We completed all the paperwork in advance. They were able to get me in for surgery on the same day."

"How?" Mom asked. "You're under-aged. You shouldn't have been allowed."

No, I shouldn't have. But money pulls strings. The world is a puppet. Carissa sighed. "Yea, I know. They turned their heads on the underage thing."

"Well," Mom said and rubbed her temples. "You didn't go through with it. So, I suppose nothing illegal was done, even though they flirted with it." She sighed. "Is that why the Cole sisters brought you home? Because you didn't go through with it and Val disagreed?"

"Yea." *That's precisely why.*

"Tell me everything."

It was another twenty minutes before Carissa was finished. She told Mom she was scared and desperate when she learned about the medical examination and recounted her conversations with Val. The arrangement with Kent's mother. The visit to the bank. Val's drop off and Gabby's intervention at the clinic.

Reluctantly, Carissa opened her backpack and exposed the ten thousand dollars in cash. Mom gasped. *I can't believe I'm doing this.* Carissa bit her lip. She hated revealing the money. Part of her was concerned that her parents wouldn't let her keep the money or would report it to the police. She was scared she wouldn't be able to use it to buy a car. But, with the cat out of the bag, and the reception as it was, Carissa felt the best course of action was to share everything.

Mom stared at the cash for a long time. Her face was locked in a glaze, calculating. *She's not going to hit me over the head and run away with the money, is she? I admit: if I saw a wad of cash like that, someone would have a headache and I'd be kicking dust on my way out.*

Mom let out a deep sigh and said the last words Carissa wanted to hear, "I'm calling the police."

No, no! Oh my God! No!

"Mom, no!" Carissa insisted as Mom stood and headed out the bedroom. "We can't. Please don't."

"We have to, Carissa," Mom said on her way to the stairs.

Carissa pursued her. "Please don't, Mom. Please don't. I'll be humiliated." Her tears swelled and streamed from her eyes. "I'm begging you, Mom. Please don't."

Mom stopped at the stairwell and sighed. "Carissa, we have to report this to the police. If we don't, he gets away with it, unreported, and can do it again. What if this is a pattern? What if someone else reported it? What if someone else was paid off to have an abortion? They can't keep doing this. They have to be stopped."

"But, Mom," Carissa sobbed. That's all she had. She didn't have an argument. She didn't know what would happen if they told the police. They'd ask lots of questions. It was too late to run any tests on her to prove her claim. It was her word against his. And maybe Val's, if she was willing to testify. Carissa wasn't sure if Val would take her side on the issue. There was a snowball's chance in Hell of that happening after today's events.

"Cari," Mom approached and gave her a hug. Held on. "When I was attacked, I didn't report it. I just held my tongue. Ever since that day, I've regretted it." She swallowed hard and breathed. "I wasn't the only one. I wasn't his first. I wasn't his last." She took a deep breath. "I should have been his last. I feel, if I said something, I could have been his last." Her eyes bore down into Carissa's soul. "I don't want you to live with that burden. I don't want you to look into the eyes of Kent's next victim knowing you could have said or done something to prevent it."

"But, it's my word against his." Carissa sniffled. "There's no one to vouch for me. Not even Val."

Mom rubbed her hands through Carissa's hair, corrected the chaos. "Well, once we tell the police, they'll investigate. Tell them everything that happened. Everything said. Everything done. They'll be able to take that information and use it to push the investigation." She kissed Carissa's forehead. "Who knows. Maybe someone else has reported something."

"You think?"

"You never know until you try," Mom said. "This could be the breakthrough they need to make a case. And maybe other girls may come forward once one of you are brave enough to do it."

"But, but I'll be on the news," Carissa argued, "and on the internet, and in newspapers. Everyone will be talking about me. I'll be a social pariah. It's what I'll be known for." She covered her face with her hands. "I'll be humiliated. Ruined. I don't want that. I can't have that. I don't want my reputation and life defined by this."

Mom countered, "Steps can be taken to keep your identity private, especially since you're a minor. Besides, do you really think they'll want this to go public? That family will do everything they can to keep this quiet."

Carissa sighed. *We're really doing this, aren't we? We're going to do this.*

"I don't want to force you into this," Mom said. "You were already," she paused, took two long and deep breaths and blinked back more tears, "already forced into this situation. But we must call the police. We can't let this go unaddressed."

Dammit. She's right. I know this. Now, I'm being selfish. Ugh. I don't want to suffer the backlash, but how many more girls will he victimize after me if I say nothing? All that is necessary for the triumph of evil is that good women do nothing.

"Okay, fine," Carissa resigned. "I'll do it."

"That's my girl," Mom said. She wiped the tears off Carissa's cheek. "Your dad's been losing it down there. I, I can't imagine how he'll take the news, but I have to tell him."

Carissa gasped. "You didn't tell him, yet?"

"I wanted to get all the information, first," Mom said. "I told him that it was something we had to talk about first. Mother and daughter. Now that we have, I'll call the police and fill him in while they're on their way."

He won't be able to look at me the same. I can't even imagine how he'll see me now. I was clean and innocent. His princess. Now I'm tainted.

"Do we have to call them tonight? It's already so late."

"Exactly," Mom said. "We should have called them sooner. The longer we go without reporting it, the less likely we are to prove anything. To be taken seriously. The only thing we have going for us now is the payoff."

The payoff? What if they take my money? Carissa sighed. *I agreed to do this. I agreed to do this. We have to report it. I know. But please don't take the money.*

"They'll come and ask questions," Mom said. "We'll probably have to run through this all over again. The whole story. They'll ask for specifics. Might even ask for explicit details. Just tell them what you told me. And if you held anything back, you make sure you tell them everything. It's important."

"Okay," Carissa said and yawned. "But I can't be up too late. I have my last final tomorrow."

Mom frowned. "What time?"

"Ten-thirty."

Mom nodded. "Okay. I'm taking the day off. I'll drop you off for your final. While you're taking your test, I'll talk to your principal and guidance counselor. Then, I'm taking you home. You're done at that school for the rest of the year. We'll figure out next semester."

What the hell? You're pulling me out of school now?

"Mom," Carissa whined. "I have classes and friends, and golf and tennis." She thought about it. "How will I get a scholarship if I'm pulled out of my school?"

Mom looked at the ceiling. "You're taking two college courses next semester, anyway. I'm going to see if I can get you in more and work out your class schedule so you can fulfill your necessary credits and be involved in sports without having to be in the same building or classroom as him."

"Oh." Carissa sighed. "Okay."

"Yea." Mom started down the steps. "I think it would be in

your best interest to spend less time at that school with the pregnancy and *him* going to the same school. Then, there's Val. I just—" She stopped and chewed the side of her cheek. "I'm going to talk to your dad and make some coffee. Take a shower. I'll let you know when the police are here."

"Okay," Carissa said. Mom walked down the stairs. "I love you, Mom."

Mom looked back. "I love you, too."

CHAPTER FOURTEEN

When Carissa stepped out of the bathroom, she heard two car doors shut. She rushed to the loft and looked out of the window. A black sedan and blue jeep were parked in the front. From the jeep walked a blond woman in a dark blue jean jacket and jeans with a white tank top. She met the man in cream khakis and burgundy polo. His black hair slicked back. His shoes were polished to a shine that reflected the moon's light back into space. The two spoke for a minute, heads bowed, before walking towards the house.

Those must be the cops. Are those the cops? Why are they in plain clothes? Is it that late? Were they off duty?

Carissa went to her room and tossed on—*wait! How do I dress for this? I mean, they're cops. Do I want to look good for cops? Will they not take me seriously if I dress down? Or will they not take me seriously if I dress too well? I mean, they're here to investigate a rape. They're not dinner guests. Son of a—dammit.*

She stared at the closet and let out a deep sigh. "Come on. Something stick out. Something speak to me."

Why am I worried about what to wear? I should be more concerned about what I'm going to say. I mean, if I don't say the right thing, they might not believe me. What if I leave something out? What if I say too much? Can I get arrested? If they don't believe me, will they charge me with filing a false report? I don't know what I'm doing. Why did I agree to this? I mean, is it better that I just keep the money and buy a car and figure out school without police involvement?

DAKOTA

Light footsteps rushed up the stairs. She could tell it was Sean. Dad was trim but generally walked and stepped heavily. Mom stepped cautiously up and down the stairs. When she was fifteen, grandpa missed a step and had a bad fall that broke his leg. She'd been afraid of falling down the stairs since and had a lecture for anyone that didn't pace themselves. Surely, the police wouldn't navigate up her stairs like that.

They probably sent him to his room. I can't imagine what he's thinking right now. I just, I can't imagine.

Sean knocked at the door. "Carissa, the police are here. Mom says to come down." His voice sounded quiet and heavy, throaty, like he could barely get the words out.

"Okay," Carissa called. It was all she knew to say. She sighed. *He'll probably never look at me the same way again.*

There was a long silence before the footsteps moved to Sean's room. He closed his door.

This is the last thing I need to care about, but I don't know what to wear. What do you wear to a police interview? I feel like a total wreck, but don't really want to look it. Hmm. Okay. No dresses. No skirts. Nothing dressy. Has to be really casual. Super casual. But not pajamas. But like pajamas? Sweats? Basic, simple sweats. And a t-shirt? Yes. A t-shirt that says, "F—k police." That would be a good start to the conversation. Sigh. *At least I still have my sense of humor.*

Carissa put on her gray sweats, white sports bra, and a white t-shirt that said "Have A Nice Day! Just Kidding, Don't" in bold black letters. *It's sad that the only clean t-shirts I have left are sassy. I guess I'm doing laundry tomorrow.* She grabbed her strawberry slippers and headed downstairs.

At the entrance, standing together, were Mom, Dad, and the two casually dressed police officers. Up close, she could see the badges attached to each of their belts. The police officers looked past Mom and Dad. The man measured her up and down with calculating eyes and pressed his lips together. The woman gave her an affirming nod.

Mom and Dad turned around and saw Carissa. Dad's face was pale and grim. He looked like he'd just been revived from the dead. In his hand was the last thing any of them wanted to see, a small bottle of cognac. *Great. Another relapse. And it's all my fault.*

Mom looked tired and defeated. Her nose was red and raw from all the blowing and wiping of her nose from crying. She reached her hand out for Carissa. There was no way Carissa could refuse the invitation at a time like this. She needed Mom to hold her hand through whatever happened next.

The lady cop stepped forward. "Hello Carissa. I'm Detective Amy Priest. This is my partner, Detective Nathan Summers." Summers nodded. "Your parents told us what happened to you. We'd like to listen and ask you some questions, if that's okay with you."

She's pretty for a cop. Like, very pretty. Why isn't she a model or actress or something? She's prettier than Val. Why would she want to be a cop?

Carissa glanced at Summers, "Yea, sure," before tightening her grip on Mom's hand. She felt like a three-year-old meeting a stranger for the first time. *Come on, Carissa. You can do this. Why am I so nervous? Why am I so scared?* "That's fine."

"Great." Priest lowered her voice to a whisper. "Would you feel more comfortable talking to us privately or in the presence of your parents?"

"Umm," Carissa glanced at Mom, whispered, "parents."

"Okay." Priest raised her voice to a normal volume. "Where would you feel most comfortable having this interview?"

I don't know. My brain is all fuzzy. I can't think. Now I have to make decisions? Dammit.

"Umm." Carissa's pointed to the closest room in sight, the family room.

"Okay," Priest said and nodded to Mom.

Mom lead the detectives to the family room. She and Dad adjusted two plough chairs for the detectives on the opposite end of the coffee table and then sat on either side of Carissa. Mom looked past Carissa to Dad and said, "Tom, how about you start some tea and grab some biscuits for the detectives."

Dad glanced at the two detectives, then glowered at Mom.

Oh great. They're fighting again.

"Please don't," Summers waved his hand. His voice was strong and authoritative. "I'm fine. Really. I just finished some Chinese."

Mom frowned. "Are you sure? It's no inconvenience at all."

Summers grinned. "Sweet and sour chicken, shrimp fried rice. Plenty of it. I'm done eating for the night. Thank you."

Mom turned to Priest. "And you?"

Priest smiled. "Thank you, but I'm fine. Just came from a dinner date."

"Tom," Mom said. "Get some started anyway. Just in case."

"Right," Dad said between his teeth and stood. He sulked to the kitchen; his hand firmly gripped his bottle of gin.

Priest and Summers exchanged a look before Summers opened his notebook and took notes. *Great. Add family dysfunction to the start of this.*

Summers cleared his throat and said, "It is standard practice in interviews for us to record and collect as much information as we can during the initial interview. We do this so we capture everything and don't have to disturb you with repeat questions as the investigation moves forward. It doesn't mean we won't contact you later on and have you reiterate details, but helps us develop a case and aggressively pursue leads. Is it okay if we record you?"

"Yea." Carissa squeezed Mom's hand again. "Sure. Go ahead."

Priest pulled a tape recorder out of her pocket, pressed record, and set it on the table. She folded her hands together and leaned forward, "If it's okay with you, Carissa, I'll be asking the bulk of the questions. Detective Summers will be taking notes. As we move into collecting more details about what happened, and the subjects involved, we will alternate. Are you ready?"

Am I ready? I don't think anyone can ever be ready for something like this, but sure. Let's pretend I'm ready.

"Yes."

2

"Okay," Priest said. "First off, I am very sorry this happened to you. We intend to take everything shared seriously. Your mother told us that you were assaulted and, as a result of that, you are pregnant. Please, tell us what happened."

Carissa breathed in and out deeply. *How many times have I talked about this now? Why does it feel harder now to tell them than it does telling Mom or Gabby or Fiona?*

"Take your time," Priest coached with a reassuring smile and nod.

She's good at this. Maybe this won't be as bad as I thought it would be.

"My friend, Val, err, well, my ex-friend Val and I were invited to a Halloween party," Carissa started. "So, we bought our costumes, ate dinner, got dressed, and went. It was crowded, or, at least, it felt like it. It was my first high school party. I'd, I'd never been to one before."

Priest listened. Summers marked a few things in his pad. *Why is he taking notes if they're recording the conversation? I guess they have to be thorough.*

"Most of the people I didn't know, but some I recognized from our high school. After we got in, Val and her boyfriend, or well, at least, the guy she was hooking up with, Jesse, introduced me to Kent." She stopped and took a couple deep breaths. Just the mentioning of his name stirred an army of emotions she'd battled for weeks and lost every conflict.

Mom rubbed her back and whispered, "It's okay. It's okay."

There was a box of tissue paper on the table Carissa hadn't noticed until Mom pre-emptively snatched and placed it in her lap. She pulled out several sheets and handed them to Carissa.

"He was very handsome and charming," Carissa continued. "He offered me drinks. Umm. Beer or jungle juice. I don't like beer. And he told me the jungle juice had a lot of strawberries in it. He knew strawberries were my favorite because of Val. She told him stuff about me. So, he made it special for me. And, when I tried it, it was really good. It wasn't too strong but was sweet and fruity. The gesture was very, uh, very flattering. I mean, that he went through that much trouble for me to make it special for me when there were so many other girls he could have done something like that for. They set us up and he was really into me." She grimaced. "I was so stupid."

"No," Priest interjected. "No, you weren't. Any girl would have responded and felt the same way you did. Such a gesture. It's very flattering. Just as you said."

"I suppose." *But I still feel like an idiot.*

"I'm sorry I interrupted," Priest said. "Please continue."

"After he gave me a cup of jungle juice, we looked around for

Val and Jesse, who disappeared. Then he suggested going somewhere quiet to talk. But there were people everywhere. So, we went to the back of his house, outside, near the pool and hot tub."

Priest frowned but didn't say anything.

"Yea, they're rich," Carissa said. "In the hot tub was his brother, Brian."

Summers's head shot up from his notepad with wide alert eyes. He forced his best poker face and turned to Priest. She listened intently.

"They suggested playing beer pong. And, well, after we played that game, we had drinks in between the games, which we won, all of them, because Kent's some kind of weird freak expert at the game, I was really, really drunk, and sick." She sighed. "It's so foggy. I can barely remember anything between the first game and finding myself in Kent's bathroom, puking my guts out. But, there I was, sick as a dog."

Priest folded her hands. "Do you remember him initiating the assault? Were you conscious?"

Carissa paled. "Yes, yes I remember." She lowered her head and glanced to see if her father was in the room. He wasn't. Then she looked to her mother who quietly encouraged her with another back rub. "I was."

"Do you feel comfortable sharing that with us?" Priest asked. Her hands were pressed against each other, tensed. Something felt off.

Cop or not, she's still a woman. Perhaps she isn't comfortable talking about it. Or, maybe she's bracing herself for the story? I don't even feel ready to share this. But I have to.

"Yea." Carissa took a deep breath. "I was just getting there. I remember puking in the bathroom alone with Kent. He held my hair. Then, I was in his bed, asleep. When I woke up, he was in the room with his brother. Umm, Brian. I heard their voices. They mentioned drugging me. Which could have killed me, ya know, because I was on my meds. I take meds for attention deficit disorder. I shouldn't have been drinking. I know. But, at some point, I know I popped another pill, because I have to. I always have to take my pills. No matter what."

She paused and breathed. "Whatever they gave me, I'm sure

it reacted badly with my meds because I couldn't move. When they started touching me, I couldn't move. I could barely open my eyes. I was exhausted, like, more exhausted then I've ever been, but mentally alert." She put her hands to her face.

Priest and Summers locked eyes, exchanged non-verbal dialogue. No one said a word. They waited for her to continue.

"I tried to fight," Carissa finally said as tears streamed down her face. She sniffled and wiped her face with the tissues. Mom pulled sheets out in rapid succession and handed them to her. Carissa blew her nose. "I just. I couldn't move. First, they were joking with each other like it was some kind of game. They thought it was funny."

She balled her fists. Her faced burned a bright red.

"Brian touched me all over. Even umm, down there. Then, he moved away and, and, Kent got on the bed and started touching me. He, he removed my clothes, flipped me over like a doll. And, I just, I couldn't move. And, after my clothes were off, he, he pushed himself inside of me. And, he did it again and again until he was finished."

Mom was crying, now. Her face buried in her tissues.

Summers scribbled notes in his pad with eyes focused down. Every visible muscle on his face was tense.

Priest's face was red but composed. "Do you need to take a break?"

"No, no," Mom said and sniffed. "Don't stop for my benefit." She passed more tissues to Carissa before collecting more of her own. She blew her nose and took deep breaths.

"I was, umm," Priest nodded her head at Carissa, "talking to Carissa."

"Oh, yes, of course," Mom said and turned to Carissa. "Do you need a break, honey?"

I don't think I've ever seen her cry this much in my life. I hope we never cry this much ever again. I hate them. This is what they've done to us. They've brought misery and pain to my family. To me. I hate them. I hope they die. I hope they get arrested, go to jail, and take a shiv right to the testicles.

"No." Carissa wiped her face with fresh tissues and took deep breathes. "No. I'll continue."

"Okay," Mom said. "Take your time." She blew her nose.

Several minutes later, both collected themselves enough to continue. Priest sat patiently. Carissa wondered if she'd ever be as emotionally disciplined as Priest.

"After he was finished," Carissa said, starting right where she left off, "he got up and left me. He just, he left me like some used up thing. He didn't care at all. He just, he just walked out and left me laying there, naked. Naked and dirtied with his, with his umm, semen on me, and in me." She cringed. "He left me in there with Brian."

Summers glanced at Priest again. Priest's eyes shifted in his direction before returning their undivided attention to Carissa.

"Brian was going to, umm, rape me as well until he realized that Kent had emptied himself in me. Then, he left, too. They both left me laying there, alone, naked, on the bed, with the door open." She covered her face. "He didn't just rape me. He humiliated me. People saw me. They were laughing at me. I think some of them took pictures of me."

Priest took out a notepad of her own and quickly jotted that down.

"Eventually, Val showed up and closed the door. She helped me up, dressed me, and we left. We were in the car when Mom called to check in on us. We went to Val's place. I, I showered and slept."

Carissa sighed and rested her head on the cushion of the couch. She felt tired. Exhausted. Almost as exhausted as that night. *Ugh. I'm pregnant. I'm going to be tired all the time. I hate this. This too is all Kent's fault. He should be pregnant, not me. Boys wouldn't be out raping girls if they could get pregnant.*

"I'm, I'm so sorry, Carissa," Priest said after a full minute of silence. She and Summers wrote detailed notes and exchanged grave looks.

After another minute, Priest looked at Carissa and asked, "Just so we're clear, could you state the full names of the assailants?"

"Umm, yea," Carissa said. "Sure. Umm, Kent Bradshaw. He's, he's the one that umm, umm, raped me." She hated saying that word. She didn't want to ever say that word again. "Brian Bradshaw, his brother, was there. He touched me. And, umm, umm, he encouraged Kent."

Priest exhaled. "Okay. Thank you, Carissa."

Summers flipped his notepad to a new page and looked at Carissa with his deep blue eyes. "Carissa, thank you for sharing that with us. You're a very strong and brave young woman to report this. It is our job at this point to take this report further and investigate every angle and collect as many details, facts, and evidence as possible. We've also been told that you were offered money to abort your child. Do you feel comfortable discussing that as well?"

"Yes." Carissa said. *The hard part's over.*

3

Two long hours later, Carissa crawled into bed and closed her eyes. She was physically exhausted, but her mind continued to race through the questions and answers of the evening, wondering if she'd missed anything. The detectives were specific and constant in their questions. The more she answered, the more they questioned. They combed through almost every conversation, every detail, every individual she spoke to before and after her rape. By the end of it, there wasn't anything else to tell. She told them everything, remembering details and conversations she'd previously forgotten.

She'd never seen a person write as fast as Summers, while Priest stuck to bullet notes and maintained eye contact and dialogue. At one point, they paused while Summers replaced Priest's tape recorder with his. They were a good team. She was impressed that they transitioned between questions and responsibilities by subtle gestures and cues. Carissa felt something she'd all but lost in the last month and a half: hope. With these two on the job, how could she lose?

There were a lot of questions about Val's involvement. She was a crucial piece of the puzzle. One specific question struck Carissa's heart like an arrow: was there any indication that Val knew what would happen to Carissa that night, if she were a collaborator or simply a friend with good intentions who knew the wrong people. Carissa would spend a lot of time asking herself that question. She wanted to move on from Val. But now their friendship was all she could think about. In the end, did Val have Carissa's best interests at heart?

DAKOTA

There was something else that bugged her. It was the way Priest and Summers responded whenever the Bradshaws were mentioned. Summers would watch Priest, who held a poker face. But her eyes. Priest's eyes would be calm one moment and intense the next. There was more going on with the Bradshaws. What if they had a history?

Perhaps I'm not the only one that's reported them. Maybe they've been pursuing this a while and didn't have any leads. Did the Bradshaws slip up this time? Perhaps.

Priest and Summers were focused as Carissa went over the details of the abortion payoff. They asked for dates, times, locations, the names of the tellers at the bank and receptionists at the clinic, receipts, and more. The more leads they got the faster they wrote and asked for more. For just a short time, the room seemed to be filled with life and energy. Mom stopped crying and listened and watched intently as it all came together.

We're going to get them. We're going to get those suckers.

The biggest piece of evidence against the Bradshaws grew inside of her. Mom said she would bump up Carissa's doctor's appointment to tomorrow morning and determine when any of the baby's DNA could be collected. The hardest part, they said, would be getting a sample of Kent's DNA to determine a match. They couldn't compel him to provide his DNA without sufficient evidence and a warrant.

Maybe, maybe not. Kent uses the locker room. I'm sure there's some way to legitimately collect a sweaty towel or his underwear. Or find out where he's eating and get a glass or something. Maybe someone I know in one of his classes can collect a piece of hair from him. I need to help with this investigation. Now that it's started, I need to do something. Maybe stab a pencil through his hand?

The detectives wanted to know if Carissa kept her panties from the night of the attack. The answer was an upsetting no. She showered, put on her jammies, and went to sleep. The furthest thing from her mind was collecting evidence. The next morning, she put on a clean pair, dressed, and watched movies with Val. Somehow, she hadn't packed the tainted panties when she left and went home. Those panties were probably put in Val's laundry and washed. And, as they hadn't talked for a month before reconnecting, it's possible they were discarded. When Carissa told the detectives this, they looked at each other and took more notes.

Carissa yawned and stretched.

Time to sleep. Tomorrow's the last day of school for me until after the new year. I wonder if Mom's going to be able to get me into more college classes. I need to get a head start on college credits but hate to leave my friends. Err. Well. Hmm. I suppose I don't have many left. Most of my friends were Val's friends before I met them. Fiona's on my side, I'm sure. I can't speak for the others. I guess we'll see who my real friends are once I'm gone.

Her phone buzzed. Like clockwork, the universe responded.

Fiona: "Was goin on??!! Val's livid! She told evry1 u tricked her in2 helpin u have sex w/ kent & blackmailed him 4 10K"

Carissa squeezed her phone. *What the hell?*

Carissa: "You have got to be kidding me!"

Fiona: "NOT KIDDING!! She doesnt want any1 to talk to u were all supposed to ice u out shes telling evbody. Evbody evbody"

She was too tired to cry. *My worst nightmare is coming true.*

Carissa: "And they believe her???"

Fiona: "The others r flippin out they don't know what 2 think but u know how it is w/ val people just go along with her + val said u pretend u were raped"

Fiona: "Did they really give u 10K?????????????"

You forgot a question mark.

Carissa: "Yea. But it wasn't my idea to ask for money. I was just trying to not be pregnant. Val suggested asking for money and got the check. I cashed it but changed my mind about the baby."

Fiona: "Well yer 10K richer but evbody hates you some1 already created a i hate Carissa group page to trash you it has like 50 r 60 likes i'll report it i got ur back girl"

Carissa: "Thanks. I'm exhausted. Call you later?"

Fiona: "Sure night!!"

I give up. Carissa sighed and looked out the window at the stars.

Look on the bright side, Cari. There's got to be a bright side somewhere in this. Gabby and her sisters are pretty cool. Maybe

this is for the best. Out with the bad, in with the good.
And with that, Carissa closed her eyes and fell asleep.

4

"I can't believe it," Priest said as she sat inside Summer's sedan. It was too cold to talk outside. His car warmed up faster than hers and had fancy, heated seats. "I sat there, writing notes, taking down the information, and the whole time, I couldn't believe it."

"I know," Summers turned on his car and cranked the heat to max. "It's something."

Something? That's the understatement of the year.

"You serious?" She asked. "It's the Bradshaws for God's sake." Summers frowned for a split second. She put her hand to her mouth. "Sorry. It's just, the timing. The timing of the incident. The timing of my promotion and transfer. The reason I came back here in the first place." She paused. "Of all the people on duty, we got that call off-duty."

Summers put on his driving gloves and bean hat and motioned her to continue.

How are you so unphased by this?

"I probably would have been home if I didn't go to that dinner," Priest said. "You, well, you find any reason you can to get out of spending time with your in-laws."

"Hey," he responded. "All we were doing was socializing and watching football. I don't watch football. And they don't expect me to ignore a call, especially an ex-cop like Mag's dad. They know, if I get a call, it's a major crime or we're short-staffed."

Priest pointed. "Exactly. Well, no. Scratch that. That part is inconsequential to the fact that I came to this city at the right time, went to the right precinct, was partnered up with you, who invited me to the right place, to meet the right guy, who invites me to dinner at the place and time I need to be near this neighborhood, to answer the call that leads to this case, to that family. This is destiny, Nate."

"I'll admit," he said. "I had chills when she said Bradshaw."

"Right?"

"And again, when I put that and the date of her attack together, I was in awe." *As well you should be.* "When God works,

God works." He shut his eyes and centered himself. "They were sloppy this time."

"Yea, they were," she said. "Very."

"This has to be done right."

"Of course," she said. "Absolutely."

Summers rubbed his chin. "Naturally, I'm taking point on this." Priest opened her mouth to protest. "I mean it. The Bradshaw's are going to lawyer up right away. The moment they hear your name, lawyers will say conflict of interest. They'll challenge evidence collection and interviews. They'll say the precinct is biased or has a vendetta against their family. The best thing we can do is have me run point. You work with me. We do everything by the book. No shortcuts. Record everything. Got it?"

Doesn't sound like you're giving me much of a choice, Priest thought.

"Got it," she resigned.

Summers looked ahead, into the street, into his own thoughts. "We have to put together a game plan and present it to Rogers. He'll have reservations about keeping you on the case. As will the prosecutor's office. Both will want to give this to Paulson. Let's make our argument convincing. Don't give them any reason to think you won't have your head on straight."

"I know," Priest said. "This is too important. I won't do anything to jeopardize this case. This is the reason I came back to Richmond."

He pulled out his phone and flipped through his contacts.

She looked at the time. "Checking in with Maggie?"

"No," Summers said. "That's next. First, I have to get in touch with a friend in New York. We're going to need him for what I have in mind."

"And what's that?"

Summers pressed the call button. "Oh. You'll see."

CHAPTER FIFTEEN

Mom knocked on the door and called out, "Carissa! Time to get up!"

Nope. Carissa yawned, stretched, and opened her eyes. She looked at the clock, saw the time, and smiled.

It was a nice change of pace sleeping in until nine o'clock on a school day. Carissa was usually up two and a half hours earlier, showering, doing makeup and hair (if she felt like it), making breakfast, eating, and then Mom or Dad drove them to school. She and Sean weren't allowed to have a relaxed morning unless they wanted to miss breakfast. Unfortunately for Sean, it was business as usual this morning. Dad took Sean to school and explained everything to him. Mom stayed home to take care of Carissa.

Thirty minutes later, Carissa stepped down the stairs to the inviting aroma of coffee, pancakes, eggs, and turkey sausage. *Always with the turkey sausage.* Mom and Dad quit red meat indefinitely after Grandpa Liam, Mom's dad, had a heart attack and Grandpa Tristan, Dad's dad, had a scare. It was poultry and low-fat seafood in the unforeseeable future for the Boisseau household.

As Carissa turned the corner, the floor squeaked, announced her presence. Mom sat in front of a full plate and waved her over, "I made strawberry pancakes."

That's all you have to say. Carissa sat across from Mom. Knowing how she liked it, Mom dressed the pancakes with banana slices and buttermilk syrup. Carissa grabbed her fork and attacked the pancakes without a word. *Oh yes, oh yes, oh yes! I love you, Mom.* She collected a fork's worth of cheesy scrambled eggs, lightly seasoned with salt and pepper, and shoved them in her mouth. She'd ignore the apple and peach slices for now. There was a tall glass of water and two smaller glasses, one with vanilla almond milk, the other with orange juice.

Wow. Mom, you've really outdone yourself. Sausage links on the saucer, banana slices on the pancakes. You have your super sweet blueberry parfait in a bowl for dessert? I love you, Mom.

Carissa teared up and said, "Thanks, Mom," between bites. Tears streamed down her packed cheeks as she chewed.

Mom smiled, "You're welcome." She set a box of tissues next to Carissa. Then, she ate.

The next five minutes was chewing, the smacking of lips, and gulping beverages. Mom ended the silence, "I made an appointment with your vice principal, Mister Hammerschmidt, and your guidance counselor for today. Then, I talk to your adviser at community college, Misses Rosewood."

Gotta secret; can ya keep it? Well, this one you'll save.

"I wish I didn't get the vice, but apparently, Miss Greenburg already left town and is spending the next two weeks in her second home in Miami. I was shocked a public-school principal could afford a second home, especially near the coast. But, her husband's practice has done very well. They're going to move there permanently once they've both retired."

Carissa didn't know anything about her principal or vice principal, and honestly couldn't care less. But it would be nice to have a second home in Miami when the snow came. She hated the winters in Connecticut. And while the winters were mild in Virginia, she could go without cold or snow at all. When Val suggested they apply to Miami University together, Carissa imagined herself at the beach every other day. And then, she thought of alligators, sharks, and the fact that she didn't really like it hotter than eighty degrees. She would be eternally hot if she moved to Miami.

I don't know. We'd have air-conditioning. That might work.

Oh, and there were hurricanes and tropical storms. She couldn't forget those.

"After the meeting today and tomorrow, we can register

your additional community college classes," Mom said. "I want to get you in as many as possible and get you out of that school and away from that boy, Val, and her friends."

Carissa frowned, chewed quickly, and then drank water to flush her food down. "But what about sports?"

Mom smirked. "I hate to break it to you, honey, but sports will be the last thing on your mind after a month or so. By the time spring comes, you're going to be showing and feeling the effects. Your hormones, appetite, and energy levels are going to be all over the place. You'll be tired half the time. I'd be impressed if you could make it halfway through a tennis match. And golf, well, let's see you maintain your excellent form with a baby bump in the way."

Aww! That means no sports scholarship.

"That never stopped Arnold Palmer," Carissa pouted.

Mom nearly choked on her food and spit some of it out on the table and in her lap. She laughed. "Oh God. You can't say stuff like that while I'm eating." She grabbed a roll of napkins and cleaned up after herself. "I'm going to have to change."

"Sorry," Carissa said but couldn't help but to chuckle. "It just came to me."

Mom grabbed a damp rag and wiped herself. "You're a great athlete, Carissa. Amazing really. But, being a mom is going to take its toll on you. I just don't see how you're going to be able to be a full-time student, athlete, and first-time mom at the same time. Plus, as we agreed in August, starting in January, you were supposed to be getting a part-time job so you could chip in on car expenses."

Oh no! I completely forgot about the part-time job thing. I mean, it registered in my head that I needed to get a car. I just, I just forgot about the original plan on how I would pay for it. So much has been going on. It just slipped my mind. I haven't even thought about where I'm going to work. Hmm. Can I get lucky and work at Mom's office as like, an assistant to the administrative assistant or something?

"I forgot." Carissa frowned. "How are we going to manage that, anyway? I'll be taking a morning class at school, then going all the way to community college, then to work? How am I supposed to get around and, well, to work to save up to buy a car? Can't I just use the money from the umm, the thing to buy a car?"

"No," Mom said and finished her glass of orange juice. "That's going to baby and college expenses. That's another reason why you have to get a job. You want to save up for diapers and daycare services. You'll need it. There's only so much your father and I will be able to do for you."

Good grief. I wish I talked to her before I decided to accept such a small amount of money. Hmm. Never did I think I'd be referring to ten-grand as a small amount of money. Maybe I should have squeezed an extra ten- or twenty-grand out of Kent's mom. Sigh. No. That's not me. As much as I need the money, I couldn't be that person.

Carissa visualized the thick stack of hundreds in her closet. *Then again, a girl's gotta do what a girl's gotta do.*

"Let's not doddle," Mom said and finished the last sausage link on her plate. "I'm going to quickly change and then we're going to your school." She stood, then paused. "Oh. And, I'm also going to set up an appointment for you to meet an adviser at VCU. It's close. You've already talked to the Cole sisters about possibly going there. You'll be able to live here your first two years if you'd like. It just makes sense."

So, yea. I guess I can stop stressing about sending out any more college applications. I've already sent my applications to the in-state schools. There's no way I can move out of state. It's time for some serious scholarship hunting; since there's no way I'm getting a sports scholarship now. Sigh.

"Yea, you're right," Carissa said and looked down at her food. It was strange. They spent the summer and a couple weekends in September touring different colleges and cities and measuring her options. Now, one drunken night made all the decisions for her. No sports. School in Richmond. Living at home for the first two years, maybe. Possibly graduating high school early depending on the meeting with the vice principal. Getting a part-time job. Her plans were made for her. Many paths for her future turned into one.

"I know this is a lot," Mom said. She stood up and rinsed her plate in the sink. "I can't imagine how you feel right now having a whole heap of responsibility and decisions dumped on you like this. But I want you to know, I'm going to be here with you, Cari. I'm going to be here every step of the way."

I'm going to need you every step of the way.

"Thanks, Mom."

Mom smiled, walked over, and gave Carissa a kiss on the forehead. "I love you, Cari." She rubbed Carissa's cheek. "Now finish that and let's get ready to go." She left the kitchen and rushed upstairs.

Carissa took another bite of her eggs and sighed, "I hope this was all worth it." She looked down at her abdomen. "Whoever you are."

Goodness. "Whoever you are?" *I have to give it a name. And, well, I'm definitely not going to keep calling my baby an it. I wonder if he is a he or she is a she. How soon can I find out? When does a fetus develop his or her gender?*

Carissa grabbed her phone and ran an internet search, "How soon pregnancy baby gender," grammar be damned. She gasped.

I can find out as early as seven weeks with a blood test. My baby is seven weeks old! I could find out today.

Carissa smiled at her abdomen and said, "I could find out what you are today."

2

It was in the car that Carissa realized she hadn't studied for her final exam. Yesterday was a poor choice of days for them to spend the night pouring over the details of her rape and pregnancy. She panicked, opened her books, and spent the car ride skimming the sections and chapters illustrated in the final exam outline.

Mom parked the car and waited for Carissa to finish scrambling through her pages. They headed inside when the bell rang. *First period just finished.* That gave her ten minutes to get to class and read as much as she could before class started.

Carissa breathed and smiled when she saw her teacher at the end of the hall. *I might have some time. I might have some time.*

Fortunately, Mister Yarborough wanted them to do well on their tests. Before any test, he gave everyone fifteen to twenty minutes to refresh themselves on the materials. Then, they spent an hour taking the test. When everyone turned in their answer sheets, he made photocopies and handed the photocopies back to the students. Afterward, he went over the test question by question and answered them. This allowed everyone to learn the answers and how well or poorly they did on their test.

"I have to run," Carissa said and clutched her backpack. "I might get twenty, twenty-five minutes of study time before the test starts."

"I'll be in the principal's office. Meet me outside when you're done."

"Okay." Carissa rushed to class. Mister Yarborough said good morning as she passed, but kept his eyes locked on Patterson High's resident botanists, Brad Sherman and Dan Hoyt. Their latest scheme was opening tea bags and mixing them with crushed pot leaves. While the teachers knew they were up to no good, they cleverly avoided detection or trouble. Their methods of consumption involved small food items, mostly breakfast or desserts, or drinks. Whenever their items were confiscated and tested, they came back negative. Months ago, Hoyt's parents complained of harassment after two confiscation efforts offered no positive results.

Whatever they're doing, they're smart about it.

As Carissa walked into her classroom, she heard Brad speak with an unpracticed British accent, "My good man. These crumpets are to die for."

Dan giggled uncontrollably and responded with his own poorly attempted British accent, "Why thank you, my friend. And must I say, this is the best tea in all of England."

Man, those guys are far gone. It's not even ten-thirty, yet.

Carissa was about to laugh until she saw Kent sitting in the front row at the far end of the classroom. Her heart sank. She froze. *Oh my God. What's he doing here?*

Kent looked up from his book and smiled, "Hey Carissa. Long time no see."

Not long enough.

This was the first time she'd seen Kent since the Halloween party, outside of her regular nightmares. She'd avoided him at all costs. Thankfully, they didn't have any of the same classes; and Kent, like most of the students with cars, ate lunch off campus, which made the food court somewhat safe. But just in case he chose to stay on campus, she ate at different spots: the tennis courts or in the bleachers of the soccer, track, and football fields. She brought sack lunches or purchased meals from the food court and then stayed off the radar by moving between locations, keeping her head down.

Never, never had Kent found a way into one of her classes nor did she ever feel he was looking for her or wanted to see her again. What changed? Was this intentional? Her gut said he was expecting her.

What do I do? Should I just turn around and leave? Yes. I can study in the hall, as loud and obstructive as it may be. I, I can't be in a room with him. I can't be in a room alone with him. Maybe I can just wait until others enter the classroom. Wait until there are just enough of us in here to where he can't see or talk to me. Find a seat where he can't sit next to me.

Ugh! But I have to study. I have most of the concepts figured out. I should know everything. But I need to at least finish my skim and answer some of the sample quiz questions at the ends of the chapters. Why is he in this class anyway? Don't ask him! Just. Just. It's best if I ignore him.

In fact, hold on! The police officer even told me to avoid contact and not engage him. What kind of a coincidence is this? The day after I talk to the police about him, he just shows up with his smug stupid face.

Carissa frowned, avoided eye contact, and sat at a desk near the entrance and away from him. She put down her bag and reached in for her headphones.

This guy seriously has some nerve being here.

"Oh, don't be like that, Carissa," Kent said with a smile. He put down his book with a clap against the desk. "I know. I probably should have called you. After all, you did give me your number." *When did I give you my number?* "But we need to talk. I thought face-to-face was more appropriate." He stood.

Appropriate? You thought a face-to-face conversation with someone you raped is appropriate? You don't get to say what is and isn't appropriate. You aren't allowed to be the arbiter of what is and isn't appropriate. You're a rotten filthy piece of shit. I should call the police. Wait. I did. We did last night. But, well, I need to get a restraining order.

Carissa pulled her earbuds out of her bag and plugged them into her ears. *Just ignore him, Cari. Keep on ignoring him.* She reached in her purse and dug around for her phone.

Kent moved across the room quicker than she knew he could move. One second, he was on his side. The next, he stood over her. The muscles in his face were tense and flexed. His eyes bore down on her.

Oh my God! Carissa fumbled with her phone, startled by his approach. It slipped out of her hand, hit her bag, and slid to the floor next to his feet. *My phone.*

Kent reached down and picked up her phone. As Carissa reached for it, he held it from her. "You're being rude, Carissa. I'm here to talk. So, let's both be adults about this and talk."

Are you kidding me right now? You're holding my phone away from me and telling me we need to be adults?

"Give me my phone," Carissa said and reached for it again.

Kent held it away. "No. We have to talk."

"There's nothing for us to talk about. Just give me my phone and leave me alone."

"You're pregnant," Kent said and crossed his arms. "And from what I hear, you believe it's mine. So, yes, we do have something to talk about."

"It is yours," Carissa mumbled.

Kent leaned in closer. She noticed a fresh tattoo on the left side of his neck. A three-headed dragon. "Wrong answer. It's not mine. And you're going to stop going around telling people that."

Is he going to hit me? Is he really going to do this in a public place with Mister Yarborough standing right outside the room?

"I haven't been with anyone else," Carissa said. Her hands trembled. She tightened them into a fist to steady them. "I was a virgin until you raped me."

"Raped," Kent scoffed. Two girls walked into the room and went to their usual seats. He leaned in closer, placing one hand on her desk, and the other on the desk behind her. He whispered, "It's not rape if you *wanted it*. Because you did want it, and you know it."

Are you on drugs? You drugged me! You said it yourself. And I was barely conscious! That is clearly rape. You must be conscious to give consent. And, when I was partially able to speak, I said, "No!" By definition, having sex with someone who is saying "no" to you is rape!

More students strolled in, yammered.

"Please," Kent scoffed. "You're just like the others. The moment you saw my big house, fancy car, pool, and the nice stuff inside my house, you were ready to spread your legs for me, and you know it. Because deep down inside, you're a *whore*." Kent ranted in a low, breathy whisper. His face twisted into a frown. Her heart raced. "You thought about what you could get out of me and you probably got wet just thinking about it. That's what you are. That's what all you girls are. You're all a bunch of prostitutes selling yourselves to the highest bidder. And you'll do any nasty dirty thing to get what you want. Either that, or you'll take as much as you can get and then slip away. But you know what, I don't play that game. I'm not going to let you waltz in, bat your eyelashes, and get what you can without giving anything in return. Nope. You come in to get yours. And I get what I want. Period. That was not rape you tight little cock trap. That was payment."

What is wrong with you? I am not a whore. I just came to have fun. You're the one who invited us. You're the one who wanted me to come. It's not like I just came over and asked for money. I didn't want anything from you but, well, maybe love. You're a psychopath. I need to get out of here.

But she couldn't, because he was leaned over her. She'd have to push herself past him and didn't want things to get physical.

How am I intimidated by him? Why am I so terrified? I know karate. I can literally kill him with one punch. She didn't know that maneuver.

"And now, you have the nerve to steal from me and my family," Kent whispered. His hands spread and pressed against the table as he moved in closer to Carissa. "My mom was kind enough to give you ten thousand dollars so you could get rid of that little mistake and go on with your pathetic life. You agreed to take the money in exchange for getting rid of the thing. Then, you reneged on that offer. You kept the money and the thing."

More students began to pour into the classroom. It was getting close to time for class to start. They whispered amongst each other and watched. But no one approached.

"So, here's what's going to happen, Carissa," Kent continued. "You're going to keep that ten thousand dollars, because I'll admit, you have a great body, and a tight pussy. That was probably the best nut I've bust this year. You make a good whore. But that's it. It ends here. You're getting rid of that baby." He reached into his pocket, pulled out a small and clear plastic container with three pills in it, and put it in her purse. "You're going to take those pills, abort it, and shut your trap. If you don't, I'm going to share pictures and video of you getting fucked all over the internet. There won't be a person in this school, in this city, anywhere, that won't see it."

Carissa's eyes flew wide open in shock. *Oh my God! You recorded it!*

Kent smiled and whispered, "Everywhere you go, people will have seen it. And it won't stop there. I'll send it to the colleges you applied for. I'll send it to your future employers. To your future boyfriends. There won't be a place you can go where that video won't follow you. And I'll hack you and send it through your email, because you're a blackmailing attention whore who likes the cock and getting paid."

"You can't do that," Carissa protested, ready to burst into tears. It took everything in her not to.

"Oh yes, I can," Kent said. "I know a guy. We've already hacked your email once. We can do it again. And again. You remember that."

You hacked into my email account? You've no right to get into my stuff! What's wrong with you?

The room was nearly full. Mister Yarborough walked into class and to his desk. He looked up at Bradshaw and frowned. "Mister Bradshaw, you might want to get to your next class *before* the period bell."

Thank you, Mister Yarborough! Please kick him out. Please. Please, please, please kick him out.

Kent looked at Mister Yarborough and gave him the biggest smile. "Sure thing, Mister Yarborough. I just couldn't help but talk to my friend here. I haven't seen her in almost two months."

"There's this exciting invention that just came out," Mister Yarborough said. "It's called a mobile phone. You can carry it around, store numbers, and talk to each other any time outside of the *classroom*."

He said I gave him my number. I don't remember giving him my number that night. Then again, there are a few things that are out of place that night. I very well could have given it to him. But I don't want him to contact me. I'm blocking his number. But do I have his number? Do I know his number?

Kent laughed. "You're right. I'm leaving." He set Carissa's phone on her desk, whispered, "Kill it or we will destroy you." He returned to his desk, packed his books, and walked out.

Oh my God! Kent is a lunatic. What am I going to do?

Carissa held on to her desk so tightly her fingers ached. Her heart beat out of her chest at a million miles an hour. Light-headed and ready to collapse at any moment, she used every ounce of willpower in her body to keep herself from crying. But water swelled in her eyes, nevertheless.

Dammit! Dammit! Dammit! I'm screwed! I can't kill the baby. I can't. What am I going to do? He's going to post a video of me all over the internet and school. Video and pictures! I'll be humiliated. I can't. I can't believe this. Everyone's going to see me naked and vulnerable. And, they're going to see my, my everything. Oh my God! What if someone shows Sean! Sean's going to see it!

People don't recover from this. I'm going to have to move and change my name. Change my whole identity. I'll have to change my hair, go by a different name, change my email account and phone number. I have to change everything so there's no way anything that is me is me but is someone else, so it can't be traced back to me.

This has to be the last day of school here for me. I just, I just can't bring myself to show my face here again after this. Who knows how many people from my school will see it? Who knows who they know? Who knows how many people they'll share it with? It'll go viral. I'll be on the news for all I know, with a blurred box over my girls and hoo-hah.

What made things worse: everyone stared at her, except Mister Yarborough. He'd already moved on to setting up the white erase board with prep questions for the exam. She turned away from her peers, tilted her head down, and let her hair conceal her face. She breathed deeply and muffled the few sobs that escaped her with her oversized sweatshirt.

I don't want to be here anymore. I'm humiliated. I'm going to be humiliated. And I'm not safe here.

The period bell rang as the last few students piled into class and took their seats. Mister Yarborough closed the door, locked it, and said, "Books out. You have twenty-five minutes to prep. Or for some of you, twenty-five minutes for a last-minute cram session." He scanned the room for reactions. "This is a final exam. It is a representation of what I tried my best to teach you this semester. Don't let me down."

Mister Yarborough paced with slow, intentional steps in a circle. "Now, usually a final exam heavily affects your grade. However, as I've said before, it's my job to teach, coach, and guide. I'm not about the tests. I'm here to make sure you actually know the material. So, if you worked hard and studied and your test results throughout the semester represent that you listened and appreciated my teaching method; if your test results this time meets or is higher than your average score; I will reward your GPA with either a plus or just push it up a total grade."

Half of the class erupted in cheers.

Mister Yarborough smiled. "Now, if you've averaged around a ninety-percent or higher. Then, you don't have much to worry about. This test won't heavily weigh on your GPA. Keep doing your best. This will be considered extra credit. As long as you get an eighty-five or higher, it'll bump your A-minus to a standard 'A'. Your standard 'A' will become an A-plus. Your A-plus will become a Lisa Simpson A-triple-plus."

A few more students cheered with a unison, "Yes!"

Finally, some good news. Carissa grabbed tissues from her purse. She dabbed her eyes and blew her nose. *I've averaged a ninety-four. I know the material. All I have to do is make it through this class. Then, I'm done. I'm out of here.*

Mister Yarborough picked up the analog timer and pressed the up button, beep-beep-beep, until it read twenty-five. "On your mark. Get set." He pressed start. "You may begin your prep."

Heads went down. Books and notebooks opened. Pages flipped. Paper crackled.

Carissa closed her eyes. *Okay. Clear your mind. Focus. Let's make it through this. Let's prep and not worry about psycho Kent.* She breathed. *I'll talk to Mom. Maybe she'll be able to get me down to only one class.*

She opened her book, took another deep breath, and studied for the last exam she'd ever take at Patterson High.

3

Mom sat outside of the classroom reading a tablet. No doubt it was one of her client's manuscripts. One of her many admirable qualities: she always read and encouraged others to read.

Carissa was sure Mom was the reason textbooks weren't a chore. She ate through them like a goat. While Dad was in meetings talking numbers, in the office working late and crunching numbers, Mom was at home reading to her. Mom took her to libraries and bookstores to meet live authors. Mom took her to an actual movie set when one of her clients, a screenwriter, was actively involved in a major Hollywood production. Carissa loved her dad, but as she looked at the ninety-seven on her answer sheet, and watched the smile spread across Mom's face at something possibly clever, funny, or diabolical in the manuscript, she knew she could attribute her academic success to Mom.

In another life, I'd consider following in her footsteps. Unfortunately, I'm not that great with people or networking, and can't write worth shit. I have no idea why I'm going into psychology if I'm not good with people. I just, hmm, I find the study of the human mind fascinating. I can't think of anything else as interesting. I suppose I should figure it all out soon. I'm starting college in what, nine months?

Speaking of nine months. Carissa felt a wave of dread wash over her. *What am I going to do about Kent? I can't possibly kill the baby. I know that now. So, what are my options? Will he follow through on his threat? Can he do what he says he's going to do? Should I tell Mom what he said, what he threatened, or assume it's an empty threat? Maybe he's just trying to threaten and intimidate me but won't actually go through with it. I mean, he wouldn't go through all of that effort just to hurt me, would he? I mean, it is his fault I'm pregnant in the first place.*

Yes. Yes, he would.

Mom looked up from her book at Carissa. Her smile faded. "That bad? Did you do that poorly on the test?" She reached for the test. Carissa relinquished it.

Sometimes, I wish I could see my own face. I wish I could see and monitor my facial expressions. I telegraph every single thought with my face, whether I want to or not. I need a poker face, but not a resting bitch face. Or, well, maybe I should try one of those. My face is too welcoming.

"I don't understand," Mom said. She looked up at Carissa with more confusion than worry furrowing her brow. "This says you got a ninety-seven. Why aren't you happier? You barely had time to study."

Carissa stared at Mom for several seconds deciding whether she should tell her what happened. *Who would it serve worrying her more after yesterday, spending hours crying and then with the police?* No. It was best to keep things to herself for a while.

Naturally, her emotions had other plans. Just when she was sure she could keep a lock on what happened, her emotions began to leak. Only, for her, emotions rarely leaked. They gushed. She burst into tears. *Dammit!*

Mom's mouth shot open. She flew out of her chair and hugged Carissa as she sobbed helplessly.

I don't know if I can go on like this.

"You're trembling," Mom said, surprised. "What happened?"

"What's this noise?" Mister Yarborough came outside as the last in his class left and saw the two. He paled. His face sank. "Oh God. I-I'm so sorry, Miss Boisseau. It's been a while since I made one of my students cry. I-I told them before the test that it wouldn't negatively affect their grade if they have a high average."

Go away! Carissa waved him away with a free hand. *This isn't about your test. My life is over, is all.*

Mom handed him the answer sheet. He studied it, frowned, looked up at Carissa, and studied it again.

"Well, that's a relief," Mister Yarborough said and handed the answer sheet back to Mom. "She's getting an A-plus. That means this isn't about me." He let out a sigh of relief, shrugged his shoulders, and locked the door. He was just about to walk away but turned around. "This doesn't have anything to do with Kent Bradshaw, does it?"

Carissa looked back at him and up to Mom. *Well, the cat's out of the bag.*

Mom's eyes nearly popped out of her sockets as she looked at Mister Yarborough. "What do you know about Kent Bradshaw?"

He doesn't know about the attack, if that's what you're asking. How would he? The teachers don't know anything that goes on. They never do.

"He's a cocky little shit," Mister Yarborough said and rolled his eyes, "just like his father. Worst man on the planet. So, I know him. Yes. More than I ever want to know." He glanced around, perhaps looking to see if anyone overheard him. He stepped closer. "He lingered after first period to talk to your daughter. I couldn't tell him I was tired of seeing his face and to take a long walk in front of a short bus but did say he should go to his next class."

"Umm, thanks," Mom said, still. Yarborough was always too comfortable and loose lipped with her. Her once told her she looked like a ginger Alicia Silverstone. She was flattered, but it made her uneasy.

"No thanks needed." He dismissed. "Whatever he said, she looked upset. But if we're being completely honest with each other, she's upset most of the time these days. Is there something we should know?"

That's not entirely true, is it? Do I really look upset most of the time? Maybe I do. This has been a shit semester.

"No." Mom stared at him, considering her answer. "We're getting it all sorted. But again, thanks for sending him off."

"Sure, no problem," Mister Yarborough said and checked his watch. "Now, if there's nothing else, I have to run home and make sure my ex-fiancé isn't moving my flat-screen out with the rest of her stuff. The couch potato claims it's hers because she watched it more than me." He walked off.

Mom watched him leave, then turned to Carissa. "Let's go to the car. Tell me everything Kent said to you."

I don't want to.

"He uh," Carissa started. "He was mad at me because I took

the money and didn't go through with the abortion." She breathed in and exhaled deeply. "He called me a whore."

Anger flared in Mom's green eyes. "That little cock shit."

"Mom," Carissa said, shocked. It wasn't in Mom's nature to swear, especially in front of her kids. But somehow, Mom being angry made Carissa feel a little better. "Language."

Mom glared at Carissa.

Carissa smirked. They shared the same expressions. It was like looking at an aged mirror image of herself.

"And what else did he say?" Mom asked.

I really don't want to talk about the threat. It'll just upset you. And, it's uncomfortable to think about, let alone speak about, the idea that there are images or video of me out there. Let's just get out of here and not look back.

"Nothing," Carissa said. She couldn't help but shift her eyes away from Mom to someone or something else. Maintaining eye contact and avoiding eye contact presented the same results. Mom could always tell either way if she was lying.

Mom's hand gripped Carissa's shoulder and dug in. *Ahh! What the?* It hurt. Mom's eyes were intense. *She means business.*

"Don't lie to me again," Mom said slowly. "What else did he say?"

Fine. Carissa sighed. *You asked for it.*

CHAPTER SIXTEEN

It was warmer than expected, and probably the last day of the year she'd be able to drive her Jeep with the doors off, so Priest insisted she drive. She parked, attached her gun to her belt—because you never knew what you might be walking into—and entered the bank.

Summers approached the bank greeter, flashed his shield, and asked for the manager. Priest captured everything. The tellers. The placement of the cameras. The number of staff on duty. The number of customers. It was a habit of hers to take in everything, wherever she was, because even the smallest detail could be a breakthrough in a case or save a life.

The greeter, a young, fair-skinned blond woman, flagged her manager. A dark, balding head with shoots of salt and pepper popped up. He eyed the guests and hobbled forward. He seemed to favor his left leg.

"Detective Summers," Summers pointed at himself. He flashed his shield for the man's benefit before briefly glancing at Priest. "And Detective Priest. Someone came in here yesterday afternoon and cashed a sizable check. We were hoping to get your cooperation in getting as much information about that exchange as possible. It is part of an ongoing investigation."

Ongoing investigation, as in started last night, and was greenlit this morning, after Captain Rogers reluctantly agreed to keep Priest on the case, despite a serious conflict of interest. She pleaded the importance of keeping her involved and said she wouldn't allow her personal feelings to affect her judgment. He wasn't concerned about her professionalism or talent. He knew she would do her job to the best of her ability. He was more concerned about her involvement endangering the case. But he'd leave her on and play it by ear once lawyers got involved.

Until then, Summers's hands had to be on everything. The less paperwork that had her name on it, the less they would have to scrub if there were issues with her involvement in the case. It was a kind gesture from a man she'd only known for a couple months.

Eh. I don't know, Priest thought. Her instincts told her Rogers was keeping something from her. His head rose and his concentration increased when she mentioned the name Carissa Boisseau. It seemed odd that a girl with no criminal background and only a year and a half residency in Richmond would peek the attention of a police captain. She'd investigate later, just to appease her curiosity. Right now, she had to focus on getting what they needed from the bank.

"Ah, yes," the bank manager said. "I know the transaction you're referring to. The check from the Bradshaw account. How can I help?"

Was he expecting us? Priest wondered.

"We're hoping you, and some of your staff, can answer some questions for us," Summers said.

The bank manager smiled. "Of course. I'd be happy to answer your questions."

"We'd also like to see the video footage," Priest said. "And have a copy spanning the time of their arrival until their departure."

The bank manager frowned and scratched his head. "I, uh, can definitely let you see it," he said. "But our security people and corporate office are the ones that handle all that stuff. I don't know what can and can't be copied or transferred. But again, we'll do what we can."

"Great," Summers said. "We appreciate your willingness to cooperate. With that said, there was also one more thing we'll need."

"I'm here to help, Detectives," the bank manager said, looked both in the eyes. "I've worked in banks for twenty years. Had a gun in my face three times in those years, two times at the same bank. You guys come through for us. I'm glad I finally get to come through for you. Name it. It's done."

We're talking to the right man.

"We'd like a photocopy of the check, Priest said."

The bank manager scratched his head. "Alright. I should be able to pull that out and give you two a photocopy. Though, I'm a little confused."

Priest raised her eyebrow. "Why?"

"Well, Bradshaw was blackmailed," the bank manager said.

Please tell me this is a joke.

Summers and Priest eyed each other.

"Oh yes," the bank manager continued. "She told me all about it. The blackmailer demanded a check, made out to cash so it wouldn't have her name on it, and without any bank penalties. The blackmailer also didn't want to open an account. Miss Bradshaw never told me the blackmailer's name. Only to expect the check." He laughed. "But you see, the young woman didn't get away that easy. We're required to report the cashing of any check of that size to the IRS. I told her to fill out a small form for me. That's what I have for you in my office."

Summers remained stoic while the bank manager patted himself on the back.

"We'd like a photocopy of that form, as well as the check," Priest said.

"Oh." The bank manager blinked rapidly. "You still want the check. Of course. Yes. Certainly. Follow me."

An hour later, Priest and Summers returned to her Jeep. Priest felt a chill and shivered. The temperature dropped ten degrees. Priest put on a jacket, hat, gloves, and wrapped a scarf around her neck.

"I guess I'll have to attach the doors now," she complained and turned down the street.

"Absolutely." Summers rubbed his hands together. "But we don't have time for that. Let's grab my car."

"Yea." Priest tightened her fists. "Can't believe she spun this as blackmail."

Summers turned the heat to max. "She won't report it until she's approached by the police. She's keeping that narrative in her pocket, just in case things turn south. She'll already have parties in play to corroborate her story. In court, and the court of public opinion, people are more likely to take pity on her if she's an innocent mom protecting her sons. Just like last time."

"Only this time, she's dealing with me," Priest said.

"Different ballgame."

Priest liked working with Summers. He was agreeable. Her last partner would have been better off as a lawyer than a police officer. He loved to argue for argument's sake. He believed in arguing both sides of an issue. While it had its momentary advantages in cases, it was incredibly annoying. He didn't know how to shut up. The man argued everything to death. She wondered what poor sap was stuck with him now that she'd transferred.

"Did you notice the anomaly?" Summers asked.

"What's that?"

Summers read his notepad. "According to Carissa Boisseau, she took her pregnancy tests on Wednesday evening. It wasn't until Thursday at lunch that Carissa approached Val to contact Janice Bradshaw. However, Bradshaw called the bank manager Wednesday morning to ensure the bank would have the funds. So, how did she know she would need the money?"

Priest gnawed on her lower lip as she put the pieces together. "Her friend."

Summers tapped his nose.

"Okay," Priest said. "Where's the connection? Who approached who? Did Val reach out to the Bradshaws when she got the pregnancy news or did they approach her sooner?"

"That's a question we'll have to ask her."

"You think she'll cooperate?" Priest asked. "We might need leverage."

"I'm sure we'll come up with something," Summers said. "We still have to follow up on the alleged illegal relationship with the store owner. You up for a stakeout?"

Stakeout! Yes. That's a great idea. Jay's been asking if he could join me on a stakeout. This would be a great one to go on, since there's no risk of danger. But I wouldn't invite him along with Nate around. Two is company. Three is a crowd. Besides, there's going to be kissing, lots of kissing. Hmm. I'll make up an excuse as to why we should wait, without saying no, and then invite Summers later, after I've gone with Jay a couple times.

Let's muster up a good excuse.

Priest frowned. "We'd be following blindly. We don't have any information on how often they meet. Where they meet. How long they meet. They could pop in and out of the dressing room in a matter of minutes. We need more information."

"I know," Summers said. "We still have to act on it. If we can catch them in the act, this can work to our favor. It's possible she's told him things, you know, pillow talk, that we can get out of him. He'll be willing to cooperate in any way he can to shorten a sentence, not be on the list, if the allegations are true."

I tried. "It's worth a try."

"What's wrong? You worried our stakeouts will keep you away from your boyfriend?"

"We haven't put the label on it, yet," Priest said. *But you're very close.* "I'm worried the Bradshaws aren't as sloppy as I thought they were. They've already established the narrative with the bank manager. I'd bet money they've done the same at the clinic. What else have they done?"

Summers shrugged. "It doesn't matter. Narrative or not, they're guilty, we'll catch them."

"We better."

CHAPTER SEVENTEEN

Mom's hands firmly gripped the steering wheel. She stared off into the distance after Carissa finished telling her about Kent's threats. She closed her eyes and said, "I'm going to kill him."

Carissa blinked. Her mouth went dry. *Shit. Does she really mean that or is this one of those moments when she's livid and saying a bunch of crazy stuff she doesn't mean? She has this weird, blank look on her face.*

"Uh, please don't?" Carissa hesitantly replied. Mom glanced at her out of the corner of her eye. "As much as I'd love to see his body trapped under a set of tires, I kind of need you to not go to prison. But, uh—," Carissa quickly fumbled for her purse, opened her wallet, and pulled out Detective Priest's business card, "we should call Detective Priest."

I should probably program her number into my phone so this isn't another coffee shop guy situation.

Mom watched the high school students getting into their cars and going off to get lunch. Carissa was sure she was keeping an eye open for Kent. Would she mow him down if she saw him?

Please don't. But please do. I'm so conflicted.

"She can do something about this," Carissa said. "I mean, he threatened me. There's got to be something she can do."

"I don't know," Mom said. "Did anyone else hear him threaten you?"

Sigh. *I don't know.*

"I'm not sure," Carissa said. "He spoke in a low voice. People came in; but he was leaned in right over me. I'm sure some of them were craning their necks to listen in, nosy as everyone is in this place. I couldn't say for sure if anyone heard anything. I'm not fond of anyone in that class. So, I don't have any numbers to ask."

Why can't I be more sociable sometimes?

"Well, that's just great!" Mom started the car. Carissa quickly looked to see if Kent was within line of sight and in Mom's crosshairs. He wasn't. *Too bad.* "That means it's your word against his, again."

Carissa slumped in her chair. *It was worth a shot at least. I hate being so powerless.*

"Call her," Mom said and looked at Carissa. "Issue a complaint."

"But you just said—," Carissa started.

"Call her," Mom interrupted. "They may not have heard what you said, but they did see him talking to you. They did see you upset. We can at least go on record saying that he's harassing you at school. We may not have anything other than his word against yours, but it's something. Maybe your teacher can confirm it."

"Yea," Carissa said. She looked down and sighed. *It feels like he can do whatever he wants. There's nothing I can do. I'm raped. I'm pregnant. And what? Now threatened, about to be humiliated to the school, the world, and there's nothing we can do about it?*

"Do you think he'll do it?" Carissa asked. "Do you think he'll share pictures and video of me to others?"

Has he already?

Mom looked at Carissa with sad eyes but didn't say anything. She didn't have to. The answer was obvious. Yes. He'd send it with a big stupid smile. Who knew what Kent was capable of and willing to do?

"I hate it here," Carissa said. She teared up again. "This is going to ruin me."

"No," Mom said. She reached over and rubbed Carissa's back. "No, it won't. We won't let that happen. We'll do something. We'll find a way to stop him. Remember last night? The detectives asked you all those questions and meticulously notated every detail. They're putting together a case. It'll work out."

It hasn't even been a day since I had all this hope that things were going to work out. Kent dashed all that hope in minutes. I hate him. This is insane. I can't believe this is my life.

"And you don't have to worry about school anymore," Mom said. "You're done at Patterson. This was your last class."

Wait. What?

Carissa stared at Mom with wide eyes. "What do you mean I'm done? What, what does that mean? What are you talking about? I still have a couple more credits to graduate."

"Chill Carissa," Mom said. She pulled out of the spot and headed out of the parking lot. "You're taking the rest of your classes at community college as we discussed. Besides, you just said you hate it here."

"Yea, I know," Carissa said. "But, if I knew it was my last day, I would have said good-bye to Fiona, umm, and Gabby, and a few others. No. Just those two. No. Maybe a few others. But I didn't even clean out my locker. I still have stuff in there. And, what about Spring season sports? If I'm not taking classes, I can't be on any of the teams. I'll be missing golf and tennis. I didn't even have a chance to tell my coaches bye. And, the swim team coach. I didn't say bye to her either."

Mom sighed. "We'll come back and empty your locker. You'll have to call everybody else. It's not like you could play tennis or golf or competitively swim while pregnant. I've been pregnant before, twice. You won't have the energy for any of that. Your sports activity will involve taking naps in the middle of the day and eating sticks of cheese with peanut butter. Your body is creating and supporting a new life. It takes a lot out of you."

Carissa frowned. *All this time being depressed about this baby; I didn't spend as much time with Miss Garrett as I should have working on my form. I pretty much dragged my ass through Fall season. I missed practices. Was on autopilot through some of the meets. Still won, though. Good thing I'm good. But now, I won't be on her team anymore. Why didn't I think this through? If I get rusty, there's no way I can stay in the amateur league, let alone get into the PGA league. I was going to use some of those potential winnings to pay off student loans.*

I feel like this is the first time in a while I've thought about this.

Mom glanced at Carissa. "I know. It feels like you're

sacrificing a lot. And you are. But trust me, once that little bundle of sunshine comes out of you, nothing else in the world will matter more."

Yea. Sure. Thanks, Mom.

"Right," Carissa said.

Ten minutes passed as Carissa stared out the window and watched the cars, the lights, and buildings. She recognized a street but wasn't sure why they were headed in this direction. "Where are we going? I thought we were going back home."

"Amy shuffled some things around and found an opening to get you in sooner," Mom said. "We're headed to see her now."

Carissa tensed. "Does she know about, umm, does she know what happened to me?"

"Of course," Mom said. "You think I wouldn't tell her? She's your doctor, my best friend, your godmother. She's family."

Of course. What was I thinking? By the time this is over, I everyone and their great grandmother will know. Homeless guys on the street will know. They'll have a billboard on interstate ninety-five, "Beware of teen pregnancy," with my face on it!

"Stop pouting."

"I'm not pouting," Carissa mumbled.

"Look in the mirror," Mom said. "You're pouting. Stop. This is going to be a big moment for you. Your first exam. And you're seven weeks in. Soon to be eight weeks."

Carissa shrugged.

Mom rapped her fingers on the steering wheel. "Carissa, you'll be able to hear the baby's heartbeat. You'll be able to see an image of the baby."

Wait. What? Carissa turned to Mom. "Really?"

"Yes!" Mom exclaimed, then wavered. "Though, I mean, it'll be a very vague image. You have to remember, he or she is the size of a bean at this point."

"What kind of a bean?" Carissa asked.

"What?"

"Well, is it the size of a black bean, jellybean, pinto bean, kidney bean, or green bean?"

Mom glanced at Carissa. "Suddenly you're Bubba the bean expert, huh?" She put her finger between her lower lip and chin, the usual place setting of her finger when she's thinking. "I'd say a pinto bean."

"That's really small." Carissa frowned. "What's the point of getting an ultrasound this early if I can't even see it?"

"I think you'll feel differently once you actually see it," Mom said with a smile. "I know I did. It's amazing to hear a heartbeat from something so small. You're lucky. With you, I had to wait four more weeks. Technology now, you have an advantage."

Carissa remembered an internet search. "Umm, so, I looked on the internet. It says that I might be able to find out the gender of the baby at seven weeks with a, uh, blood test. Is that true?"

Mom frowned and shrugged. "I don't know. I haven't kept up with that stuff in years. Haven't needed to. It's best to ask Amy. By now, she's used to being riddled with questions from moms reading things on the internet."

I feel like you're being straight with me, but also sarcastic about me looking things up on the internet. How do I respond to this? I'm annoyed.

"Okay," Carissa said.

If the internet is right, I'll give you the biggest "I told you so" face on the planet.

Mom turned right. "Hey, we're almost there. Call Detective Priest. Tell her what happened with Kent."

I'm trying to forget! Now I'm stressed again! Maybe that's what he's trying to do, stress me out. He wants me to stress so much that my stress kills the baby. That clever son of a bitch. You're not going to get me stressed! I'm going to be happy now just to spite your clever ass.

Carissa forced herself to smile.

Mom glanced at her and smiled. "Aww. I remember that look on your face. It was the look you gave me after you passed gas or pooped your diaper. You always seemed so pleased with yourself. Then you cried."

Carissa's smile evaporated. She glared. *Seriously, Mom.*

Mom laughed. "You were so cute."

Carissa pulled out her phone and dialed Detective Priest's phone number. She wanted to talk to somebody else.

2

Detective Priest listened intently as Carissa went over the

details of her recent encounter with Kent. After a few minutes, she asked Carissa to pause while she caught up in her notes. When they arrived at Amy's office, Mom parked and put the phone on speaker to listen in.

Priest was with her partner, Summers, who didn't say much of anything. *Probably taking notes, too. That seems to be a prerequisite for being a detective, good notetaking skills.* However, once Carissa mentioned Kent's abortion pills, Summers cut her off and said they were on their way. Mom intervened.

"We have an appointment to see our family doctor," Mom said. "She found an opening, also known as her lunch break, to get us in for an early examination. We'd really like to go over all of this with you but can't miss this appointment. I cancelled next week's appointment already."

"Misses Boisseau," Summers said. "It's not our intention to have you wait for us. We'd rather be there, outside of course, while your daughter is having the examination."

"Oh," Mom said. The bridge of her nose wrinkled. "Why?"

Priest jumped in the conversation. "Right now, you're holding two valuable pieces of evidence in this investigation. One of them is inside your daughter. The other is in her purse. You're going to see Doctor Amy Sanchez, the college roommate and best friend, right?"

Wow. These guys are good.

Mom shot a surprised look at the phone, then Carissa. "How do they know that? Did you tell them?"

"You told us last night, Ma'am," Summers said. "We take detailed notes."

They are on point. Perhaps there's hope, yet.

"And social media," Priest said. "We have a tech guy with a sophisticated algorithm. He provides names and identifying details. The computer does the rest. It connects all the dots, says who knows who from where and when based on pictures, tags, comments, and other parameters it can pull from the internet and select police files. He put the names in yesterday, after our discussion, and let it run overnight. We have a file on your family and the Bradshaws. It helps your profiles are mostly public. Though, I advise you to make your non-business accounts private for now, especially Carissa."

You just spoke to us last night, and now you have files on each of us? I don't know how I feel about this.

"Wow," Mom said, impressed.

I wonder how much they have. Probably not much of me online besides sports pictures. Family members from all over always want to see pictures or videos posted of my different golf tournaments or tennis matches. Oh yea. I stay in touch with my friends from Connecticut and New York. That's about it.

"Your doctor's examination will confirm the age of the fetus and window of the alleged assault," Summer said. "Any DNA evidence collected that could tie the paternity of the child to the alleged assailant will support your testimony. Your doctor will be able to inform us when that evidence can be safely collected. She also has access to a lab, which could expedite the paternity test process.

"The pills are physical evidence connecting the accused to harassment, manipulating a minor to have an abortion, and illegally providing the means to an abortion without the consent or presence of a parent or legal guardian."

That was very well put, minus the use of the words "alleged" and "accused". That boy is guilty. Guilty, guilty, guilty!

Hmm.

I like Detective Summers. I get the feeling he's one of those by the book guys. He probably reads the police code every morning while eating breakfast, something practical like fruit, egg whites, and a bran muffin. And he eats the same thing every morning, because why not? Stick with what works. His coffee? Black with two sugar cubes. He's definitely the kind of guy that uses sugar cubes. Very precise. Yep. And two sugar cubes is just right. Three sugars would be splurging. I'm stretching, perhaps. But I visualize a man that has multiples of the same suit, all pressed and in line in the closet. Multiples of the same shoes, too. And they're all shiny. He shines his shoes. That much I'm certain.

"Carissa, you coming?" Mom said with one foot out the car.

"Huh?" Carissa responded and snapped herself back into the moment.

"Let's go," Mom said.

"What?" She looked at her phone. The detectives were gone. *Crap. I was off in my thoughts again. But only for like a couple seconds. I don't recall them saying goodbye. I would have snapped out for a goodbye.*

"Carissa."

"Right, sorry." She unlocked her seatbelt and opened the door. *That's what happens when you forget to take your meds, Carissa.*

"Mom, I phased out," Carissa said. "What did they say?"

"They'll meet us inside," Mom said and looked at her watch. "Let's move. We're already ten minutes late."

Only ten? That's early for me. But yea, for you that's like thirty minutes late.

3

The receptionist, Gale, knew them well enough to flag them by without any questions. They rushed down the hallway past Amy's partners' offices. By habit, Carissa scanned the name plates on the doors. Doctors Lee, Taylor, Jacobs, and Sanchez. Mike Lee was an internal medicine specialist. Irene Taylor was a pediatrician. Peter Jacobs was a psychiatrist. Amy was the family practitioner. Carissa joked that they should make room for a dentist and slowly monopolize the medical field. They laughed and said she was on to something.

Through the first door was the spacious examination room. They recently painted the room a pale lavender to replace the plain white walls. There was still a faint smell of fresh paint underneath whatever she used to sanitize the room. Carissa admired the new look as she headed through the second, connected room where Amy sat behind her desk eating hard tacos. You could hear the crunch through the doorway. Her husband, Javier, made "the best tacos in Richmond" per Food Is Life Magazine.

Now I'm hungry. I want tacos. Her tacos.

"Great, you're here," Amy said and plopped down the taco on her plate. She wiped her hands with napkins and walked around the desk. "Javier performed his husbandly duties by having one of his delivery boys drop off some tacos." She smiled at Mom. "If he keeps this up, I might do that thing we talked about the other night."

Mom's jaw dropped. Then, she laughed. "I don't think either

of us is flexible enough to suggest that to our husbands just yet. Maybe a few more yoga classes."

Oh! No! Don't mention husbands. Don't mention husbands.

"Ew, Mom," Carissa said and covered her ears. "You do realize your husband is my dad, and some of us don't want to hear about your escapades."

"She's right," Amy said. "In her old age, my mom is a little too cavalier with the details of her and Dad. There was this thing she said they tried with pickles." She cringed. "Scarred me for life. I can't look at pickles anymore."

Carissa stared, puzzled. *Again, why? I don't want to know what they did with those pickles. But I also want to know now. I'm curious. I'm sure once I hear it, I'll wish I didn't. But I still want to know it they did what I think they did. Every time I see pickles now, I'll be wondering what happened. Is my imagination better or worse than reality?*

Amy's demeanor sobered. "I'm so sorry, Carissa." She sighed and gave Carissa a hug. Carissa hugged back. "I hoped to be the person that delivered your babies. I just, never anticipated it would be this soon, and certainly didn't want it to be like this. How are you feeling?"

"I'd be better if the son of a bi—err," she glanced at Mom, who gave her an 'I'll let it slide' look, "umm, wasn't threatening me."

"He threatened you?" Amy asked and tightened her fists. In her dress attire and doctor's coat, you'd never suspect that she took kickboxing classes in college and attended on and off for the past twenty years. "How? When?" She glanced at Mom. "You never told me he threatened her."

"It happened today," Carissa said. "Umm, how much do you know?"

Amy glanced at Mom again. Mom remained silent.

"Okay, so, she told you everything up until an hour ago," Carissa deducted.

"Yes."

Carissa's eyes narrowed. Mom and Amy talked about everything. Everything! It was a beautiful friendship. But it was annoying. *Come on! Some things are meant to be kept to yourself.*

Nevertheless, she envied them. She had a close friendship

with Val, or so she thought, but still kept many things to herself. That was who she was. She was a private person. She said nada, unless she felt the desire to. And if she did disclose something, it was about herself. It wasn't in her nature to disclose other people's life details. It was their business. If they shared, they shared. But her, she wouldn't say a thang.

I'll make a good psychologist one day.

"Fill me in," Amy said. "What happened?"

Fine. Why not? If I don't now, Mom will later.

Amy led them to the examination room. There, Carissa undressed. *How many times have I been naked in front of her?* Amy performed the physical examination while Carissa relived her experience in Mister Yarborough's classroom for the fourth time. She then summarized her phone conversation with the two detectives.

"They'll probably be here in a matter of minutes to ask you some questions," Carissa closed.

"Okay." Amy sighed. "Regretfully, this is more common than it should be. I'll know what they'll ask for." She sat. "I wish there were more women in our kickboxing classes. Every girl should be trained in martial arts so they can defend themselves." *I was trained in karate for eight years!* "Though, I'm sorry to say that doesn't help in your case."

No shit. It doesn't help if you're drugged and half paralyzed.

"Let's change the subject and talk about the baby," Mom chimed in. *Always trying to bring that positive spin to things.*

"Yes, yes," Amy said. "Let's run urine and blood tests, do the ultrasound, see that baby." Her gloved hand reached for a plastic cup with a screw-on top. "Pee in this. Then, we'll draw just a tiny bit of blood, test your Rh compatibility, as if you know what that means, and move on to the transvaginal exam."

Wait. "Vaginal?" Carissa asked.

Amy nodded sympathetically. "I understand your hesitancy. The wand we use is state of the art. It's smaller than previous models and not painful. You may feel some pressure, a little."

"Okay."

Amy collected Carissa's hand. "Vaginal ultrasounds offer the best images at this stage in the pregnancy. It helps us accurately confirm the pregnancy and determine the age and size of the fetus. It's also a great way to detect any early abnormalities." She paused. "We could do the transabdominal exam. It just won't offer the best results. We're trying to observe a fetus that's still very small. Like a bean."

"Don't get her started on beans," Mom chimed in.

Carissa shot her dagger eyes. "Beans vary in size. I'm just looking for an accurate estimation." She turned her attention back to Amy. "What kind of bean?"

"At seven weeks, I'd say a jellybean," Amy said. "Only way to appreciate it is to look and see. But first, like your mom said, we have to run some more tests. I'll ask some questions. You can ask me some questions. Then, we can capture some baby pictures."

Thirty minutes later, Carissa laid on the examination bed while Amy maneuvered the wand. It wasn't as uncomfortable as she'd expected. The unit was warm and Amy was a professional. She said she practiced on herself a couple times to know how it felt and make sure she did it correctly for others. Mom tried not to laugh but couldn't help herself. Whenever those two were together, you could always expect jokes laced with debauchery and plenty of belly laughter.

This time, their eyes were locked on the screen. Carissa stared at the small, oval, pulsing blotch on the screen and felt her heart stop, leap, skip, jump, and run. *Oh my God! That's her, or him. That's my baby. I can't believe it. Well, I mean, obviously I'm pregnant, so I believe it. But, I mean, it's just. Ugh. She was right. Though, I'll never tell her. It is different seeing an image on a screen. I can hear a heartbeat! When will I get to know if it's a boy or girl?*

"Amy," Carissa said. "I read on the internet that you could find out the gender of the baby after seven weeks. Is that true?"

"Yep. Cell-free DNA testing. It's new. While I can't offer it, I know where to have it tested. The way it works is, little bits of baby DNA make their way through the placental wall and into the mother's bloodstream. Your blood will be screened for the baby's DNA. We can determine things like gender and check for genetic abnormalities or defects early on."

Carissa frowned. "Kent is a genetic defect."

"Yes," Amy said without hesitation. "Yes, he is. Fortunately, as of right now, everything looks good. Everything checks out down there. You have a beautiful, healthy fetus with a great heart rate. And, I can confirm the age of the fetus to be just about seven weeks." She glanced at the clock, then the door to her office. "When the detectives arrive, I'll confirm her age."

They looked at Mom, who tearfully watched the ultrasound imagery and blew her nose.

"I'll upload this on a flash drive," Amy said and slowly retracted the probe. Carissa let out a sigh of relief. *That was a weird sensation.* "So, you can look back on this moment. The first images of baby, umm," she waved her hand dismissively, "I guess it's a bit early for names."

"Don't remind me," Carissa said. "I haven't the slightest clue what to name him, her." She paused. "Though, I might consider a gender-neutral name. Something like Morgan, Jordan, or Alex. That way, whatever the baby turns out to be, there's no sweating it. Instead of having two lists, one for boys and one for girls, I'll just have one master list. I could name the kid now if I wanted to, and it wouldn't make a difference."

"You could name her Junior if she's a girl," Amy said with a smile, "and Junior if he's a boy."

Carissa frowned. "Why would I do that?"

Mom chuckled and dabbed at her tears.

Carissa glared at Mom. *And what are you laughing at?*

"It's an inside joke," Amy said as she took off her glove and tossed it in the trash. "Before your time."

Mom blew her nose and laughed. "I don't think she's ready for it."

"I don't think anyone can be ready," Amy said. She and Mom laughed. *I still don't know what you're talking about.* She grabbed the flash drive and handed it to Carissa. "Alright. Every time we meet, bring this. We'll keep track of all your sonograms on this. I have a backup, just in case anything happens to this. But this allows you to hold on to it. So now, you can watch it whenever you want. Share the progress of your baby as she develops. And, for now, I'm going to stick with calling her 'she' until tests suggest otherwise."

I don't know who I would want to show this to, but thanks. Carissa put the silver flash drive in her purse.

There was a knock at the door.

"Looks like our guests have finally arrived," Amy said. "I'll talk to them outside while you put on your pants." She turned, then hesitated. "Since I'm a fervent protector of the doctor-patient confidentiality agreement, before I discuss anything with the police, is there something you want me to withhold?"

Carissa slid off the examination bed. "I don't see a reason to withhold anything."

"Great," Amy said and answered the door.

4

Carissa stared at the fetus photo and sighed. Mom hugged her, rubbed her back, and said, "It'll be okay. We'll get through this together."

Amy peeked her head in her office. "You two ready?"

"Yea." Carissa handed Mom the photo.

Amy opened the door. Behind her was Detectives Priest and Summers, notepads in hand. *Always with the notepads. These two are serious about their notes.*

"Sorry we're late," Detective Priest said. She glanced back at Summers. "We had to arrest a guy."

"He was driving recklessly," Summers said with a serious expression. His eyes focused on the notepad as he flipped through pages. Carissa loved that this man was all business. "You said Mister Bradshaw placed a plastic bottle containing three abortion pills inside your purse."

"Yea." *That's what happened.*

"Okay," he said. "Have you touched it?"

"No. Why?"

"Fingerprints," Summers said. He reached in his pocket and pulled out a pair of latex gloves. "I need to know who's touched it between the time he handed it to you and now. We'll take possession of the pills, test the container for prints."

"Okay. That's fine." *It's not like I was going to use them.*

"If there's a match," Summers continued, "it'll confirm he's been in possession of the pills. We'll also test the pills and make sure they're what you believe them to be."

Mom frowned. "What does that mean? You think she's claiming they're something they're not?"

Summers rubbed his right temple. Priest stepped forward. "He's saying there's no way of knowing what Mister Bradshaw gave her until we test it. He could have said it was one thing and given her something else."

Mom gasped and covered her mouth. "You think he's trying to poison her?"

"That's a, uh, thought," Priest said. "But let's table that idea for now. For us to charge him, we must confirm he gave you abortion pills and not something else. Giving pills to a minor is a criminal act. In the event it is something else, that can change what we can or will charge him."

Carissa wasn't sure what to do other than agree. She opened her purse and reached for the pills.

"Umm, Miss," Summers said. Carissa froze and looked up. "If you don't mind, I'd like to acquire it carefully to ensure the fingerprint is not smudged or in any other way compromised." He pulled a plastic evidence bag out of his pocket.

How much stuff do you have in your pocket?

Carissa shrugged. "Sure." She approached him with her purse.

It's a good thing I keep it organized with labels, rubber bands, and adhesive loops. If it was Val's or Mom's or Amy's purse, he'd probably just hand it back and say, "We'll take our chances."

"Hmm," Summers said when he looked inside. He pulled out the clear pill container, squinted his eyes, and examined its contents. "Exinimir plus." Priest hmphed. "Eighteen point two dash seventy-one. Noted. I wasn't sure if it was a knockoff or name brand. I'm sure tests will confirm it to be what it is." He sighed, placed the container in the evidence bag, and handed it to Priest.

Priest examined it closely. "It's the same brand."

I don't understand. Carissa, Amy, and Mom watched the two detectives. *Same brand as what?*

"Same source?" Priest whispered.

"Most likely," Summers said. He turned to Carissa and Mom. "Thank you for contacting us, Misses and Miss Boisseau. This will be instrumental in the investigation. You also signed off on giving us a blood sample."

Carissa nodded. She didn't have any words at the moment.

Never thought I'd be giving the police a sample of my blood. This feels like an episode from some twisted crime show. When did this become my life?

I suppose I should look on the bright side. Unlike the victims in the crime shows, I'm still alive. I didn't wash up on a beach naked and disheveled with rope burns and marks on my neck. Oh God. Now I'm visualizing it. I hate TV.

Amy handed Summers a sealed test tube and business card. "That's the lab where I'll be sending my samples for the test. They do excellent work and should be able to isolate the child's DNA in her blood and match it with the father's. How do you plan to get a sample from Kent Bradshaw?"

I supposed that'll be the hard part. There's no way he'll gingerly hand over his DNA like a good ole buddy ole pal of the police, "Here you go, Detectives. DNA that will prove I'm the father."

Summers pocketed the business card and put the test tube in an evidence bag. "Thank you, Doctor." He nodded to Carissa and Mom, then left.

Amy frowned. "He didn't answer my question."

Priest mouthed, "I'm sorry," to Amy and followed Summers. "Thank you for everything. We'll keep in touch. If anything else happens, and I mean anything, please don't hesitate to call." She closed the door behind herself.

Okay. That was kind of weird.

Amy stated the obvious, "They're not telling us everything."

"No, they're not," Mom said.

I thought they were on our side. What gives? They took the pills. Said it was the same brand. Same brand as what? And same source? Same source as what? Now I have all these questions. Are they working a different case? Have there been other girls? And how do they plan on getting Kent's DNA? It seems kind of weird that they just zipped out when we asked that question.

"Well," Amy said, "as much as I love you two, I have to kick you out." She smiled. "I have cold tacos to choke down before my next appointment." She looked at her watch. "In about ten minutes."

How do police acquire DNA? I mean, on TV, they'll take someone's drinking glass, find a piece of hair in a brush or comb, or issue a warrant. They operate within the constraints of the law. So who knows what loops they'll have to jump through. Unless, perhaps, they already have a sample.

"Thank you for squeezing us in for an early visit," Mom said and gave Amy a hug. "It's been—" She sighed. "I suppose I'm fortunate, having been a young mother myself, I have an idea of what she's going through. We're spending the rest of the day putting together a game plan."

Shit. Carissa gasped. *They already have a sample of his DNA, don't they?*

"If you need anything else, don't hesitate to ask," Amy said. She gave Carissa a hug. "I mean it. If you have any questions, discomforts, worries, I'm here for you. We'll get through this together."

"Okay," Carissa said. *I'm going to need all the help I can get.* "Thanks. It means a lot."

"And I'll be over the Sunday after next for game night."

"Great," Mom said on the way out. "Tell Jorge no cheating this time."

"As if that ever works." Amy followed them to the reception desk. "He doesn't listen to me. The man will stop at nothing to win."

I hope Kent's not the same way. He seems like the kind of guy that won't stop at threats and doesn't take kindly to having the police called on him. I should have asked the detectives about my safety and the safety of the baby.

"Call me when you're back in town," Mom said. "I'll keep you up to date."

"Okay," Amy said. "Love you."

"Love you, too," Mom said.

Val never loved me. I miss Gina. She was a bit skanky, and mouthy, and loved to get herself in every kind of trouble, but we had the best bond. Those were Val's selling points when I first met her. She was like Gina's twin. Except, Gina would cut off her arm and set it on fire before leaving me alone to be, to be, never mind.

They walked to the car. *I hope things work out with Gabby and her sisters. I'm tired of losing friends.*

Carissa looked up as rays of sunlight shone on her through parted clouds. *Really? Parting clouds? Rays of light as I think about my Christian friends? If there is a God, if You're really up there, that was incredibly cliché.*

CHAPTER EIGHTEEN

I'm really doing it, Carissa thought as she stepped out of the car in her sleeveless, faux-wrap black dress and black heels. She felt a chill and grabbed her black linen laced shawl. *I'm really going to church.*

Three months ago, if someone told her she would be pregnant and going to church, she would have laughed. Hard. Pregnant? She'd have to have a husband first. Church? What reason would she possibly have for going to church? She doesn't believe that hoopla.

Yet here I am, Carissa thought as she checked her purse for lip gloss. *Dressed in black, standing in the parking lot of a church with the glamour twins, their sister, and Sean. Son of uh. Why are they so freaking cute together?* She looked at Rebecca and Sean holding hands, waiting for Gabby to collect her bible and notebook from the dashboard. *I'll give kudos where kudos are due. Somehow, Becca's made an impact on Sean. He's well-mannered. Keeps himself neat. She even convinced him to get rid of his disgusting girly magazines. All Kelsea ever got was a shrug and sometimes side-eye.*

"Hold hands while you can," Hannah said. "Once we get inside, you better keep your hands to yourself. I don't want to hear anymore sass from what's her name on how I need to be my sister's keeper and keep an eye on you two."

Who are you talking about?

"Ugh," Rebecca rolled her eyes. "Just ignore her. That's what Mom said to do. Lady wouldn't know how to mind her own business if she tripped and fell in it." She looked up at the sky and added, "But we love her, right? Because she's made in the image of God."

I don't know what that means.

Gabby smiled. "Or she's a weed growing with the wheat." She locked the door with her remote and waved her phone. "Let's get a move. Mom's texting us, wondering if we made it yet."

"I told her it was going to take us about fifteen or so extra minutes to grab Sean and Cari," Rebecca said and looked at her watch. "We're on time."

"We have like two minutes to get to TBS," Hannah said and sped up, but not by much in her pink, one-inch heels. *Girl loves pink*, Carissa thought as she admired Hannah's pink, sleeveless, sheath dress. *Every time I see her, she's wearing pink.*

Whereas Gabby seems to be more of a floral girl. She wore a white dress with pink azaleas and pink ribbon belt. Her flats were white with pink roses.

And Rebecca, well. Compared to the first two, she looked a little less runway with her block-colored, cap sleeved dress. The top of her dress was white. The rest was a navy blue, which matched Sean's navy dress shirt and black slacks. *How is this happening? How am I just noticing that they're color-coordinated?*

Wait a minute. "Did you say TBS?" Carissa asked as they approached the glass door entrance. "Are we going to be on TV?"

Gabby snorted. "No silly. Teen Bible Study. We start with a little worship. Then, our facilitator goes through a set of versus and offers a detailed breakdown of some of the scriptures. After which, we break into groups and share our own thoughts about how we personally interpret the scriptures and how or if it relates to our lives."

It's like you're speaking Mandarin, right now. Carissa shrugged. "Okay."

"Yep," Rebecca said. "You're definitely brother and sister. Sean gave me the same face when I explained it to him. It's, it's kind of eerie. The expression is literally the same." *Says the sister of* identical *twins.*

"We're related?" Sean asked and looked closely at Carissa. "No. No way. She's way too freckled. Way too ginger."

I'll show you ginger. Carissa shot him a "I'll kill you later" smile. "Whereas, he's way too Asian to be my brother. Look at the straight hair. Look at the slightest bit more slant in his eyes. And his face. I mean. His lack of freckles is ghastly."

Sean stuck his tongue out.

Carissa crossed her eyes.

Rebecca laughed. "I need to spend more time with you two."

Yea, Carissa thought and smiled. *This is great. This is fun. I've gone, what, a whole hour without thinking about the fact that I'm pregnant. Ugh. And great. I just ruined that by thinking about it.*

"You think we'll run into you-know-who today?" Gabby asked Hannah.

Hannah smiled. Carissa didn't know black girls could blush but look at that. That girl was as red as brown could get.

"Do you have a boyfriend?" Carissa asked, ready to brace for the news that yet again, someone else besides her had a guy in their life. "Or someone you're like, *talking* to?"

"She wishes," Rebecca teased.

"Shush it." Hannah smirked and narrowed her eyes at Rebecca. "It'll happen. It's just not the right timing, for obvious reasons."

The greeters at the first doors said their hellos and welcomes and handed out pamphlets with the church itinerary on them. They flowed through the door and continued with the conversation.

"What reason is that?" Carissa asked as she watched Sean open the second set of glass doors for the Cole sisters. *What the hell have you done to my brother? He's being a gentleman. Are you slipping him drugs? Are you, oh my God, are you having sex with him? I mean. This is like some weird transformation. He intentionally let a door close on me just a week ago.*

Then again, hmm. I had just called him a fart and said he made a booger look brilliant. But I mean, that's what sisters say to their brothers. He didn't have to be rude.

Carissa shook her head at Sean as she followed the sisters inside. He pretended he was going to slam the door on her and smiled. *See! See! You little wanker! Eventually, they'll see you for what you are.*

"Well," Gabby chimed in. "He's twenty-five and on very

friendly terms with a blond cop that started coming here."

"I see," Carissa said after giving Sean the evil eye. "So, he's taken."

Wait. He's twenty-five? Isn't that an automatic no-can-do?

"No, actually," Hannah said with a frown. "His online profile says single. He hasn't posted any pictures of them together. I haven't seen anything that suggests they're together, together. They could be friends. All we've seen is them talking."

Gabby smiled. "Well, they are at church. Unlike Becca and Sean, some people leave the PDA at home."

Rebecca rolled her eyes and pressed herself closer to Sean, who happily leaned in and went along with it. *Of course, you would.*

"Seriously?" Hannah shot Rebecca a nasty look. "We're in the house of God now. Show some restraint."

"Oh goodness." Gabby facepalmed. "Now you're sounding like her."

"We're just holding hands," Rebecca said with a toothy, innocent smile.

"Yea, but your shoulders are touching," Hannah said and separated them. "Just hold hands like a normal person and stop being so close. You're going to get us in trouble. You can be side-to-side, cheek-to-cheek, and braid each other's hair for all I care. Just not here."

Rebecca and Sean chuckled.

Carissa laughed, "Yes. Please braid Sean's hair. I'd love to see that. I'll record it."

Sean shook his head. "Not happening."

Please. All she has to do is bat those pretty eyelashes and pout those full lips. You'll crumble like a house of cards and do whatever she asks. She has you wrapped around her finger. Ugh. *I wish I had someone wrapped around my finger.*

"We better get inside," Gabby said with her ear next to the door. "They're finishing up the opening worship song. After prayer, the lesson will start." Without another word, she cracked the door open and slipped inside.

Everyone followed.

2

DAKOTA

As they found their seats near the back, not far from the door, the youth pastor went up to the stage. He was a tall, thin brunet with glasses and short curly hair. He wore a plaid shirt and khakis. He looked to be in his early twenties. *I wonder if he's the one Hannah has a crush on.* He clapped and complimented the youth choir, then mentioned how grateful he was to be at a church that made worship a priority. They had so many gifted young people. He scanned the audience.

"I see a few new faces," he announced. "I love it. Thank you for coming. I am so happy to see you here today. Please, after this bible study is over, come talk to me. I love meeting new people. I love having an opportunity to learn new people's life stories and seeing how God's working in their lives. For those of you who are new, I'm Jon Bishop. Jon without the 'H'. Don't ask me why. If you see my parents, tell them they robbed me, and they owe me an 'H'."

The audience laughed.

"Maybe it's because I didn't take out the trash when I was twelve or something and they took it away. 'Obey your parents, and you'll get your "H" back.' Unfortunately, I was an unruly kid. My mouth could run laps around my feet. I'll never see that 'H' again."

More laughter.

"But again, it's great to have you here. I hope the text speaks to you as it does to me. And I love the series we're working on right now. It's a big one. The Book of Matthew. As our pastor shared with you last week and the week before, we're going through a chapter a week, except for a few chapters, which are longer and, or, heavier, and require two or three weeks to dig deep. In bible study, we read each chapter and spend time on each verse. Then, Pastor Brown or one of our other pastors touches on the themes and messages of the chapter of the week."

Jon took a sip of water.

"The first week, we went through the genealogy and birth of Jesus Christ, offering verse references to the patriarchs throughout the bible. I said it before, and will say it again, the path to the eventual birth of Jesus just blows my mind. I mean, to think that these very imperfect men and many unwise choices all led to the birth of the only perfect man to ever walk this earth.

I mean, Judah. The same man that had a major part in selling Joseph into slavery. The same guy that meant to cheat Tamar out of a husband and child, and then impregnated her after she tricked him.

"And this led to the birth of Perez, to Hezren, to Ram, to Amminadab, eventually leading to the birth of David. And David made some pretty interesting choices, including sending Uriah to his death, after impregnating his wife. Solomon was David and Bathsheba's second child, after their first child died. Notice, in Matthew, they won't say David was the father of Solomon by Bathsheba. They don't use her name. She is remembered as the wife of Uriah. And so, reading the bible, the old testament, from beginning to end, we have this seemingly unpredictable and chaotic history of human choices, but they all eventually lead to Jesus. Out of this crazy human genealogy, this human disorder, man's free will, God delivers order and perfection. Remember that. When things don't make sense, even when we or others make disagreeable decisions, God can and has made something good out of it. He is in control."

Strange. I don't know any of these people or what you're talking about, but part of me feels comforted by the thought. From what I heard, I thought the bible was boring. Apparently, it's got some drama. Men impregnating other men's wives and having people killed? I should check that out.

Jon took another sip of his water. "Then we touched on the end of the first chapter, the birth of Jesus, referencing Luke one, and delved into the second chapter. We reflected on the theme: obedience. The salvation of humanity, the beginning of this perfect life, starts with two young people, two teenagers a lot like you, obeying God. Mary, though confused and mystified by the concept of a virgin pregnancy, humbly accepts what the angel tells her. Joseph, questioning and doubtful of Mary's pregnancy, considers quietly divorcing Mary. But having an angel approach him in a dream, he listens and doesn't divorce her. How different would our story be if Mary scoffed at the idea of pregnancy and refused because it didn't suit her vision for her future?"

Pregnancy certainly doesn't suit my vision of my future. Sigh. *What does going through with the pregnancy mean in my case?*

"What kind of twists and turns would there have been if Joseph was disobedient, went through with a divorce anyway because he didn't trust the dream, thought poorly and suspiciously of Mary, wasn't ready to be a father, or didn't want to be the father of a child that wasn't from his loins? Imagine that."

In other words, if Joseph or Mary were even half as selfish as most of the people I've met, including myself, there'd be no Jesus, or his origin story would be different. Good grief. *If it was up to Val, Jesus would have been aborted.*

"The birth of Jesus starts with two teenagers obeying God. And throughout the second chapter, God reaches out to Joseph through dreams and warnings. If Joseph disobeyed once, it could have meant his life, Mary's life, and most importantly, Jesus's life. Yet he obeyed, they left Bethlehem and went to Egypt, then returned to Israel, and to Galilee, in the city of Nazareth.

"And there's so much we can touch on. In discussions, we wondered about the origins of the wise men. We talked about the futile schemes of men to protect their own power. We talked about the very humble beginnings of Jesus, born in a manger, and his message throughout the text on the poor, the rich, humility and meekness. Nothing anyone would expect from the child of God. He wasn't raised in a lavish lifestyle with the best horses and carriages, fancy robes, an elite education, and everything people sought after. He was born in a manger, raised by a carpenter, earning carpenter wages, and traveled by foot."

Jon paused and looked around the room. "Now, let's open our bibles to Matthew chapter three. I'll give you all seven minutes to read through the chapter. Then, we'll have a volunteer read verses one through six aloud. We'll go over the text in detail. Have a ten-minute discussion at each of the tables. Then have another volunteer read verses seven through twelve. Same. Then, the last volunteer will read thirteen through seventeen. New people, don't feel pressured to volunteer, but if you feel something stirring inside you to read, you get first dibs."

He turned off the microphone on his podium. And flipped through his notes.

Gabby looked at Carissa and frowned, "Carissa, where's your bible?"

What? What do you mean, "Where's your bible?" When the hell did you expect me to have bought a bible?

Rebecca giggled. "That expression on your face is priceless." She snapped a picture with her phone.

Gabby chuckled, "I'm kidding," and pulled a pink bible out of her purse. It matched Hannah's. The queen of pink. She passed it to Carissa. "I got you something."

Carissa gaped at the bible and accepted it. *Are you serious?* She rubbed her hands over the imitation leather. *Carissa Asami Boisseau was engraved in the bottom right corner in gold print. It's engraved! When did you get this?* Within the pages of the bible was a white bookmark. *And a bookmark!* She pulled it out.

The bookmark read: "Behold, God is my salvation; I will trust, and will not be afraid; for the Lord God is my strength and my song, and he has become my salvation. – Isaiah 12:2 ESV."

"Wow," Carissa said. "Thank you. I, I'm at a loss of words." She opened the book and fanned through the pages, breathed in the new book smell. That was how she and Mom always started books. "When did you get this?"

"I ordered it two weeks ago," Gabby said. "I mulled over the idea and prayed after you felt sick in class. The company was a little behind on engravings, apparently. I got it in the mail Thursday. It was there sitting on the table when we got home from dropping you off."

Thursday. The day Gabby convinced me to not have the abortion. Huh.

"Interesting," Carissa said.

"I thought so," Hannah chimed in while reading her bible.

"Mom said it was a sign," Rebecca said. "What do you think, Sean?"

"Yeah." Sean glanced at Carissa. She could tell he didn't want to talk about Thursday or Friday. "Definitely a sign."

Sean and Carissa hadn't exchanged words about what happened between her and Kent. It was a terrible situation. The only way he knew how to respond to the news was to punch things. After the family meeting on Friday, which was full of awkward conversation, tears, long silences, and hugs, Sean and Dad went to the basement and took turns letting out their aggressions on their punching bags. The alternative was premeditated murder.

Though Carissa stopped taking karate classes to play tennis and golf, Sean hadn't. He loved it and did well in competitions. He didn't have an interest in other sports until he discovered he might need a scholarship. That's when he started playing basketball. He was good at basketball, mostly because of his speed. He was already in excellent shape. Karate gave him quick hands for steals. But karate wasn't the only martial art he studied.

According to Grandma Boisseau, their ancestors were the sworn protectors of Japan's royal families since the early dynasties. She and Dad were strict about upholding family tradition, which meant starting karate lessons at age five. Grandma was a kyudo champion, and so were the five generations before her. Daily, she practiced kyudo and trained her children and grandchildren to do so. Sean was drawn into the allure and mystique of their heritage at an early age and imagined himself as a warrior. After he leveled up to red belt in karate, he insisted Dad plug him into jujitsu and judo. That was four different martial arts for Sean. *If anyone could whip Kent in seconds without anyone knowing what happened, it would be him.*

Carissa felt like a disappointment. She was more like her mother in her interests and activities, and incidentally shunned her heritage by not showing interest in Japanese culture. She learned the language as a child, but barely spoke it. She rarely wore the outfits her grandmother sent her; didn't pay attention to the holidays; only learned karate because Dad insisted. Instead of keeping up with karate, she played tennis and golf. Occasionally, she practiced kyudo to keep grandma happy whenever she stopped by.

"There you go," Gabby whispered. She turned the book to Matthew, knowing full well Carissa wouldn't know where to turn. "Chapter three."

Carissa blinked. Everyone was quiet.

"You drifted off, again," Sean said and returned his eyes to his black, leather-bound bible.

"Sorry," Carissa whispered. *Dammit. I hate drifting off. I'm off my meds. It's not my fault!*

She looked down at the page and hesitated. It was strange

not reading a book from the beginning. She didn't understand how you could just pick up at what looked like the seventy-percent mark. *It's almost over! It's like, hey, let's ignore the first chapters of Harry Potter. Let's start off with them playing music to the three-headed dog and sneaking past him. Or, let's start off in Twilight where Bella's hanging out with the Cullens as they're playing baseball. Maybe I should wait until they start at the beginning again.*

Just read!

What time is it?

What does it matter? Just read.

Carissa almost reached for her cellphone, but didn't, because the others would see her and wonder what the heck she was doing.

Why am I so hesitant to read? Why am I procrastinating? By the time I start, they're all going to be finished and will start the lesson. I'm going to miss stuff. Whatever that stuff is. I don't know what I'm missing. I don't know what I'll miss.

So, read it.

Okay, fine. But now, I'm worried. This hesitance to read could be a problem when I start college classes in January. I know it's because I'm off my meds. I just know it. This feels like a weird déjà vu. Like, I remember not being able to sit down and focus. My mind wandered and wandered. Like now. I want to look at the page. I do. The very moment I need to do one thing, my mind drifts and I start thinking about people, family, what I'm going to eat, what I ate, the fact that I have to work out pregnant. What's it going to be like working out while pregnant? I mean, how much can I work out? Is it okay for the baby? No matter what, I'm going to get fat. Am I going to get fat? Am I supposed to? I mean. I'll have the growing baby in my womb. Obviously, that'll stick out. I know I have to eat more for the baby. That's one thing Amy talked about. I have to start eating more and not be so reluctant to eat foods with fat. My baby needs healthy fats.

Ugh. I don't want to get fat! This is terrible. I just want to stay thin and beautiful. This pregnancy thing is seriously going to ruin my chances of getting a boyfriend. I mean, if I want to meet someone, I should do it now before I get fat. Once I have a baby and am taking classes and squeezing in some golf or tennis, when will I have time to meet someone? How can I possibly date? Who wants to date a tired, single, ginger girl with leagues of long hair and a baby in her arms? I mean, you have the pretty, blue-eyed and blonde princess looking girls like Val out there. Runway model type brunettes like Fiona. Crazy beautiful black girls like the Cole sisters. I mean, everything's full with these girls. Full lips. Full chests. Full butts. But not fat butts. Like, the good fit kind of full butts. Then, you have me. Bone and muscle. Not bad really, I suppose. I'm fit. That's attractive. My c-cups are such late bloomers, like Mom's, supposedly. She said she grew a full cup at early seventeen. I hope it's that and not just a pregnancy thing. They should have blossomed four years ago—

Wasn't she supposed to be reading?

Crap. I drifted again. Okay. I'm reading. I'm reading this time. Seriously. Let's see, Matthew three, right? Okay. Let's do this. Let's read, baby. It's reading time mother-lovers! Matthew three. Matthew three. Okay. Matthew three.

3

"So, what did you think?" Gabby asked as they filed out of the youth worship center.

Carissa smiled. "I think Sean must really like you three to sing in public."

The Cole sisters laughed.

Sean glared. "Yea, well, you're no Taylor Swift, yourself."

"I don't know," Rebecca said. "I think she sounded pretty good. There might be a place for her in youth choir."

I don't know if I'm that good. But I sound amazing in the shower.

"Yes," Gabby agreed. "You're right. I like that. When we get a chance, I'll introduce you to the youth choir director and worship minister."

I just got here, and you already have me joining the choir?

"We're in youth choir," Hannah chimed in. *Of course, you are. It sounded like I was surrounded by Destiny's Child.* "We can teach you some songs."

Rebecca gasped. Her eyes grew wide. "Yes! You can come to our place. We'll go to the basement and sing. There's a karaoke machine with gospel songs loaded in there, as well as popular secular songs. We would have a blast." She vibrated with enthusiasm. "We'll sing the songs with you. Get you practiced. Train that pretty voice of yours."

You have a karaoke machine? That's cool. I'm not usually one to sing around others. I've done karaoke once. Fortunately, it was a song I knew. So, I killed it. Hmm. I suppose in a way that's kind of cheating, but eh. Why would I humiliate myself? If I'm going to sing in front of people, I'm going to sing a song I know, and well. I'll have that song memorized so all I have to worry about is not looking like a jackass.

"Yea," Carissa agreed. "That sounds like fun."

Wait. I think we're all getting a little ahead of ourselves. I haven't agreed to come back here. I'm just checking this place out because you invited me. And, you're fun. And, well, to be completely honest, I don't know where else to go. Oh. That's a depressing thought.

"But, uh," Carissa amended, "let's see how this visit goes first, okay? For all I know, I might not even be applicable to join, considering my condition."

The Cole sisters stared at her blankly. Hannah frowned. "What's that supposed to mean?"

"Yea, what do you mean?" Rebecca and Gabby said in unison and then looked at each other.

What do I mean? I hadn't thought about it until it popped out of my mouth. But this is a church. And I am a pregnant teenager out of wedlock. Sooner or later, if I join and come regularly, I'm going to start showing. People are going to start asking questions.

"Well, I mean," Carissa started. She looked around and lowered her voice. They were in the community area, surrounded by a mix of well and casually-dressed people shaking hands, smiling, hugging, and engaged in pleasant conversation. There was no way anyone was eavesdropping. Nevertheless, she wasn't going to take any chances. "You know. My, uh, situation." She looked around again. "Won't they have a problem with me, a teenager, not married, being pregnant?"

"No," Hannah said plainly. "It wasn't your fault. They shouldn't have a problem with you. Jesus wouldn't."

"This is a place for everyone," Gabby said. "Everyone's had uncomfortable, unexpected circumstances. Everyone has a past before Christ. It's called a testimony. This is yours."

Everyone wasn't raped and humiliated and stuck with a pregnancy and the hardest decision you'll ever have to make. From what I've heard, Christians aren't necessarily the most open-minded and welcoming people when it comes to pregnancy outside of wedlock.

But I will give you credit. You've been nothing but nice to me. Your whole family has. You haven't said a single negative thing to me.

"Okay," Carissa asked. "But, does this mean I have to tell them how I got pregnant? About Kent?"

"Eek." Rebecca grimaced and pulled her hand away from Sean's.

Sean let go. "Sorry. Every time I hear his name—"

Hannah frowned. "You don't have to tell them a thing unless you want to. We're all here for you when you need us." *When, not if?* "But it's none of their business how you got pregnant. Or that you're pregnant."

"There won't be a problem," Gabby assured her. "Don't worry about it. What we are most concerned with is your salvation through Jesus Christ."

Whatever that means.

Hannah wagged her finger. "Don't lie to her. There may be a problem. You know it's gossip central up in here. Makes me sick." She paused. "Cari, don't say more than you have to. Don't feel compelled to answer. Until you absolutely trust someone, don't tell them anything private. Anything. And if they ask you a question you don't want to answer, say you don't want to talk about it or come get me. I will set them straight in a hurry. These people get in everybody's business."

Gabby shook her head. "She's so serious."

"Ooo, Han," Rebecca nudged Hannah. "It's ya boyfriend." She pointed.

Carissa looked, but had no idea who to look for. *What does he look like?*

Hannah slapped Rebecca's hand down. "Don't point!" She panicked and checked to see if they were spotted. "What if he sees you pointing at him?"

"He'll come over and ask why," Rebecca said while rubbing

her hand. "You have to talk to him in order for him to like you."
Girl has a point. "And you didn't have to hit me."

"Sorry," Hannah apologized. "But you almost—"

"Caramel latte!" A male voice announced.

Wait. What? Carissa turned to the voice and saw a dark-skinned bald man with a five-o'clock shadow. She immediately recognized him and gasped. *Oh my God! It's coffee shop guy.*

CHAPTER NINETEEN

Two months ago, Mom and Carissa surprised Amy Sanchez and her daughter, Sofia, with a birthday spa weekend. Mom got a suite at a nice hotel for the four of them. They ate room service, watched movies, sat in a jacuzzi, got hot stone massages, pedicures, and nail and hair treatments. The other three did most of the talking while Carissa listened, which made it a nice, relaxing weekend until they wanted to go dress shopping for Sofia's homecoming dance. Then it became awkward.

Sofia was invited by her new boyfriend, with whom she spent all her time. Carissa, on the other hand, was single and uninvited, except by suggestive pervs and creeps, and wanted to avoid the conversation.

When the three asked Carissa who invited her, when, why she rejected their advances, and what she was looking for, she said she was going to the bathroom and slipped out the back for a latte and scone. She didn't like any of those immature high school boys. She overheard their conversations at lunch. She knew the boys were sneakily taking pictures and sharing them with their friends. She didn't want to be another conquest dramatically dictated to 'the boys'. She didn't trust these guys. But she was lonely. She wanted somebody. Why couldn't she meet someone just a little bit more mature and together?

Next to the mall was a new coffee shop and café, Milk N' Tea. Their motto, "If you don't like flavor, you won't like us." Carissa loved them. Every brew was rich. They used two teabags for flavor and kick. Not one of her lattes felt weak or lacked substance. The service was excellent, with staff that didn't look like they wanted to stab themselves in the eyes with the stirrers she treated as straws. And best of all, drinks cost a third less than other franchises. Unfortunately, with good product, service, and prices, Milk N' Tea was always busy. *Always!* Even on Sunday afternoons, they had lines out the door.

They met on a Sunday. Coffee shop guy stood in front of her in line, laptop bag on his shoulder, reading emails on his phone. When it was his time to order, he said, "I'll have a caramel latte, medium, approximately one hundred and ten degrees, not too hot, but not iced or cold, and a blueberry scone."

Wait! Carissa stared at him shocked. "What the hell?"

He and the barista looked at her with confused frowns. He said, "What's wrong?"

"That's the exact same thing I was going to order," Carissa said. "Like, almost verbatim to what I was going to say."

"Really?" Coffee shop guy asked with raised eyebrows.

"Yes, really," Carissa said. "I like the caramel latte, but not burning my mouth like the rest of these crazy psychos." She pointed her thumb backwards at strangers. "I want it just a little warmer than room temperature. And, I was going to get a blueberry scone."

Coffee shop guy hmphed. "That's cool." He studied her for a second, blinked, and turned to the barista. "Make that two."

Carissa shook her head. "Oh no. You don't have to do that."

"I know," coffee shop guy said and pulled out his wallet. He swiped his card and accepted the receipt.

I know. Hmm. Smooth. Okay. He paid for my snack. Now what? Is he going to ask me to drink and eat with him? Do I want him to? Wait. What do I mean, "Do I want him to?" Of course, I do. He's cute. He has a nice athletic build. I wonder if he plays any sports or just works out. He has pretty eyes. I mean, for a guy. Is pretty the right adjective? Yea. I can say a guy has pretty eyes. Oh, I don't know. What was I thinking about? Oh, yea. Well, hmm. I'm curious about him now. He, he looks older than me. I mean, clearly, he is. I wonder by how much. He has, there's this, this confidence about him. I can tell he's grounded. Wait. I didn't respond.

"Umm, thanks." Carissa smiled.

Coffee shop guy smiled back and looked her straight in the

eye. "My pleasure."

Oh my! That smile. She swooned. *Ask me to sit with you. Ask me to sit with you. Ask me to sit with you.*

"Names," the barista asked.

Coffee shop guy looked to Carissa. She said her name. Then, he said, "Jay. J-A-Y. Though, the letter alone is fine if you want to save ink." The barista wrote the names on the cups. Jay extended his hand to Carissa. "It's nice to meet you, Carissa."

"Likewise, Jay." Carissa shook his hand. She was tempted to bat her eyelashes but remembered the last time she tried. She looked halfway retarded and one of her eyelashes stuck in her eye. She spent five minutes in the bathroom getting it out. When she returned, the guy was gone or fled.

Jay walked to the far end of the counter while the barista grabbed the blueberry scones.

"Are these for here or to go?" the barista asked.

"Mine's here," Jay said.

"For here," she said, gazed into his eyes.

Jay smiled again. "So," he glanced around the coffee shop, then back at her, "you here with someone?"

You. I'm here with you. Give me a reason to be here with you. Invite me to sit with you. Wait.

She checked the seating. It was a busy day to expect to find a place to sit. Couches were occupied. Chairs were filled. Tables were taken inside. There was only one table left on the patio. It had two chairs.

Oh universe. You set us up. You beautiful, beautiful universe. I don't usually believe in these things, but this has got to be—

"Destiny," Carissa said in her softest, dreamiest voice. She blinked. *Crap. I said that out loud. What the hell is wrong with me?* "I mean, no. I'm not here with anyone."

Not yet, anyway, assuming I didn't just scare you away. Ask me to sit with you. Ask me to sit with you. Ask. Does this work? Telepathy? If I repeat it again and again and again in my mind and focus on him, will he get the hint? Will he ask me to join him? Ask me to join you. Ask me to join you. Ask me to join you. Ask me to join you.

"Great," Jay said. "It looks like there's one table left outside. Would you like to join me?"

Hmm. So, if there were more tables, you wouldn't ask me to sit with you? I don't know how to respond now. I wanted him to ask me to join him because he wanted to join me. Not because there's only one table left. I suppose it would be awkward if we were both eating here and only one of us took it. Maybe he's just trying to not make it awkward. He was here first. He's being nice by letting me have it. Shit.

Two people got up, grabbed their items, and tossed their empty cups in the trash.

Well, there went that. Now there's a table in here. That's two tables. Two people looking to sit. I suppose that's that. He'll have his table. I'll have mine. Maybe it's not destiny after all.

"Looks like another table just opened up," Carissa said.

The joy on Jay's face vanished when he saw the new empty table. "Oh. Okay."

A wave of disappointment hit her like a train. *Oh. Oh wow. He really wanted to sit with me. Shit. I just ruined it. We were going to sit together, and it was going to be great. I mean, what else did we have in common besides our drink orders? I suppose we'll never know now.* She sighed. *Well, on the bright side, I didn't have to pay for my latte and scone.*

"Well, my invitation is still open, if you want to join me," Jay said as he handed her the blueberry scone on a small, ceramic plate.

"Sure," Carissa said. *Of course, I want to join you.*

"Great," Jay said. His whole face lit up. "Would you rather sit inside or outside?"

Now I'm being asked to make decisions? My head's still spinning off the fact that I'm about to sit down and talk to a cute stranger.

Carissa shrugged. "You decide."

"Okay," Jay said. "It's a beautiful day. Let's go outside."

Good choice.

They took their plates and drinks outside. He pulled out her chair. *Hmm. A gentleman.* And then sat in his own.

The view was parking lot, cars, and buildings, but the air was fresh, and the sun beamed on her face. Carissa leaned back, closed her eyes, and let the rays warm her skin.

"It's days like these that I love Virginia."

DAKOTA

Jay watched her, took a sip of his latte, and smiled. "I wholeheartedly agree. Are you a native?"

"No. I was born in Manhattan, raised in Connecticut."

"Ah. What brought you down here?"

"Umm," Carissa started. *This is always the awkward part. The part where I have to decide if I'll tell someone my dad lost his big money job and had to uproot the family. It always feels like a violation. Like I'm putting his business out there.* "My parents changed jobs when the market crashed. Some people talk about Wall Street and the economy crashing as if they have intimate knowledge of it. But they only know what they heard and saw on the news and read on the internet. My dad is an investment banker and analyst," Carissa said. "Banking kind of runs in our family. Or, at least, that's what my dad's trying to convince my little brother, Sean."

"Like father, like son?"

"Nah. Sean's more technical. He's great with computers and is always fidgeting with his own little gadgets. Anyway, what was I saying?" *Great. I'm babbling.* "Oh yea. When the market crashed, a lot of people lost their jobs. Offices closed. Some of the execs got thick paychecks, aka golden parachutes. My dad got the shaft." She paused. "Not literally."

"I would hope not," Jay said. "But it is Wall Street."

Damn, Jay. Carissa shuddered. That was *not* something she wanted to think about. "Anyway, he lost his lucrative job, some investments. After it was all over, he wanted to get out of there. There were a lot of people doing things they weren't supposed to do. Seeing it and what came of it turned his stomach against all of it."

"I can only imagine what they were up to in Wall Street," Jay said. "I've read articles and seen reports on the news. It's too bad little has changed and few were held responsible."

"Please. My dad could go on for hours about that if you let him. He knows how it all works."

Hmm. If he and I become a couple, he'll have to meet Dad. That could pose a huge problem. Dad's more than a little racist. I'm going to have to come up with a plan to change his opinion on black people. I suppose it would help if I knew someone black outside of Latoya and Daniella. Oh, and Ashley.

"But yea," she continued. "When Dad lost his job, he got depressed. He taught accounting for a while at the university, but things fell apart. I don't know what happened, but he had to quit. Mom saw the opening to accept an offer from a friend from college who wanted to start a literary consultation business. She already had clients and they were going to set up writer conferences throughout the mid-Atlantic region to acquire new talent. They work as agents, marketers, editors, content advisors, and offer additional services for those interested in self-publishing. She also wanted to be close to her best friend, my godmother, Amy. So, we moved to Virginia."

Jay leaned forward.

Hmm. I'm just talking and talking. Too much information? He's probably thinking I'm a lunatic or something.

"I hope I'm not talking too much."

Jay smiled. "No, you're great." He took a sip of his latte. "I'm listening. I want to know more. Please continue."

"Okay. It's just, umm, you gave me a look. Are you sure?"

"Yea, it's," Jay said and stopped. He mulled it over and then continued, "You said something that struck a chord."

Really? All I did was talk about my parents. "What did I say?"

"You told me what your mom does," Jay said. "I'm a writer."

Carissa blinked. "Oh, really?"

Holy cow! What are the odds that I would run into a writer at a coffee shop and hit it off? Well, actually, the chances of running into a writer at a coffee shop are about as good as running into an engineer at a construction site. But I mean, wow. Writers are Mom's favorite people. She said so herself. She'll like Jay immediately. Score! It's about time I met someone. Suck on that Sofia! You have a boyfriend and you're going to homecoming. Well, I just found a potential boyfriend, too. He's leagues ahead of yours. He's a writer!

"Yes, really," Jay said. He pointed to his laptop bag. "I come here to write. Coffee shops are the perfect atmosphere for me to process my thoughts. Sometimes I'll flesh out new scenes for my current novel or brainstorm new ideas for future novels. If I'm in a coffee shop, something's getting done. I have a queue of books I'm waiting to write thanks to places like this."

That matches what other writers have said. Whenever Mom

was at a release party for one of her clients, the family was invited. Carissa met many authors. They were all unique. There wasn't a single writer that was like the other. Their personalities went from polite and funny, to boastful and talkative, to inspiring but tight-lipped, to philosophical and angry. Some she could see herself talking to for hours. With others, she'd be bored to death. One crime author gave her the chills. Elaina Hawthorne, the self-proclaimed "Queen of Murder", spent so much time contemplating and talking about necessary details of murder, Carissa wondered if she'd committed one. Or wanted to.

"What kind of books do you write? What genre?"

"Everything," Jay said, "but mostly action and adventure, fantasy, superhero stuff, and a little sci-fi. I'm working on a series of novellas, which are about one-fifty pages each. They focus on the origins of my characters. Each novella starts by giving a little piece of the present, with interactions between the five connected to the plot of the main novel. Then, it flashes to how that character attained powers, and their introductions to the group. After all the hero origin novellas are put together, I'll either write one novella for the big bad, or include the villain's origin story in the main novel's storyline."

"Wow," Carissa leaned in. "That's a major endeavor. How long do you think all of it is going to take? How many books have you written so far?"

"Seven, total, are published," Jay said. "Two of my novellas are in the final phases and scheduled to release several months apart. So far, it's taken a year to write and edit both novellas. Each are a little over half the size of the average novel. It's exciting, considering how long my previous works took, and the fact that I split time between writing and involvement with the church."

Church. Oh man. He's one of those. But we can get past that. Nobody's perfect.

"Do you go to church?" Jay asked.

"No," Carissa said. "My grandparents on my mom's side do. Grandma's devout. But not my mom. And not me. It's not really our thing. We don't believe in all that stuff. But my dad's a Buddhist."

"Oh," Jay said and shifted his eyes to his scone and caramel latte.

Crap. Is this one of his deal-breakers? Is he one of those people where you must be in his religion to date? Gah! I was so close to happiness.

"But I mean, it's no big deal, right?" Carissa panicked. "We have different beliefs. I respect yours. You respect mine. And, I wouldn't be opposed to visiting your church, ya know, just to umm, be social and meet your friends and such."

What am I saying? Now I'm sounding desperate. Ahh! Because I am! I hate this. This is terrible. I'm already attached. I get attached so easily. This has been nice. It's been nice talking to him, even if it's been short and I'm totally blowing things out of proportion. I just, I don't know. I want this to work. I need this to work.

"Ya know, the more I think about it," Carissa started, not sure why her mouth still moved, but let it speak anyway. "I'm totally willing to learn all about it, if you're willing to teach me. Maybe there's more to it than what I've heard, and I just need someone to explain it to me."

"Really?" Jay's eyebrows rose. "You'd be willing to come and learn about my faith?"

Wait. What have I done? Does this mean I'm going to church now? Did I just commit myself to that? No, Carissa! No!

"Yea, sure," Carissa said and took a sip of her latte.

Oh my god! What are you saying, Carissa? I don't want to go to church. Then again, I didn't say how often I'd go. I can go, meet his friends, get an idea of who he is through them, and then, maybe kinda go once a month, maybe less. And this can work. There's a benefit to this. When we have kids, I can rely on him to take them to church. That's guaranteed silence for a couple hours. I can have some alone time. I can sleep from midnight until noon if I want to. Ooo. Yes. Sleep. That idea alone is reason enough to only date church guys.

"Great," Jay said. "You'll love it there. The people are really nice." He hesitated. "Well, most of the people are nice. The atmosphere is guest friendly. There's no dress code, except common sense like, come dressed and don't show off too much cleavage or any booty cheek."

Carissa laughed. *Any booty cheek. Sounds reasonable.* "I don't know. That sounds restricting. If I can't show off a full cheek, there has to be a least some booty cleavage."

Jay chuckled. "We'd encourage you to wear a long cardigan, at least until you got outside."

They laughed together. It was refreshing. Carissa felt so alive and excited that she almost wanted to cry. But no way would she allow random happy tears to ruin this perfect moment. She held them back.

After the laughter ceased, they each took a sip of their lattes and enjoyed a prolonged gaze into each other's eyes. Jay ruined the moment by asking a question she dreaded answering, "So, you told me that your dad was or is into investment banking, and your mom is in the book business, but what do you do? Are you taking classes?"

Carissa sipped her coffee. *Okay. I'm still in high school. It's no big deal. We can make it work. I mean, what, I'll be eighteen in a little over nine months, right? Yea. No biggie. But what if it is a biggie? What if he ends the conversation? What if this is a deal-breaker for him?*

Shouldn't it be?

Well, yea, kind of. I mean. I don't want a guy that's just going around cruising for high school girls. But, at the same time, he's cool so far. And I engaged him, right? Ugh! I want to see where this goes. I want to talk to him more and see if this can be something real. Which leaves me with the question: how do I answer?

"Umm, well, outside of amateur golf tournaments, I don't do anything for work, yet, but will be starting something—not sure what that will be—in January," Carissa said. She took a breath and watched his reaction. "I'm taking classes. I graduate in May."

"Nice! Congrats!"

"Yea, thanks," Carissa said and grinned. "I'm not sure which university I'm going to after that. I'm certain I'll be studying psychology. The human mind is, well, a mess." She said and chuckled.

Jay nodded. "Yes. It is; isn't it?"

"I really want to figure it out," Carissa said. "Figure out what causes people to act the way they do."

"You and the rest of us," Jay said. "There's an old book that answers that, but psychology is a fascinating field. I considered that, among other things, before sticking with my natural gift." He paused, blinked. "So, are you considering staying in-state or are you pursuing a master's program out of state?"

Oh. Master's program. No. Crap. I'm going to have to spell it out, aren't I? I mean, I was being indirect about it. But now, I just have to bite the bullet and say, "I'm in high school." Then, that'll be it. Or will it? I forget. Helena, Katelyn, Jessica Yu, Coleen, and Christine are all eighteen because their birthdays are later in the year. Just because you're in high school, it doesn't mean you're not legal. But, obviously, I'm not.

It's best to tell it like it is. Dammit.

"No, not masters, bachelor's," Carissa said. "I'm graduating high school in May and then starting college in August or September, depending on where I land." She took a deep breath as she registered shock on his face. He swallowed hard and grew tense. "I'm, umm, pretty sure I'll be in-state, though." She grinned. "We can't afford out of state tuition since a nice chunk of my college fund went up in smoke with the rest of my dad's investments during the economic big bang. But, eh." She waved her hand.

If I keep talking, this will work itself out. Just keep on talking. Keep on talking.

"There are plenty of colleges in Virginia," Carissa continued. "So, I'm not bummed out about limited options. I mean, I'm still applying in Connecticut and New York. You know, just in case a miracle happens and we trip over some extra tuition money or a scholarship. I play golf, tennis, and swim competitively as a backup." Jay's eyebrows perked up. *Yay! I did it. Keep on talking.* "Plus, I can play the piano and violin somewhat decently, and speak French, Japanese, some Spanish, a little Gaelic, and tiny bit of German."

"Wow!" Jay said. "You can speak five languages? That's amazing." He leaned forward. "I guess you're part Japanese?"

"Yea," Carissa said. "My grandma, on my dad's side, is from Japan. Born and raised. She moved to the UK and married my grandpop. They raised their family there before moving to the States for a job. Eventually, my grandparents moved back to the UK, but not before my dad got my mom pregnant. And three months later, he married my mom."

I'm just going to keep on talking.

"My grandpop's dad was French, his mom German. So, that's where the other bits come in. And, on my mom's side, we're pretty much Scottish and English heritage. That explains the red hair and freckles."

"I love freckles," Jay said and admired her.

"Really?" Carissa felt warm all over and blushed. "Great. Well, there's a lot of them to love."

They gazed into each other's eyes until Jay said something she didn't want to hear, "So, Carissa, you're in high school—"

"For seven months," Carissa interjected.

"Seven months," Jay said. He breathed and thumbed his fingers. "Okay. Here's what we can do. Let's keep talking, because I like talking to you."

"I like talking to you, too," Carissa said. She folded her hands on her lap so he couldn't see her trembling. *I'm so scared of what you're going to say next.*

Jay reached in his back pocket and pulled out a business card. "I'm going to write down my number. We can talk or text whenever you want over the phone." He wrote down his number. "I'm also going to write down the name of my church." He wrote down the name of his church, Kingdom First Trinitan Church. "You're always welcome there. I'm there every Sunday, unless I'm on vacation. So, if you decide after we're done talking today that you want to see me again and learn about my faith, come see me at church."

The last place I want to be.

"If you ever want to chat, about anything, at any time, even if it's a rant about bad drivers or old Chinese food in the back of the refrigerator—" *That was me the day before yesterday! It's like you're reading my soul. Like seriously. Who pushed it back there?* "—give me a call. I'm here for you." *Are you serious? Is he serious?* "We can be friends. Good friends. Great friends. And, after you're done with high school, and are of appropriate age, if you want to see me personally, privately again, like this, you can."

Sigh. *What do I say? Yes? No? What other choice do we have? I mean, I was totally up for sneaking around. Who would know? But, he isn't. Does it mean he doesn't like me? He doesn't like me enough to bend a little rule.*

I want a boyfriend, dammit! Can he be my boyfriend and not see me? Well, I suppose, in a way, we would be long distance. Short distance but long distance, at least until July. And I suppose, if I wanted to, I could see him at his church. That would require me to go to church. Ugh, gag, what a choice. I can't believe this. It was right here. I was this close to having a handsome, writer boyfriend. It felt so perfect. All ruined because I'm nine months too young.

"I'm sorry," Jay said. He didn't look sorry as he took a sip of his latte.

"No, it's fine," Carissa said. "I understand."

Do I? Do I understand why he doesn't want me?

"When's your birthday, anyway?" Jay asked. He seemed unphased by her disappointment. *What was his problem?*

"July," she mumbled.

"Shut the front door," Jay said. A smile grew. *Shut the what?* "Mine too! I was born in July. What are the odds?"

Carissa shrugged. *I don't know, one out of twelve?* "Yea, crazy."

Okay. Fine. I'll be your friend, dammit. If this is a sign, I'll take it. Let's be friends. But when I turn eighteen, you better not pussy foot around this. I want you to come at me like you want it.

"So, friend," Carissa said and allowed herself to relax and return a smile of her own. "What do you want to talk about?"

Two hours, three missed calls, and five ignored texts later, they parted ways. Carissa smiled the biggest smile she'd ever smiled when he hugged her. She hoped for a kiss, but knew it was a no-go. She wanted him to break the rules, but also liked him for having enough self-discipline to not.

Two days later, she planned to give him a call, but couldn't find the business card he gave her. She cried.

CHAPTER TWENTY

I never thought I'd see you again. Carissa beamed. "Oh my God! Jay!"

"Carissa, I'm glad you finally came," Jay said and gave her a hug. The Cole sisters exchanged a look.

Sweet, sweet-sweet-sweet! He smells nice. Is that cologne, body wash, aftershave? Carissa smiled so hard her cheeks hurt. "Me, too."

"I had a great time talking to you," Jay said. "When I didn't hear from you, I assumed you weren't interested."

"I, uh, lost your business card."

You should have asked for my phone number. Then, we could have stayed in contact.

Jay smirked. "Figures. Well, now that you're here, we'll have to exchanged numbers. That way, it's programmed into your phone." He pulled out his phone. "What's your number?"

Gabby gasped. Hannah and Rebecca stared.

Carissa recited her number without hesitation and grabbed her phone. When his phone called hers, she saved his number. "Jay Canus, right?"

"The one and only," Jay said. "That I've heard of. If you meet any others, let me know. There can be only one." He swiped with an invisible sword.

Carissa laughed. *I miss your dark sense of humor. It's funny how he can be such a sweet, down to earth, nice guy, but then have these random moments where he'll joke about chopping someone's head off. It's kind of perfect, as long as it's just a joke.*

"So," Jay extended his hands to the church, "how do you like it here so far?"

Carissa shrugged. "I haven't been here long enough to form a real opinion. But it's a fine place and the people are nice." She nudged her head towards the Cole sisters.

The people are nice? The people are nice? That's not a good way to describe your friends. What am I talking about?

"I mean, they're the best," she corrected. "Those three invited me here and umm, got me this, umm," she reached in her purse and pulled out her bible, "pink bible with my name engraved in it." She held it up and pointed at it. "It's engraved!"

"Wow. Engraved." Jay admired the bible's engraving. "Nice job, ladies. Thanks for getting her here."

The Cole sisters didn't say a word but stared at him and Carissa.

"Alrighty then," Jay said, returned his attention to Carissa. "Anyway, this is a great day for you to come. I'm speaking."

"You're what?" Carissa asked. "You're a speaker here? You didn't tell me you spoke at the church."

Is he like, secretly a preacher or pastor or priest or something and he's not telling me?

"Well," Jay said. "I'm not the pastor. He usually speaks. However, once in a while, the Holy Spirit puts something on my heart to offer the body of Christ, or they'll tap me on the shoulder when Pastors Brown and Wilkins want the weekend off. At least, for now, until we get more speakers."

I'm sorry. You lost me. The what of Christ? You guys have his body?

"Under pastoral supervision, we're giving select members an opportunity to address the body, share knowledge and wisdom The Lord's provided." *You're going to put a dress on a body? I'm obviously missing something.* "A more involved and constantly learning and growing church will be a greater, more beneficial church to its community."

"That's interesting." *I clearly have no idea what he's talking about. It can't be how it sounds. I'm missing something. I must be. I'm just not understanding what he's talking about. That's it. That's right.*

"I'm sorry." Jay smiled. *I miss that smile.* "You probably have no idea what I'm saying."

He might be reading my mind.

"Guilty as charged." Carissa smiled back at him. *I'm so glad I used that new complete treatment toothpaste. I'm smiling like an idiot. But my teeth are sparkling. Ping! Sparkling! Hoo-ha-ha-ha-ha!* "I have no idea what you're talking about."

"You will," Jay said. "If you're willing to learn, I can go through all of it with you." He snapped his fingers. "In fact, I'll go through some of it on the stage today. I might break script a little bit. Or a lot. However, the lesson today is on baptism. It won't make much sense out of context."

"You don't have to do that," Carissa said.

"I know," Jay said. *There he goes with that "I know" again.* "Baptism is important. And understanding why we get baptized is important. If you don't know why we get baptized, if you don't know the story and history of sin and why we need repentance and salvation, then what good is a lesson in baptism?"

"Alright," Carissa said and twirled her hair with her finger. "Okay. Well, umm, I can't wait to hear it."

"Cool," Jay said. "You won't have to wait long." He peaked his head over the crowd of church members and shielded his eyes with his hands. "I'm going to go run this over with Mike and prepare for the lesson. Sit in the front. I'd like to be able to see you."

He wants to see me! Eat that world!

"Okay, sure," Carissa said. She looked to the Cole sisters, who whispered amongst themselves. "I'll see where they're sitting and try to get us near the front."

"Great," Jay said. "I don't know what you have planned for today. If you can linger after the service, there's someone very special to me I'd like you to meet."

Wait. What? Who? Who's this special person?

"See ya later," Jay said and rushed off.

Carissa watched him leave. *Crap. Get back here! Who's this special person?*

"What was that?" Gabby asked, accused.

That's what I'm trying to figure out.

"Umm," Carissa said. She watched Jay disappear into the crowd. "Oh, nothing." She smiled. "Just, just Jay. Running into Jay.

I did not expect to see him here. I totally forgot the name of the church he went to. This is such a great coincidence."

"Coincidence," Hannah grumbled. "Hmm."

Right. There are no coincidences. This is destiny.

"How do you know him?" Rebecca asked as she inched herself between Carissa and Hannah.

"Oh, I met him at a coffee shop," Carissa said with a soft voice and blushing cheeks. "It was kind of romantic, really. He was in front of me in line and ordered the exact same thing I was going to order. Like, exact-exact, from the way he liked the drink all the way to the same flavored scone. I was so shocked; I made an outburst." She laughed. The Cole sisters looked at each other. "And then, he looked at me like I was a big weirdo. I told him he ordered the same thing I was going to order, verbatim. And get this." She allowed a dramatic pause. "He bought my order for me."

"Really," Hannah mumbled, burning a hole through Carissa's head with her eyes. *You okay?*

"Yep!" Carissa said. "After that, we introduced ourselves and ended up sitting together, talked for hours. It was great." She beamed.

"I see," Hannah said, arms crossed. *Seriously. What's up your butt? We didn't do anything inappropriate. At least, not yet.*

Gabby put her hand on Hannah's shoulder. "Hey, let's go get our seats before it starts to fill up. You know people like to claim seats like they own the place. Where's Sean?"

"Talking to Elijah," Rebecca said and pointed.

Sean saw her pointing at him and waved her over.

"Seriously, Becca!" Hannah fumed with tight fists. "Maybe if you weren't pointing so much, we would have gone unnoticed and none of this would have happened." She stormed off.

Rebecca frowned. "Don't blame me for this."

She clearly doesn't like pointing. Carissa watched. "What's her problem?"

Gabby bit her lower lip. "You know the guy she has a thing for?"

"No," Carissa said. "Rebecca pointed at him. But I never saw him. Jay came over."

"Jay is the guy Rebecca was pointing at," Gabby said and

facepalmed. "He's the guy Hannah likes. She's been gaga about him for two years now."

Oh. Crap. Well, sucks to be her. He's mine, now.

2

Entering the worship room, Carissa lost her breath and stared. *Whoa.*

It was vast, resembling a concert hall of a grand theater. Tall and curved white walls. Oakwood floors. Navy blue fabric chairs. It had three floors: the main, stage, and bottom floor. From the main entrance, a walkway stretched around the perimeter of the entire worship room with aisles for seating from top to bottom. Straight down from the main entrance was a wide, navy carpeted stairway that led to the lower and bottom floors and directly to the orchestra seating. Another walkway met the middle of the wide stairway and stretched around to the stage.

Per Gabby, when the chorus finished performing, they left the stage through that walkway and sat on the stage level. Chairs in the aisles adjoining the stage were color coded red.

On the bottom floor, at the epicenter to the stage, was an arched orchestral pit with purple chairs and a walkway that split in the middle. At that opening was a small, navy carpeted stairway to the stage. On the stage was a single standing microphone and adjustable black chair with wheels. *That's where the pastor or speaking sits.*

Behind the pastor's chair, near the far back of the stage, was choir seating. *Where they sit while they perform.*

The stage, unlike the rest of the worship room, had steel framing. Carissa could tell there was something off about the middle of the stage. It had lines as though the middle section opened.

"Does your stage open in the middle?" Carissa asked as they walked down the main walkway to the bottom floor.

"You're observant," Rebecca said with raised eyebrows. "There's a baptism pool in there. They close it when it's not in use. And, they keep it concealed because the stage isn't used solely for our services." She explained that the worship room and church hosted independent theatre, orchestra, opera, and ballet productions, and had its own music school dedicated to their worship ministry. They accepted donations and charged for the use of the facility within the confines of non-profit tax law.

"Cool," Carissa said and followed the girls. She didn't have to convince them to sit in the front. It was where the youth normally sat. Bottom floor seating was reserved for orchestra (purple), speakers (purple), teens (red), and younger adults (red). It was believed that those in their teens and early twenties should be closer to the speaker and message, as they were the future leaders of the church and world. The further away they were from the message, the more distracted they could become. The stage floor was reserved for choir closest to the stage in purple seating, and designated handicapped spots next to side entrances, but everything else was navy blue and open.

Half of the worship room was full. The choir filed in one at a time, putting on white robes handed out by a shaggy-haired boy that looked oddly familiar. Carissa couldn't place where she saw him, only that it had something to do with Val. Val was the last person she wanted to think about, after Kent or Brian.

Everyone from the orchestra was in their seats, instruments in hand, flipping through their notes or prepping their instruments for play. There were thirty in total. Half of them looked to be between fifteen and twenty-two. Thirteen ranged from late twenties to early forties.

One gentleman looked to be in his elder years with wispy, long gray hair and a goatee that made him look like Gandalf. He held a black, V-shaped electric guitar with blue lightning painted on it. She wasn't sure what to expect but grabbed her phone just in case the old man felt inspired into a hardcore guitar solo.

The last member of the orchestra, at the keyboard, had to be a prodigy. He looked like Sean when he was eight.

"Do we have a little brother I don't know about?" Carissa asked Sean. Rebecca laughed. Apparently, she'd asked him a similar question.

"No," Sean said. "But when Dad saw him, he wanted to meet the parents. Apparently, Yoshi's granddad and our grandma are distant cousins or something."

Why didn't he introduce us? It would have been nice to know we have some more family here, as distant a relative as they may be.

"That's Yoshi," Rebecca said and almost pointed, but didn't. "He's amazing. Like a little Mozart." She pretended to play the keyboard with her hands. "His sister, Hoshi, had a birthday party. We were invited over to their house. They have this beautiful grand piano. He played for us."

Gabby chimed in, "After you insisted."

Rebecca rolled her eyes. "Yea, whatever."

"He wasn't even finished with his cake," Gabby said. "We might not get invited back."

"He played, didn't he?" Rebecca said. "Hoshi loves me. She's over there with the violin. I keep telling my sisters we should sign up for the music school and become legendary musicians, but they're lame."

You're good singers. Why not start there?

Hannah turned her head. "What are you talking about? *I'm in band.* I play the flute, clarinet, and now saxophone. How many instruments do you want me to play? It's not like I have time for either with volunteering at the hospital, tutoring here, and studying."

Gabby rested her hand on Hannah's shoulder. "Chill. She's obviously talking about me, because I refused to go, you can't go, and one of us has to drive her."

Wow. You girls are busier than I am, err, or was, before I got pregnant. Ugh! Now that I'll have to cut sports out of my schedule, I suppose I could invest more time in the violin. That'll be the fun part of my schedule: violin, maybe keyboard since it involves sitting on my butt, college classes, homework, and a part-time job, if I can find one that doesn't mind hiring a pregnant teenager.

The lights dimmed as they found their seats. Carissa sat on the end. Gabby next to her. Sean next to Gabby. Rebecca next to Sean. Hannah next to Rebecca.

Yoshi opened the service with Chopin's Etude Opus 25. Carissa gasped. All eyes in the worship room turned to the young boy playing his heart out. His hands moved fast. His face tense and focused. The lights over the choir gradually brightened. That's when Yoshi transitioned to How Great Thou Art. Not long afterward, a display over the stage showed the name of the song and its lyrics. The church sang along.

CHAPTER TWENTY-ONE

After worship, prayer, and a few announcements from the associate pastor, the pastor came on stage. He was a heavier set man, short, with dark brown hair and glasses. A noticeable tan circled around his eyes. He started the service with a joke about falling asleep outside on his patio.

"I'm thirty-years behind on sleep," Pastor Mike Brown said. "My kids wouldn't let me. They made a mission of it. That being said. I shouldn't have declined the opportunity to have my grandkids over. They're just like their parents." He waved at his kids. "This never would have happened."

There was more playful commentary and the passing around of the collection plates before Pastor Brown introduced Jay Canus as a trusted friend, man of character, and appreciated leader in the church. The congregation clapped.

Wow. Appreciated leader.

Jay stood from his purple chair and walked on stage. He put his hands together, offered a respectful and short bow to the congregation, and then firmly shook Pastor Brown's hand. When the pastor was seated, Jay walked to the microphone, put his notes, bottled water, and black leather bible on a holder attached to the microphone stand, and spoke.

"Thank you, everyone, for your warm welcome. Thank you, Pastor Brown, for encouraging me to speak today. I'm not a big fan of public speaking. I say that every time I'm up here. For some reason, I keep expecting to forget what I was going to say or a clown to run behind me and pull down my pants during the lesson." The congregation laughed. "For me, public speaking was always a struggle. So, being up here is both a challenge and an honor. Thank you for giving me a chance to stretch my comfort zone."

The congregation clapped.

"Pastor Brown said it's good to open up with a joke. And, I could think of no greater joke, than when he called me a friend."

The congregation stirred and exchanged whispers. Jay started to pace.

"Prior to suggesting I speak on baptism, he invited me and a guest to his house for dinner. We showed up, promptly, at seven. Probably one of the few times I've shown up anywhere promptly, thanks to my guest. Dierdre, our pastor's wife, was in the kitchen pulling the chicken out of the oven. The dining table was set. Pastor Brown says, 'Come rest in the family room for a moment while we wait.' So, we sit on the couch and start talking. He stops us and says, 'Hold on. I'd like to introduce your guest to a dear friend of ours,' and points towards the hallway."

He stopped for a dramatic pause.

"We turn around curious, because there was no mention of anyone else joining us for dinner. And we see a brown and gold cat." The congregation laughed, Pastor Brown especially.

"He said, 'This is Wallace. How's it going, Wallace?'"

"My guest looked at me and said, 'His friend is a cat.'"

"I chuckled, because that was the last thing I expected.

"She said, 'If that cat talks back, I'm leaving you here.'"

The congregation erupted in laughter.

"I tell you: I have never seen the pastor laugh as hard as he did that night, at that moment." Jay chuckled. "You really got us there."

Pastor Brown laughed.

Jay smiled and waited for the congregation to finish laughing before continuing. "So, this is our third week in the Matthew series. Each week, in Sunday school, we're going through a chapter of the book of Matthew, verse by verse. Then, here in the worship room, we hit a major theme within the chapters. In the first week, we touched on free will versus pre-destination and how it correlates with the genealogy of Jesus Christ, as well as the fulfillment of God's promises. The second week, we touched on listening to God when He communicates with us and obedience. This week, we're on Matthew three, the introduction of the baptism of John. The baptism of repentance. Today, we'll dive into the meaning of baptism. Why do we get baptized? What does the bible say about baptism? And time permitting, I'll explain why we do full immersion baptism and not sprinklings.

"Now." Jay raised his finger. "Before I talk about baptism, I have to start at the very beginning. Some of you are visiting this church, hearing this message, for the first time. A friend who's visiting this church today comes to mind." He looked directly at Carissa.

He mentioned me. He's talking about me!

"It's important that I share the gospel from creation to Christ. After all, what is baptism without context?"

The congregation clapped in agreement.

Jay took a sip from his bottled water. "In the beginning, there was God. Our Creator. Our Father. Our Architect. The perfect, all-knowing, all-powerful diviner of everything there ever was. There was nothing created that was not created by God through His Word. God created the heavens and the earth. He defined the rules of existence and space and time. There was no life without God who created it. The universe and its various dimensions were shaped and formed. Planets, stars, nebulae, black holes, and other astronomical phenomena were of His vision.

"In Genesis, chapter one, verses one and two, God created the heavens and earth. And the Spirit of God was hovering over the face of the waters. In John, chapter one, versus one through three: 'In the beginning was the Word, and the Word was with God, and the Word was God. He was in the beginning with God. All things were made through Him, and without Him was not any thing made that was made.' So, as we begin the introduction of creation, it is important to note that we have God and the Word. In the bible, He and they are referred to as Lord God, Adonai Elohim. Individual but collective consciousness.

"Now, throughout the first chapter of Genesis, God speaks everything into existence, which coincides with the gospel according to John. Through God's Word, everything was created. God's Word is so powerful, it is life, it is alive, and anything spoken by God is. Where there was darkness, He spoke light into existence, and divided them, and created the very concept of night and day, on the first day. On the second day, God spoke the expanses of heaven into existence. He created a division between the planet and the expanse, what we understand to be our atmosphere. A shield of gases, particles, and energy that protects us from the vacuum of space, radiation, and the sorts. What the bible calls the expanse of heaven, we call space. You know, the final frontier."

There were chuckles amongst the congregation.

"Thank you, *Star Trek* fans. I knew I wasn't alone." Another sip of water.

"On the third day, God spoke the land and seas, and various forms of vegetation on the land and in the seas. On the fourth day, God spoke lights in the expanse of the heavens. A greater light rules the day. A lesser light rules the night. On the fifth day, God spoke swarms of living creatures both small and large in the waters, and swarms of birds of many kinds to fly above the earth. On the sixth day, God spoke living creatures—that includes livestock, creeping things, and beasts—into being. And God saw all that was spoken into being was good.

"Now, on the sixth day, God also spoke, aka created, man. Look at Genesis, chapter one, verse twenty-six, 'Let us make man in our image, after our likeness.' Note: Our image. Our likeness. Plural. 'And let them have dominion over the fish of the sea and over the birds of the heavens and over the livestock and over all the earth and over every creeping thing that creeps on the earth.' So, God created man in his own image. Male and female He created them.

"Before everyone goes to sleep wondering when we're going to get to baptism, I see you yawning. We'll get there." There were chuckles. "We put out coffee and water every Sunday morning. I'm not having that in here."

Jay smiled. "God created man in His image, formed man of the dust of the ground, and breathed the breath of life into his nostrils. Raise your hand if you needed that breath this morning." Half the congregation raised their hand. "From that breath, man became a living soul. God also planted a beautiful garden in Eden full of the finest trees, pleasant for the eyes and good for food, and put man in the garden. God also planted the tree of life, and tree of knowledge of good and evil.

"In Genesis, chapter two, verses sixteen and seventeen, God told man, 'You may surely eat of every tree of the garden, but of the tree of the knowledge of good and evil you shall not eat, for in the day that you eat of it you shall surely die.' God then brought every beast and bird to Adam. And whatever Adam named them, that's what they were to be called. God then created woman from a rib of man.

"Fast forward, you have Adam and Eve in the garden. Enter the serpent, a crafty creature. He asked the woman, 'Did God actually say, "You shall not eat of any tree in the garden?"' She responds that they can eat the fruit of every tree of the garden except the tree in the midst of the garden. Neither shall you touch it, or else you'll die.

"Now, I could go into detail about why one should be amiss about that last bit, but we can talk about that later, when I'm not pressed for time.

"The serpent says you will not surely die. God knows that, when you eat the fruit, your eyes will be opened and you'll be like God, knowing good and evil. Now, by saying this, the serpent calls God a liar, lies himself, and implies that God's holding out on them. You know how this story ends. Eve gets the fruit, eats some of it, and passes it on to Adam who was there with her. Then, both of their eyes are opened. And thus, sin is introduced into the world.

"Now, you might be thinking to yourself, 'Well, surely they did not die.' Now, God didn't say they would immediately die after the first bite. He said they would surely die, because the moment they sinned, he had to deny them eternal life and they would thusly grow old and die. God was telling the truth. Now, the wage of sin is death. Sin is disobedience to God. Sin separates us from God. Separation from God is a spiritual death. The moment they ate fruit from the tree of knowledge of good and evil, they were spiritually cut off from God. God is good and pure and life. Sin is evil and filthy and death. It's a deadly spiritual poison that corrupts and taints everything. And because Adam had dominion over all the beasts and birds and creeping things and livestock and over the earth, everything Adam had dominion over was also corrupted by his sin. When they sinned against God, they tainted their own flesh and souls.

"Now, as I said, because they sinned, they were denied fruit from the tree of life. That fruit would have given them immortality. God never said they couldn't eat from that tree. He only said they couldn't eat from the tree of knowledge of good and evil. But, once they sinned. Once they believed the word of a beast, of a serpent, over God, they lost their opportunity for eternal life. Otherwise, their sin nature would be eternal. They lost it that day, bad. They had a choice between life and death. But because of the craftiness of the serpent, because the fruit of the tree of knowledge of good and evil was appealing to the eye, because they did not trust and obey God, they chose death.

"And sin has been the state of the world since. After Adam and Eve were cast out of the garden of Eden, they had children. Cain, Abel, Seth, and others. Cain killed Abel. Cain was cast out and had children with his wife elsewhere. Those children had children. And many descendants of his bloodline and Seth's did many depraved things. Some of them walked with God, as in, lived a life in consistent relationship and alignment with God, but many didn't. The world became so depraved that God regretted creating man and decided to wash the world clean of men, animals, birds, creeping things, everything. God planned to wash away the sin of the world. You could almost say, God planned the world's first baptism. But Noah found favor in God's eyes.

"And so the legacy of men continued. Though the world was washed clean of men, except for a few, Noah and his wife and children and children's wives were still biological and spiritual descendants of Adam, still tainted by sin. But God had a plan for man's salvation.

"Of the descendants of Noah, he chose Abraham. Through Abraham, and his son Isaac, and Isaac's son Jacob, God created a people, a holy nation, to call His own. Israel. A nation of kings and priests and prophets that would introduce God's law and Word to mankind. Through Abraham's lineage would come a savior. From Jacob came Joseph, Judah, and Levi. By God's will, Joseph brought the sons of Jacob to Egypt, saving them from a dreadful famine. God used Moses, a descendant of Levi, a descendant of Jacob, to save the people of Jacob from slavery and oppression in Egypt, from where they took many riches. From God, Moses received the law. God created a mighty and prosperous nation through King David, a descendant of Judah. Through the royal lineage of David, the lineage of Judah, son of Jacob, son of Isaac, son of Abraham, we have Jesus Christ. Yeshua the Messiah."

The congregation clapped.

"And so we go back to John chapter one. In the beginning was the Word, and the Word was with God, and the Word was God. He was in the beginning with God. All things were made through Him, and without Him was not any thing made that was made. In Him was life, and the life was the light of men. The light shines in the darkness, and the darkness has not overcome it. Now, I just want to go back to Genesis one. Just to point out God's first words ever spoken, according to the word here, 'Let there be light.' God's Word is life, is light.

"God spoke His Word into flesh, into the womb of Mary the virgin, and gave us Jesus. Why a virgin? God wanted to use someone pure. And in Jewish custom, the firstborn is to be dedicated to God. And while some may believe Joseph to be the father, those closest to her, and Mary and Joseph knew, that who they had was a pure miracle. Absolutely one hundred percent impossible made possible. A woman cannot create a child alone. It was the hand and work of God.

"So Jesus, the Word of God in the flesh, the light of man in the flesh, life itself in the flesh, lived among us. He grew up in a humble Jewish family with a father who worked with his hands. He lived life as a human and saw life through our human eyes. He experienced what we experienced without sinning. He saw things from our perspective. He suffered. I want you to understand, God lived among us because He loves us. I want you to understand that God understands us. He understands pain. He understands heartbreak. He understands joy and laughter and everything that makes life life for us. And He lived among us for us. He lived a good clean life and did not sin.

"And after about thirty years living as one of us, it was time for Him to die for us. So, he left His normal life to begin a ministry that would lead to His death. He performed many remarkable miracles. He healed the sick. He cast out demons. He raised the dead. He walked on water. He calmed storms. He fed thousands of people with a handful of loaves of bread and fish. He did incredible, amazing, unbelievable things. And many people loved Him for it. But some hated Him. Some saw Him as a threat. As is the nature of men due to our fallen sin nature, we see something good and we just can't let it be. So men plotted against perfect loving Jesus, as they were meant to, and had Him crucified. And He let them, because He needed to die."

Why?

"'Why?' you must be asking yourself. How does Jesus dying help us? Well, the wages of sin is death. Every sin we sin is a debt. A debt that must be paid in blood. Now, without Jesus, we pay that debt with our lives. We're dead spiritually. And when we die in the flesh, we're going to our spiritual death. A life as a spirit separate from God in a place of torment, where our debt is paid with pain. That's an eternal separation from God in the place of condemnation and punishment for sin. We can't help ourselves but to sin, because of the fall of man through Adam.

"However, we don't have to pay for that debt if someone else does for us. Let's say you owe sixty thousand dollars in college debt. Well, they're going to try to get it out of you. Even take you to jail. Now, you're not the only one. Thousands and millions and billions of people are in debt and will be jailed for not paying that debt. However, let's say one day, an incredibly rich man worth billions of billions of billions of billions of billions to the," he looked at his notes, "riches in the centillions, which is an incredibly large number, decides he's going to pay off everyone's college debts for generations and generations, as long as they accept his donation. All you had to do was accept the money and him and the one who sent him. Obviously, you'd take the money, and you'd work your very hardest to make sure your family members accepted that money, and your kids accepted that money. And your friends, and neighbors, and anyone you cared about. And perhaps even strangers as your compassion compels you.

"Jesus lived a perfect life in our place and was then crucified, though He was an innocent man. In his death, His life paid a debt we couldn't afford. But only if we acknowledge that we need Him to pay for our sins and accept His sacrifice. Accept his payment.

"Now, we know the story doesn't end there. He didn't stay dead. He overcame death and rose. And since Yeshua lived, died, and rose in our place. We have risen. We are alive. Our spiritual connection with God is re-established. We are realigned with God and His Word. Through Yeshua, we are redeemed for the sins of our predecessors and ourselves."

The congregation erupted in cheers, clapping, praises and celebration. It was like sitting in the audience of a winning team at a football game. Only, this was different. His words carried weight and moved her in a way she hadn't expected. It was like something had come alive inside of her. She could feel the truth. She could feel something coming from the man on the stage. She could feel it in the congregation. She could feel it all around her. And she could feel it bearing down on her. It was the truth. He was speaking the truth. And the truth was speaking to her.

It's real. Jesus, God, angels, demons. It's all real.

After the congregation quieted, Jay continued.

"So how does this correlate with baptism? Continuing just a little bit longer in John. Let's look at chapter one, verses six through eight: 'There was a man sent from God, whose name was John. He came as a witness, to bear witness about the light, that all might believe through him. He was not the light, but came to bear witness about the light.' Now, let's turn to Matthew three."

Everyone turned to Matthew three in their bibles. Carissa did so as well.

"Now, in Sunday school, we went over John's role at this moment. John's ministry pointed to Christ. He came to prepare the way. He was part of the prophecy to be fulfilled. Throughout the years of the holy nation, prophets, told by God or guided by the spirit of truth, spoke of the coming of the Messiah and His kingdom. Now, John is telling them to confess and repent of their sins. As we know, sin separates us from God. And with the holy one coming, you do not want to be remiss. When you have a special guest, you clean up your house, clean up and deodorize yourself, and wear your best clothing. To prepare for the coming of Christ, John's ministry focused on people setting aside their sinful ways.

DAKOTA

"Humility is a very important part of living a clean life. You must acknowledge that you're sinning and that you're a sinner. Just like an alcoholic getting better must first admit he is an alcoholic. An alcoholic that does not admit he is an alcoholic cannot get better. You must first admit and acknowledge that you have a problem and need help to truly pursue and accept help. Once you have admitted you are a sinner, then you confess your sins. You call them out. You acknowledge when and where you have sinned.

"Confession, it's honestly a relief when you've let the truth out. There's something about carrying around your mistakes or vices and not facing them. Keeping them to yourself, hidden, doesn't resolve your issues. It just stays in there, building up, and you can't move on until you've put it out there on the table. Not confessing sin is like being constipated." There were giggles in the audience. "You're walking around consuming sin and it's not going anywhere. It's just building up. You feel emotionally ill and uncomfortable. You perhaps have shame that you've convinced yourself not to feel. You've probably justified it. But, when you get it out of your system. When you finally pass, you feel this great weight released. You feel lighter and relieved. Confess your sins. Let your sins pass. Confide with someone trustworthy and receptive, but most importantly, confess them to God. Don't worry about judgment. He knows everything you've ever done. Watch that feeling of relief come when you acknowledge that you have sinned. God will forgive you of your sins, but first you must confess them.

"And then, you have repentance. Once you have acknowledged you have a problem, you are a sinner, and have laid your sins down before God through confession, you decide to turn away. You choose to live a different way. I sinned. I made bad choices. Here's what I did. I'm not going to do it anymore. Repentance is turning a new leaf. Saying, 'From this day forward, I will not do what I did before.' And that's what John's message was about. John's ministry was about turning a new leaf. Setting aside your old life for a new life to come with the approach of Jesus, who would redeem us all.

"And then, you have baptism. Now, let's say you've lived your life and you never took a shower or bathed. The older you are,

I'm sure you realize how disgusting that is. Imagine the amount of dirt under your nails, caked on your skin, in your hair. Imagine the smell. Now, even if you tried your very best to avoid dirty activities. If you stayed indoors, didn't run, or perhaps even sprayed yourself with perfume, you'd smell a little better, but not by much. Because we sweat. We can get dirty just sitting still, surprisingly. That's the sin nature. So again, all these years you haven't washed yourself. You're caked with sin. That's what life is like when you're an unredeemed sinner. That spiritual dirt and grime is sin. The baptism, symbolically, is the washing away of all that dirt and making you clean. Clean like a baby. A rebirth. It's a complete refreshment.

"The baptism of repentance, known as the baptism of John, was about accepting what you are, acknowledging that you sin, turning from your old ways, and washing yourself clean and anew. Starting over from scratch. Some will tell you that baptism is just a symbolic gesture of your acceptance of Christ. I want you to understand that it's that and more. It's representative of obedience. A choice of how you're going to live your life. It's saying, 'I've done a lot of bad stuff. I'm not doing it anymore. I'm going clean. I repent. I'm a new person, fresh, and I'm not going back!'"

The congregation clapped.

"Before they knew Jesus, before His sacrifice, baptism was saying, 'I'm moving forward, repenting of sin, because something greater than I is coming and I have to be ready for it.' And then, He came. Jesus came to John. John saw Jesus, and in John chapter one verse twenty-nine, he said, 'Behold, the Lamb of God, who takes away the sin of the world!' And Jesus came to John to be baptized. John was shocked, and in Matthew three, he said, 'I need to be baptized by you, and do you come to me?' And Jesus responded, 'Let it be so now, for thus it is fitting for us to fulfill all righteousness.' And once Jesus was baptized, the heavens or sky opened to him, and John saw the Spirit of God descending and resting on Jesus. And, as if that wasn't enough, a voice from heaven spoke praising Jesus. This was done to fulfill prophecies given to God's holy nation, proving Jesus is the one they've been waiting for. Now, having witnessed this, this was the remainder of John's ministry: he bore witness of Jesus."

Jay paced more. "Now, we're talking about baptism. I've shared with you the baptism of repentance and the logic behind it. Once Jesus died and was raised, there was a new baptism. A baptism in the name of the Father, Son, and Holy Spirit. A baptism in the name of Jesus. Not just of repentance, but also complete forgiveness and cleansing of sin. A baptism of total rebirth.

"The important elements of baptism and repentance remains. Before we are baptized, we acknowledge that we are sinners and need salvation. Next, we confess our sins, repent, and accept Jesus's life as payment of those sins. At that point, God forgives and washes us clean of all past sin. Having handed over the debt of our sins to Jesus and turned away from a life of sin, we are baptized. Symbolically, when we are fully immersed under water, our whole body is washed in the cleansing sacrificial blood of Jesus. When we come out of the water, we are a new, clean, fresh person. Symbolically, when we are fully submerged under water, we are buried with Jesus. When we come out of the water, we rise with Jesus. The person we once were died on the cross with Jesus. We are resurrected with Jesus. We are born again. That is what it means to be a born-again Christian.

"Previously, we were spiritually dead and part of this corrupt world. But when we are born-again, we are part of the body of Christ and not of this world. Before we were saved, we were children of the world, sin, and the devil. But through the blood of Yeshua, we are children of God. Again, when we accept Yeshua as our Lord and Savior, we are reintroduced into connection with God. We are reintroduced into the divine, holy family. We are a part of Yeshua. He is the head; we are the body. We are a part of the kingdom of God.

"And after we have repented of our sins, accepted Jesus as our Lord and Savior, are reborn, and reattached to God, we are given a gift. A helper. The Spirit of Truth. This is baptism of the Spirit. We are born of water through baptism. And then born again in spirit through the gift of the Spirit, that resides in us hence after. The Spirit lives within us and helps us live life in alignment with God. It makes us a better person. It tugs us in the right direction. It guides us so that we are not driven by the same vices we once were. Now, we're not perfect, just better. Gradually, and exponentially better, with time. Note, I say gradually and exponentially, not instantly. As in, the curve goes up. We'll still make mistakes, because biologically we're still descendants of Adam and Eve. But upon death of our physical bodies, once we shed the flesh of men, we will be perfected in new bodies, unhindered by the sin of man.

"But back to water baptism. Some will say, 'Why get baptized? Isn't accepting Jesus enough?' Well, the first thing I want to say is that no servant is greater than his master. Point being, Jesus was baptized in water and then the Spirit rested on Him. Jesus didn't need baptism. But to fulfill all righteousness, Jesus was baptized. So, of course, if Jesus was baptized in water and Spirit, even though He did not need it, we, who are filthy sinners, should do the same, because we definitely need it. We are to follow Him. He is the example we live by. He set a perfect example. We follow that example. In Matthew three, Jesus is showing us how to fulfill righteousness. We are baptized with water. Baptized in spirit. And we are then among the righteous through the Messiah.

"Also, I like to point to John chapter three, verses three through eight. It says, 'Jesus answered him, "Truly, truly, I say to you, unless one is born again he cannot see the kingdom of God." Nicodemus said to him, "How can a man be born when he is old? Can he enter a second time into his mother's womb and be born?" Jesus answered, "Truly, truly, I say to you, unless one is born of water and the Spirit, he cannot enter the kingdom of God. That which is born of the flesh is flesh, and that which is born of the Spirit is spirit."'

"Now, some of you may say, 'Jay. What are you saying? Man cannot save himself. A man cannot save himself with works. Man needs God for salvation. Baptism is a work.' Well, yes, man needs God for salvation. God has done His part. God paid our debts for us. However, I need to remind you that in the beginning, when God made men, he gave us a job and free will. From the very beginning, we had a purpose and options. If we didn't have options, neither Adam nor Eve would have ever touched the fruit of the tree of knowledge of good and evil. We have a choice. We were given a choice. God has blessed us with the choice to accept Him or not. To accept His free gift of salvation or not. God has given us the choice of life or death. God will not force us to accept Him or salvation through Jesus Christ. You don't see Jesus forcing anyone throughout any of the gospels. In fact, the gospels clearly show people turning away from Jesus because they disagreed with what he said. He didn't stretch out his hand and compel them to stay. He let them go. He loved them. He wished they would stay and listen to him and repent. But it's their choice. Just like it's our choice to acknowledge we're sinners, confess our sins, repent of those sins, let Jesus pay for our sins, be forgiven of our sins, and be washed clean and born again in water and spirit. If we believe, we know what is asked of us and we do it.

"People confuse the meaning of salvation through works. There's this idea that if you're doing the right thing, being a good person, checking all the boxes on the list, like charity and volunteer work, you're fine. You go to Heaven. That is works salvation. We should do those things because we want to, they're the right thing to do, but they don't guarantee salvation. Jesus is the way to salvation. Baptism isn't a work; it's a doorway.

"Jesus gave us a great commission. In Matthew, chapter twenty-eight, He tells us to make disciples of all nations, baptizing people in the name of the Father and of the Son and of the Holy Spirit. Clearly, baptism is important. In Mark, chapter sixteen, verses fifteen and sixteen, He says, 'Go into all the world and proclaim the gospel to the whole creation. Whoever believes and is baptized will be saved, but whoever does not believe will be condemned.' Again, believe and be baptized. There is an important connection between those two. That's three gospels, Matthew, Mark, and John. Throughout the book of Acts, what did His apostles do? They baptized.

"Now, having said that, there have been exceptions. God is a god of mercy and compassion. In Luke, chapter twenty-three, verses thirty-nine through forty-three, when Jesus was being crucified, there were two criminals who were also being crucified that day. One man mocked Jesus. The other man acknowledged that Jesus was an innocent man, recognized Jesus for who he was, and asked, 'Jesus, remember me when you come into your kingdom.' And Jesus replied, 'Truly, I say to you, today you will be with me in Paradise.'

"Now, what happened in that conversation? First, the man acknowledged that he and the other criminal were sinners, criminals. Humble acknowledgement that he's a sinner and recognition that they were getting what they deserved. That's pretty close to confession of sins. Two, he recognized who Jesus was and that he needed Him. In that moment, he knew the only hope there was for him was the innocent man next to him. I believe, in that moment, that man, in his heart, regretting everything he had done. He was repentant, or borderline repentant. I believe that man had an honest fear and respect for God. He made bad choices worthy of crucifixion. However, in that moment, Jesus saw in that man what was needed for salvation. Jesus in his love and compassion of the man who humbled himself and accepted his punishment, accepted him into the family. There was certainly no way the man could be baptized, unless he was washed later, after his legs were broken.

"What I'm saying is: baptism is important. Otherwise, Jesus wouldn't have made it part of the great commission and his teachings. John wouldn't have made baptism a part of his ministry. Jesus's disciples wouldn't have baptized people. Baptism is for man, from God. A gift in the path to righteousness. Before one puts on new garments, he must take off the old ones and wash himself. Then, he can put on the new garment. And Jesus's perfect blood cleans eternally.

"Baptism is very real, meaningful, and powerful. Which brings me to one more thing: we should not create boundaries to baptism. There are some churches that establish a set of rules like you must become a member of that physical church. No. That's not right. You should have a conversation with a person and make sure they're fully informed of what a baptism represents. But you shouldn't make someone fill out forms and sign up. No. That's inappropriate. If anyone accepts Jesus and wants to be baptized, you baptize them then and there.

"Some churches may make you take a class or classes before baptism. I think it's good for a person to have a complete understanding of baptism and what it represents before they get baptized, so that person is not baptized in vain. However, I feel that can be handled in an intimate, personal conversation. On a corporate church level, I don't have a problem with a class as long as the class offers a complete understanding of baptism and is immediately followed by baptism. And that class should be for those that don't already have an understanding. I'd hate for someone to be forced to go through a class if they already understand the principles of baptism.

"It's also been implied that there are a few churches who make you pay for baptism. If you go to a church, and they want to charge you or someone you know, please pray for that church. They are disrespecting God's *free* gift. No one should ever be charged for a baptism, ever.

"Having said that, some have it in their heads that you have to be in a physical church to be baptized. You don't. You can fill a bathtub with water at a comfortable temperature and carefully baptize someone there. It is encouraged to do it in a natural body of water; so, you can go to the beach and baptize people at the beach like Jesus. You can baptize people in the pool at school or a gym or at your friend's house. It's not about where you do it. It's about people surrendering their sins and lives to Christ.

"Listen everyone, God loves you. God created this beautiful, rich world for us. And man screwed it up and has been screwing it up ever sense. But God has never completely given up on us. He's loved us in all this time. He's fought for us. He's guided us. He gave His only begotten son for us. He's lived for us. He's died for us. He overcame death for us. He's given His Holy Spirit to help us. Whatever pains or vices or demons you're enduring in your life, remember that it's not because of God. It's because of man's dysfunction. But there's a better way. There's a better life. That is life through Jesus, the Word, through whom all things were created, with love. Lean on Him. When you make a mistake. Lean on Him. Confess. Repent.

"And if this is the first time any of you have heard this, or if you're hearing it for the second, third, fourth, fifth, sixth, seventh, seventy times seventh time, and you finally feel compelled to confess your sins and surrender them to Jesus who lovingly paid for them, please come forward. There is a better life, a new life ahead for you. You can come forward now, or if you're shy, after the service. We have our senior pastor and associate pastors and youth pastors up here ready to have that conversation with you. We're here to talk. We're here to love on you. We're here to work with you through whatever you're going through. We're going to be baptizing people today for the next hour.

"We don't make it a public spectacle. It's a real, intimate thing we don't take lightly. But any of you are free to watch and support and participate in the baptisms. We love it when people come up and enthusiastically engage in the process of bringing people into the body of Christ. It is a joyful day whenever someone accepts Jesus into their life. And if you're at home, we encourage you to come to our church and be baptized. Six days out of the week, we have someone here to baptize you. Monday through Friday, it's nine to five. Sunday, it's after service to about one o'clock. You're also free to come and talk and ask questions.

"With that, I'd like to thank you all for coming. Next up, the worship team will sing while we talk with whomever comes forward. Pastor Brown will go over announcements and close us in prayer. Thank you."

Jay gave a respectful bow and walked down the steps. There, he, Pastor Brown, and a few others greeted people from the congregation as they approached.

Carissa watched and smiled.

CHAPTER TWENTY-TWO

"So, what did you think?" Gabby asked as the service ended and people filed out of the worship room.

I don't really know what to think anymore.

Carissa shrugged. "I'm not sure. It's a lot to take in. He went through a lot."

"Yea. He did, didn't he? That was a creation-to-Christ sermon. I think he did great, considering he amended it to the lesson at the last minute."

"Yea." Carissa chewed the inside of her cheek. "Totally."

Gabby watched her. "Did you understand what he was saying? Were you able to follow?"

I think so. Carissa sighed. "I mean, I've heard some of it before. My grandma on my mom's side is a Christian. She'll talk about God occasionally. I just haven't heard it like that. He was very specific, repetitive, but also kind of casual about it. Most of it wasn't hard to follow. I just, you know, I don't know. I didn't believe. But, part of me believes."

"Is that so?"

"Yea," Carissa said. "I felt something while he was speaking. It, it's hard to explain. I could feel he was telling the truth. I mean, I kind of believed somewhat, a little, that maybe God was real. I believe in karma and destiny and stuff. Even though my current circumstances have made me question all of that lately." She sighed and put her hand on her stomach. "Now, it's like, what he said, his words affected me."

"What do you mean?" Gabby asked. "Affected you how?"

I don't really understand it. Carissa frowned. "When he started, it was just words, ya know? He was talking about creation and the Word and describing God in a way I hadn't heard before nor understood. And I was like, okay. He's explaining the religion. Then, he went into the Adam and Eve story everyone's heard. I was thinking, 'Yea, yea, yea. We've all heard that story before.'"

She paused.

"And, well, I don't know, maybe it was about the sin stuff. I've made bad choices, but never really felt like I was a bad person. But I think about other people. Some of the choices they make. Like Val. It just. I don't know. Lately, it feels like there's more going on than just people being crap people. Like there's something deeper, below the surface of it all. Something tangible I never saw or felt before until now. This world is screwed up. I mean, what, what happened to me. That was just, they were so, so, disgusting." She sniffed and blinked away tears. "They're monsters."

"Okay." Gabby gave Carissa a hug. "It's okay."

"Kent threatened me a couple days ago," Carissa said.

Gabby gasped. "Did you tell the police?"

"Yea," Carissa said. "But there was this look in his eyes and eerie feeling in his presence. I think about that night when he, when they." She shook her head. "A tiny part of me, a voice in the back of my mind, knew I shouldn't go to that party, but I went anyway because I wanted to go. And now, now, I can just, I can see it clearer now. In his eyes. Kent's eyes. The evil. And, when I look at Jay, when I watched him on the stage. I saw something else entirely different. The look in Jay's eyes, in your eyes. Just being around you, in this place. I feel a presence. Pure peace like a cool breeze that settles right in my heart. It's something powerful and, I don't know, uplifting. It all feels so real." She took a deep breath. "It's all real."

"Very much so."

"After, uh, after Kent did what he did, I felt so, so dirty," Carissa said. She crossed her arms, held herself. "I felt polluted, inside and out. I felt filthy. Still do. And, well, now I just want to be clean. I want to feel something else other than dirty. And, again, for a moment, when Jay was speaking, I did. I felt that dirty feeling go away. His words made me feel clean. He gave me a sense of hope that I don't have to feel filthy anymore."

"Well, that's a start." Gabby smiled. "Jesus is the way." *I'm pretty sure a poster outside says just that. I guess that's the church's slogan.* "Does this mean you believe in God, now? Do you believe in Jesus?"

I'm still trying to figure that out.

"I should, shouldn't I?" Carissa said and shrugged. "Maybe. Jay invited me to church. If I hadn't lost his business card, I might have come here when you invited me. I never would have been raped. I wouldn't be pregnant. It's like, I had a good choice, and it was taken away from me. It just slipped through my fingers, or out of my purse. And, with you, I was making a choice between good and evil, but didn't realize it. And, I feel so stupid. I made the wrong choice. I had a choice between you and Val. I chose Val." She sighed. *And I was laughing at you while doing it.* "Now, my life is turned upside down."

Gabby sat silently, pondering what was said.

"I just wish I could go back and make a different decision," Carissa said. "That's all I've wanted for the last two months. I wish I never went to that party."

Gabby pressed her lips together, frowned. "We don't know what waits ahead of us. But part of our faith is believing that God will use the bad this world throws at us for our good. I hope, in time, you'll see God's work on your behalf with clear eyes." She rubbed Carissa's back. "He's brought you here. He's given you new friends and a loving community. Sometimes, bad things happen to guide us to the good things."

Carissa frowned.

"You're here now," Gabby said. "Let's move forward. We're all here for you."

You keep saying that. I guess we'll see. Carissa looked around. Most of the congregation was gone. Hannah, Rebecca, and Sean were nowhere to be seen. *Where is everyone?*

"Where'd Sean, Rebecca, and Hannah go?" Carissa asked.

Gabby pointed to the stage. *Don't point or Hannah might murder you while you sleep.*

"He's decided to get baptized today," Gabby said. "I heard him whisper to Rebecca during the service. He's probably in the back changing into the white garments they provide for baptisms."

A small crowd of people waited at the stage for the baptisms. In the crowd was Jay. Next to him, laughing and smiling, was a blond-haired woman in a black, polka-dot dress. She rested her hand on his shoulder and whispered something in his ear. He laughed.

"Wait a second," Carissa said and moved forward to figure out what the heck was going on. "Who's that with Jay?" Was this the friend or guest that was with him and Pastor Brown? Was she the blond lady the Cole sisters were talking about?

I was in denial. I can't believe it. He is seeing someone. Look at her. She has her hands all over him. Well, I am not going to let this happen. I'm about to bust that relationship wide open.

Gabby followed her. "Uh, Carissa."

Carissa worked her way through the crowd. Gabby followed. When they made it to Jay, Carissa called out to him. He turned around and so did the blonde.

Carissa gasped. It was Amy Priest.

Aww, shit.

2

"Carissa," Jay said when he saw her. "You're still here. Great. How'd you like the lesson on baptism?"

Amy's eyes moved between Jay and Carissa.

Carissa wasn't sure what to do or say. Normally, in this situation, she'd clearly mark her territory, whether it was hers or not, with a hug, playful flirtation, holding his arm or hand, or something. But this was different. She couldn't make waves with Amy. Amy was investigating her case and would know exactly what she was doing. That left her with only one option. Be nice.

"It was a lot to take in," Carissa said. "Some of it, I couldn't follow. But, it made an impact." She looked to Gabby, who stood beside her. *This has got to be some kind of joke.*

"Well, an impact is all I can ask for," Jay said. He rested his hand on Amy's lower back. "Amy, this is Carissa. She's the one I told you about. The one I met at the coffee shop who had the same order as me."

Amy frowned at Jay, whispered, "*She's* coffee shop girl?"

DAKOTA

"You know her?"

This is weird. He told her about me? What did he say? What does this mean? They must have a close relationship if he's telling her about other people he's talked to. Or not? But the way we spoke at the coffee shop, it seemed like he was interested in me. We were flirting and everything. The only issue that existed was that I'm seventeen. How long have they been together? Was he talking to me while dating her? I mean, he gave me his phone number an hour ago.

"We've met." Amy reluctantly extended her hand. "Nice to see you again."

A handshake? Really? Yea, sure. Let's make this more awkward than it already is.

Carissa shook it. "Yea. Nice to see you, too."

The hell it's not. What's going on?

"You've met?" Jay asked. "How do you know each other?"

Ugh. Of course, he had to ask. Now, she's going to tell him. Can she tell him? I mean, I don't know. I don't know the rules. Once you tell a police officer something, does it become public knowledge?

"Umm," Amy scrunched up her face. "All I can say is that I met her while on duty." Jay glanced at Carissa. "She's not a person of interest or anything. It's nothing she did."

Phew. Well, whether she's dating my guy or not, I owe her for that one. Dodged a bullet there. But not for long. I mean. What am I going to tell him when I start to gain weight and show my pregnancy?

"You serve thousands of people," Jay said. "Naturally, you'll come across people you meet in the line of duty."

Amy grinned. "Precisely."

Phew part two. That's a wrap. Maybe I can get around this. Maybe I can get around him knowing I'm pregnant. I mean, when I start to show, I can wear baggier, bigger clothing that doesn't show the bulge. There are some materials that are thick and misleading. And it's winter, so that's perfect. Sweaters and layers are necessary. And, well, when spring comes it'll still be somewhat chilly at times and rainy. I can totally wear a sweater until summer. By the time summer gets here, and I'm really showing, I can just be "busy" but stay in contact until the baby comes. Then, I can hide the baby until he's fallen in love with me.

Probably the most asinine thing I have ever thought, ever.

"So, how did you two meet?" Gabby asked.

Oh. Yea. I should have asked that question.

"My partner brought me here." Amy pointed at Summers, who stood watch next to Pastor Brown. *If these people don't stop pointing, Hannah will kill us all.* "He keeps an eye on the pastors, makes sure no one tries anything. When I told him I was raised in a Baptist church up until I went to college, he invited me. I'm still new to the area. I just moved down here at the end of October for my reassignment."

The end of October. Are you freaking kidding me? I can't believe this! The end of October has literally screwed my life.

"Instead of waiting for the service, the welcoming committee suggested I step into a Sunday school class. She said the lessons from Sunday school are usually linked to the sermon. Jay's class was the closest one. I went in. There was an open seat next to him. I sat and listened. After it was over, we talked."

"I mostly asked her questions," Jay said. "I'm fascinated by her line of work. Before I committed to writing, I wanted to be an investigator. Still kind of do."

So, if I become a cop, you'll be fascinated in me? Sigh.

"His next project is about a police officer in the seventies," Amy said.

Yea, he told me, probably the weekend before he told you. Dammit! I can't believe I lost that business card.

Jay smiled. "Yea. The character happens to have a connection to the strange. Those in his department consider him the expert, the go-to on strange. They don't believe in the supernatural stuff or don't want to. So, in a nearby small town where they've never had a single crime outside of jaywalking, there's been a murder. I'm not gonna say who. When he gets there, he sees the civility of the town unraveling before his eyes. He discovers there's a lot more going on outside of the realm of the human eye. It'll be quite fascinating. I'll provide more details once I finish it. It's nice bouncing ideas off the head of an actual police officer who's aware of the procedures in that time."

"How's that?" Gabby asked.

"My grandpa is a retired cop," Amy said. "He used to tell me all his cop stories, including how both complicated and simple operations and procedures are now than they used to be." She smiled and thought. "He was so proud when I joined the force. I think he cried a little. Though, he was way too macho to ever admit such a thing. He said it was too windy and dust got in his eye."

I don't care about your stupid grandpa. This totally sucks. How is it you met him just after I met him? It's not even fair.

"So, that was it," Carissa said. "You met in Sunday school."

"Yep," Jay said. "She was new. She sat with me. I invited her to lunch. She counteroffered and invited me to lunch with her and Detective Summers. After it was over, we exchanged information and things developed from there."

Great. You had lunch.

"Speaking of which, I'm hungry," Amy said. "Are you going to baptize someone, or can we scram?"

"Hmm, I'm starving too." Jay put his finger to his lips. "After going through that lesson, I really should baptize someone. I haven't had an opportunity to, lately. It'll only take a few minutes. Which means, I have to run back there, change into my white garb, baptize someone, and then come back. So, a half an hour? That sound fair?"

"It'll probably be an hour," Amy said, "but sure. I'll get something from a vending machine. I live off that stuff at the office, anyway."

"And, I'm off," Jay said. He gave Amy a peck on the cheek. "It was nice seeing you again, Carissa. You as well, Hannah."

Gabby frowned. *Oh, she hates that. But they're identical twins. Both athletic. They sound almost the same. Hard to see a personality.* "I'm Gabby."

"Oh! Oh, I'm sorry, Gabby." Jay cringed. "She's usually the one that talks to me."

Because she has a thing for you. And I have a thing for you. And you seem to be totally oblivious or playing it cool.

"It's okay," Gabby said. "It's an everyday thing."

Jay left. Amy and Carissa looked at each other. An awkward silence loomed.

"So, uh, how long you and Jay been together?" Gabby asked.

I love the fact that she's being nosy and asking the questions I want to ask but won't ask. We make a good team, Gabby. We make a good team.

"Well," Amy checked her watch, "officially, about twenty minutes ago."

Wait. What? Twenty minutes ago? Are you playing with my emotions right now? How twenty minutes ago? Did you become a couple right after the service?

"I don't, wait, what?" Carissa asked. "You haven't been dating for the past two months?"

"Not that it's something I should be sharing." Amy glanced around and leaned closer. *Is this a secret?* "We met and became friends about seven weeks ago. But, I had just left a serious relationship. Part of the reason why I moved here. That and the promotion to detective. I wasn't ready to jump into another relationship. But, he liked me. I liked him. And, I didn't want to miss a good opportunity just because I left a bad situation. So, we went on dates whenever our schedules didn't conflict. It wasn't anything serious. I kept the door open for either of us to pursue other things, which I could tell upset him."

Great. You just keep that door open. I will slip in and—

"And, then, today, he said something right before going on stage about a coffee shop girl finally visiting the church. That made me think I should probably act fast before that someone else snatched him up." She chuckled. "Didn't know that was you. But, it got me thinking. He wants to be with me. He's a great guy. I feel secure and safe with him. He's trustworthy, unlike the last guy. What's my problem, ya know?"

Oh my God! I can't believe it. He mentioned me! Dammit! He mentioned me and you panicked and asked him to be your girlfriend. I mean, asked to be his girlfriend. Though, the first one would have been kind of funny. Hahaha. Would you be my girlfriend, you beautiful, beautiful man, you? No. That's not funny. None of this is funny.

"So, I told him I was ready to be his girlfriend," Amy continued. "He only dates to marry, which means he won't waste my time. And I'm serious about investing in our future. Hearing that, his face lit up. We hugged. And, that's it. Twenty minutes go." She grinned.

I want to hit you over your pretty, blond head. But you're a cop and working on my case. God. I hate that you're so pretty! And he's yours now. And somehow, it's my fault! My being here screwed me. Just my luck!

"Good for you," Carissa said, smiled. It was a fake smile. All three of them knew it was a fake smile. But she kept it up. "Good for you both."

There was a tense, thick silence.

"Sean's getting baptized," Gabby said, thankfully changing the subject. "Her brother, Sean. He's dating my sister. Rebecca, not Hannah. He's dating Rebecca."

"That's nice." Amy checked her watch. "I'm happy for your brother. And your sister."

"Thanks," Carissa and Gabby said.

More silence.

"So, how's the investigation coming?" Gabby asked. Both Carissa and Amy glared at her. *No, you did not.*

"I can't talk about that here," Amy said. *Thank you. I don't want anybody to hear about this.* "Nor is it appropriate to go over the details of an on-going investigation."

Gabby frowned. "That doesn't seem fair. I feel like I should at least be kept in the loop. After all, I'm the one that talked her off the ledge. I was at the clinic. If it wasn't for me, she would have gone through with it."

"Gab!" Carissa said, looked around. *Keep your voice down!*

"Follow me; I need to take a statement from you," Amy said and pulled a notepad out of her purse. *God forbid if this woman doesn't carry a notepad wherever she goes.*

A half hour later, Amy finished questioning Gabby as Sean and Rebecca walk on the stage in the provided white tees and pants. They stepped into the bath and Rebecca baptized Sean in the name of the Father, Son, and Holy Spirit.

CHAPTER TWENTY-THREE

Christmas was only a few days away. Carissa wasn't looking forward to facing her extended family, who would have loads of questions about her pregnancy.

In an attempt to distract her, Mom, Dad, and Sean reminded her of their annual, three-day gift shopping extravaganza. Three days of shopping, wrapping, teasing each other with hints, and hiding presents around the house. On the first day, Mom and Carissa bought gifts for Dad and Sean, and others, and Sean and Dad bought gifts for the ladies, and others. Mom and Carissa pooled their money together and bought Sean a new winter clothes and a Kyudo set. Dad's gifts were a new watch, some shirts and ties and socks on sale. Mom bought one other gift she said Carissa shouldn't see.

It's a shame I followed her anyway and saw the store she entered. I understand now why people douse themselves in gasoline and light a match. There are things people should never know about their parents. Ignorance is bliss.

On the second day, they switched partners. It was a father-daughter and mother-son day. After a long overdue one-on-one lunch, Dad and Carissa bought Mom a new bookcase to go with her current collection. She thought the set was no longer for sell. Dad's investigation confirmed the collection was only renamed, repackaged, and advertised as new because of one new piece. They bought the new piece. Dad also bought Mom a gold necklace and locket with a picture of the two of them when they were college sweethearts. The engraving on the front said

"Forever", and on the back, "Tom and Kate". *Aww. How sweet!* Dad bought Sean more clothes, these dressier than the last, since he was outgrowing most of what he owned and tearing up the rest. *Kid's taller than me now. That's just wrong.*

The third night, they bought the last few gifts for extended family and friends. Those gifts they wrapped together. Carissa was shocked by the number of gifts they got over the three nights. The previous two years, gifts were scarce. They all saved up this year to make up for the last two.

Sean apparently blew most of his money and bought Rebecca a yellow gold promise ring. The boy had a thing about buying girls jewelry. She hoped he'd manage his money better after Kelsea. But he was set in his ways.

When Rebecca sees that ring, she is going to freak out. I know I would.

Halfway through the wrapping, Mom set off to make her signature crispy chicken parmesan pasta with creamy cheese mashed potatoes, corn on a cob, and side salads. Once Carissa was finished wrapping, she chopped vegetables and pleaded with Mom to keep her pregnancy hush-hush.

Mom hugged Carissa and said, "I know you want to keep this to yourself, honey. I personally don't want to talk about it anymore than we already have." She teared up. "It breaks my heart every time I think about it. But they're *family*." She tightened her hands around Carissa's. "They're part of us. We'll need them and their support through this whole thing, especially once the baby comes. You'll see. We're there for them when they need us. They're here for us when we need them."

That's the common line I've been hearing, "I'm here for you." The only time I needed someone to be there for me was the one time no one was there because Val was too busy whoring herself off to what's his name. I can't remember the guy's name. She probably can't either at this point.

What I don't need is to be the subject of pity and family gossip in Virginia, Connecticut, New York, the UK, Japan, Germany, and France. Last thing I want is my rape to become international news.

"They weren't there for us when Dad lost his job," Carissa said and stopped cutting vegetables to see Mom's reaction.

"When we had to move here."

Mom nibbled her lower lip, took a deep breath, and went back to managing the pots on the stove. "That's because we weren't the only ones that lost money. And you know some of their money was tied into his investment accounts. Even though it wasn't his fault, they had legitimate hard feelings."

"Yea," Carissa said. "And he's been working constantly since and made most of it back for them." She flung her hands in the air. "We barely saw him before and hardly see him now because he's always working so much, trying to make things right with family. For all the help they are, they're not helping this family any." She turned back to her vegetables and started chopping again. "I don't want them to know, except, maybe grandma."

"That doesn't count," Mom said. "She already knows. We talked to her about it."

"Duh," Carissa said and regretted it immediately. Mom gave her the evil eye. "The other one." *Please try and keep up.*

Mom shook her head. "This is your secret, but since a new baby is coming into this family, it's not up for discussion. Eventually, you're going to give birth to that baby. They'll want to know where the baby came from and would be mad we didn't tell them sooner. Plus, we're going to have a baby shower, because babies are expensive. We need all the support we can get. I mean, we're paying for your college and the baby. You'll need a crib, clothes, toys, pampers, food, daycare, child-proofing accessories, breast-pumps, and let's not mention the unexpected that comes with babies."

Carissa opened and shut her mouth. *Dammit. How dare you have a good point? You should have told me that before I decided to keep it. Man. We needed more safe-sex and baby talks. Not that it was my intention to get pregnant anyway. Not like I had an option to make him use protection. Why don't vaginas come with teeth? I feel like vaginas need teeth.*

"Fine," Carissa mumbled. "We can tell them."

I'll just get started on the telegram. Tell the whole world that I got knocked up by an ass in a tuxedo who drugged me while his brother egged him on.

Mom hugged her again. "It'll be fine."

People keep saying that. You should stop lying to me.

"Sure."

At the end of the three-day shopping extravaganza, the Boisseaus packed for the road, went to bed early, and slept until four in the morning, Christmas Eve. Dad drove until they made it to New Jersey, got gas, and let Mom drive the rest of the way to Connecticut. It was snowing, bad. It was almost impossible to see more than a few yards ahead. *When it snows, it blows.* The radio said they were expecting thirteen inches. But Mom loved driving through the snowy weather and New Jersey and New York traffic. Dad said it was the only mental illness she had that worked in his favor. Carissa and Sean laughed as Mom shot Dad an "I'll kill you" glare.

They arrived at Uncle Liam's house in Ridgefield, Connecticut a couple hours before dinner. Grandma Ava, Mom's mom, and Aunt Carrie, Mom's younger sister, came out to greet everyone with hugs, especially Carissa. They examined her in detail and talked about how good she was looking, how to stay that way, and how to get her figure back after the pregnancy, making sure to comment on their successes. That conversation dragged on inside and while they unpacked in the designated girl's room, a room with two deluxe queen-sized beds and a cot. Aunt Carrie was the first to flaunt how tight and fit she was since she and Aunt Jessica, Uncle Liam's wife and Mom's sister-in-law, joined a spin and bodyworks strength class. Carissa's various cousins ooo'd and ahh'd as Aunt Carrie flexed. Grandma casually slipped in that she preferred to workout "the old-fashioned way".

What does that mean?

Some grimaced. Others burst into laughter.

Does that mean what I think it means?

Once the post-pregnancy body conversation ended, there was the pregnancy conversation. They all went on and on about their experiences with different kids. Things to look out for. Things to avoid. Discomfort or pain she should call the doctor about, or not. Comfort foods, exercises. Carissa listened to it all, overwhelmed and underprepared.

Am I ready for this? Do I really want to do this?

The conversation continued at dinner after Uncle Angus, Mom's second oldest brother, and his family showed up. What was she going to name the baby? Did she want it to be a girl or boy? How was the police investigation going? Why hadn't they done anything about it yet?

Sean tried to bail her out by announcing that he'd been baptized. Grandma took the bait and gave him a big hug and kiss on the cheek and praised God, but then turned her attention right back to Carissa. When was she going to be saved? Did she believe in Jesus? Did she meet any cute Christian boys at church? Only a good Christian boy with the love of God in him was going to be willing to raise another man's child and offer a stable home life.

Carissa locked her eyes on Mom and stared at her, hoping to telepathically transmit how annoying these last few hours were for her. *Why did you have to tell them? I haven't had a moment of peace since I got here.*

What did Mom do? She smiled. *You're smiling right now? You think this is funny? This is not funny! I just want some peace and quiet and to be left alone. I did not want this.*

After dessert, the adults and young people separated. The girls talked amongst themselves. The boys played violent video games and talked trash. The younger kids played with their various toys and watched the older kids. Carissa hid in the bathroom for twenty minutes until someone had to pee and couldn't wait any longer. *Go away. There's a perfectly useful bush in the backyard.* Then, she put on her jacket, gloves, hat and snuck outside.

Grandpa Liam, Mom's dad, rested in his chair on the porch watching the snow fall. He wasn't allowed out unless he wore his complete fur outfit: coat, hat, gloves, leggings, and boots. All fur. Grandma's orders. He looked like a brown bear with a large beer stein full of eggnog rested on its lap. A small bead of sweat ran down his forehead. *You poor soul.*

"Hey Grandpa," Carissa said and sat in the chair next to him.

Grandpa smiled and pulled a plush, heated electric blanket out of a big paper shopping bag. He said, "The tradition continues," and passed it to her. It was already warm. "For a moment, I thought you might have reached that age where you forget about old pop-pop and wanted to hang out with the girls."

Every year, family came together for four days around and

on Christmas. They bounced between Uncle Liam's, Uncle Angus's, or Grandpa Liam's house. Carissa could stick with the pack for most of the day, but after dinner, she needed a break. She needed to recharge. Like clockwork, she would sneak out of the house, on to the porch, where it was quiet. Grandpa would always be there doing the same thing. They were cut from the same cloth, he had said.

"Never gonna happen," Carissa said and snuggled up in the warm blanket.

The purpose of sneaking out was to appreciate the quiet. When the sky was clear and starry, they appreciated the majesty of it all. Other days, like this one, they watched snow fall and listened to the wind. But today, this time, Grandpa had other plans.

"When your mother got pregnant with you, she was scared to tell us," Grandpa said, breaking the code of silence. "She didn't tell us until she was showing."

I considered that.

"Your grandmother was so upset with her. Not because she was pregnant. Well, maybe a little bit of that, but mostly because she waited so long to tell her. Your grandmother wanted to be the first one to know so that she could brag about having a grandbaby to all her friends. And she kept it to herself that your dad proposed, which she insisted happened immediately after she found out she was pregnant, because she didn't want to be publicly humiliated." He took a sip of his hot cocoa. "You know what I was worried about?"

What's most important to Grandpa?

"The Celtics making the playoffs?" Carissa asked with a grin.

Grandpa laughed and then let out a heavy series of coughs that worried her sick. After he composed himself, he said, "Well, that, yes, definitely. Larry was retiring that season and needed to end his career in the championships, or at the very least, in the playoffs. Talk about the end of an era. But, umm. What was I going to say? Umm, yes, I was going to say that I wasn't worried."

Really? Your daughter gets pregnant by her college boyfriend, out of wedlock, and you don't worry?

"Why not?" Carissa asked.

"Faith," Grandpa said and took a very deep, calming breath.

He closed his eyes and smiled. "Every time I wanted to get riled up or started to think about how she would take care of the child, if she would get married, would it be a healthy baby, what if Tom's not the right guy for her? I mean, he isn't a Christian. Despite our efforts, your mom wasn't a true believer. So, what about our grandchildren? Does this mean they won't be believers? But every time I thought of something that would make me worry, it faded away. It was replaced by peace, and faith. I knew things were going to work out."

Alright. Is this where I hear things are going to be okay for the five thousandth time? I expected something more from you, Grandpa.

Carissa shrugged. "So, everything's going to be just fine, right?"

"Eh, eventually," Grandpa said.

Wait. What? Carissa frowned. "Eventually? What do you mean 'eventually'?"

"Exactly what it means in the dictionary."

Now wait a second here. "Isn't this the part where you cheer me up and tell me everything's going to be okay?"

"You don't need cheering up," Grandpa said. "You need faith. Things work out in the end, as God uses all things for our good, but everything's not going to be okay or fine or easy all the time. Things are going to be challenging, exhausting. Character building. Being a parent may be the hardest thing you'll ever have to do, and you're starting very young. Younger than your mother and grandmother. It's going to be a trying couple of years."

"Okay," Carissa said. "So, does this mean you're worried about me and not my mom?"

Grandpa shook his head. "No. I'm not worried about you. I feel that same peace I did when I found out your mom was pregnant. Now, if I felt any differently, if I felt a stirring in my spirit, I'd have a lot more to say on the matter. But, I don't. I feel calm. You're going to have to climb a very steep hill, especially when dealing with the biological father. But, God willing, life is going to be beautiful once you make it over this hump."

He paused. "You know, the way you used to take care of your little brother when you were younger, and the way you watch over him and your cousins now, especially when you think no one's looking, I have the feeling you're going to be an excellent mother. You don't have to worry about that either. You're going to be a terrific mom."

Really? You think so?

Tears collected in Carissa's eyes. She hadn't realized how much she needed to hear that. She gave Grandpa a hug.

"Thanks, Grandpa."

2

Early Christmas morning, Carissa woke up, ran to the bathroom, and puked her guts out. *Ugh. Please end soon.* When she opened the door, Mom, her aunts, and cousins were up and watching her.

Great. An audience. Should I do a little dance? "This is the greatest show on Earth!" Kick. Kick. Jazz hands.

On her way back to bed, commentary on morning sickness began. She didn't want to hear it. She didn't want to talk about it. She was exhausted and nauseous, and wanted to go back to sleep. Their words were efficiently drowned out by a pillow over the head.

"You shouldn't do that," someone said. "You'll deprive yourself of oxygen, which deprives the baby of oxygen."

If you don't shut up, I will deprive you of oxygen. Just let me go to sleep!

It didn't take much work to fall back to sleep. The day had just begun, but already felt like she ran a marathon and followed that with a singles tennis tournament. Her body ached. She could barely move. This was the worse it had ever been.

What happened to just a little nausea and morning sickness? If this is how I'm going to feel this whole pregnancy, I quit.

Mom brought Carissa a banana-strawberry-pineapple smoothie blended with strawberry ice cream and insisted she eat an omelet, just to build her strength. As she took her first sip, she beamed and stretched out her weak arm for a hug.

You are the best mom ever.

By ten o'clock, the young ones opened all their presents. The teens and adults watched and waited on grumpy, pregnant Carissa before opening their own. Eventually, Uncle Angus, a large and hairy man jokingly referred to as half-man and half-bear, a very ginger bear, picked her up out of bed, cradled her like a baby, and carried her into the family room. Then, the rest of the family opened their presents.

Most of Carissa's gifts were for tennis and golf. Tennis balls. Golf balls. A new sand wedge. Polo shirts. Sporty skirts. Sports bras. Tennis shoes. Most of the items were from her public wish list she forgot to update or remove.

Ha! Jokes on me! None of this will fit because pregnancy will make me fat. And once I have a baby, and am in college, there's no way I'll be able to play sports. Thanks everybody! Thank you so very much.

Sigh.

I guess I can't get too upset. It's not like any of them knew until two days ago.

The last gift, the best gift of all, was from Grandpa. Mom walked her to the bathroom and Grandpa sat outside and kept her company. When she finally stepped out, he looked around to make sure no one else was looking and handed her a small wrapped box.

She accepted the box and looked around, confused. "You're not usually the mysterious type. What's up?"

"Open it and find out." Grandpa smiled and rubbed his hands together mischievously.

Should I be concerned? I don't want to be concerned, but I'm concerned.

Carissa unwrapped it. It was a Ray Bans sunglasses case. "Ray Bans! Wow! Thanks, Grandpa." She gave him a hug. "You and Mom must be in sync. I just saw a kind I wanted Monday. I couldn't get them since we were getting presents for everyone else. Are these the red ones?"

Grandpa shrugged. "Why are you asking me? Just open it."

Fair enough.

She opened the sunglasses case, and her jaw dropped. *That's not a pair of sunglasses.* She looked up at Grandpa with wide eyes. "Oh my God. Oh... just... oh my God! This, this is, this can't be. Are you serious?" Her voice raised to a near scream.

Grandpa hushed her and looked around. "Hey kid, I'm trying to keep this quiet," he whispered. "If the others get wind of this, you're going to have a lot of jealous cousins." He thought about it. "And aunts, and uncles."

I can't keep this secret. I've kept a lot of things secret. I am the secret keeper. But I can't keep this secret. This is what I've wanted for the last two years.

"I can't believe it." Carissa stared inside the sunglasses case. "Are you sure?"

Grandpa chuckled. "That's what your grandma said. And then, when I told your mom, that's what she said. You Cowden women are consistent. That's for sure."

Okay.

Mom came around the corner. "Sean's about to open his presents. Come on you two." She looked at the sunglasses case. "And hide that before someone sees it."

Carissa closed the sunglasses case and looked around for a place to hide it. *But where?* She quickly stuffed it in her shirt. It stuck out over her bra.

Mom snorted. "That's ridiculous." She plucked it out. "I'll put it in your purse. Come on."

My stupid nosy cousins better not go through my purse. I can always tell.

Carissa and Grandpa followed her to the family room.

Sean was happy with his new clothes, but more so with the kyudo set. Dad proudly bragged about Sean's kyudo skills. Uncle Liam said it was okay for him to fire one arrow inside the house, just to demonstrate to the family.

Aunt Jessica quickly objected, "No, he cannot."

Carissa pulled a tennis ball out of her gift pack and handed it to Uncle Liam. "Here. Use this."

This will technically destroy one of my presents. I hope whoever gave it to me doesn't get offended.

Sean opened the screen door, sucking all the heat out of the room, and instructed Uncle Liam to throw the ball at a tree a few meters from the house. After putting on his boots and jacket, Uncle Liam stepped out, to the right. Everyone except Uncle Liam collected behind Sean in anticipation. Uncle Liam threw the tennis ball. Sean launched his arrow and pinned the tennis ball to the tree.

The room erupted in applause.

Sean smiled, happy to get the attention. He held it for twenty minutes as they pointed at things in the yard they wanted him to shoot. Aunt Jessica apprehensively listed items in her yard she didn't want damaged. *Good luck with that.*

Carissa yawned, laid back on the couch, and fell asleep.

Two hours later, Carissa woke up to see family dressed and putting on their coats and hats. *I guess I'm not going to the movies.* It was another Cowden Family Christmas tradition. After morning breakfast and opening presents, they went to the movies. The usual choice was whatever new Christmas-themed comedy released. Three hours later, they would return, eat, and have a game night.

Three more hours of sleep. That's fine with me. Especially since I can go to the movies anytime I want now. Thank you, Grandpa!

Mom chose to stay home, watch Carissa, and help grandma prepare sandwiches and soup for when everyone returned.

Grandpa didn't want to go to the movies. He said it was a waste of money for him to go since he'd probably fall asleep during the movie anyway. Uncle Angus said Grandpa snored loudly the last time they went to the theater. Half the theater was mad at him. He hadn't gone back since.

Poor Grandpa.

As everyone filed out, Carissa called out for Dad and gave him a long hug. She squeezed him extra tight.

"Get some rest, Munchkin," Dad said and kissed her forehead.

He hasn't called me that since I was like, eight. Carissa grinned, barely able to keep her eyes open. "Okay."

Dad let go of the hug and said, "I love you, honey."

"I love you, too, Daddy." She smiled and yawned and closed her eyes.

It was the last time she saw her father alive.

3

Thomas Boisseau and his son rode down Main Street on their way to the movie theater when a red truck drove through the Main Street and West Lane intersection at full speed and smashed into their sedan. The driver's side took the full impact of the hit. The sedan was pushed off the road and rolled into the ditch. Sean hung upside down, barely conscious. Thomas,

DAKOTA

broken from head to toe, whispered his final words to his son, then breathed his last breath.

CHAPTER TWENTY-FOUR

In Winter,
  there's cold,
  still silences,
  and death.
  It's not the last
  of the seasons,
  but the first.
  In death,
  there is beginning.
  From nothingness,
  there is life.
  This has always been
  the way.
  Death comes
  and resurrection is not far behind.

It didn't feel real. Nothing felt real anymore. But there Carissa sat, in the front row, dressed in black, at the wake of her father. Mom, a total wreck of cries and tears, sat beside her. Sean sat as silent and still as a stone, with Rebecca holding his hand. At the podium was Dad's younger brother, Pierre, telling stories of his childhood. He was two years younger but looked like a carbon copy.

Two days after the accident, the Boisseau family landed in Connecticut. Uncles Liam and Angus took turns transporting

DAKOTA

family from the airport. It was the first time both the Cowden and Boisseau family were together since Mom and Dad's wedding.

Grandpa and Grandma Boisseau were the first to arrive. Grandma was broken up, and barely spoke. Dad was the second youngest, but her favorite.

Pierre, his new girlfriend, Sabine, and his daughter, Lisa, arrived a few hours later. He looked shaken and tired. It had only been two years since his wife passed. Dad had introduced the two in high school. Now two of his favorite people were gone.

The rest arrived within an hour of each other. Uncle Akio and Aunt Sabrina, with their five daughters, flew in from France. Uncle Aiko and Aunt Katsu and their three children, and Aunt Alana and Uncle Yori and their three daughters, flew in from Japan together. Dad's uncles Gunther and Halbert, and his Aunt Heidi, and a few cousins flew in from the UK and France.

The amount of family support and attendance was overwhelming. Any hard feelings between Dad and family after the financial crisis and his alcoholism were mute. They all came together to remember the affectionate child, comedic teen, focused adult, and loving father that was Thomas Boisseau.

By the time Boisseau family arrived, the wake and cremation were scheduled. Mom didn't want Dad to be cremated, but knew it was what he and grandma wanted. Carissa felt a deep stab in her heart. The man she hugged only two days ago would be a pile of ashes. She would never see or speak to him again.

Her father, the man that held her and rocked her to sleep; the man that read her bedtime stories; the man that played princess tea parties with her; the man that sat her on his shoulders; the man that tucked her in and kissed her on the forehead; the man that helped her with her math homework; the man that danced with her at daddy-daughter dances; the man that taught her how to play and excel at golf; the man that was her rock when she needed a shoulder to cry on; the man that never made her feel anything other than loved, was gone.

When Pierre left the stage and sat next to Sabine and Lisa, Sean was called to the podium to say a few words about his father. He sat silent, still, for a half minute before going up. He avoided eye contact, and instead kept his eyes down. He'd barely spoken since the accident. He came out with only a few bruises, scrapes, and cuts. The greatest damage was to his psyche after watching the life leave his father's eyes.

The moment Rebecca was told Sean and Carissa's dad died, she threw the remainder of her allowance and Christmas money into a one-way ticket to Connecticut. She showed up the day after the accident and didn't leave Sean's side.

"I thought, when I came up here, something would come to me," Sean said and closed his eyes. "I didn't prepare anything to say." He took deep breaths. "The last words. The last words that came from his lips, I hoped that I could repeat them. I hoped that I could make sense of what it was he was asking of me. And, share that knowledge with you. Now that I understand, I'm not sure what I'm supposed to say."

He tightened his fists.

"Father always told me that men at peace within are like stones. Durable. Still. Silent. Patient. Timeless. Calm. And sometimes cold. Under great pressure, our final form is precious and unbreakable."

Grandma Boisseau smiled. Those were the words of her grandfather and father, who passed it on to her brothers and sons. She was glad her sons were passing it on to theirs.

"I am a stone," Sean said. It was echoed by the Boisseau men. He stood still and silent for a few seconds, then returned to his seat.

After the wake, family came together to discuss how they could help. Some offered monetary support. Others were willing to visit more often. Pierre offered to spend New Years with them in Richmond. Grandma Boisseau also offered to stay in Richmond for a longer period and help around the house. She wanted to spend more time with her grandchildren and oversee Carissa during the pregnancy; even if it meant spending time with Kate, the woman who kept her precious son in America.

Carissa's pregnancy was no longer a secret, but not a single soul had an issue with it. Grandma Cowden, who hosted both families from Japan in her summer home, filled them in on what Carissa had been through in the past two months. Rape, depression, nightmares, threats, and being pressured into an abortion. The woman didn't spare any details that were given to her. As much as Carissa insisted on her privacy, she was too grieved to care.

I am a stone, Carissa thought and gazed out of the window into the snowy abyss. There were no more tears left to cry. She could barely feel at all.

2

Carissa waited in the driver's seat of a sleek, silver station wagon, the new car Grandpa Liam bought her, while Mom, Sean, and Rebecca said their farewells.

She couldn't attend the cremation. It cut her deep that Dad was dead, lying in a coffin. She hated that Dad's body was burned to ash, put in an urn, and might be placed at home. When Great Grandpa died, Dad wanted a piece of him at home. His ashes were distributed amongst multiple family members. There was an urn of him at home, too. It made her uneasy. Now, she might take Dad home, too. She wanted a part of him with her, but not like this.

Grandma Boisseau wanted to put most of Dad's ashes in a larger, family urn. Carissa saw it when she visited their home. It was large, with a family crest embroidered with gold lettering in old Japanese. She said their family was once prominent. The shadow guard of Japanese royal families and nobility since the first dynasty. The ashes of their family members for the last ten centuries were stored in that urn. Something about it made her want to scream. She believed in ghosts and spirits and couldn't imagine what would happen if it were ever disturbed.

What solidified her belief was the dreams. Whenever she stayed in their house, the guest room was not far from the Room of Honor, which held most of her family's relics. She had the most vivid dreams. Some of them were pleasant memories of living off farmland, feeding animals, laughing with family, and falling into the arms of the one she loved. But other dreams were full of suspicion, fear, and a few required the bloodying of her sword.

What's wrong with me? I watch too many movies. That's what's wrong with me. None of that was real. It was just in my imagination.

But didn't you say it yourself, after Jay's speech, that you knew it was real? All of it. Couldn't you feel it? It's as real as real gets.

Sean opened the back door for Rebecca, closed it once she was in, and walked to the other side. His face was still and stoic. *I've never seen him like this before. I don't know what to do.*

It pained her soul to lose her father. What was it like for Sean, being next to him, watching him die? What was it like feeling his breathing slow and stop, seeing the light in his eyes dim? What were his last words?

Sean never said. And as much as she wanted to ask him, it wasn't the time to ask. Not in this state. She had to give him time.

"So, I guess this is it," Carissa said. "We're going home."

She looked to the back, loaded with their luggage. They'd stayed longer than intended. While it was nice to be with family, sticking around after the cremation wasn't going to work. They needed to get home and figure out what to do next. Figure out how to live without Dad. They would have to reign in a new year without him.

Uncle Pierre insisted on visiting and celebrating the new year. After repeated assurances that they'd be fine without him, Mom eventually caved in and said he could come. It would be nice for Carissa to spend time with her cousin. "She always wanted a little sister."

The most uncomfortable part of Uncle Pierre's visit would be the physical similarities between him and Dad. They were both younger duplicates of their eldest brother Akio, a spitting image of their father. Pierre's face was slimmer, muscled, hardened. Dad's face was always softer. There was a warmth and tenderness in his face and personality they lacked.

Mom knocked on the driver's side door. Carissa rolled down the window.

"I'm driving," Mom said. It wasn't a question. It wasn't a suggestion. Her voice wavered, but only because Carissa could tell the woman was holding back tears. Her hands trembled. *Are you okay to drive?*

She loved driving. Carissa had no idea why, but Mom did. The more challenging, the better. Snowstorm? Driving with a smile. Rainstorm? Slow, steady, and cackling. Hailstorm? Bring it on, baby. The woman would drive around a tornado without flinching, probably laughing like a mad woman. She loved the movie *Twister* and watched it at least once a month. And so, while Dad drove some, it was her that insisted on getting behind the wheel.

So, what if Carissa wasn't exhausted, nauseated, and slightly ill? What if she was feeling right as rain and wanted to go to the movies? Mom would have gone as well. Mom would have driven through the snow with a big goofy smile on her face. Would she have died? Did she blame herself for his death because, maybe, had she driven, Dad might not have died?

Sean said they had a green light. They were driving fine. It was the red truck that sped through a red light. Did it matter who was driving?

It mattered to Mom. Because that meant it could have been her. She could have died. Did she want to die in his place? Did she wish she died in his place, because she loved him and wanted him to live? Was she relieved it was him instead of her? What was going through her mind? How could she resolve these questions in her mind and the pain of losing the love of her life?

Carissa let Mom drive.

Minutes later, as Mom turned on to interstate eighty-four, Carissa realized something was missing.

"Mom," she looked to the back, not recalling anyone carrying Dad's urn. "Where's, umm, where's Dad's urn?"

Mom kept her eyes straight, driving carefully. She swallowed air and said, "He's going with his mother and older brother, Akio. It's, it's what he would have wanted. She's going to put him in the family urn, with his father, and grandfathers. Your Uncle Akio is going to put some of his remains in a smaller family urn for family members he's closest to at their home."

"Oh," Carissa said. A moment of relief was followed by an ache and pressure in her heart. It felt like two hands reached inside her chest and choked her heart. She teared up. He was really gone. Even what was left of him, taken way.

"I'm sorry," Mom said. "It would have been nice to take part of him home. To have him with us. But, Virginia was never his home. He didn't really want to be there. And I know he didn't want that to be his finally resting place."

She breathed deeply. "After you and Sean went to college, he wanted us to live in England for a while and be a couple train rides away from half his family. Now, he gets to be with them."

Dad loved his family. That's what drove him to work so hard. It made sense.

"I understand."

"He's always with us," Mom said. "We have plenty of memories at home. Pictures. Videos. Personal moments we can hold on to in our hearts and minds. I like to believe the best parts of him will stick with us. The best parts of him are in you."

Yea. I suppose.

"I'm taking him home with us," Mom said and rubbed the back of Carissa's head. "You two are all of him I need."

3

It was late when they finally made it home. Dropping Rebecca off was difficult. She insisted she stay with Sean one more day. Her parents refused the request. She held him for five minutes, gave him a kiss on the corner of his lips, told him she loved him, and went inside. For the first time since his father's death, Sean grinned.

Thank you, Rebecca. God, I'm so glad Kelsea cheated on him. Finding Rebecca was the best thing that could have happened to him. She's so much better than any girl he's ever liked. He better not screw this up or so help me...

The inside house lights were on when they arrived. Carissa didn't remember leaving any on. Mom and Dad set a timer for lights on the outside, but not inside. Or did they? It seemed so long ago. Everything was a blur. But there were other oddities.

First, paint cans were on the porch. There weren't any when they left. Why would there be? Second, the paint on the front of the house was still wet. Who painted the front of their house while they were gone? Why? Third, the porch chair grandpa bought three years ago was missing.

What the—? I loved that porch chair. Sitting on that chair is like having grandpa around when he's not around.

"Why are the lights on?" Sean asked as Carissa opened her mouth to ask the same question. She looked at him and then Mom. "And, what's with the paint?"

Really? You're quiet almost all the way home, and when you finally have something to say, you steal my lines.

DAKOTA

"It's been a long day," Mom sighed. She unlocked the door and deactivated the security system. "Let's bring in our luggage and call it a night. I'll explain it to you in the morning."

"But," Carissa said. "What about grandpa's chair? Is it inside?"

Mom teared up. "Just wait until the morning, Carissa. I need to rest. I can't have this conversation tonight." She gave Carissa and Sean a hug. "Could you bring the bags in?"

"Sure," Sean conceded. As Mom walked away, his eyes examined the front porch. "Something's wrong here."

"Yea," Carissa said. "I got that much."

Sean leaned close to the paint without touching it and pulled out a small flashlight he kept with him. *I always wondered why he carried that around. I guess for situations like this.* He turned around and scanned the street.

"Do you recognize that car?" Sean said and nudged his head. "The one across the street. It's not the Sanderson's car."

Carissa squinted. It was a black sedan. She didn't recognize the make or model. The windows were tinted.

Sean stepped off the porch and walked towards Carissa's station wagon. She followed him half a minute later, but he was gone.

Okay...

"Sean?" Carissa called out. Nothing.

What the—? Where'd he go?

She searched the car. Not there. She searched behind the house. Not there. She looked back to the sedan and saw a shadow rapidly approach it from behind the Sanderson house.

What the—? Is that? Is that Sean? How'd he get over there so quickly?

He had a quill of arrows on his back and bow in his hand.

What are you doing?

Sean tapped on the driver's side window with is arrow, aimed and ready. As the window lowered, so did his arrow. It was Detective Summers.

4

In the morning, Carissa, Sean, and Detectives Summers and Priest sat around the kitchen table while Mom prepared coffee and hot chocolate. Carissa wasn't allowed to have coffee. Sean hated it. The detectives said they lived off it.

After Mom distributed the drinks and sat, Summers started, "On Christmas morning, your neighbor, Jeff Sanderson, stepped out to get his newspaper. He looked up and saw your house."

He laid seven photographs of their house on the table, one by one. The first two pictures were a straight shot from the road. Picture one was wide span. Picture two zoomed in on the porch. WHORE, in big, bold, red capital letters, was spray-painted on the front of their house, next to the door. The gray, fabric porch chair was covered in red spray paint. *Grandpa's chair.* The second three pictures were close-ups of the mailbox. One each for the top and left and right sides. Someone drew red penises with a fine paintbrush. The final two pictures were from the right side of the house. One picture spanned the entire house. One picture focused on more spray paint. In big letters, it read, "Carissa loves the cock. But it will cost you."

Carissa felt like she'd been punched in the gut. Her face red. She thought she might get sick. *Why? Why are they doing this? I didn't do anything to them.*

Sean's knuckles cracked under the table, startling her. He fumed.

Mom was exhausted and distant as she sipped her coffee. Dark bags swelled under her eyes. She hadn't slept but spent most of the night crying.

Poor Mom.

It wasn't the first night she slept without him. But she laid in their bed, for the first time, aware he wasn't going to sleep beside her ever again. She smelt his scent in the pillows and sheets. Clung on to them and wept. Come laundry day, his scent would be gone. His musk was in the air. But eventually, even that would fade away.

When she finally slept, just for an hour or so, he was in her dreams. Maybe that was all she would have left of him. In that case, all she wanted to do was sleep.

Summers snatched up the pictures and put them in a manila envelope. He set it to the side and pulled out another envelope.

"There were also pictures left in the mailbox," he said. He avoided eye contact. "Images of an intimate nature. If you want to see them," he slid the envelope across the table, "they're in there."

Oh no. Oh my God. They've seen me naked. Those bastards put pictures of me naked in a mailbox. How many people have seen them? How many more will see them? I can't believe this! Why are they doing this to me? What did I do to deserve this?

Carissa didn't know what to say. She didn't have any words. She gaped at the envelope and reached for it with a trembling hand. Two months had passed since that terrible night. If she opened that envelope, how much of that night would flood back at her? What would it be like to see herself in a drugged state? Lying there, helpless, naked and used.

"There are six images total," Summers said. "Four of you, alone. Two with someone else, edited, to conceal the other party's face and any identifying marks." He paused. "There was also a note."

"A note?" Carissa asked. *Of course, there's a note. The psychos always wrote a note to toy with their victims.*

Summers pulled out a photocopy and read, "I don't make threats. I make promises. Do as you're told or face the consequences. This is your final warning."

The room was silent. The threat hung in the air.

"Your final warning?" Mom repeated. "What's that supposed to mean?"

My life is going to be even more of a living nightmare. That's what it means.

"He's trying to intimidate her into taking those abortion pills," Summers said. "He's threatening to go through on his promise of humiliating her."

Priest, who had been unusually quiet, chimed in. "As difficult as this may be to believe, it helps your case."

"How so?" Mom croaked before clearing her throat and sipping some more coffee.

"He admitted to the possession of sensitive images when he confronted Carissa in her classroom," Priest said. "He also threatened to share those images. This note, this vandalism, corroborates that statement." She nodded to Summers.

He said, "You told us multiple pictures were taken of you by voyeurs. The images here make it clear Kent and Brian took images of you as well, while in the act. There is no doubt more images, including unedited images with Kent's face in it, are stored somewhere. We have more than enough grounds to form an invasive IT investigation. When it comes to the possession and distribution of underage pornography, which is what this is, we have more leeway to aggressively infiltrate suspected computers and hand-held devices. All we need is a little evidence to get a warrant. We can walk in their house and take every computer, recordable DVD, and external hard drive. We'll need a separate warrant from a different judge to access Brian's devices. However, we're working on that, too."

"An IT specialist who handles sensitive cases scheduled the first flight he could," Priest said. "He's in route now. He should be landing in an hour. He'll be helping us with the next phase of the investigation."

"Next phase?" Mom lowered her coffee cup. Her grip tight. "What's been done so far? They've impregnated my daughter, almost pressured her into an abortion, and vandalized my home. Something has to be done."

"Can you arrest them?" Carissa asked. "Can you at least drag them in for questioning?"

Priest and Summers exchanged a look. Summers nodded. Priest pulled out an eight by five inch hardbound notebook with a pink cover and golden spiral. A diary. *This is new.* She rested it on the table and took a deep breath.

"I know this isn't easy," Priest said. Her hand and eyes rested on the notebook. "The patience we're asking of you. I've been there with my sister's assault." *Really?* "I hope you understand that we're approaching this investigation in the best way we see to secure a conviction." Her eyes shifted to Carissa, then Mom, then Sean, and finally, back to the notebook. "What we need is more information. Since we're working with the greatest degree of subtly, it'll take more time to collect what we need. I don't want the Bradshaws to know we're on the case until we already have something concrete to hold them on. We don't want them to know about the investigation until we're already on their heels, inside their computers."

She opened and closed the diary. Felt the cover. "We've laid out a solid plan of action with timetables. There are people we need to interview we can't risk interviewing, yet. People who'll tip them off the moment they're out of our custody. If we're too hasty, if we make a move before we have the right pieces in place, they will lawyer up. They'll pay people hush money. They'll destroy evidence. Whatever it takes, they'll do it. To prove rape, we need evidence. So, it's best to play the strategy game. Let them think they're getting away with it just a little bit longer. Once our tech specialist gets here, that's when the next phase, the more aggressive phase of this investigation begins."

"They trashed our house," Mom said. "They have to know we've called the police at this point. I don't see how this plan can work. Wouldn't they have seen the police around our house?"

Summers shook his head. "No."

Carissa and Sean looked at each other.

"What do you mean, 'no'?" Mom asked.

"Well," Summers said, "we didn't have a patrol car drive to your house. We had an unmarked car arrive. The officer, dressed in suit and tie, took the front, side, and mailbox pictures with his high-def camera. We had a casually dressed service crew come in, fix some things, and collect evidence, footprints, fingerprints, things of that nature. Detective Priest collected the items from the mailbox. We had our officers come in a moving truck, in casual clothing, and collect the porch chair that was urinated on and spray painted—"

Urinated? They urinated on grandpa's chair!? No one said anything about them urinating on the chair. Those animals! I am going to kill them. I'm going to rip off their filthy little peckers and beat them to death with them.

"For all they know, the insurance company visited," Summers said. "I bought the paint. Me, Officer Graham, your doctor friend, her husband, and two of your neighbors repainted the house. There was no trace of official police involvement in any of this."

Wait. You painted our house? That's, that's, so unusual. I don't understand. Police officers don't do that. Why would you do that?

"You painted the house?" Carissa asked.

Summers shrugged. "I used to paint houses with my dad during high school and for extra money in college. I painted my own house. And family members' houses. I know what I'm doing.

It was the least I could do, considering what you've been through."

"Why?" Mom asked.

"Surely," Summers explained, "the Bradshaws have to be asking themselves the same question. To their knowledge, you haven't reported the rape. Carissa didn't have the abortion but kept the money. She left school after being threatened. And, when they vandalize your home, you don't call the police. Instead, you remove the chair and have your house painted. It looks like it never happened. They must be confused. They're probably halfway suspecting you don't want to get the police involved. I think they'll keep testing the waters. But also, possibly. Without police involvement, that leaves them thinking they can do whatever they want. They've already been sloppy. I want to keep them sloppy. Keep their guard down."

"Hmm." Mom seemed to perk up and nod, agreeing with his logic.

"The longer we can maintain the illusion there's no police involvement, the better," Summers said. "They've tied their own nooses. Now, we just need them to put their necks in them."

Carissa couldn't help but to smile at the idea of Kent hanging from a rope. There was hope, yet.

"The good news is: we'll be cataloging the DNA from the chair's fabric and cross-referencing it with the DNA from your child. If there's a match, we'll have DNA evidence that the father of the child was at the scene of the crime and urinated on the chair. Once we can match the DNA with a person, we can tie him to the rape, vandalism, threats, and inappropriate pictures."

Mom let out a sigh of relief. "Thank you so much."

"My pleasure," Priest said.

Finally. Carissa watched her family take the news well. *Maybe things are going to work out after all.*

5

In the afternoon, after a long nap, Carissa nibbled on a strawberry breakfast bar and staggered into Dad's office. It was as he left it. Nothing was disturbed. She wondered how long it would stay that way. When would the decision come that it's time to clear Dad's office out? Who would be the first person to claim it as their own? Would they leave it as it is like a memorial?

She looked at the family portrait on the wall. On his desk were pictures of each of them. The picture of Mom was from their one-year anniversary. She posed in Times Square with an ice cream cone in her right hand and chilly dog in her left. Her face twisted with her tongue out. She looked so young and free and silly. It was hard to reconcile that image with her mother this morning.

The picture of Sean was from his first karate class. The boy had to be three years old. He stood in horse stance with an eye on the camera and a big smile. Carissa grinned and wiped the dust off the frame. Dad kept telling Sean to drop the smile and look serious, disciplined. Dad wanted to capture the image of a child warrior. The more he wanted Sean to look serious, the more Sean laughed. At that age, it was hard for him to take anything seriously. The kid would laugh at paint drying. Now, he took everything seriously, except his sister.

The picture of Carissa was from her first day of kindergarten. She didn't want to go. Mom and Dad took her together in hopes they could calm her down. She cried all the way there, in the office, when they left the office, and at the door to kindergarten class. The image was of Carissa clinging on to Dad's leg for dear life. Both of her arms and legs were wrapped around his left leg. Mom brought the camera hoping her mood would change. She wanted to capture the image of a smiling kid holding a sack lunch and heading off into the educational world. Instead, she was embarrassed. But, some part of her still felt the need to take a picture. Capture that moment in life when little girls were inseparable from their parents. From their daddies. That moment would pass.

Carissa teared up.

She loved his choice in pictures. They captured their true selves. Mom's spirited humor. Sean's untamable joy. Carissa's attachment to those she loved.

She sighed and leaned back in his chair. If she could see him one more time, what would she say to him? What could she say? It was when you wanted to say something of value and consequence that you couldn't.

Her eyes shifted, almost on their own, to the bottom drawer

of his computer desk. It was slightly cracked open.

Carissa righted herself and opened the bottom drawer just a little bit, just to peek. Not that he was going to storm in and ask her why she was nosing around where she shouldn't. There was no real need for stealth anymore. The man's secrets were no longer his to keep. She pulled the drawer completely out and noticed a card sitting on a stack of papers.

Wait a second. Is that—is that what I think it is?

She reached down and grabbed the card. It said: Jay Canus. Author. Independent publisher.

Get outta here. This can't be—

She turned the card over. On the back, a handwritten phone number, "Kingdom First Trinitan Church", and little hearts Carissa drew around his phone number, filled in with pink highlighter.

The business card I thought was lost. I can't believe it! Dad had it the whole time! How did he get it? I remember putting it in my purse. Then it was gone. I was never able to figure out how it went missing.

She stared at the card, glanced around the office. She wouldn't find any answers. The man who knew why it was in his desk drawer was gone. He would never tell her how or why it made its way out of her purse and in his office. In the drawer. But she could come to her own conclusions.

CHAPTER TWENTY-FIVE

"Oliver!" Summers called out and waved his arms. "Over here."

Anywhere but the airport, it would have been impossible to miss a man of his stature towering over the crowd waiting for friends or family or leaving the gate.

Priest watched a short, thin, balding man with a laptop bag and one piece of luggage march straight past them. He wore earbuds. She waved and yelled after him. "Detective Courier! Detective Courier!" The man kept on walking. "I don't think he heard us."

"No, I heard you," a voice said behind her.

Priest whipped around, startled.

Behind her was a brown-haired man with three large pieces of luggage. He wore an *Albert Einstein* with his tongue out black tee. The shirt was tight enough to cut off his circulation and advertised his large pecks, washboard abs, and muscular arms.

Oh Jesus.

Her eyes widened as she took in his handsome face. His hair was tied into a ponytail. He did not look like a bookworm, workaholic tech specialist turned detective. He looked like a runway model that forgot to shave.

"You thought that was me?" Oliver asked and put his hand over his heart. "Honestly, I'm offended."

Priest rolled her eyes. The man didn't have a digital fingerprint. No social media accounts. No pictures of him in any of the articles about his family. Even his driver's license picture was inaccessible. The man was a ghost. How was she supposed to know what he looked like?

Summers smiled and shook Oliver's hand. "Good to see you, bud."

"Nathan, my man, picking me up from the airport." Oliver pulled Summers in for a hug and pat on the back. "I hope Maggie doesn't get jealous. Didn't she have to take a taxi last month?"

A month ago, Summers was busy with a break-in at a jewelry store and couldn't get away to pick his wife up from the airport. Instead, she took a taxi and met him at the crime scene.

Summers chuckled. It was like watching two ten-year-old boys reuniting after summer break. "Naw. She'll be jealous when I drop you off. Because she wishes she could send you packing."

Oliver laughed. His white, perfect teeth gleamed. *Good grief.*

Summers handed Oliver the case summary report and grabbed two pieces of luggage. "Thanks for coming. I know you've been busy. I hate to pull you away, especially with your recent complications at work."

What complications?

"No problem, man," Oliver said. "It was perfect timing, honestly. When you told me the details of this case, I wanted to hop on the plane right away. Almost used my dad's private jet. We'll get these guys."

"Curious," Priest said. "What about this case pulled you away from a trafficking task force?"

"Can't say, yet. But trust me when I say, you've struck oil."

He grabbed his final piece of luggage and followed them outside to the car.

2

"That pretty much wraps up everything that's happened so far and where we are in the investigation," Summers said and pointed to the case board in the conference room. He and Priest wrote key events, points, and their action plan. "Here's our action plan. Amy?"

She stepped in without hesitation.

"First pieces of evidence: one, the check from the bank," she pointed at the notes. "We know what the money was used for and where it went. Two, we have the emails of the clinic appointment: request, payment, and approval. Enough to get a warrant for the clinic's records. We'll hit them first and nail whoever approved her abortion. It's probably the same person that supplied Kent Bradshaw with the abortion pills."

She pointed to a photo of DeQuan. "Next, we're talking to DeQuan. He can verify Carissa was at the party and testify that the Bradshaws hosted the party and provided alcohol to minors. Considering he's royalty at their school and connected to a broader social network, we're hoping he'll be able to provide us with more details about that night, rumors, and pictures. If anyone has videos or pictures of her, they'll have shared it with him. He has three younger sisters and is on Carissa's brother's basketball team. I think we can appeal to his humanity, get him to see things from our point of view. His involvement would help this investigation."

"What if he doesn't want to cooperate?" Oliver asked and sipped from his travel mug.

Priest pressed her lips together and thought. "We'll try our best to be convincing. If he doesn't cooperate, we'll find a way of encouraging his cooperation. Any assistance you can provide would be greatly appreciated."

Thumbs up from Oliver.

"After talking to DeQuan, I plan to have a sit down with Valerie Caulfield," Priest pointed at a picture of Val. "We need a clearer understanding of her involvement. According to Carissa's testimony, the Bradshaws contacted Caulfield first to invite both to the party. We're confident Caulfield contacted the Bradshaws about the pregnancy. The Bradshaws contacted the bank and prepared funds around the same time Carissa informed Caulfield that she was pregnant. Once evidence and clinic testimony tie the Bradshaws to the clinic abortion attempt, we'll get their phone records and determine who contacted who first. From there, I'll have meanable evidence to weigh Caulfield as an accomplice and pressure her to provide us with all the details we need to tighten the noose around the Bradshaws."

"Question," said Detective Frank Paulson, head detective of the sex crimes division. He ran the previous case implicating the Bradshaws and wasn't keen on Summers and Priest taking lead. Despite her request, Rogers refused to exclude Paulson from the briefing.

I'll probably regret this but... "Sure. Let's hear it."

"So far, you've based your entire case on the testimony of one person, right?" Paulson asked. "With no witnesses or physical evidence like blood, semen, or bruises. Nothing proving a lack of consent."

Priest took a deep breath. Yes, they were building an entire case on the testimony of one person. She understood how loose of a case they had without concrete evidence. It was hard to prove rape, especially months later. She also understood how much pressure was on Oliver's shoulders to find digital evidence without violating anyone's rights.

"Yes. But as I'm sure you know, Detective, the testimony of the *pregnant* victim paid ten thousand dollars by the accused carries weight."

"Oh, but of course." Paulson rolled his eyes. "I just had to put that out there. All you have is the testimony of one girl. What if this girl is blackmailing them? Her own friend says she's a liar. You need something solid like witnesses, evidence, just to get through their wall of lawyers. If this goes to court, as if we have enough for charges, we're going to have to stick solely with what we can prove."

"The more evidence we acquire, the more we validate her testimony," Priest said. She felt herself flexing her right hand. A tick when she was losing patience. "The interviews were recorded and time-stamped. As we collect evidence, that is timestamped. It'll work in her favor. It will, one, make it clear that our case is validating her original testimony; two, show her testimony isn't being shaped by the evidence. It will prove that everything she said was true, assuming everything she said was true."

And for all our sakes, I hope this girl is telling the truth, the whole truth, and nothing but the truth, so help me God, Priest thought. *Justice for my sister depends on it.*

Paulson shook his head. "Just as long as this isn't about your personal vendetta to prove their guilt. We didn't have anything on them last case but a girl's diary and torn dress. We didn't have enough evidence for a judge to sign a warrant for the DNA sample of what little we could test after the abortion and removal of the fetus. And even if we had, the evidence would only have proven he was the father."

Personal vendetta? "Listen. Your failure to acquire evidence—" Priest started, nose flared.

"We'll have something solid, soon," Summers interrupted and signaled her to calm down with his eyes. An outburst was all Paulson needed to lodge a complaint that Priest was too emotionally involved. "Witnesses that say Carissa was there. Pictures that will link her to the crime scene, Kent's bedroom. Enough testimony to say she was drinking alcohol and intoxicated. If she was intoxicated, she can't give consent. In his home, his bed, intoxicated, it'll at least give a judge sound enough judgment to get us a DNA sample."

"Umm," Oliver raised his hand, "are we going into the boy's locker room and taking a strand of hair from a brush in his locker?"

"You're jumping ahead," Summers said. Oliver shrugged. "But yes. Either with a warrant or through the special privileges of school administration, we'll use every legal means to acquire Kent Bradshaw's DNA. He gave her abortion pills on school premises. That's reason enough to search his lockers."

"That's a stretch for a warrant," Paulson scoffed. "This action plan has more holes than lace panties."

"Moving on," Priest pressed and took a deep breath. She couldn't let Paulson get under her skin again. "Oliver had a great suggestion after we picked him up from the airport. Please share."

Oliver rapped his fingers on the table. "If we can tap into the social network, get access to shared and tags pictures, we should be able to watch the party play out. Arrange the images and video based on the GPS tracking data and timestamps. Add existing media on the internet from previous mansion tours, we might be able to nail down where the people in the party were, follow Carissa's steps, and catch Val and Jesse on the move. Maybe some voyeurs captured something useful."

Priest glanced at Oliver. *By something useful, you don't mean footage of them having sex. Useful or not, I don't want to see that.*

"Can you do that, legally?" Summers asked. In the last two hours, what Oliver could do without a warrant was asked fifteen times. They couldn't afford shortcuts. Any evidence recovered illegally would be tossed out as inadmissible.

"Well, here's what I suggest," Oliver said wrapped his fingers against the table. "First approach: we find willful participants to give us access to their online profiles, devices, and files. From there, I can identify other individuals at the party, anyone who received or shared inappropriate pictures and press those people to come forward as witnesses and give me access.

"Second approach: we have an eyewitness account of two students discreetly watching and sharing sex videos and pictures in the computer lab and on their phones. She's confident someone mentioned a Halloween party and a fellow student is in the video. The teens trade and sext media with each other. If we get access to the school computer lab, I can fish through the computers and network storage for something we can use. Hopefully, whatever I find will be useful for this case.

"Third approach: I intend to set up a server for Carissa's new email address, since her current one is being hacked. I can set traps. I can dangle bait, like sending a group email detailing her email address has changed. The hacker will try to hack her new email.

"Once he or she accesses the server illegally—through a trap door of my design—and mistakenly downloads something nefarious—cue evil laughter—I'll climb into the window they've opened and observe and take whatever I want. The moment we have proof that her email was hacked and track the IP and location and device information and user activity, we can get a warrant to seize the hacker's computers and other devices. If, while tapped into their computer via nefarious virus, I find something illegal, we can then claim recordable disks, jump drives, and hard drives. Anything they could have saved backup copies to. I've done it before, many times. No lie. I will also be able to see if there's anyone else he's hacked or exploited. I'm sure they'll be more than happy to prosecute."

In the last ten years, Oliver bounced between cybercrime, homicide, sex crimes, organized crime, vice squad, and white-collar crime divisions. He'd built up a reputation and was now the highest demanded IT specialist in New York. Two years ago, the FBI tapped him to work in a federal trafficking task force in conjunction with NYPD's cybercrime and vice divisions. If he said he could do something, she believed him.

"Great," Priest said. "That's exactly the kind of stuff I like to hear." She tried not to look at Paulson but could hear him shifting in his chair. She smirked. "That's brilliant."

Why Captain Rogers didn't rip the case out of her and Summer's hands and put it in Paulson's, she didn't know. All she could do was thank God he didn't. The man would never have reached out or had access to Oliver. He never would have pursued a digital angle. He would have told Carissa there was nothing they could do because she waited too long to report the incident. The vandalism? Sorry, no witnesses. The inappropriate pictures of her in the mailbox? There was nothing connecting them to the Bradshaws. Paulson would have buried his head up his ass, sat in the sand, and let the waves wash over him.

Priest's right hand balled into a fist. She took deep breaths. "Pictures and video were taken before, during, and after the rape." She tapped the warrant items on the board. "Those are our primary objectives. We want to get ahold of all of them, anyone who's ever seen them, and cease all distribution. We're talking justice for Carissa. We don't need anything lingering out there to haunt her." She took another deep breath and nodded to Summers.

Summers pointed at the board. "Which brings us to the recent vandalism. We're comparing the DNA from the couch with the small DNA sample collected from Carissa's blood. In theory, they're able to pull the baby's DNA from the mother's blood. We'll see. If it matches the DNA from the couch, we'll know the father of the child was at the scene of the crime. If it matches, we have vandalism and harassment."

And if we can match the fetus DNA we collected from my sister's womb, it'll be enough to prove someone in their family got her pregnant.

"It's always nice when suspects assist in the investigation," Oliver said.

Summers sipped coffee from his *World's Best Husband* coffee mug. "We still have a lot of work to do. Our focus is discretion. Keep this investigation quiet before the Bradshaws catch wind and lawyer up. Let's make progress without making waves.

Otherwise, the sharks will circle, destroy or conceal evidence, and eat this case alive."

I don't like the idea of the case being eaten alive but agree. The slightest whisper carried over a breeze implicating their desire for digital evidence could mean instant deletion. Lawyers could guard financial and phone records behind hearsay, police bias, and slander arguments. Carissa's a nobody compared to the Bradshaws.

They're already accusing her of being an opportunistic gold digger looking to get knocked up and earn an easy payday. Exactly what they said of my sister.

"Questions?" Summers asked.

Oliver raised his hand but didn't wait. "I'm to assume we've already looked through traffic cams between the Bradshaw and Boisseau residences?"

"Yes," Priest said and pointed to a short, Hispanic man with a buzzcut in the back. He had his feet up and sipped from a *Mysterious Ways Brew* coffee cup. "Chip scanned the traffic logs Trevor sent us. None of the Bradshaw vehicles could be identified. But they could have easily taken side streets that don't have them." She paused. Oliver probably had no idea who Trevor was. "Trevor's our correspondent for city transportation requests."

"I figured as much," Oliver said and rubbed his scruffy chin. "What I don't understand is, why Carissa?"

Priest blinked. "What do you mean?"

"What's their motive?" Oliver asked. "Why drug and rape her when they're high profile bachelors who can get a girl without coercion?" *They wouldn't be the first.* "Think about it. Handsome, rich, socially connected guys like this have lines of eager girls dangling off their balls. I would know."

Some of the guys in the room chuckled.

Priest glared. Oliver was the son and heir of a retired cop who used his wife's family's connections to open a large tech firm called Courier Technologies, Inc. They made state of the art law enforcement and military gear, as well as general consumer products. Last year alone, their company made five billion dollars in gross profits. He was one of New York's most eligible bachelors.

"In all of our discussions, we haven't talked motive," Oliver said. *Because it doesn't make sense. It never does.* "There's got to be a reason why they chose this specific girl, investigated her, reached out, had her brought to the party, made it look like they were a couple or 'hook up', and raped her. It serves no purpose. They have more to lose than gain. It's just as much a mystery as the last girl. She wasn't popular. She didn't play sports, unlike Carissa. And, the only reason she went to that party was an extended invitation through a friend. Same M.O. But why invite her? It's not about sex. Two other questions: what makes this and the last girl different than the others? And why not leave her be afterward?"

Summers leaned forward. "Go on."

"After the rape," Oliver continued, "after they've found out she's pregnant, they try to pay her off. She decides to keep the money and the baby. That would piss anyone off, surely, but it's only ten K. A drop in the bucket. He could have told her to say she got drunk, passed out, and didn't know who the father was. Keep the money. Keep the baby. Don't contact us ever again. Why intimidate her into aborting the child when she hasn't gone to the police?"

"Simple: she could fleece them out of more money," Summers said. "Demand child support."

"She can claim Kent's the father," Oliver responded. "But she'd need DNA evidence. As we all know, you can't force DNA testing without proof of a physical relationship. Even a lousy lawyer will say a person is not compelled to provide DNA evidence based on hearsay or to prove their innocence. And, okay, let's say she does have a witness and proves that Kent is the father. Without a thorough police investigation, like ours, she can't prove rape, which is really hard to do. All she would get is child support for eighteen years. For these people, again, that's barely a drop in the bucket. Twenty to thirty K a year, plus medical visits. That's chump change. Let's round it up to fifty K, as if she could ever get that. It would hurt, but it's still chump change for the Bradshaws. She can't ask for more than that."

Priest's head perked up. She knew where he was headed.

"They can drop a half million in a trust account and move on with their lives," Oliver continued. "Better yet, challenge her for custody, make it a long fight, and drown the Boisseaus in court fees. Instead, they took drastic measures, threats and vandalism, at the risk of her going to the police. All over a bastard child. Unless, unless there's more to it."

"You're saying there's a greater consequence than child support," Summers said.

"For them, absolutely."

"That's stupid," Paulson announced. *You're stupid.* "You're overcomplicating this." Priest frowned. "It's not like they were married. All she could ever ask for is child support, bare minimum. She's not entitled to anything else."

"*She*, wouldn't be entitled to anything else," Priest said and pointed at her belly. "But what about the child?"

Oliver winked. "Being a man of some convenient wealth—" *You look like an attractive street person.* "I know a thing or two about inheritances. We should dig into the Bradshaw family's will and testaments for the current and last three generations. My bet is their inheritance doesn't include a separate clause for legitimate and illegitimate children and, for some reason, they don't have the ability to change that. There's your motive."

"Motive for the threats, not for the rape itself," Priest noted.

"Inheritance isn't automatic," Paulson scoffed. "You have to be written into the will."

"Not always," Oliver smiled. "Knew this guy that was almost written out of his inheritance when it was dramatically revealed that he was a bastard, infidelity three thousand. Still got a piece of the pie because grandpa was non-specific about equal share among his descendants."

Priest wrote *inheritance* on the board.

It doesn't explain why they targeted Carissa, but their reaction to her pregnancy; the attempted payoff for the abortion; and the intimidation. Who knows what they're capable of or willing to do to prevent Carissa's child from getting an inheritance?

Her mouth went dry. If bribery, threats, public humiliation, and vandalism didn't work, they'd resort to harsher measures. Carissa could be in more danger than anticipated.

But if an unwanted pregnancy came at such a high cost, what motivated them to target her in the first place? Why didn't Kent or Brian use a condom and prevent a pregnancy?

"Makes sense." Summers said. "For them, an abortion or accidental death are their only options." He looked to Priest.

They went after my sister. They raped her, got her pregnant, and then forced her into the abortion. It was all too much for her. She was always so sensitive, quiet, and vulnerable. She couldn't handle it. Who knows what else they said and did. They said they'd share pictures of her if she didn't go through with the abortion, told anyone. Between that and the guilt of the abortion, that's why she killed herself. If she killed herself. All so they could protect their inheritance. In theory.

But again, the question remains: why? Why target my sister? Why target Carissa? Why get them pregnant, then try to destroy their babies and lives?

"They have more to lose than I anticipated," Summers said.

Priest plopped down in her chair. "And a strong motive for murder."

Paulson scoffed. "Right now, all you're doing is spitting out unsubstantiated theories and assumptions."

"I hate to say it," Oliver said, "but he's right. We're getting ahead of ourselves. It's best we stick with what's right in front of us for now."

"Agreed." Priest stood. "I'll get started on the warrant for the clinic. We'll nail them on conspiracy and coercing a minor into an illegal abortion and go from there."

Summers looked at his watch. "That's it. Let's get to work."

3

Oliver waited until Priest and Summers were the only ones left in the conference room. "Paulson's going to be a problem. I hate to say this about another cop, especially one in the sex crimes depo, but he's taking a serious piss on this case. Is he in their pocket, or just a grade 'A' asshole?"

"I don't know." Priest hoped they didn't have a rat. That was the last thing this case needed.

Summers swatted that idea out of air like a gnat. "Rogers listened the whole time. I sent him a text, penny for his thoughts. 'Paulson's all ego,' he said. This is a high-profile case. Paulson wants it. If we take the Bradshaws down, it makes him look bad because he didn't get anywhere on your sister's case. It makes him look even worse if you solve her case after only being here for three months."

Makes sense. He bombs and then I swoop in and come out the hero after being a detective for three months. My ego would be bruised, too. But it's not about egos. It's about justice. If Paulson can't get his head out of his ass and do his job, he better stay out of my way.

"I already knew the answer," Oliver said, fingers rapidly at work on his keyboard, "I just wanted to hear your responses. Here are my thoughts, also known as the truth. One, there's a telling tattoo on the back of his neck. When you have a second, check it out. Two, Paulson never investigated the Patterson clinic. There were three clinics in the area that offered abortion services. Wouldn't have taken more than an hour to canvas all three. The fact that he visited the two other clinics, but not Doctor Green's clinic, *the closest clinic*, means something.

"Three, he didn't treat the diary of an alleged suicide victim as credible testimony. Four, he accepted her suicide at face value. According to the logs, he didn't request a viewing of the body, the coroner's report, or a copy of the autopsy. The bruises on her neck were completely disregarded. Was he asleep on the job? No. He's dirty. I'm getting him out of our way."

Priest blinked rapidly. "Out of the way?"

"How?" Summers followed.

Oliver typed a stream of commands on his laptop. "A friend from Internal Affairs was waiting for him outside the conference room. I gave him a peek at Paulson's financials. There are a few irregularities."

Summers frowned, looked over Oliver's shoulder. "Internal Affairs? Was that really necessary?"

"Ask me that two weeks from now."

"We're asking you now," Priest said. "I'm not sure who you're used to working with. But here, we like answers."

"And you'll have answers in two weeks," Oliver parried. "Sooner depending on how quickly you can get me access to the Bradshaw computers, and I find what I need. Their connections. Which reminds me. I figured out how I can get Bradshaw's DNA." He smiled and rubbed his hands together.

Oh, that smile makes me nervous.

"I'm always open to ideas," Summers said. He shrugged at Priest with an apologetic grimace. "Let's hear it."

So, we're just moving past the fact that he tossed Paulson over to Internal Affairs and not demanding any extra details? My sister never got justice because of his lazy work. I want to know what he's done.

Oliver pointed at his shirt. "I can be a substitute teacher." Priest and Summers blinked at him. "You said Kent accosted the Boisseau girl in class. So, we'll use the classroom against him. When the new semester starts, I can substitute teach one of his classes. I'll get close enough to pluck a hair or, if he sheds, pick a hair off his shirt. Maybe he'll leave DNA on his desk. Leave a water bottle. Sneeze or something."

"Hmm," Priest said, "A substitute teacher could get us some fingerprints. Too bad Rogers won't go along with it. Not without serious convincing. This has never been done on such a small, shot in the dark case." She rubbed her chin. "Maybe some Skins tickets could sway him. You might have a solid plan."

Oliver smiled. "Excellent."

Summers pleaded with her to reconsider with his eyes. "A solid plan? Really?"

"Hear me out," Priest said. "I can't go anywhere near that school, or the Bradshaws, without being recognized."

Patterson High was her alma mater. She was the captain of girls' varsity tennis and won the singles district championship two years in a row. She was co-captain of the soccer team. They were national semi-finalists three years in a row, finalists her senior year. She also played basketball. Pictures of her and team lined the halls. Trophies dominated the cases.

Only a few years ago, she had a breakdown after her sister died and made a scene at the school looking for someone, anyone, that could help her sister's case. Three years later, it was still fresh on some minds.

"But he's a stranger," she added.

"And getting stranger by the minute." Summers smiled at his friend. Oliver snorted.

"If Captain Rogers signs off on it," Priest continued, "and the school administrators okay it, you'll have to get that DNA. Find a hair. Give him a tissue to blow his nose. Jerk him off. I don't care. Something. We'll need something. We can't come out empty-handed."

Priest and Oliver looked at Summers and waited for him to cave in. The man had a heart the size of a whale when it came to his friends and colleagues. He couldn't disappoint if he wanted to.

"This is completely outside of protocol for a case like this," Summers sighed. *I know.* "But if Rogers signs off on it, let's do it."

"Sweet." Oliver pumped his fist. "Now, I have to find a lizard and transmogrifying school bus."

The hardest part would be convincing anyone to let this goofy man educate their children.

CHAPTER TWENTY-SIX

On New Year's Eve, no one was in the mood to celebrate. Mom made breakfast, socialized until she couldn't keep herself together anymore, then spent the rest of the day in bed, in tears. Uncle Pierre ordered pizza for lunch, movies on demand, and sat on the couch with Sean. Amy, Mom's best friend, took care of dinner. Later in the evening, Mom dragged herself downstairs and went over the fine details of losing a spouse with Uncle Pierre. He helped her find and print off the necessary paperwork, explained their insurance policies, claim processes, fund distribution, and taxes.

Thank God for Uncle Pierre. In her condition, I wouldn't be surprised if she couldn't write her own name.

While Uncle Pierre tended to legal matters, Elisabeth followed Carissa. She helped with chores and talked about school, a boy she liked in her math class, when she would finally grow in her boobs, makeup application, everything that came to her mind. Carissa didn't mind the distractions from her problems. She liked it when Elisabeth visited. She always wanted a little sister. Elisabeth was the closest thing she had.

Rebecca spent most of the visit putting together a vision board and plotted her and Sean's agenda for the entire year. Things they were going to do. Concerts they were going to see. Books of the bible they were going to study. She filled a large, folding poster board with pictures from news articles, magazines, and printed lists. She also brought a monthly-weekly planner. Sean went along with it watching her in awe.

Sigh. *I wish someone looked at me that way. Well, someone did. But, I lost his phone number. Only, it wasn't really lost, was it?*

How can I be mad at Dad now? Okay. So, he went in my room and stole away my chance to be with a great guy. I don't know his reasoning. I just know he's gone now. I won't get an explanation from him. Maybe Mom? Will Mom tell me, if I ask, if she knows?

Sigh.

As midnight crept closer, Uncle Pierre called them outside and opened a box full of fireworks. Sean's eyes lit up. They each took turns lighting sparklers, launching tiny missiles, and watching the lights and explosions in all their various designs. Some of the kids in the neighborhood came out to watch. Uncle Pierre, a constant lawyer, was reluctant to let any of the neighborhood kids touch the fireworks. He offered fireworks to the parents while, in great length and detail, removing personal liability for any accidental damage or injury to any person or property. He went on for five minutes. The looks on the neighbors' faces was priceless.

Amy interrupted, said, "Don't worry. If anything happens, I'm a doctor," and shot Mom a "Can you believe this?" eyeroll.

For the first time, Mom smiled.

After all the fireworks were lit, they went back inside and watched Time Square's New Year's Eve celebration. As the ball dropped, Carissa cried. It would be the first year of the rest of her life she'd be without her father. It would also be the year she became a mother.

While everyone else went to bed, Carissa, Rebecca, and Elisabeth broke their diets and ate ice cream sundaes with chocolate syrup, nuts, sprinkles, chopped strawberries (for Carissa), and a cherry on top. Then, they all snuggled up in Carissa's queen-sized bed and talked about what was next.

Elisabeth, Rebecca, and Sean were the same age. After seeing what Rebecca and Sean had, Elisabeth made it her new year's resolution to get her first boyfriend and find love. Rebecca said the best way to find love was to first find Jesus, who was and is the greatest example of love man could know. Elisabeth had no idea what she was talking about, so Rebecca went through the gospel of Jesus Christ, Yeshua the Messiah, in detail.

While they spoke, Carissa thought of Jay.

DAKOTA

What am I going to do about Jay? Should I say something or wait? Maybe this is just a silly crush. Maybe I should I move on. No. I don't see how I can. I don't want anyone else.

I don't understand how spending just a few hours with him can mean so much to me. Yet, when I think of love, relationship, he's the only one I can think of. He's the first one that comes to mind. I can't say there haven't been other guys that caught my attention. Or wanted my attention. There's just something about him. Something that tugs at me.

So, what am I going to do?

He has a girlfriend, Amy, the detective. If I try anything, what would happen with her? She's handling my case. I can't just, just go behind her back. And, he definitely wouldn't go along with it. Would I want him to? Would I want him to leave her for me? What would that say about him?

But what if he loves me, too? I mean, he met me first. He liked me first. And he was so excited when he saw me at the church. I could tell, just by the way he looked at me, the way our eyes connected, that there was something real.

I must do something. I know that. He was mine first. He'd be mine if the business card hadn't been taken out of my purse.

Sigh. *I don't know what to do, but I can't do nothing.*

Maybe... I'll just talk to him. Who knows, maybe, somehow, they've broken up, or will break up. Maybe he'll realize that it was me he wanted all along. But he couldn't have me because we had no means of contact. So, he started seeing her. This would have been a lot easier if he took my number.

I'll, I'll text him. That's what I'll do. Just, a fun, innocent text. I could say, "Happy New Year." That's innocent enough. It'll open the door. There's nothing wrong with wishing someone a new year. It'll just get the conversation started.

Yes. That's it. That's what I'll do. And, we can talk about what we did for the holiday. Talk about the new year. Maybe, possibly, we can meet for coffee again.

But that should be his idea. He'll have to suggest it. That way, it's not me going after him. And, this way, I'll be sure he wants me and not her.

Okay. That's what I'll do. That's the plan. I'll text him.

2

Carissa excused herself and went to the bathroom with her phone. She sat on the toilet and pulled together enough courage to text him.

Carissa: "Hey Jay! Happy New Year!!!! ☺"

She waited while checking herself in the mirror. Had she gained weight? A little. It was hard to tell. As tired as she felt half the time, she still tried to stay in shape for tennis and golf. No matter what anyone said about how busy she would be, she needed to stay involved in sports. She needed to keep up her game. It wasn't just about her love of the sport. It was about money now, too. She could make good money if she worked herself into the professional league.

She'd try her best to be a mom, work part-time, and study full-time. But, how would she manage that? Women usually took months to years off from work to tend to their children. If school didn't work out, if she was too tired or busy with the baby to have a job, she had to be able to do something.

There was no way she'd let a baby get in the way of making her dreams come true. In fact, the baby would be her incentive to work harder and make a name for herself. She was a single mom with a dead dad who wouldn't be able to take care of her. She needed all the help she could find. Tennis and golf were her backup plan, her part-time job.

She checked her phone.

Hmm. No reply. I wonder if he's out doing something. I wonder if he's with her. What if they're, like, making out? Oh. What if it's more than making out? That would be terrible!

But, wait, I don't know. Do Christians do that? I mean, they're not married. He's pretty, uh, vocal about his beliefs. From what the Cole sisters say, sex outside of marriage was a big no-no. You think they'd do that if they're not married?

I don't know. She's pretty. Like, crazy pretty. And it's a holiday. New Year's is probably one of the more romantic holidays. I mean, you're starting a new year together. A fresh start. She was probably his New Year's kiss. I wish I was his New Year's kiss.

She stared at the phone.

Son of a—

I feel stupid. He doesn't like me. He's with his girlfriend, not thinking about me.

She huffed, grabbed her phone, and left the bathroom. As she walked into her room, the phone chimed and vibrated. She froze mid-stride to the bed and stumbled over her own feet. She caught the bed and saved herself from a fall.

Elisabeth and Rebecca stopped, turned. Elisabeth laughed. "Are you okay?"

Carissa righted herself, then picked up her phone. "Does my dignity count?"

"Let's say, no," Elisabeth said with a smile.

"Then, I'm perfectly fine," Carissa said and checked her text.

Jay: "Hey Carissa! It's great to hear from you. Happy New Year!"

She beamed and reread the text again.

He's happy to hear from me! It's great to hear from me. What else should I say? He has his phone in his hands right now. I need to figure out what else to say. Or, maybe he'll say something. Should I wait for him to say something else? Will he say more?

"Who are you texting?" Elisabeth asked with watchful eyes.

Carissa felt Elisabeth and Rebecca examining her. "Oh, you know, just a friend." She shrugged, smiled, put the phone in her pajama pants, and slipped into bed.

She couldn't restrain her joy.

I'm not lying. It's not like I'm lying. He is a friend. Kind of. Sort of. We're just getting to know each other. I'd call him a friend. A male friend. Perhaps, maybe, possibly, in the future, he'll be a friend, that is a male, with romantic implications. But he is a friend.

Elisabeth shook her head. "I know that face. I've seen that face. That's not just any friend. That's a boy, isn't it?"

In the literal sense, yes. Though, he's more of a man than a boy. But do I say that? I mean, Rebecca is right here. If I tell her that I'm talking to Jay, she'd probably tell her sisters that I'm texting Jay. Do I want that? I don't want this to be an issue between me and Hannah.

Then again, when he and I do eventually see each other, it'll still be an issue. And who cares. He didn't have a caramel latte with her. He didn't give her his phone number. He didn't give her a hug. They've barely spoken, right? She hasn't said a word to him about her feelings.

Hmm. Now that I think about it, had I not commented on him ordering what I was going to order, we probably wouldn't be talking right now. That means he likes a girl that speaks up. What did Dad always say? Take the initiative or lose the opportunity.

"Kinda, sorta," Carissa said and pulled out her phone. The two leaned their heads forward and looked at the name on the screen after she plugged in her password.

"Jay?" Rebecca said in shock. "You're texting Jay?"

Yep.

"Who's Jay?" Elisabeth asked. "Is he cute?"

Yep. Totally. Carissa nodded.

"He's a guy from our church," Rebecca said. "And, from what Gabby says, and how it appears, Jay has a girlfriend." She gave Carissa a hard look. "A detective, in fact. The same one working on your case, right?"

Well, she and her sisters all have one thing in common. They don't mince words or beat around the bush. She went straight for the guilt trip. Thanks.

"Yea, but it's not like that," Carissa said. *Not yet, anyway.* "I just wished him a happy new year. He responded the same. And we're friends. Friends can talk."

"Mm, hmm," Rebecca said, stared.

I love how black girls say, "Mm, hmm." I can never, ever, duplicate that.

"See, watch," Carissa said. "We're just going to have a short, pleasant chat."

Carissa: "What are you doing for New Year's?"

The girls leaned in and waited for a reply.

Jay: "Well, after referencing one of my favorite TV shows, Castle, for the nth time, I convinced Amy to bring me along for a stakeout. Now, we're waiting. What about you?"

Hmm.

They are together. I was right. Dammit. But I mean, it's not like they're doing anything romantic. They're in a car, watching who knows what, probably bored out of their minds. If they were at a party, with friends, drinking champagne and laughing or at home, together, kissing and grinding after watching the ball drop, maybe I'd be jealous. Maybe. Sigh. Definitely. No doubt about it.

But a stakeout? That sounds stupid. She's going to bore him out of his mind. I give them a week or two. Tops.

"A stakeout?" Elisabeth asked. "On New Year's Eve?"

"I know, right?" Carissa snorted. "Totally lame. I'd definitely make sure he had a better time on New Year's." She could feel Rebecca's glare. "You know. As a friend."

"Mm, hmm." Rebecca doubted. "As a friend."

Elisabeth snickered. "As a friend! Right. And boys look at dirty websites for research purposes."

"Researching that bootay." Carissa reached over and slapped Elisabeth's butt. Elisabeth's head fell back on her pillow as she burst into laughter.

Rebecca rolled her eyes. "Are you going to respond or leave him hanging?"

Oh crap. You're right. Wait! I thought you didn't want me to talk to him. Ah, whatever.

Carissa: "Spent time with family, friends. Having sleepover with the girls. Trying to unwind. Lots been going on."

Jay: "It's great to spend time with the ones you love. I hope you're having fun."

Jay: "You say a lot's going on. Is it something you're open to talking about?"

Carissa froze.

Why did I say a lot's going on? Now what am I going to tell him? I can't tell him I'm pregnant. That'll scare him away. Do I tell him that my dad just died in a horrible car accident? Do I tell him my house was vandalized and that someone peed on my grandpa's porch chair? Do I tell him there are nasty sexual pictures, and perhaps video, of me out there being distributed by rapist rich boys? Man. My life is shit.

"He seems considerate," Elisabeth said.

Rebecca agreed. "What are you going to tell him?"

Nothing. Absolutely nothing. Carissa shrugged. "I haven't a clue what to tell him. But I know how to stall and turn this in my favor."

"How?" Rebecca and Elisabeth asked at the same time.

"This," Carissa said and typed.

Carissa: "Too much to talk about. Don't know where to start. Especially in text. Can I see you? Soon?"

"You didn't," Rebecca said, mouth hung open.

"I did," Carissa shrugged. *Sometimes a girl's got to take the initiative.*

Elisabeth smiled. "That's so bold. I'm never like that. I'm always so shy." She sighed. "Maybe that's my problem. I haven't dated any guys because I didn't put myself out there."

Carissa blinked and momentarily had a flash of when she and Val bought their costumes from *For Every Occasion*. She was in shock and awe of Val's confidence, the way she boldly went after that married man. In the end, Val got what she wanted. He kept the phone number, gave her a call. They were a secret item now.

Was that what she wanted with Jay? Did she really want to instigate a secret relationship with another woman's man? Was she going to be like Val? Could she look at herself in the mirror if she was?

"My dad told me: it's better if the guy pursues," Rebecca said. "What we should do, as women, is make ourselves available. We should be present, close, beautiful, and not sending mixed signals. However, he should be the one who pursues us. Not the other way around."

Jay: "If you ever want to talk, you can find me at church on Sunday. I'm always available."

Jay: "As of now, I couldn't and wouldn't meet you anywhere else. I am in a committed relationship with Amy. So, a private meeting would be inappropriate."

Crap.

Jay: "Still, I would very much like to know what's going on in your life and be of service however I may without the appearance of compromising our integrity in the process."

Crap, crap, crap. Triple the craps.

Jay: "I hope you understand."

What about that wouldn't I understand? You're in the car with her. Obviously, you want to talk to me. But as you said, you're not available at the moment. If anyone saw us having a private meeting, they would talk. I got it.

"Well," Elisabeth sighed. "At least you tried."

Carissa shrugged. Disappointment clear on her face.

Is it wrong that this makes me want him more?

Rebecca repeated uh-huh as she read Jay's texts. "Well, he's right. He does have a girlfriend, and you are seventeen. Let's not forget that. It would be inappropriate for you to meet in private. He did the right thing. That's something to be commended." She turned to Elisabeth. "Now, let's get back to Jesus."

I haven't even responded, yet. What do I say? How do I respond? Maybe I won't. Maybe I'll leave him hanging. It's kind of petty, but I mean, whatever. I've lost him.

Carissa yawned and slipped under the covers with Elizabeth while Rebecca talked about Jesus teaching, healing the sick, removing demons, feeding thousands with several baskets of bread, walking on water, and raising the dead. Elisabeth listened intently, wide-eyed like she was being read a bedtime story.

But it was hard for Carissa to pay attention. She kept looking at her phone, hoping Jay would change his mind and profess his unequivocal love. That text never came. So, instead, she wondered what the new year would bring.

She was pregnant. Alone. Fatherless. She would juggle a part-time job, school, and whatever else life threw at her. When would things get better in her life?

And by get better, she realized, she meant: when would there be a loving guy in her life to make her feel loved and safe, and take care of her needs so she wouldn't have to worry about life alone? When would she have a confidant that she could trust? She needed someone with whom she could share all her fears, worries, doubts, and experiences.

She wanted someone with whom she could finally lay all her cards on the table and feel safe, loved, protected.

New year, you better do me right. I can't take anymore.

Carissa closed her eyes, tried not to cry.

God, don't let this year break me down.

Her phone chimed.

Jay: "Meet me on Sunday. We'll talk. Whatever it is you're going through, I'm here for you."

Carissa smiled.

3

Gabby, Hannah, and their parents came over the next day with a gift basket to add to the collection of gift baskets, edible arrangements, casseroles, lasagnas, pies, flowers, and cards that came in from Mom's friends, clients, coworkers, and neighbors. *Where am I going to put all this stuff?* They came to treat Mom to a day off from motherhood, but also to invite her to church on Sunday.

At first, she was hesitant, even resistant to the idea of doing anything or going anywhere church-related. But by the end of the day, after spending time with the Coles, she changed her mind.

While Uncle Pierre mulled over the details of Dad's estate and insurance, Mister Cole helped fix things around the house. Afterwards, he and Sean played basketball. Mister Cole, a former pro basketball player, was the boys' basketball coach of Yarborough Academy, a private school.

Gabby and Rebecca challenged them to a "boys versus girls" game. Mister Cole firmly declined them, saying he didn't want to deal with any hard feelings on the way home after stomping them profusely. They played with competitive quips, teases, and jeering until Mama Cole called the girls inside to help with dinner. The boys were only two points ahead.

"It's not over," Gabby said.

Mister Cole said, "It was over before it started."

Carissa laughed. They were such a competitive family. Game nights were a laugh riot at their house.

Mama Cole and the girls made soup, sandwiches, and salads for lunch; crispy, egg-battered chicken, chicken broth gravy, mashed potatoes, macaroni and cheese, green beans, and corn for dinner. Everything tasted amazing. *I'm visiting them more.*

During dinner, Mister Cole slipped in a few Christian dad jokes.

"How do you make holy water?" Mister Cole asked.

Carissa shrugged. "I don't know."

"You boil the Hell out of it." He laughed.

"Dad, stop," Hannah complained. "You're embarrassing us."

Mama Cole chuckled and said to Mom, "See what I have to put up with?"

After a week of despair, Carissa saw a little more life in Mom's eyes. She grinned.

The Coles left after dinner. On their way out, they encouraged Mom to come to church on Sunday and invited

Uncle Pierre and Elisabeth to join them.

"Come make some new friends, hear a positive message," Mama Cole said. "You need to get out of the house. Away from all the memories."

Mom hesitantly agreed. As did Uncle Pierre.

By the time the Coles are finished, my whole family will be going to this church.

4

The days turned like wind-blown pages. For the first time, the Boisseaus were going to church as a family. One by one, they piled into Carissa's station-wagon.

Mom wore a long, black-topped flower dress and black flats. Carissa wore a white dress shirt with a black suspender skirt and black flats.

They looked at each other and grinned. Sunday was Flats Day. It would always be Flats Day. Mom made a rule for herself: never wear heels on a Sunday. It was the only day of the week she intentionally didn't have anything to do outside of relaxing and the occasional last-minute shopping. But that was it. If she had to wear heels, to her, it meant she was doing too much. Carissa thought it was smart and adopted the rule.

Sean wore a light blue dress shirt and black slacks, which was set aside two days ago by Rebecca who insisted they color-coordinate. Carissa thought it was the funniest thing ever. The girl ran his life. But he'd never been happier.

Props to this girl for being organized. I'm not sure what I'm going to wear until ten minutes before it's time to leave. Or, ten minutes after.

Uncle Pierre and Elizabeth slid in the back seat with Sean. Carissa bumped into Mom on the way to the driver's side. Mom held her hand out. "Not yet, you're not. Give me the keys."

Are you serious?

"Mom," Carissa whined. "I have a license. I know how to drive. I've driven plenty of times. I can do it."

"I know you know how to drive—" Mom started.

"Then why won't you let me?" Carissa argued.

Mom stared at her. "You're seriously going to ask me that question after your father just died?"

You used the Dad Just Died card? Of course, you did.

Carissa sighed. "He drove to and from work every day for years. So do you." She frowned. "It was a fluke. A stupid fluke because some loser wasn't paying attention and didn't know how to drive in the snow with ice patches in the road."

Mom looked her in the eyes. "I'm driving." It was a command. She extended her hand and waited for the keys.

But it's MY CAR!

"Ugh. I don't know why grandpa got me this car if I can't drive it," Carissa pouted. "I won't be able to drive before I'm too fat to get behind the wheel." She put the keys in Mom's hand and stomped to the passenger's side.

I've begged them for a car, or help getting a car, ever since we got to Richmond. I get a car and now I can't even drive it. All because some idiot shithead didn't know how to drive in the snow and killed my dad. This is so stupid.

Mom rolled her eyes and shook her head. "Carissa." Carissa opened the passenger door. "Carissa."

What do you want now? Carissa looked up with narrow eyes. "Yes?"

"Here," Mom said and passed the keys across the car.

Is she playing with my emotions right now? I'm barely holding it together and can't afford her changing her mind again.

"Before you get fat," Mom said. There was a grin somewhere behind her stone expression. It was the face of a woman that didn't want a repeat of the worst day of her life, but also wanted peace with her daughter.

I suppose this means I won't be able to drive in my third trimester. But whatever. We'll fight that battle when we get to it.

Carissa drove, cautiously. She stayed two or three miles below the speed limit, looked left and right and double-checked before any turns, and let people pass if they looked like they were in a hurry. She didn't want to give Mom any reasons to change her mind.

When they made it to the church, she found the Coles' usual parking spots and put herself a few cars from theirs.

"This is a church?" Uncle Pierre asked as they entered the building, impressed. "I've never seen a church like this before."

"That's because it wasn't designed like a normal church,"

Sean said. "It's the architectural fusion of a university's main campus building, lecture hall, and concert hall. According to the leadership, they never had any intention of operating or looking like a traditional church. It's a school, training grounds for their commitment to the great commission."

The leadership called Kingdom First a university of spiritual development, enrichment, and missionary education. Once you were a member of the church, you had a curriculum. They scheduled open classes, readings, and lectures each day of the week for people wanting to hear or study various books of the bible in detail. A person could go to church any day of the week and study something new.

What was most important, for them, was consistent lessons and guidance on how to build relationships, utilize your potential, embrace your purpose, set a proper example, and have the essential conversations that teach and show Yeshua.

"So, this is some kind of new age church?" Uncle Pierre asked.

"That's one way of looking at it," Jay said as he approached them from around the corner. He walked with his hands clasped behinds his back. "We're focused on what we're called to do and be and grow with God along the way. We take a hard look at scripture, align ourselves according to His word, and figure out how our talents can best serve the great commission. Then, we take action."

He pointed at the mission statement on the wall. "We study. We grow. We teach. We lead. His Word is our truth, our water, our seed."

Uncle Pierre shrugged. "Okay."

That's exactly how I responded when I heard this stuff. I'm glad I'm not the only one.

Jay smiled at Carissa.

Did he just read my mind?

"In short, we're not the kind of place where you only show up on Sunday, listen to someone talk, sing a little bit, have a little bit of introspection, and then pat yourself on the back for being a regular Christian. We expect more out of our people than regular attendance and tithes and offer them more so they can be more. But two definite and important things are that no one who attends our church leaves not knowing The Word or their purpose. If you don't know your purpose, how can you effectively and intentionally serve God as He intended?"

"Sure," Uncle Pierre said and looked at the rest of the family.

Oh brother.

"My Uncle Pierre has no idea what you're talking about," Carissa said. "He's never attended a church service. Not once a single day in his life."

Uncle Pierre shrugged.

"Oh, sorry," Jay apologized. "It's easy for us to get caught up in our Christian speak. Welcome to Kingdom First." He extended his hand to shake. "I'm Jay."

Mom gasped. "You're Jay Canus?"

Ut oh. I suppose they had to meet eventually.

"Yes." Jay smiled. "That's me."

She glanced at Carissa. "The one who gave my daughter the business card."

Is she about to go off on him for talking to me?

"That's... right."

"Author of The Shadow-blood Series?" Mom continued.

Jay nodded hesitantly. "The same one. All of the above." He snapped his fingers. "Oh right! Yes. Carissa said you're a literary consultant and agent. It's a pleasure meeting you." He shook Mom's hand.

She had a business card out of her purse within seconds. "Here. We should talk. I remember reading your complaints about the beginning of your career, the difficulty you found in establishing your name, networking, and promoting yourself. You've become very successful, but I can still help you with that."

Phew. I thought she was going to have a fit about him talking to me. I mean, I know I'm not eighteen, yet. But I mean, come on. One, we just had a coffee and scone. Two, he didn't know my age until after we talked for a while. Three, when he eventually falls madly in love with me, and asks me to marry him, I'll be eighteen.

"Thanks," Jay said and put the business card in the breast pocket of his shirt. "I'll stay in touch. I'm writing outside of my known genre in my next book, after the superhero series. It'll be slower paced. Mystery. Psychological. A pinch a horror. Not too much. I'm not into that, though you'd think otherwise having read my series."

DAKOTA

"I've read all of your books," Mom said, her eyes locked on him. "Twice."

Wait. I'm not liking where this is going. Where is this going?

"Wow," Jay said with a smile. "Thanks! Reading them once is an honor to me. Reading them twice. That's flattering. Thank you so much. I'm delighted you enjoyed my work."

Mom nibbled her upper lip. "But I have to ask you. Why does it feel real? How do you do it?"

"I beg your pardon," Jay said. His face still, tense.

"When I read the series, it felt real, like it *actually happened*. Like I was reading history. All of those people, and the creatures, the shadow-bloods, were real."

"Who's to say they aren't?" Jay asked. He wasn't joking.

Let's just call this the end of that conversation. You're dominating too much of his time. That's my job.

Carissa gripped Sean by the shoulder and nudged him between Mom and Jay. "So this is great and all but Sean, don't you want to show Mom and Uncle Pierre where Mister and Misses Cole meet for adult Sunday school?"

Mom frowned at Carissa, probably because she was being rude.

You're damned right I'm being rude. I don't care. I really don't need you two talking about books right now.

"Of course," Jay said and looked at his phone. "Please, don't let me stop you from getting to class. Time is ticking. I have to get going myself."

"Yea," Carissa continued. "If we keep gabbing, we're going to be late." *We already are.* "Er. Sean, you show Mom where the Coles are. I can show Lizzie where Becca, Gabby, and Hannah are. Jay, I'd like to have a sidebar with you about that thing we were supposed to discuss."

Mom frowned at Carissa but quickly corrected her face for Jay. "Call that number. I'd love to have you visit our office, meet for lunch, talk about books, and what series you have planned for the future."

Mom! This is a church. We're not here to talk business!

"Thanks," Jay said, patted his breast pocket. "I'll definitely do that." He turned to walk away and paused. "Oh, and Carissa, Misses Boisseau."

"Kate," Mom corrected. "My name is Kate."

"Of course," Jay said. "Kate. Communion is a time when we come together as a body of believers and recognize and remember our Lord and Savior, and his sacrifice, through the symbolic consumption of his flesh and blood."

You do what?

"What was that again?" Uncle Pierre asked, bewildered.

Mom smirked. "I know what communion is."

"Right." Jay grinned at Carissa and Uncle Pierre's facial expressions. "I should have phrased that differently. I'm better on paper. That's why I don't speak much here. But we drink the fruit of the vine, grape juice, and eat unleavened bread prepared here in the church. The grape juice is His blood. The broken bread is His flesh. In the last supper, during the Passover celebration, Yeshua ate with His apostles and told them to eat and drink in remembrance of Him. Then, he was tried and killed and rose. His blood paid for our sins. By His blood and flesh, His sacrifice, we are spared from the condemnation of our sins.

"It's biblically tied to the first Passover feast, when God saved the Israelites from slavery. You've heard of the story of Moses, yes?"

Sort of. Grandma made me watch that Charlton Heston movie. The one with the burning bush.

Everyone affirmed hearing the story.

"Right. The first Passover feast was before the final plague. As Moses was commanded by God, he threatened to take every firstborn in the land of Egypt. Then, Moses told all the people of Israel to take an unblemished lamb for each household. They would eat the flesh of the unblemished lamb with unleavened bread. The blood of the lamb would be placed on their door posts. When the angel of death came to take the firstborns of every household, he ignored the households of those who had the blood of the lamb on the door posts. Those who did not have the blood of an unblemished lamb on their door posts lost their firstborn.

"It also ties to the story of Abraham and Isaac. Abraham was told to go to the top of a mountain and a sacrifice would be provided. At the top of the mountain, Abraham was tested to give up his only son, sacrifice his son to God. Abraham was just about to do it when God stopped him. And then he provided Abraham with a lamb.

"So it was then, it is now. Yeshua is the unblemished lamb of God, His firstborn, His only begotten Son, provided for us. Yeshua lived a perfect life as a sacrifice for our sin. The only way we can be spared final judgment is through His blood on the door posts of our hearts, minds, souls, and lives. As the Jews have a Passover feast to remember their being taken out of slavery in Egypt. Us Christians have a communion to remember being taken out of slavery of sin and death. When it's time for us to stand before God in judgment, we are spared."

Jay stopped and smiled.

The Boisseaus stared at him.

I like him. But he doesn't just talk. He tells stories.

"Oh right, of course," Jay laughed. "Back to my original point. Apart from Sean, who was recently baptized, none of you are to partake in the communion. It is only for those who believe in Yeshua and have accepted Him as your Lord and Savior. Otherwise, it's a disrespect of His sacrifice. For you, it would be meaningless consumption of his flesh and blood without belief or reflection. You're just drinking juice and eating unleavened bread."

"Alright," Mom said and glanced at her family. "I won't touch the stuff."

"Yea," Carissa agreed. "No juice for me. Got it." She looked back at Uncle Pierre and Elizabeth. They exchanged a confused look. "It's a lot to take in. But it'll all make sense."

Or so I've been told.

"Great." Jay looked at his phone, "I have to run. I hope you enjoy bible study, err, Sunday school." He trotted off.

Don't forget to talk to me later about US!

Mom nudged Carissa with an elbow. "I see why your dad kept his business card."

Are you already fishing for a new husband? Chill, Mom.

5

After the service, Carissa waited for Jay. It was annoying. Just when it appeared he was done talking to people, another person approached him. At this rate, someone would drag her out so they could go to lunch. She frowned.

Will you people shut up and leave him alone for a moment?

Whatever conversation they had was brief. Jay pointed towards the exit and moved with intention. She subtly walked in that direction to follow him. When he was out of view, she sped up so she wouldn't lose him.

She rounded the corner and caught him entering an office just before he popped out of view again. She looked to see if anyone was watching her before she approached the office. *Jay Canus* was on the plaque next to the door. His title: *The Architect.*

Since when does he have an office? He said he spoke sometimes. He didn't say he was an architect. I thought he was an author.

Carissa turned the handle slowly. It was unlocked. She inched the door open and peeked inside. The spacious office looked vacant. But there was another door open. She slipped in quietly and closed the door behind her.

The office had a white, long, plough couch. The walls were a glossy and reflective white. His desk, bookcases, and the shelves attached to the wall were all glass. The chairs were a gray metal with soft, white cushions. *A bit strange that there's so little color in his office.* Her eyes caught the small flower plants on each of the shelves and on his desk. *Oh. I see what you did there.*

The more she thought about it, the church did seem to have more glass furniture than any building she'd been in. It was usually wood, plastic, or metal.

This guy sure has a thing for glass.

The sound of drippling water came from the second room in the office. She crept across the carpeted floor and peeked her head into the other room.

It was a bathroom. Jay was sitting on the toilet.

He looked up. Their eyes connected for three seconds before he reacted, "Hey! What are you doing in here?"

Shit. Carissa turned around and ran out of the office.

6

I am such an idiot! Carissa fumed as she turned the corner and disappeared herself into the crowd of people. *I can't believe I just walked in on him like that. This is so embarrassing. Why couldn't I just text him and ask him to meet me somewhere in the church? He probably thinks I'm a stalker or something for following him.*

Does he know I followed him? Maybe not. Maybe he just thought I found his office and let myself inside.

I am a stalker, though. I snuck around and followed him to his office. But it had to be done so I could catch him alone.

That, umm, really doesn't make it sound any better. Whatever. *A girl's gotta do what a girl's gotta do. It's not like I saw anything. He sat there with his pants to his knees and cellphone in hand. I mean. Nothing was exposed. It's not like he exposed himself to me or anything.*

Though, I mean. It would have been nice if he had.

She smirked.

What am I going to do now? He won't want to talk to me now. Sigh. *I'll rejoin Mom and the others. They've got to be wondering where I am.*

She swiped her phone. She had fifteen unread texts and three missed calls.

If any of those are from Mom, she's going to kill me.

She gave her texts a quick glance. There were three from Gabby, two from Rebecca, one from Sean, five from Elizabeth. *Seriously, Liz.*

Mom texted her four times. *Dang it! She gets so impatient when I don't text back.* Two texts asked for Carissa's location. One told her to put her phone on vibrate instead of silence next time. The other said, "Look at your phone, Carissa."

Perhaps she's relying on some underlying human instinct that motivates us to do things we can't explain. Some sixth sense, third eye stuff.

It looked like Mom, Gabby, and Rebecca left voicemails.

We are in church. We're supposed to silence our phones during the service. I just forgot to unsilence it. Sue me.

She unsilenced her phone and returned Mom's call. "Hey Mom, I'm sorry. I had my phone on silent. I was just trying to track down a friend here. But, I, uh, caught him at an awkward moment."

"We're waiting outside," Mom said. "The Coles suggested a Korean-American chicken place on Broad Street. It's supposed to be really good."

Oh yea! I've been there before.

"Oh, I know the place," Carissa said. "The spicy chicken is the best. You're going to love their pot stickers."

Mom smiled over the phone. "She sold me on it the moment she said pot stickers. Get out here, kid. I'm surprised you're not hungry already."

On cue, Carissa's stomach growled. She was hungry. Starving. Ravenous. *What the?*

"You're like a witch doctor or something," Carissa said. "My stomach growled the moment you said that."

"Don't make me turn you into a toad, My Pretty," Mom said, imitating the voice of the Wicked Witch of the West.

Carissa bust out laughing. *This woman is too much.*

"Okay," she said. "I'm on my way." They both hung up.

She turned around to see Jay standing behind her. She froze. *Oh crap!* He didn't look happy. But he didn't look mad. His face was a blank canvas with a wrinkle peeking out of his forehead. His arms were crossed.

"Is there a reason you were in my office?" Jay asked.

Carissa's heart sprinted to its maximum velocity. She felt lightheaded. Her thoughts were a blur as she tried to grasp what words to say to the man. "I, I, I just wanted to talk to you. I saw you go into the office and hoped we'd get a chance to talk things out."

She felt tears rush to the surface and tried her best to bat her eyes, fight them off. She didn't want to make a scene. The last thing she wanted was to make a scene.

Jay sighed. "You should always, always knock." He made eye contact. "If my office door is closed, you should always knock."

Carissa head bobbed rapidly, repeatedly. "Yes. Of course. Of course."

He grinned. "It's embarrassing getting caught with my pants down."

I know the feeling.

"That's at least once a week for me at home," Carissa said, forcing a smile on her face. She took long deep breaths to calm herself down now that she knew Jay wasn't going to yell at her. He didn't seem like the yelling type but walking in on someone on the toilet revealed parts of people you didn't know. "I'll think I'm alone in the house and then, suddenly, Sean's walking past and yelling, 'Close the door!' All I'm wondering is: when did you get home? The house was empty. I never hear him coming up the steps."

Jay chuckled. "Sounds like your brother is a ninja."

"He is!" Carissa said with wide eyes. "I mean, the kid is trying to learn all the martial arts he can. I've noticed his studies have slowed since he started dating Becca. But he wants to learn as many as possible. He's the closest thing to a ninja I know."

"Wow," Jay said. "That's awesome. Do you know any martial arts?"

Not as much as I should. Sigh. *After what I've been through with Kent, I need to learn more. I wonder if I can recontinue my karate classes while pregnant.*

"Yea, I know some karate and kyudo."

"Cool."

"But I don't practice enough to improve as I should," Carissa said. "I was thinking that I have to pick it up again. My father wanted us both to be more than capable of defending ourselves and someone else, and to teach our kids the same."

Jay scanned the hallway. "Where is your father? I thought that was the man with your mother until you called him your uncle." He watched her, waiting for an answer. "Could he not come?"

No. This is not what I wanted to talk about.

"No." Carissa looked down and away as her emotions raced back to the surface again. "My, umm, my father died. He was killed in a car accident last week."

I'm about to cry. Dammit! We were supposed to talk about us!

Jay blinked rapidly and processed that. "I'm sorry. I'm so, so sorry, Carissa." He looked around the crowded hallway.

I'm making a scene.

"Would you like to talk about it somewhere, less exposed?" he asked.

You mean, in a less public place so people won't see me crying my eyes out. That would be nice. It was what I wanted. Now I have to go.

She wiped away tears. "No. I can't." She sniffed. "My mom's

waiting for me outside. We're going to lunch."

"Okay," he sighed and peered into her watery eyes. "I'll walk you to your car."

"Alright," she responded, looked up at him.

Jay collected her hand. *He's holding my hand.* They slipped through the thinning crowd of people to the exit. He held the door until she passed and then followed.

The hot sun beamed down on her before a cool breeze sent shivers through her body. *Good grief, it's cold.* She put her arm around his, collected his body heat. He radiated it like a nuclear reactor.

"Where's your family?" Jay asked and scanned the parking lot with a hand shielding his eyes from the sun.

Carissa pointed towards her car. She saw the Cole sisters next to their car. Mom and Uncle Pierre talked to their parents. Elizabeth and Sean waited next to Carissa's station wagon.

"Join us for lunch," Carissa said as they walked. "It's been too long since we've talked." She squeezed and hugged his arm. Gazed into his eyes as he looked down at her. "You know, really talked. Like the last time at Milk 'N Tea."

Jay sighed. "Carissa, you know I can't do that."

She frowned. "Why not? We're friends. You can have lunch with friends, right? No one has to know how we feel for each another."

He closed his eyes and stood silent for a second.

"I'm going to tell you a short story," Jay said and gently pulled his arm away from her. "Because I need you to understand why I can't do what you've asked of me. Why I need this to remain as it is: a friendship confined to church. It's also the story of why I built this church."

Tell me a story? What is this? I don't want to hear another story, especially if you're putting restrictions on our friendship.

Carissa teared up again. "No, Jay. I don't want that. That's stupid." She threw her hands up as anger exploded out of her. "Why are you doing this? Why are you being so, so like this towards me? You *like* me! I know it! I can *feel* it! I can see it in your eyes. Why don't you just admit it and let things happen?"

"Because I have a girlfriend, Carissa," Jay said. His face tensed up. She could see him take deep breaths to maintain his calm. *I need him to lose his calm.* "An amazing one, at that. I've wanted what I have with her for a very long time. I can't pass that up. I can't put that aside, especially when the alternative is something I can't allow to happen."

Can't allow it to happen?

"Why not?" Carissa argued. "Why can't you? We have a connection. There's chemistry. She's not better than me. You think she's better than me?"

Jay frowned. He scanned the parking lot for spectators. *He's embarrassed of me. He doesn't want to be seen with me.*

"You're seventeen, Carissa," Jay said. "It doesn't matter what I think or feel. What you think or feel. This, whatever it is, cannot happen now."

Carissa stomped her foot and huffed. "I don't care! It doesn't matter."

Jay watched her miniature tantrum. "If you care about me, you'll have to care, because it matters to everyone else."

"It doesn't matter what everyone else wants or thinks," Carissa said. "Isn't this about us? Why do you care so much about what other people think?"

I can't believe this. Why is this happening? Why can't he just be with me? None of that other stuff matters. He met me *first. He liked* me *first. He's supposed to be with* me, *not her. I need him. She doesn't. I'm pregnant. She's not. My baby needs a father, a good man. My needs are greater than hers. That makes me the priority.*

Ugh! First Dad takes my business card. Then she gets in the way. Now he's saying he can't be with me because I'm only six months shy of eighteen. It's so stupid.

"I'm in a position of authority where I must live by example," Jay said. "I can't afford to make impulsive decisions based on feelings or give people the wrong idea about me and a young woman like yourself. Besides, as I told you, I care about Amy. It sucks that we're in this position, but it is what it is. I care about you. If things were different, if I was single, if you were a little bit older, we would be together. But circumstances are as they are. Friends is all we can be right now."

Carissa scoffed. "Whatever."

Jay looked to the sky and took a long deep breath. "Anything that is meant to happen will. I need you to trust that if God wants us to be together, we will be together. Nothing can stop that. If we're not meant to be together, we won't be, but someone more suited for you will enter your life."

He's rejecting me. I can't believe this.

"Bye Jay." Carissa stormed off.

"Carissa," he called after her.

She turned around. "What?"

"Just because I can't be with you, it doesn't mean I can't be here for you," Jay said. "If you need anything, or want to talk, I'm always here for you."

Sigh. *No, you're not.*

Carissa walked away.

CHAPTER TWENTY-SEVEN

It took a thick stack of paperwork and three phone calls from Captain Rogers before Principal Greenberg let one of their detectives work undercover as a substitute teacher to investigate a student. After more prodding, she also allowed access to the computer labs, any information stored within, and network storage. Greenberg wasn't sure how far they were stretching the law, but so far, no one thought it was illegal.

They're public computers owned by the city or county school board. So, not illegal, especially when used for illegal means.

"We believe this student poses a danger to his peers and has already been engaged in an alleged sexual assault and distribution of inappropriate, underage images from that assault," Rogers spoke over speakerphone. "During our time at your school, we'll be asking several students questions and getting the lay of the student's social networks. We only ask that you be discreet and not let anyone know that our detective is anything other than a substitute teacher."

Priest crossed her arms. *I hate that we so casually use the term "alleged".*

Greenberg hesitantly agreed under the condition that they would immediately depart if their investigation compromised the education of her students or disrupted the educational process.

Rogers promised there would be no disruption and ended the phone call. "Nate, I'd feel a lot more comfortable if you were the undercover. There's no question that Detective Courier is an incredible resource, but he's a bit of an, uh, unfamiliar element. I just made a promise I'm not sure I can keep."

That's one way of describing him.

"You have nothing to worry about," Summers said with a reassuring voice. "I wouldn't have gone along with this if I didn't believe he'd act with incredible focus and professionalism. Besides, the man has two doctorates. He won't let us down."

2

Oliver walked into class in pleaded khakis, white dress shirt, and navy-blue vest. He put on a pair of glasses and admired himself in the mirror. "I own this look."

Over the earpiece built into the glasses, Priest said, "Yes. It's refreshing seeing you dressed like an adult. I almost mistook you for a professional." She took a sip of her coffee.

"Joanne? Is that you?" Oliver asked.

What? Priest squinted. "No. This is Amy. Detective Priest."

"Oh, phew," Oliver said and fixed his hair into a ponytail. "All this nagging. I mistook you for my ex." He smiled in the mirror.

Priest gaped.

Summers snorted. "Okay, you two. Ollie, students should be coming in at any moment. How does the room look?"

"Great," Oliver said. "Jeremy from forensics swept the room. It's spotless. The moment anyone puts their hands on the desks, they'll track. We'll know who is who, assuming they don't bounce seats. But even then, we'll know. I'm keeping track of where Bradshaw sits. Taking a picture when he settles. Here's hoping his prints match the pill case and pictures."

"We can only hope," Summers repeated the sentiment. "I'll have Jane go in between periods to help you collect fingerprints and any DNA, hair, something."

"Jane, Jane," Oliver snapped his fingers. "Oh. You mean the recruit that looks like she just fell out of the womb."

Summers laughed.

Priest turned to the back of the van and smiled at Jane. Her baby face was why Rogers assigned her to the case. Dressed in her black "e equals leave me alone" tee, blond hair in a ponytail, and tight jeans, she looked like a high school student easy. She could fool anyone.

"I'm in the van, ya know," Jane called out.

"I know." Oliver smirked.

Priest chuckled. "Anyway, as planned, I'll be monitoring you from the van. Nate and Jane will be in the computer lab for the data scrubbing. Jane leaves for the print scrubbing and then rejoins him afterward. You meet them during lunch period."

"My favorite part of the day," Oliver said. "Searching for boobies on public computers. When will they learn?"

"When we find something concrete and know the user that accessed it," Summers said. "We're looking specifically for pictures of Carissa. But if we find anything else, anyone else, especially minors, we'll catalog it and track down the user. I have a feeling one of these pimple-faced pervs has a collection and will roll over on the source."

"We were all pimple-faced pervs at that age," Oliver said.

"Speak for yourself," Summers said. "I had clear skin."

Murmuring came from the hallway. The door opened. "Students are coming," Oliver whispered. "Time to shine."

3

The period bell sounded. Oliver closed the door.

"Mister Yarborough will be away for a few days," Oliver began and walked with his hands clasped behind his back. He made eye contact with each of the students as he walked. "In the meantime, you'll have me."

Someone called from the back. "Who are you?"

"I've been asking myself that for a long time," Oliver said. He walked to the dry-erase board and wrote the first name to come to his mind. "I am James Brown. And before any one of you asks, yes, I feel good."

The class laughed.

That's not the name we gave him. Priest leaned forward in her chair. *Why the audible?*

"For your first assignment, I'd like you to take out a piece of paper," Oliver said and wrote his assignment on the board. "Tell me how much better looking I am than all the other substitute teachers you've had."

4

Lunch didn't come fast enough. After three hours of watching Oliver make a damn fool of himself, she needed to take a break. She took a bite out of her chicken sandwich and waited for Summers and Jane to fill her in on the details of the data scrub.

"I don't know why they still have a computer lab," Jane said. "All the students get laptops. They can easily go home and print things."

"And that's precisely what they use it for," Summers said. "Printing. But there are those that use it for social media, watching videos, and—" He pulled up an image on the screen. The young girl didn't look old enough to go to high school.

Priest turned her eyes. "Good lord."

"Yes, He is," Summers said and closed the image. "There wasn't a lot on the hard drives, as we suspected, which made scrubbing exceptionally easy. It went fast. We got through thirty computers, recovered and copied every file, in less than two hours. The largest haul was the network storage. Some of it's still downloading. After we collected all the data, we connected it to Oliver's laptop. Blew through it with his special software in thirty minutes." He tapped the flash drive. "We got images; time stamps when the files were accessed; logins for the students that accessed the computers at those times. We even got logins and passwords to some of their social media accounts."

Priest leaned in close. "Are we allowed to look?"

Summers pointed at the image file on the screen and said two of his favorite words, "Probable cause."

Hours later, the team regrouped at the precinct. Rogers stepped out of the office as soon as they arrived. "What do we have?"

Summers debriefed Captain Rogers on finding the social media logins and passwords, and image files.

"Keep me updated," Rogers ordered. "Especially if you identify the young women in the photos, and immediately if one of the young women happens to be my daughter." He returned to his office and made a phone call.

Priest grabbed one of Oliver's laptop bags. "Let's relocate to conference room B."

Oliver made three laptops shadow images of the computer lab computers, borrowed the cookies from the scrubbed computers, and used them to log in as the students. From there, he opened another piece of software that catalogued the friends lists and captured profile, private, and public images from all the females on the friends lists. He commissioned facial recognition software to determine if any of the naked images matched the females in the friends list. He said the process could take several minutes to a couple hours depending on how many pictures they accessed.

While Oliver put his software to work, Priest cross-referenced student groups, sports team rosters, and public profiles for commonality and connection between the young men who accessed the images. She needed to piece together the social network, know who to talk to, who to press.

We only need one weak link to bust this case wide open. Every group has one.

"What about the girl?" Jane asked and pointed at a profile picture. "This girl accessed three of the pictures. Casey Nichols."

A girl into the other girls? Possibly.

Summers accessed her profile. She kept her password saved in the browser. And that was the break they needed.

"What's this group?" Summers pointed. "Pumas Uncovered."

"Our mascot, I mean, Patterson High School's mascot is the puma," Priest said.

"Click it," Jane ordered, leaned over their shoulders. There was an impatient forcefulness to her tone.

Summers shot Jane side-eye and clicked the link. It was a closed group, invite only. Casey was a member. Each post had teaser images and clips of girls undressed, but with censor bars over their breasts and genitalia, and various girls' faces. Some shots were taken from a locker room. Some shots were taken in private residences. There were shower scenes. And sex tapes.

As he scrolled down, his face reddened. There had to be at least a hundred posts, each attached to a link and detailing item and subscription costs for the uncensored versions. Videos cost extra. Links sent them to more teaser content or a password-protected website: pumasuncovered.xxx

"They're selling the images for profit," Priest scoffed. "I can't believe it."

"Believe it," Oliver said as he joined the rest of the group.

"This is the first case I've had in a while where they're not selling people." He scratched the back of his neck. "At least, not yet."

Not yet? You had to say, "Not yet." If this is the first case you've had without someone being sold, I can't imagine what you see on a regular basis. Then again, you are from NYPD's vice squad.

"Well," Jane said, "whatever they're selling, they're going to jail."

Obviously. The questions is—

"Who?" Summers asked. He clicked through the social media profile. "Who's going to jail? That's our next question. We need to find the group administrator. Determine the sources of the images. Get the name of every member of this group. Every subscriber on the attached links. All of them are going to answer for this."

He stepped out to inform Rogers. Rogers stormed in behind him four minutes later, clicking through the images.

As much as it would help our case if he found a photo, I really hope he doesn't find his daughter in there. It just, I don't know how he'd react to it. How hard is it for him to be a father and a cop? Separating his fears and protective instincts, and preventing them from interfering in his investigations? I can't imagine how I'd feel right now if I had a teenage daughter.

Priest closed her eyes.

"She's not there." Rogers let out a sigh of relief. "Do you have access to the other site?"

Oliver shook his head. "Not yet. She didn't access it from the computer lab. So, we don't have her password."

Rogers shrugged. "So? Do what it is you do. I know what you're capable of." He pointed at Oliver. "Hack it."

"Sir," Summers said. "You know we can't do that without compromising our investigation."

"No," Rogers said. "Probable cause. Look." He pointed at the title. "Patterson Pumas. Local high school. Students looking up pictures. Same high school. You've already found sex images. There's your connection."

"I can write it up and see if a judge feels we have enough," Priest said. "But if we hack it now, we lose everything."

"We'll get in there with a warrant, Sir." Summers spoke with confidence. "We gotta play it safe."

DAKOTA

I know how he feels. If there's even the slightest chance that there's a picture or video of my sister on that website, I want to know. But hacking the website compromises the investigation. Sigh. You know it would. Fruit from a poisonous tree...

Rogers resigned. "You're right." He marched towards the door. "Find me what we need to get a warrant."

Oliver rubbed his chin. "We need to identify one of the girls in the pictures as a Patterson High student. Preferably, a minor. A minor would allow us to take down the page and arrest anyone associated with it, no questions asked."

"You can barely see faces in these," Priest complained.

"But, you can see some," Oliver said. "My bet is that the only faces visible are the girls that are eighteen or older, seniors and graduates. They're not complete idiots." He pointed to his head. "If we can identify one Patterson High student, eighteen or not, on school premises, that's enough for a warrant. It ties the website to the school. There's reasonable suspicion to search their content for identification and age verification purposes."

Summers cracked his knuckles. "Well, let's get to work."

They spent the rest of the night calling in favors; saving images from the social media website; crafting digital access warrants; and finding domain provider contact information. The to-do list was larger than their team.

Priest yawned.

That's what tomorrow is for. This case has steam. This case has wheels. Enough backing to have access to more resources. Rogers signed off on two extra people to do the footwork. All we have to do is take what we have and put it to good use.

Tomorrow's question: Does this new evidence tie in with Carissa's case, my sister's case, or are we moving on a completely different set of tracks?

Oliver will tell us if any of the girls in the pictures match the girls in the friends lists. We need to identify the girls in the pictures. The pictures on the lab computers, as well as the pictures on the social media website and subscription website. If just one of the girls is a minor, we can take the whole site down.

If Oliver doesn't get any leads, I'll reach out to Carissa. Maybe she knows one of the girls. I can reach out to one of her friends, too. That Gabby girl from church. She's social. Her sister, too. It might not be their circle, but they're associated with a lot of groups.

This sure would be a whole lot easier if the school had a photo registry of the students—

Oh, of course. Why didn't I think of this sooner? I was on the yearbook committee many years ago. I should contact the company that makes the yearbooks and get their digital registry and copies for Oliver. We can identify any student that's been there in the past ten years.

She made a note in her pad, turned off her bedside lamp, and laid down in bed. She looked at the alarm clock and groaned. It was two AM. She had to be at the school in five hours. Why'd they work so late?

Her phone blinked. *Well, it's not like a few extra minutes of checking texts will make much of a difference.* She grabbed her phone and slid her finger along the touch-screen. There were three texts from Jay.

Jay: "I missed you tonight. Are we still on for tomorrow?"

Jay: "Hm. The crime must be fierce tonight. Don't be a hero."

Jay: "Wait. Should I say that to a cop?"

She smiled. *No. Probably not.* And texted back.

Priest: "I'm not sure… I'm exhausted. Busy day in office. Got home 20 mins ago. That major case I was talking about is taking off."

Priest: "Must get up early. 6AM. I'll be running on negative empty 2morrow. Can we reschedule?"

She put her phone down and fell asleep.

5

Priest staggered into the back of the van, two large cups of coffee in hand, and slumped into her chair. Summers' head was leaned back, a cap over his eyes.

I can't believe he's here before me. He must have got like three hours of sleep.

She set his coffee in a cup holder and sipped from her own. She breathed in the aroma and couldn't resist smiling. She loved coffee and decided to zip by Jay's favorite spot, *Milk N Tea*, for their unique, house blend. This rare indulgence was her way of celebrating.

DAKOTA

We struck oil yesterday. I barely slept four hours and don't want to move this morning. But it was all worth it.

In addition to the monumental discovery from computer lab scrubbing, Jane got usable fingerprints from Kent's desk. Priest made a note to check in with Jane to see if there were any matches to the prints taken from the pictures left at the Boisseau residence.

What's most important is matching Kent's prints to the plastic case with the abortion pills.

They didn't find Kent's DNA. Not even a hair. But, an hour later, Oliver came in with a plan, and ten packs of bubblegum.

"I'll be putting cinnamon incents on my desk and giving the students cinnamon bubblegum to test a theory about cinnamon's effect on cognitive functions as they brainstorm."

I suppose that's one way of getting his DNA.

Priest frowned. "How do you expect to get the gum back?"

"Well, to not piss off the other teachers, they'd have to turn it in to me or I'd collect the gum before class ended," Oliver said.

"That's a lot of gum to track," Priest said. "How will you know which is his?"

"Keep in mind, the only gum I'm tracking is Kent's," Oliver said. "I'll take a plate around the room, make sure everyone puts their gum on it. I was thinking of keeping a toothpick handy. When he puts his gum on the plate, I'll turn my back to him and stick the toothpick in his gum. That way, I know which is his. I'll also try to make sure his row is last."

"What if he and the other students don't want to chew the gum?" Priest asked.

Oliver shrugged. "Then, we're back to waiting for him to shed or sneeze or blow his nose."

Or I could punch him in the face and give him a solid nose bleed.

"Who knows?" Summers said, coming out of his nap. "Maybe God made him the kind of guy that sticks his gum under the table."

"Let's hope so," Priest said with her mind already moving towards the next topic on her agenda. "How's your facial recognition tech working?"

"Overnight, it wasn't," Oliver said with an apologetic face.

"Some unexpected updates restarted the computer and interrupted the process. Then, the computer went to sleep. I'll get it working while I'm in class today."

"Good." Summers rubbed his chin. "What are the odds this ties into the Bradshaw case?"

"Slim to none," Oliver said. He gave Summers a slow nod. "That doesn't mean we don't pursue it."

Should I ask what that's about?

"If we can tie him to the website," Priest said, "and determine it's his means of distributing Carissa's pictures and video, assuming he is, we have proof to arrest him for distribution. We get the video itself. We have proof of rape."

"What if we don't find any connection between him and the website?" Oliver leaned back in his chair and pressed the tips of his fingers together. "What if he didn't submit it online? What if one of the witnesses did? You know, the guys that snapped pictures of her after Bradshaw was gone."

Summers tapped his upper lip and considered that. "Our goal is to find something and a person attached to that something, so we can perhaps find out who shared images of Carissa. That objective hasn't changed. If we find her pictures, we trace recipients back to the source. Hopefully it leads to Bradshaw, if not Bradshaw, a witness at the party. Someone had to see him come and go."

Oliver and Priest agreed.

"You think they'll talk?" Oliver asked.

"Whether they talk or not, pictures or not, we'll need the gum spit DNA to tie him to the pregnancy," Priest said. "We can't prove rape without a photograph, video, audio, or confession. But, at least we can throw a wrench in their gears and prove that Kent is in fact the father. Let's not forget about the inheritance question."

Oliver grinned. "You going to put him in cuffs and drag him on Maury?"

"If we could, I would," Priest said. "But do whatever you have to. Just get that DNA."

"Whatever I have to." Oliver rubbed his hands together. "Did Rogers say how long the warrants are going to take?"

"Longer than it should," Summers grumbled. "There are

some shower clips that may be from the girl's locker room. Jane's going to take pictures of the girl's locker rooms and bathrooms. Run comparisons. If we have a solid match, we can get a warrant."

"That was definitely the east wing girl's locker room," Priest said. "I exclusively showered in there. West wing showers had the absolute worst water pressure."

"Stop," Oliver said. "You actually took showers?"

What's that supposed to mean?

She wanted to sniff herself but refused to give him the satisfaction. She smelled fantastically of orange zest. He was obviously trying to get a rise out of her. "Nate, since you're running by the office, I have an idea. Before I fell asleep, I thought about getting images of the students from the yearbooks and running them through facial recognition. See if they match the girls from the pictures and clips. When I woke up this morning, I realized that I wouldn't have to go through a third-party. The students and teachers have custom photo ID cards made. They use them for identification, access to certain rooms, and in-school purchases."

"Girls and boys," Summers clarified. "Underage boys in those images would give us the same warrant access." He glanced at Oliver. "I have a meeting scheduled with Greenberg to go over our discovery in the computer lab. After that, we're going to have unlimited support from the school and staff."

Oliver blinked rapidly and rubbed his five o'clock shadow. "But, we have to keep this hush-hush. She needs to give us what we ask for without telling anyone why. There's most likely at least one staff member who has access to that site."

Oh. I would hope not. But I'm not naïve.

"You think a teacher or someone in administration might be providing or viewing the images?" Summers asked.

"You know what I do," Oliver said with a straight face. "Sadly, I have personally arrested ten educators for illegal possession and distribution."

Ten? Did you say "ten"? Maybe I am naïve.

"If you've checked the news lately, a lot of students and teachers are hooking up. For every incident reported, there are a hundred more that aren't."

Summers agreed.

"Not to mention the slimy guys that approach the students and offer them gifts or grades in exchange for favors. One teacher was responsible for a disappearance. The sex trade is new and old money. They have access to a lot of young women and their information, habits, interests."

Therefore, why I became a cop. To stop guys like that.

"I agree with your concern," Summers said. "I'll voice it during our meeting. Tell her, if anyone asks what we're doing, why we're here, stonewall them. Stonewall them hard. And if there's pressure from above her paygrade, she should tell them we're trying to identify a victim. Keep it cryptic."

Smart. Technically, some of the girls in the pictures are victims. Plus, the term victim *is broad. It could be assault, rape, murder, or something as menial as petty theft. No one would suspect it's related to the website.*

"Hopefully, she'll agree and keep this locked up tight," Summers said. *And isn't the gossiping type.* "If we can get a copy of the student identification files, how long would it take you to run them through facial recognition?"

"Barely any time at all," Oliver said. "I've got three laptops networked and working together as one. You give me the files. They should be able to identify the students in the images in one hour, max. I still think we should get those yearbook pictures. Wouldn't hurt to have more images to reference for when we do get access to the secured website."

"I agree," Priest said. "I'll make a few calls."

"Great," Summers said.

"God willing, the principal will spare all of us some time and identify one of the girls during your meeting," Priest said.

Summers tapped his nose, then rested his hand on his heart. "From your lips to God's ears."

Oliver glanced at his watch. "Well, time to get to class." He exited the back of the van, raised a finger, and turned around. "Oh, I forgot to mention. Last night, a name sounded familiar. So, I checked my class roster. Guess who's in my first period."

Priest shrugged. Summers took a sip of his coffee and waited.

"Not one guess?"

Priest rolled her eyes. "Bob Sagat."

Oliver smiled. "I'll accept it. The answer is: Casey Nichols."

Summers leaned forward. "So, she and Kent are in the same class. So are a couple hundred other students. That's probably a coincidence. I won't assume a connection without something else."

Fair argument.

"Well," Oliver said and scanned the parking lot. He looked like a high school girl ready to spill juicy gossip. "After figuring out she was in my class, I checked her address. She and Kent only live a couple blocks from each other." He raised his hand as Summers was about to speak. "Also, based on pictures in her account, she was at the party on the night in question." Priest opened her mouth. He waved his hand. "Also, two weeks ago, there was a status on her page. 'Flix and chill w/ K.' It wouldn't surprise me if they were hooking up."

I hate this new hookup culture. Why can't people just date and commit? It's a lot less messy.

Then again, him hooking up, or at least, somewhat involved with a girl, or a revolving door of girls, may give us some leverage if one of them turns on him.

"Keep an eye on them," Priest said.

Oliver winked, "I can do one better," and closed the door.

Priest scratched her eyebrow. "Should I be concerned?"

Summers nibbled his lower lip. "Probably."

CHAPTER TWENTY-EIGHT

Summers sat in the principal's office waiting for Greenberg to end a phone call with a concerned parent. He fought to stay awake and wished he had more than three hours of sleep and a short nap in the van. He was running on empty but needed to be at his best when talking to Greenberg. This case was too important for him to coast through it like some of his other cases.

It wasn't as though he didn't take his job seriously. He simply didn't lose sleep over them. Cases typically worked themselves. Find the facts. The facts didn't change. The evidence didn't go anywhere, most of the time. All losing sleep did was make a person less sharp.

Yet, with this case, he felt rushed, as though there was an invisible ticker. He needed to solve it as soon as possible, not just for Carissa's sake, or Priest's sister, but something else. There were higher stakes.

Why else would Oliver come? He was the kind of guy that dropped anything for a friend in need. But he was also ridiculously busy. Asking him to leave his job to handle a local rape case when the man was involved in New York's major crime division, a federal sex crime task force, and international slave trade investigations was asking a lot.

Yet, Oliver was unexpectedly available.

"Ollie, I've got a very sensitive case I'd like to send your way. Any help or advice you can give would be most appreciated."

"Sure," Oliver said. "I've got a couple minutes. Let's hear it."

Summers provided the core details of the investigation he could share. After he was finished, Oliver repeated the name of the assailant and went silent.

After an uncomfortably quiet sixteen seconds, Summers asked, "You still there?"

Oliver said, "Hold on, buddy."

"Okay."

Ten minutes of silence followed.

Summers tried not to get impatient but couldn't help himself. He had work to do. "Should I call you back? I can just call you back."

"No, no, don't hang up," Oliver said. "Just hold on tight. Shoot me an email of what you have. What you can share."

It was policy to digitize and backup their notes. He sent the files and waited five more minutes in silence.

"Sweet baby Jesus on ice," Oliver finally said. "Unbelievably convenient timing. I'm so glad you called me, Nate. I'm currently between cases right now and can be down there in a couple days. Call it destiny."

"Um, thanks." Summers leaned back in his chair and took another sip of his coffee. "I didn't expect this. I just wanted some advice."

Fast typing was audible over the phone. "Trust me. After this case is over, I'll be thanking you."

What's that supposed to mean?

"I'm scheduling my flight. I'll call you later to work out our game plan. See you soon."

Click.

Summers hadn't realized at the time what they were up against. What they were looking at. But now, with the discovery of this website, he questioned the stakes of the investigation. A common rape investigation turned into a discovery of an online porn site exploiting teenage girls. What more were they going to stumble across? And again, why did it feel like there was a ticking clock?

After this is over, he's going to be thanking me? What does he know?

It was Oliver's idea to not approach the Bradshaws after Carissa's house was vandalized and the pictures of Carissa were discovered in the mailbox. It didn't make sense, at the time, but now he was beginning to understand.

What if the pictures from the vandalism were also on the Pumas Uncovered private website? What if the site connected to something bigger? Where was the money going?

What does Oliver know that he's not telling me?

"Coffee?" Greenberg asked while shoving a coffee cup in his face. "You look like you need it."

"Thanks," Summers said. He'd have to put more thought to his questions later. Right now, he had a job to do. He accepted the coffee, blew, and took a sip. It was heavily creamed and sweetened, just how Priest liked it. He, on the other hand, liked something stronger. He liked coffee to slap him in the face. "I appreciate it."

Greenberg wasn't a mind reader, but her wise blue eyes watched and weighed his reaction. "I wasn't sure how you liked it. But I've never offered a single soul straight, black coffee and received a positive reception."

"It's fine," Summers said and stood. He sipped more of it, happy to have more caffeine. "Are you free now?"

"Last time I checked, I'm charging the county over forty dollars an hour," Greenberg joked and opened the door to her office. "But, I'm available to you at no additional cost."

Forty dollars an hour? I should have become a high school principal.

"Thank you for meeting me," Summers said and pulled out a notepad with prepared questions. "I'm sure you have a busy day ahead of you."

"Yes, I do." Greenberg sat behind her desk. She leaned back and folded her hands in her lap. "I've already heard some very interesting remarks, and complaints, about our substitute teacher. It seems he doesn't take his role very seriously. But there's no need for damage control, if that's why you're here. The other staff seem to find him amusing. They've started a pool: how long will he last before I fire him?"

Sounds about right.

"I'm glad he's living up to my expectations," Summers said. "But that's not why I'm here."

Greenberg shifted in her chair. "What's on your mind,

DAKOTA

Detective?"

Summers reached inside his jacket, pulled out a manila envelope, and set it on his lap. His eyes never left Greenberg, catching her every reaction. Though he didn't suspect any involvement in the website, he had to keep an open mind. He saw too many cases go awry because officers and detectives hadn't kept an open mind.

Greenberg's eyes were on the envelope. She didn't show any signs of anxiety but leaned forward just a little bit.

"What's that?" she asked.

And so it begins.

"First, I truly want to thank you for giving us an opportunity to place our detective in your classroom as a substitute," Summers said. No matter who he talked to, he found it beneficial to stretch out deliverance of information, just to measure their anticipation. "And thank you for allowing us intimate access to the computer labs. It's opened a completely new investigation for us."

Greenberg raised an eyebrow.

"When we combed through the lab computers and network, we hoped to find anything that proved inappropriate images of a specific student were being traded by the other students," Summers said. "After scanning, we've discovered images of others are being traded."

Greenberg sighed. "Detective. This school has hundreds of high school boys from ages thirteen to nineteen. If they weren't exchanging inappropriate images, that would be breaking news. With the hormones racing through this place, the hyper-sexualization of women, this new age of women wanting to," she used air quotes, "'*liberate* themselves' and '*embrace* their sexuality' by showing off way more than they should and advertising their sexual escapades, it's to be expected. What I want to know is: what have you found and is it worse than trading pictures of naked celebrities or sexts?"

Suspicion lessened.

Summers opened the envelope and took out the pictures: censored images of young women and screenshots of profile accounts. "We're working on identifying the young women. If you can, it would help our investigation." He passed the pictures across her desk. "We first discovered the pictures in temporary files and tied them to student logins. Those students have more pictures in their network accounts. We were able to access a social media profile through stored account and password information."

Greenberg hesitantly glanced through the images, frowned.

"When we accessed one of the student social media accounts, we discovered a group named Pumas Uncovered," Summers continued.

She looked up. "Pumas. As in, the Patterson Pumas."

"Yes," Summers said. He found and pointed to the screenshot of the group page. "There are more than two thousand posts of inappropriate pictures and videos."

Her hands started to tremble as she looked at one of the pictures.

Summers leaned forward to see what picture she was looking at. "Do you recognize someone?"

Greenberg shook her head. "No. I just, I wasn't expecting this." She put down the pictures. "You said there are *thousands* of these posts? Of *my* students?"

"Our tech guy used a special software to download all the videos and pictures. He hopes to get some geodata from the images and videos. Determine where they were taken and by whom. Device identification. There's a lot to go through."

And it'll take a lot of time. Time we don't have. We could use at least three to five more people in on this case to help us sort through everything. Either that or share this case with Paulson, which I'm not going to do. Amy would kill me for thinking about it.

Greenberg passed the pictures back to Summers. "Thank you for putting the censor bars on the pictures. That's more than I wanted to see."

"We didn't put the censor bars on these pictures," Summers said. He put the pictures back in the envelope. "They did."

She frowned. "I don't understand."

"They're posting some media with faces and parts fully exposed while censoring others."

Greenberg leaned back. "Is there something special about the ones not being shown?"

DAKOTA

Summers wasn't ready to share their theory just yet. "They're selling their content. The pictures and videos link to another website. It could be a marketing and sales thing. Show some. Hide others."

Greenberg's frown began to wrinkle her entire face. It aged her. For a woman in her late forties, she had incredibly smooth skin. He wondered what product she used. His wife was constantly shopping for face creams to avoid looking as wrinkled as her mother. Her mother had a face with a thousand laugh lines and infinite chins.

"The most important thing is identifying the young women so we can take this group page and website down," Summers said. It was time for the ask. "We can report the group to the social media site. With their help, we can take control of it to get access to all the subscribers. But we can't take down the private website without proof those girls and boys are from your high school. We have the facial recognition software. We just need something to cross-reference. Names and pictures."

Greenberg blinked and brightened. She understood what he was asking for. "You want access to our student database."

Summers nodded. "Yes. I'm aware you take pictures of all your students and provide student IDs. We need access to their information. Names, pictures, and if possible, addresses."

"Addresses?" she asked. "Isn't that a bit much?"

"To correlate the geodata from the pictures," he explained. "If we can match the geodata from the pictures and video with the students addresses, we'll know who, when, and where they took the pictures and made the videos. With your help, not only can we identify the girls, but also the entire network. Students, or others, are taking these pictures and uploading them. But even if we can't identify some girls, we can identify their homes. Get their parents involved."

Greenberg sighed. "That's an awfully large request you're asking of me, Detective." She bit her lip. "But it makes sense."

Summers agreed but said nothing more. She was mulling over her answer. He didn't want to press her. He told her what he needed and why. Considering the sensitive subject of their investigation, he suspected she'd say yes. But the breach of privacy for hundreds of students alone was a practical reason to deny his request.

"Okay," Greenberg said. "I'll give you what you ask."

"Thank you," Summers said and pulled a portable hard drive out of his jacket pocket. He set it on her desk and stood.

Greenberg stood as well and led him to the door. "How's Amy holding up? I suspect she's hoping to find some evidence that will, in some way, provide justice for her sister?"

Careful what you say.

Summers took a deep breath. "She's doing well. This case has her on pins and needles. I've never seen someone more committed to finding answers than her. But it's not just her. I'm sure you're aware that several of the officers and staff at our precinct have daughters enrolled at Patterson."

"Of course. Of course. I'll contribute in whatever way I can to calm their nerves. Who knows. Perhaps all this cooperation will get me out of a parking ticket one day."

Summers grinned. "If this case goes in the direction I think it's going, we might just give you a free parking pass."

Her eyebrows perked up.

"Just don't get carried away," Summers said. "If I find your car parked in the middle of an intersection, I'll revoke your parking privileges."

Greenberg laughed. "But that's the best spot."

Summers chuckled.

"I'll get all the information you need on a drive," Greenberg said. "Come back to the office after lunch."

"Great," he replied. "Thanks."

Summers left the office and looked at his watch. Lunch was in three hours. There was a lot he could do, but sleep called.

I'll break the news to Amy, then sleep. At the pace this case is moving, I might not sleep tonight.

2

"Welcome back," Priest said as Summers opened the back door of their surveillance van. "How'd the meeting go?"

Summers yawned. "She signed off on access to the student registry. Pictures, names, addresses, all of it. I'm to pick up the drive after lunch."

"Perfect," Priest said. She wagged a piece of paper. "I have some good news, too."

"Let's hear it."

"Sarah from crime lab compared the print from the abortion pills case with the print from Kent's desk." She pointed to the results. "It matched."

Summers pumped his fist. "Thank you, Jesus. Solid evidence."

"My sentiments exactly," Priest said. "This just got real."

He rubbed his chin. "Let's not get too excited just yet. It's proof he gave her the pills but—"

"It's enough to get a warrant for his home, for his school lockers," she said, "especially school lockers, since he gave her the pills at school. Maybe we'll find a comb, half drank water bottle, a sweaty jock strap. Something with DNA. I'll see how far we can go in our warrant." She paused.

With DNA, we can prove he's the father.

Her eyes widened. "Heck, Nate. With that print and the money trail, we've got them. They pressured her into an illegal abortion. Charges can stick. All we need to do now is confront the clinic directly."

"Perhaps, but evidence could also support their blackmail narrative," Summers said. He lacked her enthusiasm. "I'll call the precinct to work up a draft warrant. Our favorite judge can rubber stamp the search warrant for the locker and clinic. We'll determine if the pills we have match their inventory. Check their records. See who signed off on the abortion. See who paid."

"Perfect," Priest said and grabbed her keys. "I'm tired of being stuck in here. Jane can take over at the van. She has spare keys."

"We're going now?" Summers sagged in his chair.

"Of course! Why would we wait?"

"Because it could take hours to get the warrant," Summers yawned, forced himself into an upright position, and followed her. "I have a feeling this is going to be a long day."

"You can sleep in the car."

3

The moment signed warrants landed in her hand, Priest felt a power rush. Things were finally in motion. Evidence, warrants. She held justice like a baton and planned to squeeze the

Bradshaws as hard as she could and bludgeon them with it.

"We're here," she said to her napping partner as she parked. *Now all we have to do is get them to roll over on Janice. We get access to her finances, phone records. Hopefully, we'll find something that ties them to the purchase of the abortion pills years ago. Don't worry, Sis. We almost have them.*

Chip, in his standard police uniform, and Sarah, their crime lab specialist, a short brunette in black suit and tie, parked and got out. Four other uniformed officers, Red and Brice, and Thomason and Marsh, got out of their squad cars and approached Summers and Priest.

"Doctor Green came back from lunch an hour ago," Brice said and pointed at a green Porsche. "That's his car." He rolled his eyes.

Hmm. We'll have to take a close look at his financials.

Summers pointed towards the building. "Red, I'm going to need you to watch the back entrance, just in case Doctor Green decides to slip out. Brice, you'll cover the front. Sarah, Chip, you'll follow us. Thomason and Marsh, you'll hang tight at the entrance, just out of sight, until I give the all clear. Depending on how cooperative they are, I might pull Red in to help us collect what we need or keep an eye on the staff. We're checking medical records, admittance papers, financial records. Anything connected to Carissa Boisseau. Captain already has Henrick and Conway waiting to secure their phone records, depending on what we find. Any questions?"

I have a question. But I won't ask in front of everyone else.

No one else had questions.

"Alright, let's have a moment of prayer," Summers said. Everyone huddled together while Summers spoke a prayer over the group. That was his thing. Before entering hostile territory, interviewing a victim or suspect, or an arrest, Summers insisted on a prayer for the men and women in blue and those in the community, including the perpetrators.

After he was finished, Summers said, "Let's move," and led the way.

Priest walked by his side and whispered, "You think, depending on the answers we get here, Rogers will officially reopen my sister's case?"

Summers opened the door and held it for her. "One case at a time, Amy."

Right.

Inside, straight ahead was the reception desk. Four women stood in line at the first window. At the second window, a receptionist was on the phone. Another phone rang beside her. Seven people sat in the waiting area with magazines and cellphones in hand.

"Perfect timing," Priest said. A mischievous smile grew on her face.

Summers frowned. "I'd think you were being facetious if you weren't smiling."

A busy day meant they wouldn't have time to play interference on the investigation. They'll be under pressure to help their waiting clients. She could always rely on human impatience to turn up the heat.

If it was up to me, I'd make sure we held things up. Have them an hour, maybe two hours behind on their appointments. Put as much pressure on them as possible. If they tried to shift the blame on the police, we'd just say they're not cooperating with a rape investigation. Or they're "allegedly" helping a rapist and his family pressure a victim into an unwanted abortion. That'll put black marks on their social status.

"We have a warrant," Priest whispered. "They have to cooperate. And, I think they'll do whatever they can to avoid causing a scene during a busier time in the office."

"No." Summers disagreed. "We want them to cooperate. If we're going to get them to work with us, turn on Janice Bradshaw, we need them on our side."

They'll work with us whether they want to or not.

"Nate," Priest whispered. "If the Cole sisters hadn't stopped her, Carissa would have gone through with the abortion." She huffed. "Who knows how many illegal abortions they've performed? Who knows how many other girls have been pressured into taking pills this clinic provided?"

Summers raised his palms and softened his voice. "I know. I know. I understand. But if we go in hot, they'll clam up and involve lawyers. They might still do that. Let's at least start with honey. Ask to see what needs to be seen. Video. Any record of

Carissa being here. Approval paperwork and who signed off on it. Be polite." He smiled. "If that doesn't work, you can twist arms and wag the warrant."

"Good cop, bad cop," Priest said and let out a breath. She flexed her fingers and calmed herself. "I suppose that never gets old."

"Nope," Summers said and walked straight to the reception window, ignoring the line. "Good morning, Ladies." He pulled out his badge and waved it at the women waiting in line, then the receptionist. "I'm Detective Summers. I'm here to see Doctor Green."

The receptionist, Sharice, examined the badge, said, "Hmph," and turned to the other receptionist. "Bonnie. Call Green to the front."

Bonnie put her hand over the receiver of her phone and said, "He's in the middle of a procedure. I can't call him now."

Well, let's put that warrant to good use, then.

"When will he be finished?" Priest asked and flashed her badge.

Bonnie looked at her watch. "He went in about five minutes ago." She scrunched her face. "So, I'd say he'll be back there for another twenty. Doctors Sanders or Thompson might be available."

"Who's the senior partner at this clinic?" Summers asked.

Sharice said, "Doctor Green."

"After Green?" Priest asked, impatiently.

"It's Doctor Thompson," Sharice said. "Then, it's Doctor Sanders. But Sanders is still new. He only joined us three months ago."

Summers and Priest exchanged a look, then said, in unison, "We'd like to speak to Sanders."

A few minutes later, Summers and Priest stood in Doctor Sanders's office. If it could be called an office. Priest suspected someone emptied a small storage closet and squeezed in a desk and three chairs. There was no knee space. He didn't have windows. There was enough wall space for a few framed diplomas. A singular framed picture on his desk.

Sanders was young, clean shaven with dark brown hair and bright blue eyes. While they waited for him to finish with his patient, Priest scoured the internet for information on him. They were the same age. This was the beginning of his medical career. She wondered how long it would last working with guys like Green.

If they're guilty.

"After the latest upgrade, our security footage is automatically streamed, recorded, and stored in the cloud through our security firm," Sanders said. "It allows us to access live footage, keep tabs on the staff and any patients, record any escalations or incidents. It also helps us identify protestors who may decide to vandalize us or harass our clients."

Vandalism will be the least of your concerns once we get the footage of Carissa's arrival and departure.

"Do you record audio and video?" Summers asked. "Or just video?"

"At the reception desk, both." Sanders said and logged into his computer. "We've found people will say just about anything to get what they want and then try to sue us later. Shut us down. It's also a good way of making sure our staff are delivering all the correct information." He pulled up the current feed.

Summers gave a subtle head nod to Priest.

"Doctor," Priest said on cue. "We appreciate you helping us out with this case. The footage we're looking for is on December seventeenth. A young woman had an appointment at four-thirty with Doctor Green."

Sanders stopped clicking. "December seventeenth, you say?" He turned from his screen to the detectives. A wrinkle matured on his forehead. "Doctor Green left earlier that day. Something came up. So, he reassigned all of his new patients to me."

"When did he do that?" Summers asked. He glanced at Priest. "Reassign his patients."

Is it possible Doctor Green intentionally made a deal with Janice and then left it to Sanders to do the illegal procedure? What a jerk.

"Umm, the appointment was made late, around lunch," Sanders said. "I remember it specifically because he signed off on it in a hurry, then made a b-line for the door. Just out of the blue he said something came up and I'd take his patients. It was quite unusual, especially for him."

Priest leaned in closer, invading the man's space. "Unusual how? Was there anything else unusual?"

Sanders nodded. "Well, it's unusual for him to leave when he has patients. I mean, from what I hear, and from what I've seen, the man's all about filling the waiting room, getting as many clients, err, patients, as possible. And then, he takes most of the patients because he's the senior partner. He's the name and face of the clinic." He shrugged. "He'd sooner not show up for the birth of his firstborn child than to miss out on an opportunity to make some money."

That's exactly the kind of stuff I need to hear. You'll make a great character witness. I'm glad we're recording this.

Priest checked her recorder before adding the necessary quote in her notepad.

"But, there was also the protest," Sanders said. "I bet he didn't want to be around for that."

Summers pulled out the paperwork for Carissa's appointment and planted it on Sanders' desk. "Was this the new appointment he made before he left?"

Sanders flipped through the paperwork. "Yep. That's the one. The blackmail girl, right?" He pointed at Carissa's name. "The one who's trying to take advantage of the Bradshaws."

Priest went red. *I want to choke someone every time I hear that false narrative. It's the same thing they said about my sister!*

"That's one of the complaints we're investigating," Summers coolly replied. He pointed at the appointment. "It says the appointment was prepaid. Is that common practice?"

Sanders swallowed, hard. "Well, I wouldn't call this a common situation. It's not often a mother calls and schedules an abortion for her son's blackmailer. But, we do process medical paperwork, insurance claims, and pre-authorize credit cards to make sure the funding will be available. It was a same-day appointment. Green took care of all of it."

"That is unusual, especially when the young woman is a minor," Summers said. "When was the patient's mother contacted?"

Sanders shrugged and looked at the record. "Looks like the mother's consent was provided the same time Misses Bradshaw called. There's a contact number for her." He pointed. *That is not*

Kate Boisseau's phone number. Priest wrote it down in her notes. "And there's her signature on the parental consent form."

I hope Carissa didn't forge her mother's signature. That's the kind of complication I don't need right now.

"I'd like a copy of that," Priest said. "And any fax number or email address used to transmit it."

"That's all in the medical records," Sanders said as if he was talking to a novice.

"Okay." Summers rubbed his chin. "Let's see the payment records. The credit card used, the time of the transaction, the amount, all of it."

Sanders hesitated but complied. He pulled up a second screen and typed in his password, which Priest committed to memory. Carissa's patient records appeared after a few clicks. "That's it right there." He pointed at the screen.

"Print it off," Priest and Summers said at the same time and looked at each other. Smiled.

Sanders blinked rapidly. "I guess you two work together a lot." He pressed print.

"Great minds," Priest said, pointed at her head. "Please print all of it. The correspondences, the approvals, the login name of whoever authorized it. And the contact name or number of the person who made the appointment and payment. All of it."

Sanders swallowed hard but did as he was told. "Detective, are we being investigated? Do I need a lawyer?"

Priest wanted to laugh but didn't. She merely smiled and patted him on the back. "If there's one person who won't need a lawyer, it's you."

"We're just following up on everything," Summers said. "She didn't go through with the abortion but kept the money. That might have been her plan all along. We need to know all the details, including the most intimate ones: how much money was involved and who signed off on everything. To understand the scope of the loss of assets, we need to see the whole picture."

Playing him like a fiddle.

"Okay," Sanders said. The crease in his forehead relaxed. "That makes sense." He printed off the rest of the documentation and handed it to them. "You'll probably want the release form and logs for the abortion pills, too, right?"

What? Oh, hell yea. Thank you, God.

Summers looked up from the documents so fast she heard something pop. "Of course, we do."

Sanders clicked and printed the rest of the forms.

"When did the request come in for the abortion pills?" Priest asked. She was curious. The Bradshaws had to acquire the pills the same night Carissa was supposed to have the abortion. Otherwise, they couldn't have pressured Carissa the next morning.

Sanders pulled up the request timestamp. "It was done about an hour after she checked in for her appointment." He clicked it a couple times. "This was the unusual thing. Doctor Green called after she left. Said the reason code for the appointment was logged wrong, even though he was the one that put it in. He said it was supposed to be a pill pickup instead of a surgery. That's an impossible mistake for a doctor to make, but whatever. Maybe that's why she didn't go through with it." He scratched his head. "Anyway, someone else came to pick up the pills in her stead."

Priest and Summers looked at each other and then asked, again in unison, "Who?"

"Kent Bradshaw," Sanders said. "The father."

♪*Hallelujah! Hallelujah! Hallelujah-hallelujah! Halle-heylujah!* ♪

Summers pulled an evidence bag out of his jacket pocket and pointed at the pill container inside. "Are these the pills?"

The color faded from Sanders' face as he looked at the evidence bag. His mouth fell ajar before he flexed it a couple times. "Can I see?"

"Sure," Summers said. "Gloves?"

The desk drawer was yanked open. Sanders pulled gloves out of his desk, passed two to Summers, then wrestled a pair on shaky hands. Summers slipped in his gloves and retrieved the pill bottle. He carefully opened it and took out a pill. He gently placed it in Sanders's hand.

After a quick examination, Sanders returned the pill. "This, this looks like the capsules we use. I'm not sure why someone removed the bottle's label. How do you have them—?" He gasped. "Is she dead?" He swallowed hard. "Is she dead like the other girl? Is this a murder investigation?"

My sister. He's talking about my sister. Whatever he says, at this moment, could be used to reopen my sister's case.

Priest checked her recorder again. It captured the entire conversation up to this point.

Coolly, Summers raised his eyebrow and asked, "What other girl?"

"I'm not sure I should say anymore," Sanders said with his head down.

Priest put her hand on his shoulder and softly said, "Listen. Nothing you have said or done incriminates you. On the contrary, your assistance so far has been invaluable. As long as you continue to cooperate and share what it is that needs to be shared, you have absolutely nothing to worry about."

The forty-seven seconds of silence that followed felt like a half hour. But after taking a deep breath, and swallowing hard, Sanders told them what they needed to know. "The ladies in the front like to talk. One of them, Sharice, was here when the other girl, the one on the news who killed herself, came in. It was just like this." He took a breath. "The Bradshaw mother called and prepaid. Green authorized the procedure. The girl came in with Brian Bradshaw and filled everything out."

And there it is. I can reopen my sister's case. We never knew where the abortion took place. We didn't have anything tangible to say where it happened, how it happened, or who was responsible. We didn't have anything. This is how I get justice for my sister.

"Brian Bradshaw was with her, in the clinic?" Priest asked.

Sanders confirmed. "According to Sharice, yes."

"Do you have footage?"

He shook his head. "They switched security companies two years ago, and only held surveillance footage for about two or three months before discarding them for hard drive space. The only time they needed to review or hold footage was if there was theft, vandalism, damages."

Makes sense. I would have loved to have Brian on tape with her. Up to this point, he was able to deny he was the father. Deny everything. Now we have potential testimony that he was present. A witness.

We should find out who else was working that day. Two eyewitnesses are better than one.

"I'd like to have a copy of her medical records, admittance papers, everything," Priest said. "It's only been four years. You should still have a physical copy or digital record on file."

Summers protested with his eyes but said nothing.

One case at a time, I know. But I can't pass up this opportunity. I just can't.

"This clinic holds records for up to five years," Sanders said. "So, it should be there. However, I don't know her name."

"Dakota Marie Priest," Priest said and maintained eye contact.

Sanders froze and stared at her for several seconds before swallowing hard. "Yes. Of course. I, uh, I see now." He looked to Summers, then back at Priest.

He quickly printed and handed them all the paperwork requested of him.

"Here's a USB drive for the surveillance data and aforementioned digital records," Summers said as he passed him the device.

"Of course." Sanders mashed it into the computer. Beads of sweat matured on his forehead. "You are investigating us."

Neither Summers or Priest confirmed his suspicion. They simply watched him as he provided what they needed.

All the color was gone in Sanders's face. "That girl, Carissa. She's dead, isn't she?"

"No," Priest assured him. "She's alive."

Sanders sighed, relieved, and quietly finished duplicating the necessary files. "I suppose I'll call my lawyer now."

Summers rested his hands on the table. "That won't be necessary, Doctor. You're not the one being investigated. The Bradshaws are. So is Doctor Green. From everything you've said here, there's no reason to believe you had any involvement in what they were doing."

Sanders didn't look convinced. He kept his eyes on the computer screen. Priest watched as he copied the requested files. She smirked as the copy finished. He unplugged the USB drive and slid it across the table to Summers.

"Listen," Summers said as he accepted the USB drive. "We're

grateful for all your help. In fact, we'd like you to continue to help us by testifying in court as a witness." He pulled his business card out of his breast pocket and slid it across the table. "You'd be telling everyone exactly what you told us. There would be no legal repercussions towards you what so ever. We can assure you of that, assuming everything you've told us is the truth."

"But I'll be out of a job," Sanders resigned.

Or running the place.

The door to Sander's office burst open. A short, slim, bald man stood at the entrance. "Detectives? Your visit is a bit unexpected. I wish you'd called first. I could have set aside some time for you."

Priest calmly smiled at Green. "Doctor Green," she reached out to shake his hand. He shook it. "I hope our visit hasn't startled you. We're investigated a blackmailing case."

Green frowned. "What? Blackmailing who? Me?"

"Allegedly, someone is blackmailing the Bradshaw family," Summers said with a straight face.

Sanders's jaw nearly fell to the floor as he watched Summers spin their visit, yet again. But he said nothing.

Green's blinked, examined their faces. "Really? Is that so?"

To throw off any suspicion, Priest chimed in, "It seems the Bradshaws have friends looking out for their best interest."

"What does that have to do with us?" he asked. His eyes locked on the paperwork in Summers' hands. He glanced at Sanders. Sanders shrunk in his chair.

"Misses Bradshaw reached out to you, of course," Priest said. "We just came to verify whether the girl showed up to fulfill her end of the arrangement or if she took the money and fled." She rubbed her chin hoping to look contemplative. "It's possible she might demand more."

Green looked at Sanders. "Did you get what you came for?"

Summers subtly slipped the USB drive, still in his hand, into his pocket and stood. "Yes. She was here, checked in, then left. Looks like she was carrying the money with her. Not exactly the smartest blackmailer I've ever seen."

"But criminals are dumb." Priest smirked, locked eyes with Green.

"Are they?" Green stated more than asked.

Summers exited Sanders's office. "We'll investigate this further. Who knows? She's probably done it before. Assumed if she got away with it once, she can do it again."

Priest agreed and repeated herself. "Criminals are dumb that way."

"Hmph," Green said and narrowed his eyes to a squint.

"You took the call from Janice Bradshaw, right?" Priest asked, watched his eyes. "You arranged Carissa Boisseau's procedure to get the Bradshaws out of their uncomfortable situation." She pulled out the report and pointed at it. "You signed off on it. Right here, authorizing the abortion, right?"

"Well, I mean, I took the call," Green sputtered and looked between her and Summers, then shot dagger eyes at Sanders.

"You are such a good friend," Priest said and smiled. With a soft voice, she continued, "She's so lucky to have you."

"What?" Green's entire face twisted in confusion. "I don't know what you mean."

"You're too modest, Doctor," Priest said and stepped closer, invaded his personal space. "I wish I had a friend who was willing to put himself out when asked. I mean, what you did, orchestrating an abortion for a minor without the consent of the parent. Putting your whole practice in danger. You must be close. Very close."

Green stared at her.

"If you choose to cooperate," Summers said, "the prosecutor would be willing to work with you. But, the moment we walk out that door, we're taking this to the judge for an arrest warrant."

Green tightened his fists and steamed. "You don't have enough to arrest me. It's not like she went through with it."

"We also have the records of Dakota Priest," Priest said and pointed at the paperwork. "An abortion performed by your clinic, at the behest of Janice Bradshaw. She was also a minor. Her mother was neither inform nor consented."

His face fell. His shoulders slumped. The breath escaped from his body. It was at that moment she knew they won.

"What do you need me to do?"

Over the next hour, Green confessed everything.

CHAPTER TWENTY-NINE

Oliver and Jane were in the van when Priest and Summers returned. They smiled and pointed at a piece of gum in an evidence bag.

"Got'er done!" Oliver announced and took a swig of his canned iced tea. "It was simple really. I halfway followed the lesson plan and then quizzed the students. If they got the answer right, I gave them a candy bar. If they got the answer wrong, they got a stick of gum and had to chew it in shame. Because I'm a dick. But anyone with gum had to toss it on their way out of class so the other teachers didn't piss and moan if it ended up stuck on their desks."

"Smart," Summers said and gave Oliver a fist bump. "How'd you know which was Bradshaw's?"

"I kept a close eye on him. Handed him purple note paper. He spit it in there. We're solid. We got it. Now all we have to do is compare it with a viable bio sample from the fetus." He put his pinky finger next to his mouth and faked evil laughter.

Jane chuckled.

"After your antics in class yesterday, I wasn't sure what to expect from you," Priest said before dropping their clinic notes on the table. "Thanks for coming through. Proving his fatherhood is one more nail in their coffin. We got a confession from Green, confirmation from his subordinate, and documents and video from the clinic proving the entire abortion scheme was arranged by Janice Bradshaw without the consent of Carissa's mother. We also have documents and video proving

Kent Bradshaw acquired abortion pills from the clinic, for Carissa."

She filled them in on what happened at the clinic.

"Cheap move interviewing the new guy," Oliver said and laughed.

Priest smirked and shrugged.

"We're interviewing DeQuan next," Summers said. "Carissa's brother, Sean, is a teammate of his. They're not close friends, but close enough that I hope we can get through to him. He was one of the few people she recognized. He can corroborate she was at the party, hosted by the Bradshaws, and provide eyewitness testimony that Carissa was drunk and unable to consent. We can prove rape."

"Pictures will help," Priest chimed in. "We know people took pictures at the party. He'll know who else was there. He's a local celebrity, most likely linked to the other guests in social media. We can get pictures of the party, maybe get DeQuan to rollover on who provided the drinks, hit the Bradshaws with providing to minors."

"One of the people taking pictures had to catch a snap of Carissa," Oliver said. "Once we identify those posting pictures, we can encourage them to surrender what they have."

"That's something else we'll learn," Summers said. "Whether anyone's shared illicit images with DeQuan. Athletes get access to everything. If anyone's seen pictures of her, the sports team has."

"You can get help from Coach Campbell," Jane said. "He's a solid guy."

"You're right," Priest said. "DeQuan's their best player. The coach will cooperate and insist DeQuan does as well. Last thing they need is bad publicity about him being at a party where there's a rape and him not cooperating in a police investigation."

"He can kiss his career goodbye," Summers said.

"Or, he'll fit right in," Oliver said and shrugged as everyone looked at him. "Please. You've seen the news. Some of these athletes don't know how to behave these days. They used to be role models. 'I wanna be like Mike.' Now they're in murder investigations, cheating and beating their spouses."

Maybe like, what, five high-profile athletes?

"Anyway," Priest said. "We should head to the coach's office before lunch is over and get his cooperation." She opened the van door. "You can pull DeQuan out of class. With the coach with us, if he agrees to help, we're likely to get all the information we need to bury the Bradshaws."

"Before you go," Oliver lifted his finger, "I've got some sweet, sweet, juicy gossip for ya."

"We've got to get to the coach," Summers said. "Give it to us after we interview DeQuan."

"Well, at least answer this one question for me, do you still plan on having that late-night surveillance on Caulfield and married dude?"

Summers snapped his fingers and turned to Priest. "He's right. We never planned a time for that surveillance."

"It's fine," she said. "I can tail Caulfield."

This was the first time she'd ever seen Summers pout. "Without me?"

It's a me and Jay thing. It's his way of going out on the streets with me without being on the streets. Quell that writer's curiosity and give us some alone time. I'm doing my job and on a date at the same time. It's kind of nice.

"It's late work, off duty," Priest said. "I don't want to pull you away from spending time with your wife, especially when you two are trying to uh, you know." *Make a baby.* "You don't have to join me."

"You bet I do," Summers said. "If you catch her and the store owner together, that's leverage to get Caulfield to rollover on the Bradshaws. Did you want to go alone?"

We're all adults here. What I'm about to admit shouldn't surprise any of you.

"No," Priest said and grinned. "I'm going with Jay."

Summers stared at her without speaking for five long seconds. "Definitely explains why I wasn't invited. It's more of a make-out session than a stakeout—" He stopped. "You know what. I'm not your dad. I'm sure he's a gentleman. I'm just going to drop it." He paused. "Has this been going on for a while?"

"Just a few times," Priest said.

"Oh," he said, blinked. "Have you seen anything, yet?"

"A penis," Jane whispered.

Oliver laughed. Summers put his hand over his mouth to hide his smile.

Glad we're all adults here.

Priest blushed. "*No*. We followed her to a guy's house. Not the store owner. Some other guy from her high school. Football player, wide receiver, name's Jake Blanchart. No ties to the Bradshaws or Boisseaus. Doesn't register as a person of importance in our investigation."

"Sounds like Caulfield's the real wide receiver," Oliver joked. Jane spit out part of her sandwich and chuckled with him. "Clean up on aisle two."

Let's get focused, people. "You had a question about the surveillance."

"Yes," Oliver said after they regained their composure. "Today is the day you want to follow her."

"Why is that?" Summers and Jane asked simultaneously. *Jinx.*

"Two cheerleaders in my class were trying to figure out where they were going to eat after practice," Oliver explained. "One asked what Caulfield suggested, since she's the queen bee this year. The other said she was meeting up with some guy. The first girl laughed and said, 'It better not be Jake.' The second said, 'No it's a much older guy this time, even more scandalous than Jake.'"

So, if we follow Caulfield after cheerleading practice, we'll catch them. Priest's eyes widened. "Are you sure that's what you heard?"

"Oh yea," Oliver said. "I take great pride in my eavesdropping skills. It gets better."

How could it get better? If we have leverage on Caulfield, we're close to more leverage against the Bradshaws. My sister is no longer rolling in her grave. She's damn near jumping for joy and doing cartwheels just about now.

"Well, Kitty Jenkins just happens to be Jake Blanchart's girlfriend," Oliver revealed. "And, guess who she briefly dated before Jake?"

"Kent Bradshaw," Summers guessed.

Oliver tapped his nose. "According to the gossip queens, she ended it with him when she found out he slept with a drunk girl at a Halloween party. Invited her and everything."

They're talking about Carissa. Priest's leaned forward. "Really."

"Go on," Summers said after a brief glance at Priest who was nearly coming out of her chair.

"It gets better," Oliver said.

How? How could it get any better than this?

"Someone who was at the party sent her a video as proof," Oliver continued. He leaned back in his chair, put his hands behind his head, and smiled. "Merry Christmas, ya filthy animals."

We need to get our hands on that video. See what's on it. If it's damning enough to break off a relationship with one of the richest bachelors in Richmond, it's got to be more than enough to somehow use it against him. Now all we need is the testimony of DeQuan that he greeted her at the party and Bradshaw provided alcohol.

"Jane," Priest said and hopped out of her chair. "Find Kitty's class next period and any extracurriculars she has after school. I want to talk to her as soon as possible. I have pictures and video of Caulfield entering Blanchart's house and a kiss as he greets her. Should be more than enough to get her assistance against both Bradshaw and Caulfield."

"Hell hath no fury." Jane gave a thumbs up.

Summers let out a long yawn and grabbed his tall coffee. "Let's get going before I fall asleep."

2

It was Joe Campbell's sixth year coaching Pumas Basketball. In his first year, he turned a failing team into district champions. The next two years, they were regional champions. The following year, they were state champions. The year after that, they were semi-finalists. Hopes were high that they'd make it to the finals, maybe even take the national championship.

Campbell, a former pro basketball player himself, successfully put together a prime team and trained them extensively. At first, many parents and administrators thought he was too tough on the boys, too strict. Now, everyone worshipped him. Hopes were high. The school buzzed with excitement whenever the basketball team was mentioned. They were close. This year, Coach Campbell would take them to the gold. They were ready to take it all.

DeQuan was their most valuable player. He averaged thirty points a game and scored most of the points in regular season and early playoffs. His advantage was size. At six feet and ten inches, it was customary for someone to play as a forward or center. Not DeQuan. At home, he was trained day in and day out on three-pointers. His father, Steve Jacobs, said, "I raised a shooting guard expecting him to stop growing at my height, but he shot up like his grandfather." The end-product was a kid that shot from anywhere on the court. He had range but could power himself in for a short shot or dunk if he needed to.

Being such an essential element to their championship run, Priest knew the coach would do everything in his power to get DeQuan to cooperate competently and quietly. She was not disappointed.

"Shit," Campbell said as Priest and Summers showed their badges. "This is not what we need right now." He pushed away his two chicken and lettuce sandwiches on a paper plate. His wife prepared his lunch every morning. Beside the sandwiches was a single-serving of orange juice, bottled water, apple, and two chocolate chip cookies. "Which one was it, what did he do, and what's it going to take for us to resolve this quietly without turning our nationals campaign into a shit show?"

Priest and Summers looked at each other, silently signaling with their eyes who would go first. Summers yawned. That was her cue to take point this time around.

"It's about DeQuan," Priest started.

Campbell tossed his hands in the year and let out a stream of cuss words before tossing some paperwork on the floor. "I knew it! It was too good to be true. We were this close." He put his fingers so close together she was sure they were touching. "With his scoring average and the other boys stepping it up, I knew we'd take the championship this year. With DeQuan out, we've lost our best scorer and three-point defense. Not to mention, it's going to mess up our energy. Do you have any idea how important energy is in basketball?"

Priest played junior varsity basketball for a year before she accepted it wasn't her thing. You needed momentum. If your team lost confidence, even for a minute, the game could turn against you. "Coach—"

"What did he do?" Campbell interrupted. "Was it drugs? No. Can't be. Because he's too smart for that. I refuse to believe he's dumb enough to throw away his whole career to get high. Is it possession? Because if it's possession, you've got to know it can't be his. I know kids do some dumb shit, but not when they have scouts so far up their asses choosing a meal is a group decision."

Summers sat in front of the desk. "Relax, Coach."

"What? Did he steal something? I mean, I don't know why he would. His dad's doing well for himself, finally. But I don't know what kind of friends Quan has when he's not with the team."

"Take a breath, Coach," Priest commanded with a little more steel in her voice. She sat in the chair next to Summers. "Just listen first. We need your help to talk some sense into him. We knew you'd be the man to talk to before we approached him."

Campbell nibbled his lip and then slid his sandwiches forward to continue eating. "Alright. What's going on?"

Priest waited for the man to take a bite of his sandwich before starting. "On Halloween night, there was a party at the Bradshaw manor. There were a lot of high school students present, drinking. One of those students was drugged and then sexually assaulted."

Campbell put his hands over his eyes. He looked like he was about to cry.

"It wasn't DeQuan who assaulted her," she quickly dismissed. The last thing she needed was their hero coach to have a breakdown or heart attack on her watch. "But he was there. Her greeted her as she arrived at the party. He's a potential witness to what happened there. We need to know what he saw at that party. You and I both know this isn't the first time a young woman has been assaulted at one of these parties." She wavered, thought about her sister.

"There are also pictures of the assault, of the young woman, being distributed. We need to know if he's seen or received any of those images. If he has possession of those pictures or had anyone share images of the party itself and other participants, or non-incriminating pictures of the young woman and the

Bradshaws at the party, we need access."

Campbell considered her request. "How old was she?"

"Seventeen," Priest said.

"So, if he did have such pictures in his possession, he would be in possession of—"

"Child pornography," Priest said. "Yes."

"If he admits he has these pictures, wouldn't he incriminate himself?" Campbell asked.

What are you, his coach or attorney? I suppose these days you have to be both.

"Listen, we're not interested in that," Priest said. "Anything he's in possession of, his presence at the party, it's water under the bridge. We're after a bigger fish. A whopper. If he helps us out, you can trust we won't use his possession against him. We'll keep his involvement in this investigation as quiet as possible. He'll be an anonymous source as far as the courts allow, able to prove alcohol was provided to minors which led to the rape of a minor by those providing that alcohol. We can already prove who's the father." *Hopefully.*

Campbell rubbed his chin. "Sounds like you have it figured out."

"We do," Priest said. "We want a party guest to paint a broader picture, let us know who else was there, maybe give us brief access to his or her social media account so we can see any posted and shared pictures at the party."

"What about the girl?" Campbell asked. "The victim. Can't she do that?"

"She's not socially-connected. We suspect that's what made her a good mark. She's still relatively new to the city, to the school. Even though she's involved in several extracurriculars and even an amateur sports league, she says she doesn't know many people. The only person she knew at the party was the person that invited her. We suspect that individual is somehow involved."

"Okay," Campbell said. "Give me a moment to process this."

"That's fair," Priest said. Summers agreed.

Six minutes later, Campbell finished his lunch, stood, and shook their hands. "Alright. But I want to be there when you talk to DeQuan."

DAKOTA

"Deal."

3

Ten minutes into third period, Priest, Summers, Oliver, and Coach Campbell stood outside of Oliver's class.

"We're ready for DeQuan," Priest said and nudged her head towards Campbell. "Coach will be present during the interview to ensure DeQuan's complete cooperation."

Campbell peeked his head in the room and waved at DeQuan. DeQuan shot a thumbs up and stood. He put his notebooks in his bag, flung it over his shoulder, and gave everyone the peace sign on his way out. Priest had a feeling this wasn't the first time Campbell pulled DeQuan out of class.

"Great," Oliver said and whispered. "I have a feeling he has what you're looking for." Wink.

Not sure if I should be relieved or worried by that statement. Is he an optimist or did he do something?

"We'll let you know what's revealed," Priest whispered as DeQuan approached. "Assuming he agrees, be ready to plug into his social media account and track any tagged or linked photos that trace back to the party."

"Of course."

DeQuan fist bumped the coach and stepped into the hallway. After a quick examination of Priest and Summers, he said, "You're cops. What's this about, Coach?"

Campbell looked down both ends of the empty hallway and pointed right towards his office. "Let's go to my office. There's something these detectives need of you that's best discussed in private."

Priest and Summers followed.

"Good luck," Oliver closed the door.

Campbell pointed his thumb towards the door. "What was that about?"

"Beats me." DeQuan shrugged. "Probably flirting with lady cop, here. Man's gotta shoot his shot."

Campbell laughed. Summers smirked at Priest.

So long as he doesn't suspect Oliver is a cop, he can think whatever he wants.

Minutes later, they were in Campbell's office. Campbell sat in his chair, DeQuan across from him. Priest sat next to DeQuan. She turned her chair to face him, scooted back to give him space. Summers sat on the couch to Priest's right sipping coffee he commandeered from the teacher's lounge.

Campbell briefed DeQuan on what happened at the party and what the detectives needed from him.

"Man, bitches be gettin raped all the time," DeQuan said. "That ain't got nothing to do with me or my career."

Priest pulled out her pen.

Campbell hopped out of his chair and almost leapt over his desk. "Don't quote him saying that!" Priest's pen froze over the notepad. He sat, took a breath, and glowered at DeQuan with still, authoritative eyes. His face was tense, red, making it clear he meant business. "Tell them what they want to know."

DeQuan sighed. "I don't know much, but someone is lying out of their ass."

"What do you mean?" Summers asked, his notepad out. He quickly scribbled DeQuan's remark.

Priest waited, ready with her notepad, watching DeQuan's facial expressions and body language. Her voice recorder rested on the table between her, DeQuan, and Campbell.

DeQuan frowned. "Carissa's best friend, Val, has been going around saying it was all a setup. She's saying she didn't realize it at the time, but the moment she invited Carissa to the party, Carissa was plotting to sleep with Kent and get knocked up. But Kent was the one asking about her before she was invited. Weird questions."

Priest shot Summers a look.

First, Val is a snake. I'm taking her down. Second, this confirms what Carissa told us. He's confirming the conversation Carissa and Val had later that night, after the rape.

Summers signaled two fingers as if he were a telepath. When it came to partners, perhaps there was a little telepathy by proximity. "What did he ask about her?"

"Everything there was to know about her," DeQuan said.

"Specifics."

"Her interests, her likes," DeQuan said. "What she wanted to study; where she's going to college; what kind of food she likes. He wanted to know her favorites. About her friends." He paused.

"Go on."

"Kent, he wanted to know if she had a lot of friends, connections," DeQuan continued. "If she knew any people he knew. People's opinions of her. It was weird to me because most guys ask: does she have a boyfriend or is she hooking up with anyone? But I didn't know anything, and her little bro, Sean, wasn't interested in telling me more than the basics. He said she wasn't interested in football or basketball players. I think he didn't want me or any of the other guys hooking up with his sister. He always got hot in the face when guys asked about her. I don't blame him. I get the same way with my sisters. If these jokers want to get with one of my sisters, they best be prepared to get their ass beat."

Summers made note of that. As did Priest. *Precisely what we hoped he'd say.*

"And after your talk with Sean Boisseau, Kent invited Carissa using Val and Jesse as his proxy," Summers said.

"Yea," DeQuan said. "Kent told my brother Nate he wanted to get with her and I knew her brother. He planned to invite her but needed to know what he needed to know. I told Nate she didn't have concrete plans and he told Kent. Days later, she showed up at the party dressed like a red angel or something."

Red angel?

"A fairy," Priest corrected. "She was dressed up as a fairy from the Tinkerbell series. She had fairy dust."

"I don't follow that shit," DeQuan said. "She had wings and cleavage. That's all I know."

Of course, that's what you would notice.

Summers leaned forward and pressed his pen against the notepad. "Now, for the record, where was this party?"

"At the Bradshaw house."

"And who specifically hosted the party?" Summers continued.

DeQuan looked to Campbell. Campbell nodded for him to answer the question. "Kent Bradshaw and his brother, Dragon."

Priest noticed a micro-expression. The shortest frown matured and disappeared from Summers' forehead. "And Dragon is?"

"Brian Bradshaw."

"Thank you," Summers said and noted it. "Now, there was alcohol at this party, right?"

DeQuan glanced at Campbell, again. And again, Campbell advised him to answer. "Yea, man. Of course, there was alcohol. It was a party."

"Right." Summers marked a check next to the question. "And who provided the alcohol at the party?"

"A number of people," DeQuan said. "Some brought their own. Some was already there at the house."

"And the alcohol already there at the house was provided by whom?" Summers asked.

"The Bradshaws."

Yes! Priest smirked. *We got them on providing.*

Summers gave her a barely detectable head shake before continuing his questions. "How do you know it was provided by the Bradshaws?"

"Kent told me I didn't have to bring anything because he would provide, just as long as I let people know I was coming. He knew more people would come if I came, especially my female fans. Any guy I invited had to bring two girls. Any girl had to bring a friend. Gotta get the right ratio. When I arrived, he had a stash prepared just for me." He snapped his fingers. "Oh yea, he also made jungle juice. He was proud of that shit. Said it was heavy on strawberries like I enjoyed fruity drinks. I told him to get outta here with that gay-ass, fruity-ass shit and got a beer."

This time, it was Summers that smirked. He forced it behind a serious demeanor and jotted down more notes.

"Just to confirm," Priest intervened. "Jungle juice has alcohol in it."

DeQuan glared at her as though she were the village idiot. "Yes, *Detective*. Jungle juice has alcohol in it. A lot of it. He said his was a mix of rum, vodka, a little whiskey, and a sprinkle of tequila. Dude was acting like he was a jungle juice connoisseur and shit."

"Thank you," Summers said and noted the ingredients. "Now, you and Carissa spoke when she first arrived. Did you see her any time after that in the party?"

DeQuan shrugged. "Yea. I played her and Kent in beer pong. But, my girl couldn't shoot for nothing. I had them down to two cups all by myself. And then, a little bit after that, I saw her and him dancing. But she was tore up by then. She could barely stand. I saw them one more time, sitting on the couch when I was on my way to use one of their rooms for a little sidebar with ma girl. When we came back, they were gone."

Priest and Summers looked at each other before adding to their notes.

He's the witness we needed. Carissa being fall-over drunk means she couldn't consent. Once we compare Kent Bradshaw's DNA to the fetus's, and they match, we have ourselves a closed case. But we'll need more than just DeQuan's testimony, especially if we intend to keep him out of the spotlight. Part of the deal of getting his support and testimony is preventing his involvement from affecting his potential basketball career.

How could I consider that as a priority when we're dealing with a rape case? We gave coach our word.

"This is all very helpful, Mister Jacobs," Summers said. He reached in his pocket, pulled out a second, smaller notepad and pen, and rested them on the table. "Would you mind writing down the names of some of the other party guests who may have witnessed Carissa's and Kent's interactions?"

DeQuan glared at Campbell. Campbell gave him a hard look and pointed at the pad and pen. DeQuan let out a loud sigh, resigned. Priest was glad Campbell was present. She half expected DeQuan to say he wasn't a snitch. Perhaps he was thinking just that. But, he wrote down six names and extended the notepad to Summers.

"Please, hold on to it," Summers said. "We're not quite done with it, yet."

DeQuan again locked eyes with Campbell before putting the pad back on the desk. He stared out the window, at the football field, and waited for the next question.

Summers made a few notations, then asked, "Have you heard anyone say they saw Kent Bradshaw and Carissa Boisseau enter a bedroom together at the party? Or saw Kent leave the bedroom she was in before she was found naked in bed?"

"Yea. Two of my boys, Eric and Freddie, were upstairs when Carissa was brought up drunk. They said she, Val, and Kent went into Kent's room. Kent left, then Val, then Kent came back with

Dragon. Then—" He hesitated. "You not gonna come down on my boys Eric and Freddie are you?"

That depends on what you have to say next. If they were outside the room when Kent and Brian entered the room, they were possibly outside when the two left. That means they're the closest thing we have to witnesses. It also means we have a problem. Because they're also the gawkers who saw the aftermath. And instead of helping her, they took pictures.

If ya boys took pictures of that girl after she was raped, and have been sharing those pictures around school, I will rain hellfire down on them so hard, God Himself will amend their story in the Holy Bible.

"Tell us what happened; we'll see what we can do," Priest said. She used her most concerned and endearing face.

"Coach."

"Tell them what they want to know, Quan," Campbell commanded. "You have your whole future to think about here. You help them out, none of this gets back to you. Now, I'm counting on you to do the right thing. I can't protect you if you don't cooperate."

Summers leaned forward. "You have sisters. What would you want to happen if one of your sisters was that girl in the room? What if someone raped," he glanced at his notes, "Sharonda or Jasmine? Left her laying there on display and then threaten her into having an abortion. Would you want someone to stay quiet? Would you want little Sharonda left pregnant, humiliated, and without any justice?"

DeQuan's nostrils flared, his hands firmly gripped the arms of his chair. He eyeballed Summers for five seconds and then surrendered, arms slouched. He said, "Dragon and Kent went in with a camcorder and shut the door. Whatever they did in there, they recorded the whole thing." His skin reddened. "When they finished, they left her with the door wide open. Kent first, then Dragon. Dragon said, 'She's all yours boys,' and walked off. Eric and Freddie couldn't believe it. They started taking pictures of her. Eric wanted to go in on her."

Priest's hand tightened around her pen into a fist. *I'll lose my badge. I'll probably lose my life. But before this investigation is over, I am going to kill Brian Bradshaw.*

DAKOTA

DeQuan wrote down a few more names. "Some other guys were up there, too. Thought it was funny. Started taking pictures. Those pictures have been going around the school." He took out his phone, flipped to the images, and rested the phone on Campbell's desk. "She just laid there. They would have run a train on her if Val hadn't come up there. According to the guys, Val said she didn't agree to a train bang and told everyone to get out. Shut the door behind them."

I hate Val. I hate these boys. I hate everybody. You'd think I'd be used to this by now. But, every time I think humanity can't sink any lower, they take out a shovel and start digging.

DeQuan paused and stared at the pad of paper. "Val doesn't realize how close she was to having a train run on her, too. But she's off limits."

Summers and Priest connected eye contact for two seconds.

"Off limits?" Priest asked.

"Yea," DeQuan said. "Like I said before, she's helping them out. Val's been spreading the word around about Carissa pretending to want Kent to pop her cherry, lying about taking birth control pills, getting pregnant, claiming rape, and blackmailing them. This whole production is shady, because it's all coming from one side. Haven't heard a peep about anything from Carissa. Probably has something to do with the mysterious sex tape Brian and Kent made but hasn't shared. At least, not with me."

I hate girls like Val. There's at least one or two in every group that will scheme and completely stab you in the back without remorse or afterthought. I must get that sex recording. I know they still have it. It's got to be somewhere on their computers, in their possession.

"May I?" Priest asked and pointed to DeQuan's phone.

"Go ahead," DeQuan said, no longer showing any signs of resistance.

That's more like it. We've got names, narrative, and now pictures.

Priest looked at the pictures and her heart sank. Carissa was naked in bed. She looked more like a doll than a person the way her limbs were awkwardly twisted, eyes open, mouth parted. She felt a cold chill as she saw the horror in her eyes.

She flipped through more of the pictures. There was no change in Carissa. Only the angles of the camera changed. There was also a short video clip. She pressed play.

Male voices laughed in the background. A squeaky voice loudly requested a condom multiple times so he could "go deep on a bitch".

Another male voice said, "Man, you can't trust any pussy after a Bradshaw's been in it." Laughter.

The camera slowly approached Carissa. She lay immobile but alive. Her chest rose and fell as she breathed. But that was the only movement. She didn't blink.

A third male voice crudely said, "Damn! The dick was so good she just layin there." Laughter. "Girl ain't movin a muscle."

"She in shock," someone else yelled.

The squeaky voice said, "Man, get out the way. She ain't seen nothin til she seen this."

"She won't see nothin, because it's so small." Laughter.

"My newborn nephew got a bigger dick." Lots of laughter. The camera shook as the person who held it laughed.

"Eric, put that away; you're embarrassing yourself," someone yelled. More laughter.

"I'm about to go in her," the squeaky voice insisted.

The camera moved up real close before a female voice yelled, "Hey! What do you think you're doing?" The video ended.

This is damning. The video Brian recorded will obviously prove this was a rape. But this, this in and of itself is damning. She does not look in her right state of mind. If I can identify the voices of the guys in the room...

Obviously, Eric's the guy with the squeaky voice based on what he said. We'll have to confirm that. I'm interviewing him next.

Priest passed the phone to Summers. He took a deep breath, mumbled something under his breath, and scanned through the pictures, watched the same video. He handed the phone back to Priest, his face still and stoic.

"Are you able to show me who sent you which pictures and the video?" Priest asked. "Like the ones sent to you from Freddie and Eric. Text messages and emails?"

"Yea, I can do that."

"Thank you," Priest said. "We're going to be taking a copy of these pictures and the video."

DeQuan sighed. "I know."

She took a picture of DeQuan's phone with her phone. She snapped a picture of each of the pictures on his phone, the detailed properties, and recorded the video in its entirety. Then, she connected her phone to his phone and transmitted a copy of the pictures digitally.

"Have you shared these with anyone else?" Priest asked. She hoped his answer was no. *Distribution is a hard transgression to turn a blind eye to.*

DeQuan shook his head. "Naw. I don't send pictures. People send pics to me. I ain't sending no pics of nothin to nobody. And I don't need to send that around. It's gettin around on its own."

This is going to make my job a lot easier, or harder.

"We'll need to look through your text messages," Summers said. "Access your social media and email accounts for any other pictures of you or anyone else at the party."

Campbell chimed in. "You're asking for a lot, Detectives." He stood. "Now, he's been willing to cooperate. He's certainly given you more than enough to go on. I don't see a reason to dig into his accounts and messages."

Priest's head turned slowly to Campbell like a scene from a horror movie, no emotion on her face. "We're talking about the possession and distribution of child pornography. Images taken immediately after she was raped. We expect him to provide us with all the information regarding what he has, how he got it, who sent it, and then we're going to go down the list until everyone who has had possession of it and transmitted it, is charged and convicted, except for our dear friend, DeQuan."

Campbell swallowed hard, glanced at the phone, and sat. "It's your choice, DeQuan. But I encourage you to do what she says."

DeQuan shrugged. "Let's just get this over with, man. I don't want to have nothin to do with any of this. I got places to be."

Sounds good to me. So do I.

CHAPTER THIRTY

Captain Rogers was at the elevator as the doors opened. "I want to hear it all."

Can we get off the elevator first?

"The entire interview," he said. "I want to see the pictures. The video. The documentation from the clinic. Everything. I've already called the Prosecutor's Office. They'll be here in about an hour. I want to be up to speed and ready to talk charges."

"Conference room B in ten minutes?" Summers asked.

"Why ten minutes?" Rogers complained.

"He has to pee," Oliver said. Summers shot him an elbow straight to the ribs.

Rogers's face tensed up like a six-year-old boy that didn't want to wait until the morning for his Christmas present. "Alright. But be quick." He smirked. "Only two shakes."

Oliver laughed. "Anymore and you're just playing with yourself."

Oh my God. Priest rolled her eyes but grinned. She didn't want to relax. The case wasn't over until it was over. A million things could happen between today and conviction. But a lighter mood was to be expected after their latest discoveries. This was what her previous office called a Golden Day, especially after what Jane and Oliver uncovered in the locker room. She couldn't wait to reveal it in the conference room.

She didn't have to wait long.

Ten minutes later, they were in conference room B. Priest and Summers quickly ran through recent developments with captain, their team, and newly assigned officers.

"As you can see, we've made leaps since our last meeting," Priest said. "This morning, Summers and I went to the clinic on Patterson and had a productive conversation with Doctors Green and Sanders, as well as their receptionists. Not only have their documents solidified Carissa's complaints and story, it also helped shed light on a previous case, my sister's. We now have documented proof that Janice Bradshaw orchestrated the successful abortion of my sister's baby as well as the planned abortion of Carissa's. We have eyewitness testimony from a receptionist and nurse. She's worked at the clinic for six years and was there, on duty, when Brian Bradshaw walked my sister into the clinic for the abortion. The receptionist described her demeanor as terrified.

"We also have video of Kent Bradshaw picking up abortion pills the night Carissa did not go through with her abortion. He accepted a pill bottle. We have his fingerprints and the bottle. There is a match. The information from the bottle we have matches what they provided. There's no way they can deny Kent was the provider of the pills, especially once we have Mister Yarborough's statement that Kent stayed behind after class to confront Carissa."

Jane quickly ran copies of the clinic documents and passed them around. Priest turned on the flat screen and played security video of Kent accepting the abortion pills.

"Doctor Green confessed to his involvement as an accomplice with Janice Bradshaw in both abortions and agreed to testify for reduced penalties," Priest said. "I recorded our entire exchange, as well as our opening interview with Doctor Sanders. Let's listen."

She played the entire interview. After it was over, she smiled. "In addition to the testimony of the bank manager, who says Janice Bradshaw authorized the check for Carissa, we have the abortion attempt portion of the investigation wrapped up."

Oliver gave her two thumbs up.

Summers stepped in. "Our next interview was with DeQuan Jacobs, a local high school basketball celebrity. He told us what he knew and saw that night. Gave us second hand information about who was where and when. He saw Carissa not long before she was taken to Kent's room. From his observation, she was so inebriated she could barely stand. Two of his friends were upstairs when Carissa, Valerie Caulfield, and Kent entered the room. Caulfield and Kent left the room, and Kent and Brian Bradshaw returned. Brian Bradshaw had a video camera in hand.

"The two friends were also outside when Kent and Brian left the room. They took pictures of Carissa with their phones after her rape. Someone else recorded a short video. We have the contact information for all the individuals that sent DeQuan photographs and video. We're waiting on warrants. We'll be making arrests, taking possession of their phones, the works. As you'll see from this video, we have enough for an arrest warrant."

Summers played the video taken from DeQuan's phone. After it was finished, he flipped through the shared images. Then, he turned off the flat screen.

"Kitty Jenkins, an ex-girlfriend of Kent Bradshaw, saw the same video, and confirmed that Carissa was in Kent's room, on his bed," Priest shared.

"We'll have a specialist corroborate our observations," Summers said. "When the prosecutor comes, he'll determine if our current evidence will win us a solid conviction."

Captain Rogers nodded. "Great job. How are we coming on the website? The girls?"

Summers nudged Oliver. "You're up."

Oliver stood. "I have good news, bad news, and more good news. Good news: with the help of the school we've run student ID images through facial recognition and successfully identified about fifty-seven students over a time frame of five years."

"Fifty-seven?" Rogers asked, his nose scrunched in disgust.

That was my first reaction.

"More are matching," Oliver said. "There's reason to believe we're going to find images of twice or three times as many."

He took a sip from his water bottle.

"Pumas Uncovered is a group dedicated to sharing naked images and video of students from Patterson High. It's linked to a password-protected website which is more than likely their payment platform with additional, uncensored content. Jane's pictures of the girl's locker room shower and walls and lockers matched with the setting of some of the pictures and videos on the media site. Many of them are taken by individuals. However, most are taken from a fixed position. When I saw this, I realized there was a good chance that someone has skillfully hidden a secret camera in the girl's locker room and has been observing and recording them shower, change, et cetera. Being in a fixed position, there was also the possibility of an ongoing livestream."

Makes me sick. Something like this could have happened when I was going here.

"Wait," Rogers said. His face reddened. "Since you're telling us this, I'm to assume that you've removed it and recovered the images, video? My daughter probably showers in that locker room."

Priest and Summers looked at each other, Rogers, and then at Oliver. They would have to leave it to him to explain.

He's not going to like this.

Oliver clasped his hands together. "That's the bad news." He paused and thought about it. "We found it but haven't removed it."

"And why the hell not?" Rogers asked.

"We don't know who placed it there," Oliver said. "No doubt, their prints will be on the hidden camera, but unless they're in the database, we're not going to get very far. It's a member of the faculty, or a janitor. That much, I know. It has to be. From what the device settings are telling me, that specific camera has been sharing pictures and video from that fixed position for two years. Regular downloads like clockwork. But I can't remove the camera until after we've tracked this person."

"So, what are you going to do to find the person?"

Oliver smiled. "Well, first, I want to thank Jane for her incredibly selfless and shameless acts of vanity." Jane frowned. "Before she realized the camera was in there, she took pictures of herself in the locker room to get a better idea of the angles some of the naked pictures were taken. That allowed me to get a better fix on where the camera was. Whoever watched her probably thought she was taking pictures for a boy. Her actions would never register alarm from the camera owner."

"I was dressed in those pictures, by the way," Jane said and glanced around the room. "Completely dressed."

No one suspected otherwise.

Oliver winked at Jane and continued, "I slipped in, found the camera, and accomplished a remote interface. First, and foremost, what they're using isn't cheap. We're talking about a hidden camera that will cost you several thousand dollars." He passed around the product picture and specifications. "It has complex programming functions, motion detection, night-vision, thermal imaging, water resistance, steam resistance, timers, schedule systems, improved streaming capabilities, and about several hundred gigabytes worth of onboard memory. And the resolution?" He whistled. "This camera has incredible, high-definition resolution. You could see the hair follicles of the pimple on my left butt cheek through my jeans. This is the *real* shit, right here."

Rogers's face grew redder. This was not the news he wanted to hear. Priest hurriedly sent Oliver a text.

Priest: "What's wrong with you? His daughter could be in those pictures."

Oliver's phone buzzed in his pocket. He checked his text and glanced at her. "That's hyperbole, obviously. The images are crap. Things are barely visible. You can hardly see anything. Don't worry about it." He put down the specs.

"Anyway, the great thing about complex technology is that it's easier to hack. This camera stores video until its scheduled upload or whoever placed it sends an upload-download command. Then, it transmits everything it has to the owner and or a remote server. Now, I've uploaded a virus. The next time the upload-download happens, the virus will also be uploaded-downloaded. It will send out a distress call during standard internet activity on that computer. We'll know the computer and user information, where it's located. The virus will also transmit that person's computer activity, web history, keylogging, passwords, webcam, everything."

Captain Rogers stopped frowning. His eyes widened. "Good God."

Yes, He is.

Oliver pointed at his laptop. "But wait, there's more! I

installed another virus that imprinted and imprints itself into the images and video, especially the streaming video. Whatever website they show up on, they'll again cry out to me. I will be able to know and locate anywhere it is posted or shared or viewed. Also, anyone that views those images will be infected by the virus. That beautiful virus is going to send out its distress call as well, also sharing the computer information, location, and aforementioned goodness. If that person doesn't have access to the absolute best internet security and firewall software money can buy, it'll also open a backdoor to whatever device they're using.

"Assuming everything goes according to plan, we'll be able to find out who it is that set up this camera today or tomorrow morning. It's probably the same person, or one of the persons, administrating or supplying pictures and video to the social media or private site. The media uploads are scheduled to happen as early as eight o'clock every morning, Monday through Friday. They're also scheduled to begin after each class period. And around five in the afternoon, after many practices. The content on that person's computer, and backup storage, has to be enough to put this person in jail for several lifetimes.

"In short, tomorrow morning, when the owner and his viewers connect to watch naked high school girls, not only will we be able to track the person using the hidden camera, but also be able to track the website and individual users and viewers. The entire network." Oliver sat and put his feet up on a chair. "Case closed, bitches."

"Not quite yet," Priest said. *But we're almost there.* "There's still the matter of Carissa's case and the rape video. We need to get a search warrant before we arrest them, so they can't release it in retaliation."

Summers stepped in. "When drafting that warrant, we'll have a little bit of latitude on the location of the video, as the search can fall within the realms of trying to prevent the destruction of evidence and the video may not be confined to a particular device, like the video camera. It could be on a PC, phone, remote server, or any number of other storage devices. We must have sufficient and reliable information to authorize the search. Then, we'll have to find the device."

"This is where the more aggressive phase of our investigation begins," Priest said and pointed towards line items on their agenda board.

"We've been tiptoeing around the Bradshaws collecting clues, interviewing people, swearing them into silence under the threat of arrest for impeding a police investigation," Summers said. "But after tomorrow, our days of running silent are over. Assuming the virus works, Oliver and our cybercrimes division are going to be very busy arresting every person who's had access to the locker room video stream and filing charges. It'll probably include whoever's been passing around pictures of Carissa. I don't know how many students are involved, but suspect it'll be enough to make waves."

How many could there be? Enough.

"That's why, first thing tomorrow morning, we're interviewing the young men that recorded Carissa and took pictures after her rape," Priest said. "We need them to flip on Kent and Brian Bradshaw and agree to testify. We'll already have a warrant to search their possessions for any additional images or video they have that could expose the truth of what happened that night. If things go according to plan, we'll be able to arrest the Bradshaws tomorrow on a variety of charges."

Summers turned to Jane. "While Amy and I interview the young men, Jane and Chip will be drafting additional warrants needed and meeting with the judges to collect them." Jane and Chip nodded. "We don't have evidence that the Bradshaws are in possession of the sex tape, yet. We're stationing Chip outside the judge's office. Once Freddie and Eric serve as eyewitnesses of Brian carrying a video camera into that room, we'll send that audio testimony to Chip. With everything else, their witness testimony will get us a search warrant."

"And that's when we pounce," Priest said. "Once we have a search warrant, we're going to ambush them. We're going to hit their home, Kent at school, Janice's office, and Brian at college at the same time. We'll be coordinating with the local police in Williamsburg to simultaneously detain Brian and search his apartment. It should go off without a hitch."

"Let's not forget the arrest warrant for the group administrator of the Pumas Uncovered site, once we get his or her identity, and breach the private website linked to the social media site," Oliver said.

"Sounds like tomorrow's going to be a busy day," Red said.

Priest couldn't help but beam at the progress they've made. "The arrest of one of the richest families in Richmond. Arresting whoever is responsible for illegal recordings of young girls in a high school shower. Arresting a bunch of high school students exchanging child pornography. Yea. It's going to be a busy day. Not to mention a media madhouse." She looked at Captain Rogers.

"Don't worry about me," Rogers said. "I'm ready for it. So long as you do things by the book," he glanced at Oliver, who shrugged, "we shouldn't have any problems."

I'm not sure why there's been so much scrutiny towards Oliver. He's a bit goofy, but so far, Oliver's done everything by the book. He knows leagues more than any of us do about digital crime, and there's obviously more to him than meets the eye. That doesn't mean I won't ask questions every step of the way. This case is too important.

"Before any of us gets too excited about tomorrow," Summers said, "there's a lot of planning to do. I don't know how wide a net we'll cast tomorrow for the students. We've put together a game plan on who is arresting who and where and have everyone split into teams. We'll be assigning team members shortly. Team leaders are on the board."

He pointed to the dry erase board.

"We'll need to know the whereabouts of every member of the Bradshaw family and other key players. I'm going to issue discreet drive by and tailing orders and monitoring rotations from this point until the moment of the arrests."

"Discretion is key," Priest said. "You're going to ruin our day if you tip off the Bradshaws before we pounce. You've done this hundreds of times, but as always: identify and observe. Subtle stakeouts."

Oliver snapped his fingers and asked, "You're still going on your stakeout tonight, right?"

My second reminder of the day. I'm surprised Jay hasn't reminded me.

"With everything we have, we might not need to," Priest said.

Besides, in Val's case, being a lying, conniving little tramp is not illegal, unless you're under oath. As much as I'd like to arrest her for setting Carissa up for rape and pressuring her to consider an abortion, I wouldn't have anything but circumstantial evidence and hearsay to go on. Perhaps, once we get access to Kent or Janice Bradshaw's phone records and message history, it'll be a different story. Hmm. Note to self: Write a note to yourself to include their phone records and text messages in the search warrant.

"I strongly encourage it," Oliver said. "It'll prove fruitful. Trust me. Call it a hunch."

Anytime someone says, "Trust me," that's when you should worry.

Priest frowned and looked at Summers. He shrugged. "I'd trust his hunch."

I'd trust it if I believed it was just a hunch. With Oliver, this is more than a hunch. He's not telling us what he knows or how he knows it.

"Sounds like I have a long night ahead of me," Priest said. She picked up her cup of coffee and looked at the other officers in the conference room, and asked, "You have anything else, Nate?"

Headshake. "That's that," Summers said. "Any questions?"

No one had any.

"Great," Summers said. "That's a wrap. We'll update some of you on your tailing assignments in three hours. When we're finished with the prosecutor, team leaders will convene for a brief rundown of our arrest plan. The rest of you will get your group assignments via text or phone call as we've established them. Don't turn off your phones." He turned to Rogers. "Anything else, Captain?"

"Nope," Rogers said.

"In that case, let's get to it."

2

Three hours later, Priest sipped coffee and analyzed their arrest plan. The first arrests of the day would be Freddie and Eric, DeQuan's boys. Reduced penalties if they rolled over against Kent and Brian Bradshaw.

We'll need all the witnesses we can get.

Summers and two uniforms would then have the honor of arresting Kent Bradshaw, while Priest arrested Janice.

The look on her face when I lock those cuffs on her wrists will be so satisfying.

Sarah and Jia from crime lab would comb the Bradshaw mansion for computers, cameras, video cameras, hard drives, and storage devices or disks. They would also scan and swab Kent's bed and bathrooms for traces of Carissa's prints, hair, or DNA.

Officers Conway and Red, accompanied by Oliver, would arrest the locker room camera owner. From there, they would work with the county and city police to track down anyone who had access to the video stream and associated illegal content.

Officers Brice and Henrick would make the drive to Williamsburg in the morning and work with Williamsburg Police to arrest Brian Bradshaw and transport him to Richmond.

With the major players in custody, Officers Conway and Red would each lead a team of three to arrests others who received or shared media of Carissa.

Priest leaned back in her chair, anxious to put her feet up, and looked across the table. Summers went home to take a nap after the meeting with the prosecutor. He insisted on joining her later for the Valerie Caulfield stakeout. She refused. The case work was done for the day. The man needed to sleep and spend time with his wife. Anything that came up from Oliver's gossip girls and "hunch" wouldn't be anything more than what she could handle.

Perhaps Jay will get to watch me arrest a guy. I wonder if seeing me in power like that will turn him away or turn him on. Maybe we can do some cop and criminal sexy roleplay someday. He's made some shockingly playful and imaginative insinuations, with marriage as a prerequisite. I wonder which one of us will start to cave in first.

Me.

"I've got some good news and bad news," Oliver said as he sat in Nate's chair and rolled it over to hers, almost bumped their knees.

Why so close? Priest frowned. "Well, let's hear it."

"We got the warrant, flexed our muscles, and the social

media site gave us access to everything," Oliver said. "The content, member lists, admin names, access to member and admin private profiles, phone numbers, emails, addresses, IP addresses, passwords, mothers' maiden names. You name it. If they had it, we got it. We even have access to the link between the media site and their smartphones." He shifted in his chair like a little boy guilty of something and hoping his parent won't find out.

"Are you kidding?" Priest asked and perked up. "That's not good news. That's great news. That's just more names to add to our arrest warrants. What's the bad news?"

"We've got about two hundred scumbags that need their teeth punched in, and unfortunately, I only have two fists," Oliver said before kissing his fists. He forced a smile, but his eyes said he'd rather be anywhere in the world than in that chair. "Sasha and Natasha are going to have bruises."

Priest snorted. *You would name your fists. But what's going on with you? Something's up.*

"Any luck with the other site?" she asked, curious. "The password-protected one?"

Oliver put his hand on her desk and looked into her eyes. "Yes. The warrant came through for that as well. That's the real bad news."

"What?" Priest frowned. "Does the warrant not give you what you needed?"

"Oh no," Oliver said. "It does. Absolutely. We got the green light to hack the website. It's hosted on a secure and encrypted private server in a home residence. Connor and I were able to bypass its firewalls and encryption, download some of its content, and track its source location. You know Connor from cybercrime. Gifted kid. Not as fast as me, because that's impossible, but we tore through their encryption like a fat kid through a candy wrapper."

I don't understand why you're being weird about this. We just got a huge win.

"Okay," Priest said, annoyed again. "What's the address? Bradshaw residence?"

"Sadly, no. The residence server hosts the website but is only a relay for a separate private server which stores all the material uploads. It's registered under FRTY I&E in an office building downtown. Tenth floor."

"We need to go to that location, now, and secure the private server," Priest said. "If you can do your magic, we can track and arrest anyone that connects to that website, that residence server, private server, and download its questionable content. This sounds like great news. What's your problem?"

Oliver sighed. "What I found on that server is what I need to talk to you about. What I'm going to show you is incredibly difficult to see, and you're not ready for it."

What are you talking about? I'm not ready for it? What do you mean I'm not ready for it?

He looked at her with fixed, concerned eyes. Any sense of humor, joke, was removed from his face. Priest swallowed her spit. She knew that expression. She gave it her first day working homicide when tasked with telling parents their seven-year-old girl was found floating in a river with a rope around her neck.

Shit. Priest felt a cold chill run down her spine. *What is it? What could be that bad?*

"Before I tell Nate, or anyone else," Oliver said. "I needed you to see it first. It's only right."

See what?

"What is it?" Priest asked, scared to know, but angry he wouldn't just spit it out. "Stop beating around the bush and tell me already!"

"It's your sister," Oliver said. "I recovered raw video of your sister."

She blinked. "What?"

One raw memory stuck with Priest for years, playing in a loop, despite therapy and alcohol: her sister's black coffin lowering into the dirt. *Dakota.* A frail, lifeless form rested eternally in her favorite pink dress. Her silver tiara fixed on her head, parted long blond hair. A blush of pink permanently marked her cheeks and lips.

She hated the idea of another nightmare repeating itself in her head, but what was her alternative? Not review the evidence? She needed to see it. How bad could it be?

Bad. She swallowed hard. *It could be really bad.*

Priest fought for even breaths and let out a whisper. "Show

me."

CHAPTER THIRTY-ONE

In conference room B, Oliver's laptop plugged into the flat-screen. A still image of Dakota in an unfamiliar room blurred. He shut the door behind them and dimmed the lights.

Priest sat, uneasy about what she was about to watch, only knowing that it was something she had to see. She needed to know what happened to her sister, no matter how much it hurt to know. No matter how much it hurt to see.

"Are you ready?" Oliver asked.

She nodded, inaudible. *Could anyone ever be ready for what I'm about to see?*

"Here goes," Oliver said and pressed play.

Dakota's dimpled smile filled the screen before the camera zoomed out. She stood, posing in a short, white, cocktail dress. Her golden blond hair was in curls. Dazzling but fake diamond earrings reflected the light in the room.

"So, what's this about?" she asked with a rich Southern accent. She sounded so much like daddy and grandpa. "You record all your party guests?"

A male voice said, "Only the special ones. You did win our costume contest."

She smiled, proud. "I don't know how. I mean, there had to be at least two other girls at the party dressed like Monroe. Can't say I got any points for creativity."

"It's how you wore the dress, babe," the male voice said. "I mean, you're so beautiful and sexy. Those girls don't hold a candle to you."

Dakota grew red and gushed. "Really?"

"Oh yea," he said. "You blew those girls out of the water. If you ask me, you're the prettiest girl at this party."

She rolled her eyes. "Now you're just messing with me."

"No, I'm not," he said. "I'm serious. You've got it going on."

Dakota watched him with fixed eyes. "I think you're just saying that. I mean, if I was really as pretty as you say I am, I would get a lot more attention."

The camera moved closer to her. "I don't know about those other guys, but, I think you're fire, girl. They're probably intimidated by you."

"Hmm," Dakota considered. "Perhaps."

The camera was fixed in place with an audible click. Then, a muscular male approached her from behind the camera. He towered over her, which she was used to. Dakota was only five feet, two inches.

"I, however, know a good thing when I see it and go after it," he said, his big hands rubbed her shoulders and arms. "I want to be with you."

Dakota stiffened. "Uh, you mean, like, go on a date? Or are you implying something else?" The skepticism in her eyes made it clear she already knew what he was implying.

He chuckled. His hands moved to her hips. She exhaled, blinked rapidly, and blushed again. He said, "I'm thinking a lot more than a date."

"So." She guided his hands from her hips and took a deep breath. "What you're saying is: you want me to be your girlfriend. Officially."

"Oh, absolutely," he said and returned his hands to her hips. "Don't you want to be my girlfriend?"

She fixed her hands on his. "I've never had a real boyfriend before. My daddy won't let me. He's been watching me like a hawk ever since I turned fourteen." Again, she took his hands off her hips. "That and guys haven't shown that much interest in me. Some said I was too skinny. Others said I had a black girl's butt. Neither complaint corroborates the other. It's hard to figure out what boys want."

"You have a beautiful ass," he said before reaching down and cupping her butt with his hands. "Those guys don't know what they're talking about."

She turned a deep red. "I can't believe you just grabbed my butt."

"Well," the male voice said, "I'm your boyfriend, right? Don't I get ass grabbing privileges?"

She frowned and removed his hands from her butt. "No. I never made it official."

"Well, it's official," he said and returned his hands to her butt, gripped her butt cheeks harder, and pull her against his crotch. "I'm your boyfriend."

"Brian." She grimaced and forcibly removed his hands. "If you *ever* want me to be your girlfriend, you're going to have to curb your enthusiasm and be gentle with me. Unlike some of these other girls, I was raised to take things slow."

"Slow," Brian said. "You want to take things slow?"

"Yes. I'm not like the other girls you're used to. I expect to be respected. I don't rush into things. I take things slow."

"Like, slow as in, soft kisses?" Brian asked and lightly caressed her cheek. "Or slow as in, gentle pumps from behind while you bite down on a pillow?"

Dakota frowned and took a step back. "Slow as in, maybe we should talk about this later, when you have a clearer head."

"I'm just kidding." Brian grinned and stepped closer. "I just get excited being around you. You excite me. I've never felt this way about someone before. It's hard for me to control myself. See?"

He pointed to the bulge in his trousers. She simply stared at it, perplexed. Then she looked at him hesitantly.

"I think I should go," Dakota said and took a step back.

"Please stay," Brian said. Every time she backed away, he stepped closer, kept them within inches of each other. "Let's talk for a while."

"No. You're obviously looking for more than I'm able to give you right now. Besides, Kylie is probably wondering where I am. I should go see if she's okay. She was drinking a lot."

Brian sighed. "I thought you wanted to be my girlfriend."

Dakota hesitated. Her eyes shifted down and then up again. "I guess I didn't know what that meant."

"Well, can't I at least get a kiss?" Brian asked. "Then, we can talk about going on that date. A real one. A serious one. I know this great restaurant we can go to. I'd make it extra special with flowers and music. I'll even get us a limo."

Dakota looked past him towards the exit. "To make up for your disrespectful behavior, it would have to be the finest meal short of dinner in the Buckingham Palace."

"And the kiss?" Brian persisted. He had a one-track mind and was missing a wheel. "Have you ever kissed a guy before?"

"A kiss?" She frowned at him. "Have you not listened to a word I said about taking it slow? What are you, thick?"

Brian's hand swung around and slapped her hard on the side of her face. Her eyes and mouth shot wide open in shock as she fell back to the floor and tumbled. Tears burst from her eyes.

"You hit me!" Dakota cried. "You asshole!"

He stepped forward and reached down, but she kicked at him.

"Don't touch me!" she yelled. "Get away from me!"

"Don't kick me, you bitch!" Brian yelled and kicked her in the stomach. "Stupid cock tease whore." He kicked her again.

Dakota curled into a ball on the floor. "Stop!" she pleaded and gagged. "Stop, Brian! Stop!"

"I will stop when I damn well please!" Brian yelled and kicked her again.

"Please!" Dakota sobbed.

Brian stopped and stood over her, fists balled. He huffed and puffed and looked back at the camera. "For the fraternity," he said and returned his attention to Dakota. He knelt, picked her up off the floor, and carried her to his bed.

"Leave me alone," Dakota demanded and struggled against his grip. "Let go of me and leave me alone."

Brian dropped her on the bed. "I will do whatever I damn well please, and you will like it."

Dakota twisted and rolled towards the other side of the bed. Brian reached out and grabbed her ankles. He pulled her closer to him. She kicked her feet in a running motion to release his hold. He released one of her ankles and punched her in the hamstring.

"Ow!" she yelled and kicked at him again. Brian swung and hit the same spot. Dakota cried out in pain. Her arms reached back to protect her leg. Brian yanked her toward him, climbed on the bed, and pressed his body weight on top of her.

"If you fight me, I will break you," Brian threatened. His hot breath in her face. "You know I can. I will beat you so bad you won't be able to walk outta here."

Dakota pushed with all her strength against him. He put his hands around her throat and squeezed. She blinked rapidly, flailing her legs and slapping her arms against his.

"I can snap your neck, bitch!" Brian yelled. "Stop fighting me."

She balled her hands into fists and struck against his arms. The frail phalanges met thick muscle. He didn't flinched. He squeezed harder and harder until her legs slowly stopped kicking, fists slowly stopped swinging. He let her go and she gasped for air. Coughed.

"Don't be stupid," Brian commanded. "I can kill you if I want to." His left hand tightened around her throat again. He balled his right hand into a fist and held it over her face. "You give me any more trouble and I'm going to beat the shit out of you. Do you understand?"

Dakota nodded and sobbed.

Brian released her throat and straightened himself. He reached under her skirt and slid her panties down her legs, past her heels, and on to the floor.

"Don't," Dakota pleaded. "Please don't do this."

"What, did, I, say?" Brian asked and clenched his right fist.

She put her hands up to shield herself. She sobbed, "Okay, okay."

Brian grabbed her waste and turned her over on her stomach. He unzipped her dress and tugged and pulled it off her on to the floor. He unclipped her strapless bra and tossed it behind him, leaving her bare.

"Brian," Dakota cried.

"Are you serious?" Brian asked and slapped her butt with an open hand.

She put her face into the sheets and wept.

He rolled his eyes and took off his pants and boxers. "You're crying now. But in a minute, you'll be moaning like a whore."

Dakota looked back at him with a scowl. He spanked her again. She yelped.

"Eyes forward!" Brian commanded and took off his tank top. He lifted her hips and positioned himself behind her.

"Please don't," Dakota asked and sobbed. Her whole body trembled.

"Too late," Brian said and forced himself into her.

A minute later, he pulled himself out of her and got off the bed. He looked down at his crotch and swore, "God dammit! I forgot the condom."

Dakota remained silent and still.

"Did you hear what I said?" Brian asked and pointed at her. "All your fighting made me forget my condom."

She said nothing.

Brian grabbed her hair and pulled her head up to meet his. "Listen, and listen good. When you leave here, you will say nothing. You will tell no one a goddamned thing. If you do, I'm coming after you. And you know what will happen when I find you?"

Dakota shook her head, slowly.

"No?" Brian asked and tugged at her hair. "Okay. If you say anything to anyone, I will beat you to death. Got it?"

Dakota nodded.

"You better pray you don't get pregnant," Brian said. "Because if you do, I will beat you until you lose the child. Understand?"

She nodded again.

Brian tugged at her hair again. "Are you sure?"

Another nod.

"And I won't just stop at you," Brian said. "I know where you live. I know where your sister lives. I will make your life a living hell. Understand?"

One more nod.

"Say you're not going to say a word," Brian ordered her.

"I, I won't say a word," Dakota mumbled.

Brian tugged at her hair. "Awfully quiet. I can't hear you."

"I won't say anything," Dakota sobbed.

Brian tugged her hair again and then pushed her head to the bed. Her head bounced and she cried out. He grabbed his camera, looked directly into it, and smiled. The video ended.

2

Priest staggered into the bullpen and collapsed into her chair. The rape video was the hardest thing she'd ever had to watch. The moment he put his hands on her she needed to take a break. Each time, she didn't know how she could see anymore. How she could endure it. But she had to, for her sister. It was the evidence she needed to finally get justice. And she would get justice. No matter the cost.

Her eyes shifted to a locked drawer. It held her firearm. She unlocked the drawer, opened it, and stared at the pistol issued to her five years ago.

I'm going to kill him, she resolved and grabbed her gun and extra clips. But as she got to the elevator, and the doors opened, Jay walked out holding a dozen gardenias and a cup holder with two tall Milk 'n Tea cups.

Jay.

"Hey Beautiful," Jay greeted. "Ready for our stakeout?"

Priest froze and blinked away her tears. "Jay, you're here." She looked at her watch. "Early."

"For once, right?" He handed her the gardenias. "And just like last time, I brought us snacks." He raised the cup holder. "And drinks. Coffee with two percent milk, extra sugar, and a swirl of mint for you and green mint tea for me, to keep us sharp." He pointed at his hiker backpack. "I brought some surveillance gear and bottled waters. Freshly ordered chicken sandwiches and side salads are in the car."

Priest hid her face in the gardenias and inhaled. She had to regain her composure before she completely lost it.

Your timing couldn't be worse. I can't go on this stakeout. I have to get to Williamsburg and empty every clip I own in his chest and head. He raped Dakota. He's the reason why she's dead. I'm ending this once and for all. Right now.

"Also, I uploaded the best works of Rossini, Debussy, and Chopin for lovely background music," Jay continued with pride. "It's going to be the best."

The best.

Priest took deep breaths, forced herself to maintain her composure, and manufactured a smile, "Thanks, but we can't do this tonight. Something's come up. New evidence. We'll have to do this another night."

"Priest!" Rogers called from across the room and marched forward with purpose. Oliver was not far behind him.

If I don't get outta here, he's not going to let me go. Dammit, Jay. Of all the days, you chose today to be punctual.

"You're not going to Williamsburg," Rogers said after a quick glance at her sidearm. "I just had their police chief on the line. They're keeping an eye out for Bradshaw's vehicle. We'll get him. But someone with a cool head will get him."

"Captain, please," Priest pleaded. She could feel her strength waver and façade crumbling. Her eyes watered. "I have to do this. I need to get over there and look him in the eyes as I read him his rights." *I'm not reading him shit.* "Put cuffs on him." *On his corpse.* "It's the least I can do."

Rogers shook his head. "I can't let that happen."

"Please," Priest begged. "What if it was your daughter? What if she was in that video? Wouldn't you want to go after him?"

"Of course," Rogers said. "And that's pricelessly why you can't go. Because if that was my daughter, my sister, my wife, I'd put a bullet in his head without a second thought. And I'd probably put a second in his head afterward, just to make sure."

Why are you conserving bullets?

Priest glared at Oliver as he gave Jay a 'sup head nod.

You should've kept your mouth shut until I left. Why'd you go straight to the captain?

Of course, she realized the captain needed to know. Assuming she tried to arrest Brian, instead of shooting him on sight, *fat chance of that*, Rogers had to contact Williamsburg police, communicate a change in the cross-jurisdiction arrest and transportation orders, provide them with the necessary information, and finalize the arrest warrant in motion.

"If I can't arrest him, at least let me be there when he's arrested," Priest pleaded. "Let me watch them shove him in the back of a cruiser."

"No," Captain said. Priest opened her mouth to protest. "And that's final. They're transporting him here. You'll get to see him behind bars, tomorrow. And you'll get to see him in court, in front of his peers, being charged with everything we can find in the book, and then some."

Priest sighed and glanced at Jay. He stood still, cup holder still in hand. His concerned and loving eyes watched her. She felt a wave of calm rush over her. It made no sense how her pain washed away.

"Okay," Priest resigned. Her shoulders sagged. "Fine."

Rogers let out a sigh of relief. "Let's be smart about this by figuring out how and why that video is on that server in the first place, and what else is on there."

"We *have* to secure the private server tonight," Oliver added. He glanced at Jay. "Before we do anything about the Bradshaws or anyone else, we need what's on those servers. Everything depends on it."

"What exactly?" Priest asked. *What could be more important than beating Brian's cold dead body with my pistol until he can't be identified?*

"The office building's owned by wealthy, powerful people. Bad people. They're the reason why your sister was raped. The moment they get wind of what's happening with this case, the open window we have right now to stop them will close fast. We're going to need a warrant and plenty of officers and squad cars squatting on premises until I copy what we need and remove and secure the servers. The moment we're on site, the private security will inform the owners. The owners will call the mayor. You'll understand soon."

Rogers's entire face frowned. "They'll call the mayor? For what?"

"To squeeze his balls," Oliver said. "That video, the hidden camera, it's only the tip of the iceberg. This ties into a lot more than Carissa, Dakota, and that website. We're talking your missing persons reports. Trafficking." He put his hand to his mouth and rubbed his lower lip. "I've been following leads for years. This is finally my chance. Trust me. Once we get to that server, I can explain everything. But we need to lock it down."

Priest sighed. "This is a mess. We don't have officers and squad cars to spare on the night shift right before our big grab tomorrow. It'll take at least three hours to get that warrant this late."

Rogers swatted down her concerns. "Don't worry about people. I can authorize overtime, no problem. I've had five officers asking about it. Christmas debt. I can call Bob and get Richmond City on site, since it's their jurisdiction. Get our warrant genie to put something together in a jiffy. Oliver, detail everything technical we need to request. Oh, and contact our favorite judge, the rubber stamper. I'll think about who we can drag in to cover the server overnight."

Not me. That's for sure.

Jay stepped forward. "Why not us?"

What? Priest, Rogers, and Oliver turned to Jay.

"I already brought dinner, snacks, and coffee for a stakeout," Jay said. "I don't mind a late-nighter for justice's sake."

You don't, but I mind. I can't be there overnight. I'm exhausted as is. We have a long day tomorrow. We're taking down the Bradshaw family and half the pervs in town. Not to mention, I'm going to have to contact the Boisseau family.

Rogers's eyebrows rose. "That's quite an offer, Pastor, but I'm going to need a well-rested Detective Priest tomorrow."

Captain just called him pastor. He's not a pastor.

"How about this?" Priest started. "We get the warrant, pop over there, Oliver downloads everything on the server, and then we have an overnighter, other than me and Jay, squat on the server."

Oliver slipped in. "Not enough terabytes in my arsenal to download everything. But I'll download anything pertinent to our current cases, and then some."

"Sounds great," Rogers agreed. "I'm going to call Samantha and tell her I'll be running late. Let's get this warrant in motion as soon as possible." He trotted off.

"Pastor?" Oliver said. "Since when did you become a pastor?"

Jay shrugged. "I mean, technically, the moment we accept Yeshua as our Lord and Savior and are baptized by water and Spirit, we're born again into the body of the Messiah and adopted into a holy royal family and priesthood. Keyword being priesthood. So, though inaccurate, his sentiments are correct. Pastor, priest is interchangeable depending on denomination."

Oliver patted Jay on the back. "You don't change, Jim. Not one bit." They hugged.

"Good to see you, too," Jay said.

You don't change? Good to see you? She wasn't sure why she

DAKOTA

felt her worlds colliding, but she did. "You know each other?"

Jay hesitated. "Umm, yea."

"It's complicated," Oliver said and called the elevator. *It's complicated?* "How long is it going to take to get your warrant genie the specifics?" He glanced at his watch. "We have to pop in on Caulfield and married dude. Umm, Bastard."

Bastian. His name is Bastian. But I'm inclined to agree.

"About ten to twenty minutes, hopefully," Priest said. *You're not getting away that easy.* "How did you two meet?"

"We're not permitted to talk about it." Jay sipped his tea. "Discretionary protocols. How about I meet you two in the Jeep? I have to make a phone call."

Discretionary protocols? What the heck?

"Sure, we'll meet you there," Oliver said to Jay and looked at Priest. "While your genie is putting together the warrant for the server, I'm going to grab my laptops from the cybercrime lab. I'll call you to share what it needs to say. We might need to make a quick stop to grab some external hard drives if we're going to copy the server's hard drives. At least ten terabytes. Maybe more if you have room in your car."

The elevator door opened. Oliver stepped in. Jay leaned forward, kissed Priest's lower lip, and said, "Love you." Then, he got on the elevator. She stared at them as the elevator doors closed.

Love you? He just told me he loves me for the first time. The timing couldn't be worse.

CHAPTER THIRTY-TWO

Cheerleading practice ended ten minutes before Priest got to Patterson High. Through gadgetry Oliver refused to disclose—*perhaps it's best he doesn't reveal his methods*—he was able to track Val's movements.

"She's left school and is headed north," Oliver told her. "Turn right."

Priest rolled her eyes and turned. She hated following directions without knowing where she was going. She hated GPS units. She hated backseat drivers. She wanted to look on a map, plot out her route, and go. She needed to see where she was going, as well as alternative routes.

After a few turns, they were a safe distance behind Val's car and followed her to *For Every Occasion*. Priest parked in the lot next door and turned off her headlights.

Jay passed her a small pair of binoculars. "Here."
You have binoculars...
"When did you get these?" Priest had to ask.
"After our last stakeout," Jay said, reached into his backpack. "You said to come prepared. How are we expected to catch anything with our bare eyes at this time of night?"
"Police have only done it for the last two centuries." She lifted the binoculars and watched Val. *But these do help.*

Val stood at the store entrance with her phone to her face. A minute later, the door opened. A man reached out, picked her up, spun in a circle, and kissed her.

Click-click-click.

Priest's head swung around. Jay held a camera with two long lenses attached. "You brought a camera, too?"

Click-click-click-click-click. "Of course." Click-click-click.

Of course. Mister Private Eye over here. What have I started? Focus. She looked back at the storefront. They were gone. "Looks like they've gone inside."

"Let me see that," Oliver requested and reached his hand between the front seats.

Jay passed the camera.

Oliver flipped through the images. "Nice. That's enough for an arrest. But you'll have to arrest him. You know. For reasons."

Jay unbuckled his seatbelt. "Citizen's arrest it is."

"He was talking to me," Priest said, half-smiling at the audacity of her boyfriend, and unbuckled her seatbelt as well. "You're staying in the car."

Jay pouted. "Couldn't I at least, like, be around for moral support or something? Snap some pictures before you bust in and catch them red-handed."

"Or boob-handed," Oliver added, "in this case." He pointed at the camera. Jay chuckled.

Priest stared at the two. *These two are ridiculous.* But she appreciated the comedy relief. An hour ago, she was in tears and prepared to commit first degree murder. "Fine. Come along. Take some more pictures. But you're staying outside."

Oliver and Jay got out of the jeep and crept in a half-squat behind Priest. At the entrance, Jay straightened and scanned the store with his camera zooming in and out. "Oh, goodness sweet mercy," he said and turned around. His eyes were wide. "I can't take a picture of that."

"I can," Oliver said and grabbed the camera. "For justice." He peeked in and pointed his camera. "Oh wow. Yep. That's illegal." Click-click-click-click-click. "That's also illegal." Click-click-click-click. "Somebody is going to jail, jail, jail. All the way to jail." He jigged.

"A lot safer than home when we tell his *wife*," Jay cheered. Oliver gave him a high five.

Priest stared. *How do they know each other?!*

"Good news for you, Amy," Oliver said. Click-click-click. "You don't have to worry about handcuffing Bastian. She's done that for us." He gave her a thumbs up.

"I can't believe this," Priest mumbled under her breath and called it in. "I need a squad car at *For Every Occasion.* ASAP." She hung up. "Give me that camera."

"I've taken more than enough." Oliver handed it over. "With these shots, we might as well drive him straight to prison."

Priest snorted. *If only it worked that way. It would save us all a lot of paperwork.*

"You two get back to the jeep," she said. "I'll wait for a squad car or these two to leave the building. Whichever comes first."

Jay frowned. "What if they see you and try to take the back exit or emergency exit?" He looked at Oliver. "Shouldn't we cover those until they're in custody?"

Priest stared at him. *Who's the cop here?*

"He has a point," Oliver said.

I know. Priest glared. "Fine. But if they go through the back or emergency exit, you're not allowed to stop or apprehend them. Don't touch either of them. Just move out of the way and call me."

It's not like we don't know who they are or where they live.

Jay reached in his pocket and pulled out a whistle. "I have a whistle. I'll blow my whistle."

"You brought a whistle?" Priest asked. *Of course, you brought a whistle. And binoculars. And a camera. What else did you bring with you? A batarang? What didn't you bring?*

"Of course. You said come prepared. Don't all police officers carry a whistle?"

But you're not a police officer. Sigh. *I'm going to have to make this our last stakeout. It's going to break his heart but, this has gone too far. I did not expect him to get so into this. Though, I shouldn't be surprised.*

"Yea, if you're directing traffic," Priest said.

That's when Oliver pulled out his whistle. "Oh! Will ya look at that? I came prepared, too."

For what?

"That doesn't count," Priest argued. "You're obsessed with Kindergarten Cop. You probably brought his sunglasses, too." Oliver reached in his pocket and put on the round, black-framed sunglasses Arnold Schwarzenegger wore. She sighed. "You know it's too dark for, ugh, whatever. Just go behind the building and wait to see if anyone comes out. I'll call you when I have them in custody. Call me if they come out the back."

The two nodded and walked towards the back.

"And please don't blow your whistle," Priest added.

Oliver called back. "Blow our whistles. Got it!"

Children. I'm working with grown children.

Fifteen minutes later, a squad car drove into the parking lot. The officer stopped in front of Priest and lowered his window. "Are they still inside?"

"Like rabbits," Priest grumbled. She recognized the officer. Diaz. "I've got two guys in the back, one civilian, one consultant slash detective slash vice squad. They're standing watch just in case our love birds make a run for it. But I've got places to be, and don't feel like breaking the door. I'm hoping they'll quietly surrender without a hitch."

Diaz smirked. "I see you're an optimist."

Right? "I'll approach the door. When I wave, you flash your lights and give your siren a quick chirp. I'll knock on the door and show my shield. If you see me run, it means one of them is making a run for it. That's when you hop out and cover the front. Got it?"

"Got it."

Priest walked to the door and waved. Diaz flashed his red and blues. His siren sounded. She knocked on the glass door and showed her badge and shield.

Val hopped off Bastian and scrambled for her clothes. Bastian, with one hand still cuffed to his roller chair, followed suit and reached for his pants. He called out to Val. She didn't listen, but slipped into her shirt, halfway pulled up her skirt, and rushed towards the back, shoes in hand.

Well, looks like we have a runner. I hope she doesn't run into Jay. That's the last thing I need tonight.

Priest signaled Diaz and sprinted around the back. She heard a whistle screech followed by a loud scream. It sounded female. She hoped it wasn't Val's scream, considered the alternative, then hoped it was.

I pray to God that's not how Jay screams.

Priest swung around the corner and saw a half-dressed Val,

skirt around her ankles, sprawled on top of Jay. Oliver stood over them.

Well, this image is going to be stuck in my head.

"Is everyone okay?" Priest asked. She wasn't sure for whom to be more concerned.

"Surprisingly, I'm comfortable in this position," Jay said— *Really?*—and reached for his back. He winced. "Ahh, man."

"Not to be confused with 'amen'?" Oliver asked. The two looked at each other and laughed. *So, he's fine.*

"Up, Miss Caulfield," Priest commanded, hands on her hips. "And pull your skirt up."

Val stood, pulled up her skirt.

"You have the right to remain silent. Anything you say can and will be used against you in the court of law. You have the right to a court appointed or otherwise attorney. If you cannot afford one, one will be provided for you. Do you understand your rights?"

"I didn't do anything," Val whined.

"Yea, sure." Priest rolled her eyes. *That was a lot of nothing you two were doing on that chair.* "How'd you end up on the ground?"

"She burst through the door," Jay said and rubbed his back. "Screamed and toppled into me after I blew my whistle. Guess I startled her."

Of course, you did. She wasn't expecting two guys waiting outside, in the dark, with whistles.

"That question was for Miss Caulfield," Priest clarified and returned her attention to Val. She pointed. "You and I have a lot to talk about."

Val's mouth dropped open and closed as she tried to find the words. "I, uh, uh, I, I didn't do anything wrong. It's, he, him. I'm a minor. He, he took advantage of me. It's all his fault. I haven't broken any crimes. I'm, I'm a victim."

Please.

"You haven't committed any crimes," Priest maintained eye contact. "Is that so?"

"I mean, like, yea. I can't be charged with anything. I'm not the one that did something wrong. He is! I'm a minor."

"Did you know it was a crime to setup Carissa Boisseau to get raped by Kent Bradshaw? It's called conspiracy. People that know are talking."

Val paled. She swallowed hard.

"We know you contacted the Bradshaws when you found out she was pregnant. You helped orchestrate the money exchange for the illegal abortion. You drove her to the clinic, then abandoned her when she refused to go along with it. People have confirmed you're spreading a rumor that Carissa intentionally got pregnant to blackmail the Bradshaws."

"No," Val barely whispered before backing away. Was she going to make a run for it, again? "You, you're wrong."

"You've also been pressuring her friends to shut her out," Priest said. "Especially Miss Rogers. You said not to talk to Carissa unless she gets the abortion and stops, 'blackmailing the Bradshaws'. You're using social pressure to force a person to get an abortion."

Val licked her drying lips. "Telling them to not talk to her is not against the law. She's, she's bad news."

"Talk about the pot calling the kettle black," Oliver scoffed. "People who live in glass houses shouldn't ride married guys under a spotlight while throwing stones."

Priest closed her eyes and balled her fists. *I'm talking to a suspect, you daft prick. Shut up!*

"You know what's bad news?" Priest said and pulled out her handcuffs. "I have to take you to the precinct."

"No, I don't want to go to jail," Val whined. "You can't arrest me. Call my mom. You can't arrest me without my mom. I want a lawyer."

Lawyer, naturally. That means we'll have her detained for an hour or so before either get access to her. Hopefully someone else can swing by the judge and grab the warrant for the office building. We'll also need a warrant for the specifics of her phone. I must search Val's phone for text messages and phone records that fill in the gaps, verifies or refutes the current narrative. How will I access her phone?

Simple. We'll access Bastian's phone. He'll willingly give us access for a plea deal. No doubt they've shared at least a few inappropriate pictures. If she sent him anything with nudity, it gives us grounds to access her phone. Her messages. Messages specific to their arrangement. We can't risk her deleting any correspondence between her and Bastian or the Bradshaws once she gets access to her phone again. To prevent her from tampering or deleting evidence, we have the right to preserve said evidence. That's the opening I need.

But what if I tried a different approach?

"Lawyer or not," Priest said, "we're arresting them. If you don't want to cooperate and help us take down the Bradshaws, we'll do this the hard way. You can call your lawyer while we process your charges. You can join them in jail."

Val blinked rapidly. "Wait, wait. Take down the Bradshaws? That's what this is about? You're saying, if I help you take down the Bradshaws, I won't be charged for anything?"

I didn't say that, but it sounds like your slippery ass is about to try to make a deal. As much as I'd love to see you behind bars, you'd probably get a slap on the wrist, anyway. Community service. House arrest. Whatever. I'm better off having you spill the entire deal and put the final nail in their coffins.

"Perhaps," Priest said. Cooperation would suit her needs and tie up the case nicely.

Final nail? The video of my sister will put Brian behind bars for the rest of his life. If God would be so kind, maybe it could put him under the needle? But there's no capital punishment for rape in America, yet, and no capital punishment at all in Virginia.

"Okay, fine." Val perked up. "I'm not getting paid enough to go to jail."

Not getting paid enough. You're such a slimy little worm. I can't believe I'm considering leniency. But the Bradshaws must go down for Dakota and Carissa. You'll get yours. It's only a matter of time. Girls like you always get theirs.

"Tell us something we need to hear and let's go from there," Priest said.

2

Val waited impatiently in the interrogation room until an officer escorted her mother into the room and closed the door behind them. Priest watched the two from the other side of the one-sided glass and listened to them bicker.

"You were caught having an affair with a married man?"

were the first words out of Katherine Caulfield's mouth, her face hot and cherry. "I should slap you in the face! I can't believe you'd put me through this shit after what your father did to me. You want to be a homewrecking whore like Brenda?"

Well, that escalated quickly.

"I should have made popcorn," Oliver said and scooted his chair closer. He took a bite out of his apple.

Where did you get that apple? We don't have apples. Nowhere in the station do we have apples. We didn't stop for apples on the way. Did you take that out of someone else's lunch?

"No," Val pouted and lowered her head. "I don't know why. I just wanted him, and figured, if he went along with it, it was on him, not me. He's going to jail. That's his fault."

Katherine stared at her daughter. "And what's this about Carissa being raped? You said she stopped talking to you for no reason. Just iced you out."

"Well, she didn't have to stop talking to me," Val said. "It wasn't my fault. I didn't tell him to rape her. I just set them up. How was I supposed to know he was going to do that? It seemed like a beneficial arrangement for all of us. I just wanted to help her out. Get her some love. You know how much of a prude she was."

Katherine rolled her eyes. "Everyone's a prude compared to you, Kendra, and your father. It's like Sam and I are the only ones in this family that can keep it in our pants."

"I bet you twenty bucks she's having an affair," Oliver said and reached for his wallet. "Double or nothing it's someone in her office."

Priest was all business. "Nope."

"Whatever." Val crossed her arms. "Maybe if you opened your legs more, Dad wouldn't be sniffing around fat bitches."

Katherine's mouth hung open in shock. Oliver cackled.

"That's my cue to go in there," Priest rushed out. *I was not expecting a showdown.* She swung one door shut and the other open, stepping in just in time as Katherine approached Val with an open hand. "Sorry for the wait. Paperwork."

Katherine spun around and nearly fell but caught herself on the table. "Detective." She straightened herself.

We're all going to pretend you weren't about to strike your child. I don't need child services taking away my suspect before she rolls over on her co-conspirators.

"Priest," Priest said. "Amy Priest." She shook Katherine's cold, frail hand. Katherine's bones gave under her grip. She released quickly. "I believe the officers have informed you of the situation with your daughter and Mister Bastian Braun, the owner of *For Every Occasion*." Katherine nodded. "And her involvement in the rape of Carissa Boisseau."

"Yes."

Priest motioned for Katherine to sit while she took out her notepad and pen. After Katherine sat, she sat. "We've put together a very strong case against the Bradshaws. We have actionable intelligence and are prepared to make an arrest with what we have. What happens to your daughter, whether she cooperates or not with the final details of our investigation, determines if she gets pulled into the net we're about to cast. While on her way to the station, she agreed to cooperate. However, we needed you present, as she is still a minor."

"Right." Katherine leaned forward, listened. "What do you have on the Bradshaws?"

Nope.

"That's not how this works. Val's verifying what we already know and filling in the gaps. She'll be a key witness. In exchange, she won't be charged as an accomplice for arranging Carissa's meeting with Kent, helping put her in Kent's bed while she was heavily intoxicated, where he later raped her, informing the Bradshaws that Carissa was pregnant, and helping coordinate and coerce Carissa into an illegal abortion."

Katherine's head twisted so fast at Val, Priest flinched. "An abortion? Are you serious? You convinced Carissa to have an abortion?"

Val frowned. "She didn't go through with it."

"She didn't go through with it," Katherine repeated, fumed. "You're just like your sister. It makes me sick. You know how I feel about abortions, especially after Kendra snuck behind my back for hers."

"Right," Val scoffed. "It wasn't because she didn't want to have a kid in college. She did it to spite you. Because everything is always about you."

Good grief. Let's focus you two. I don't have all night.

"If we can get back to the matter at hand," Priest said. "How about we get started with the interview so you two can get home at a decent time. It is a school night."

"As if that matters to her," Katherine grumbled. "Whoring all hours of the night."

Priest blinked and pressed her lips together. *Alright then.* She pulled out her voice recorder and put it on the table. She pressed play. "Valerie, as you've already been informed, I'm recording this interview. Please identify yourself."

"Valerie Caulfield."

"Great. Valerie Caulfield, do you agree to cooperate with the Carissa Boisseau, Kent Bradshaw rape investigation?"

Val let out a long exhale and mumbled, "Yea."

"Speak up," Katherine commanded.

"Yes," Val said, frowned.

"Thank you," Priest flipped open her notepad. "Tell me how this all started. From what we know, Kent Bradshaw reached out to you. You were contacted by him first, right?"

"Yes, I was," Val said.

"What did Kent want?"

"Kent was fishing for information about Carissa," Val said with her eyes down. She stared at the plain metal table in the interrogation room while her mother fumed beside her. "He was really into her. Like, really, really into her. He wanted to know everything I knew about her and wanted pictures of her. Video. Everything I had. So, I told him what I knew and agreed to introduce them, bring her to the party, if I could come along and be in his inner circle." She paused. "He agreed. He said if I set everything up, I'd be like a member of the family."

Katherine glared at her daughter.

"Who wouldn't accept that offer?" Val asked. "Their money has money. They own houses in New York, California, Florida, Berlin, Paris. They have a condo in Vegas on the strip. Said I could go on a trip with them or on my own to any of them if I wanted. They'd be good to me."

Priest, as usual, took detailed notes. "And when he spoke to you, did he say what his intentions were towards Carissa?"

Val shrugged. "He obviously wanted to hook up with her. I

told him she was a virgin. And he'd have to navigate around her hesitation to lose her virginity. But, she always wanted a boyfriend and was very curious about sex. She's seventeen. It's senior year. We're all about to go off to college. She needed to lose her virginity."

She needed to lose her virginity. Right. Priest tried not to roll her eyes. *I didn't lose my virginity until sophomore year of college and to some barely sober linebacker, no less. Regretted every second of it. And by every second, I mean the ten seconds he lasted.*

Sigh. *That's so depressing. I should have held out for someone else. Someone like Jay.*

"Did he say he wanted to have sex with her?" Priest pressed.

"He said he wanted to hook up with her," Val said. "So, yes."

Priest made her notation. "Okay. So, you two went to the party. You arranged the introduction. What happened next?"

"We had fun," Val said. "There was music and dancing. I went off with Jesse to dance, drink, and," she glanced at her mom, "talk."

"Talk," Katherine scoffed.

Yea. Sure. I bet there was a lot of "talking" that night.

"Did you check on Carissa and Kent? And if so, how often?"

Val frowned when she concentrated. "Yea. I'd occasionally see how things were progressing. They were having a lot of fun playing beer pong and, between games, dancing. She didn't have an issue with him being handsy on the dance floor. She told me if felt good. But she showed reluctance about anything further. He needed to close the deal in order for things to 'go as planned'. Whatever that meant. He said it was very important. Getting laid is always *very important* to guys. But this was different. Anyway, I told him to keep up what he was doing. I'd never seen her so relaxed."

"Eventually, she had too much to drink, right?"

"Oh yea," Val said. "I didn't know she could take so much. She surprised the hell out of all of us. But eventually, she could barely stand and walk. She said she was feeling sick. We had to drag her upstairs. He insisted on his room. Said he had his own personal bath. Of course, he does. Then, she got sick in his bathroom."

Welp. There we go. She was drunk, couldn't stand on her own two feet. She had to be dragged to the bathroom to vomit. She was too intoxicated to consent. That's rape. Not that she's a very credible witness. But, it'll stick.

"About what time was this?" Priest asked.

"A little after twelve," Val said.

Priest marked the time. "You're sure."

"Yea. We had to watch the clock cause Cari's mom had a stick up her ass. We had to leave by one."

Priest glanced at Val's mom. Their eyes connected for two seconds before Priest returned to Val. In those two seconds, she communicated what needed to be communicated. *You should be setting more boundaries for your daughter.*

"So, Carissa got sick," Priest said. "What happened next?"

Val scrunched up her nose. "Well, she had to get herself cleaned up. I couldn't have her smelling nasty and Kent was pressing me to make sure she didn't have vomit breath. I stuck with her while she washed her face and brushed her teeth. He had some spare, new toothbrushes in his bathroom. In plastic. She gargled mouthwash and was good. Then, she wanted to take a nap, so we put her in his bed."

Priest noted both Val and Carissa's stories matched to this point. "Alright, so she was in Kent's bed sleeping."

"Yea," Val said. "That's how I left her. I closed the door behind me and she was good."

Priest made sure she locked eyes with Val as she asked the next question. "Okay. So, we have a drunk, sleepy Carissa in Kent's bed. Did Kent tell you he was going to go in the room with her?"

Val nibbled her lips and shifted in her chair.

Oh don't you start clamming up now. I don't want to have to press you on this. You need to tell me. And you need to tell me now.

"Val," Priest said. "Did Kent tell you he was going to go in the room with Carissa?"

Val sighed. "It was less than an hour until one. Jesse wanted to," her eyes shifted to her mom, "do stuff before I had to leave. So, I went off with him. I mean, she was in there snoozing. I wasn't going to babysit her. She had a bucket."

"You didn't answer the question," Priest said.

Another sigh. "He said he would check up on her while Jesse

and I did our thing." She looked down and then up. "I said, 'Sure you are.' But, I didn't think much of it. I didn't think he'd go in there, screw her, and then leave her lying there naked on the bed for everybody to see."

"But that's what he did."

"Yea. He said, before she got sick, she said she wanted him to take her virginity."

"And you believed that?" Priest asked. She restrained her desire to look at the two-way mirror.

"No." Val returned her eyes to the metal table. "But what was done was done. I was livid at first, but then, you know, I was scared. I didn't want to get in trouble. It was my fault she was there in the first place. And then, he called me when we got home and told me to make sure she got cleaned up." She pointed towards her lap. "Everywhere. He told me to dispose of her panties, too. He offered me some money to keep me quiet. I guess he sobered up a little bit and wanted to cover his tracks."

He offered you money. These are the details I needed. "How much?"

"What?"

"Money," Priest said. "How much money did he offer?"

"Well, he said two thousand at first," Val fumbled with her fingers. "But when I hesitated, he said five thousand."

Her mother nearly fell out of her chair. "Five thousand?!"

Val nodded.

Priest checked the voice recorder to make sure it captured everything. It did. Not that she couldn't rely on the surveillance cameras and recording equipment in the room. "And you accepted."

"Of course," Val said. "I'm not going to pass up on five thousand dollars. I should have asked for more. It's not like refusing the money would undo what happened or my involvement. I considered splitting it with Carissa. I was going to treat her to a spa day and fancy dinner. But she ditched me. So, I said screw it and kept it for myself."

Can you blame her? Her friend sold her out.

"Okay," Priest said. She would need another notepad soon. "So, just to clarify all of this, Kent Bradshaw paid you five thousand dollars to stay quiet, make sure Carissa was cleaned of any physical evidence, and to get rid of Carissa's soiled panties."

"Yes. Err. No."

"No?" Priest doubted.

"Well, he paid me to stay quiet. But, after offering five thousand, I had to deliver the panties as proof in order to get the money."

Makes sense. Can't take a girl like Val at her word. "And you gave him Carissa's panties."

Val smirked. "Not exactly. You see, once I realized Carissa was probably never going to talk to me again, I figured I might as well get as much money out of this as I could. So, I gave him my panties instead and got five thousand in cash."

This girl... Of course, she did.

"I see," Priest said. "And they didn't challenge you? They didn't know you gave them a different pair of panties?"

"No. We wore the same panties that night."

"The same panties?" Priest asked. "I'm not following."

"After Cari and I got our costumes from Bastian's store, I insisted we get some new underwear. I wasn't going to have my girl hooking up with Kent in some two-year-old, busted up, unsexy panties. Girl didn't have the right panties for the night. So, I insisted we get something for me. When we got in the store, I found a buy one get one free sale. We split the cost. We both had the same pair, same color: black, laced, just slightly different sizes. There's no way they would be able to tell the difference."

Priest noted that. *If she gave them the wrong panties—*

"Are you saying you still have Carissa's panties?" Priest asked, leaned forward. She needed an admission of possession. The panties were crucial evidence. If Val had the panties, a refusal to relinquish them would be obstruction of justice. Therefore, the moment Val said yes, she would get possession of those panties one way or the other and bury Kent with them, assuming his DNA matched with the DNA they had on file and that of the fetus.

Heck. At this point, we have enough to compel him to provide a DNA sample.

Val flexed her jaw. "I kept them just in case Carissa went to the police. I knew those panties were worth more than five thousand dollars, especially if there was an investigation. If those panties got in police custody, Kent would get arrested, convicted, and do some hard time. They'll pay real money, a couple hundred thousand dollars, maybe even a million, to keep those panties out of your hands. I'd be set for years."

Wow. Just, wow. You've admitted your blackmail plot. Priest looked at Katherine. *If this is her now, I can't imagine what she's going to be like in college, or as an adult.*

"Those panties are crucial evidence in this investigation," Priest said. "We're going to need you to turn them in." She turned to Katherine. "We'll have a uniformed officer at your home when you return to collect that evidence."

Katherine glared at Val and agreed, "Of course. We'll get those to you right away."

Val sighed. "Another loss."

"Let's continue where we left off," Priest said, ignoring her last remark. "The Bradshaws paid you hush money and bought panties they thought were Carissa's. Then, what happened?"

"Nothing for a bit," Val said. "They checked in to see if she said anything. If she was going to make a fuss. I told them she shut me out. She shut everyone out. I hadn't heard a peep about what happened. I just as easy assumed it was all over until she contacted me telling me she might be pregnant."

Priest made a note. "That's when you contacted the Bradshaws."

"Yea. They told me: if anything came up, call them. A pregnancy? Oh yea. It would only take one paternity test and they'd have to shell out a whole lot more than five thousand. We're talking inheritance money. We're talking child support, medical expenses, and if necessary, legal ramifications if they decided to challenge anything she asked of them. They told me, if it was true, I had to convince her to have an abortion. They said they'd arrange everything and had a doctor friend who could give them pills or do the surgery. They said he's done it before."

Doctor Green. "His name?"

Val shrugged. "They didn't tell me a name and I didn't care to know. I just wanted to know what I was getting out of all this."

Of course, you did. Always the opportunist.

"Did you get anything out of it?" Priest asked.

Val frowned. "No. They were going to give me another five thousand cash, but Carissa didn't go through with it. She bailed."

Aww. Poor you. You didn't get your blood money.

"I see," Priest said, fighting the urge to smirk. There was no time for pettiness. "Now, let's step back. I need to confirm a few things. After Carissa went to your place with her pregnancy tests and confirmed she was pregnant, who did you contact? Kent or Janice Bradshaw?"

"I contacted Kent," Val said. "But his mom stepped in and took over. She was pissed, too. After all, she's the one shelling out all the money. Kent didn't get his inheritance until like a week or two ago, when he turned eighteen. Not to mention, this is the second time their family's been involved in a rape scandal, ya know."

Oh yes. I know.

"Anyway, she said Carissa wasn't having that baby," Val continued. "And if I cared about my friend at all, I needed to convince her to get rid of it."

That sounds like a thinly-veiled threat. Priest made a note of that. *Perhaps it's Janice that influenced the vandalism on Carissa's house. I wonder if she'll consider stronger measures if this case goes public.*

"So, you convinced Carissa to get the abortion," Priest said.

"Not at first, but it didn't take much convincing when Carissa found out her mom made a doctor's appointment for her. She didn't want her mom to know she was pregnant. So, she agreed to go through with it. She got ten thousand dollars out of it and didn't even go through with it. Did she tell you that?"

"Yes," Priest said.

So far, Carissa was completely upfront with her, which was good. The last thing she needed in a major case was a victim and key witness that lied or withheld information. The difference between a good and bad investigator was asking the right questions, sometimes multiple times in different ways.

"How did Janice and Kent respond when you told them Carissa didn't go through with it."

"They were livid," Val explained. "I mean, ten thousand may not be a lot of money to them, but it's a lot of money to give away without getting what you agreed upon. Kent's mom said I was useless. And since I didn't get Carissa to come through on that abortion, I wasn't going to see the five thousand we agreed on. She was going to shut me out and blackball me anywhere she had influence."

Oh, boo hoo. What? You won't be able to go to one of those bourgeois country clubs or ballroom parties? I bet you're heartbroken.

Priest yawned. She couldn't help it. And she hated that Val saw it. "Did Janice Bradshaw give you any inclinations that she planned on retaliating with vandalism or violence?"

"Uh, what?" Val blinked. Shock registered on her face. "No. I mean, she was incensed. Intimidating. She made a subtle comment about having the ability to make a person disappear. But, I mostly got the feeling she meant business about her money. She didn't say anything to me. You think she's the one that trashed Carissa's house."

Solid eye contact. Priest communicated no emotion. "Isn't she?"

Val looked away.

"Let's move on," Priest said. She trusted her hunches, and the hunch was telling her Val had suspicions, but nothing iron clad. She didn't want to start entertaining conjecture. She wanted to focus on hard, cold facts. "What did you do next?"

Val shrugged. "There wasn't much else I could do. But Kent said there were some pictures and videos going around. A rumor, too. If anyone asked me what happened, I was to tell them that Carissa went to that party to have sex with him, to trap him. I was supposed to tell people she lied and said she was on the pill so she could get pregnant and blackmail the Bradshaws for money. Then, that she took the money but didn't get the abortion, and asked for more money. As long as I went along with the program, and we put enough social pressure on Carissa to have that abortion, things would work out for all of us." She sighed. "This is all a disaster."

But, you went along with it.

"What happened after that?" Priest continued to prod.

Val frowned. "What do you mean what happened after that? Nothing else has happened. Carissa left school. She doesn't talk to me and the girls anymore. My part in all of this is done."

"Not quite," Priest said and put away her notepad.

"What do you mean?"

Priest looked directly into Val's eyes and said, "You're going to testify against the Bradshaws in court. You'll tell all of them what you just told me." She turned to Katherine. "We'll also need phone records, text messages. Everything that will corroborate what was said here tonight."

"Of course," Katherine said. She grabbed Val's phone and handed it over to Priest.

"Mom!" Val protested.

"Shut up," Katherine commanded. "You're in enough trouble as it is, whoring yourself around town. And I'm pressing charges against that grown ass man you've been having sex with."

Val complained. "There's private stuff on that phone."

"Yea," Katherine said. "I'm sure you took some pretty trashy pictures of yourself and sent it to him and God knows who else." She looked at Priest. "Please delete them."

Hmm. Priest looked at the phone. *Trashy pictures on her phone. I wonder if any of these would show up on that private server or that Pumas website.*

"As long as they aren't evidence against Mister Braun, or tied to any ongoing investigation, you can trust we won't make any copies," Priest said. "The phone will be returned to you, as is, and you can dispose of the images."

"Thank you," Katherine said, ignoring Val's angry stare.

Priest examined the phone and then passed her notepad and pen to Val. "Please write down all passwords or PINs."

Val stuck her lip out in protest.

Katherine put her foot down. "If you want to have a phone at all after this, give her what she asked."

Val wrote sloppily and then slid the pen and pad away. Priest made sure it worked before continuing.

"You're also going to have to go to school with Val tomorrow, so she can change classes," she said.

"Why?" Katherine asked. "I don't see what any of this has to do with her school."

"Bastian Braun is the husband of Elizabeth Braun, her English teacher."

"What?" Katherine stammered. "Your teacher's husband?"

Laughter could be heard from the other side of the two-way mirror. *Thank you for your continued professionalism, Oliver. I suppose this is my cue to leave.*

"Thank you for your assistance, Misses Caulfield, Valerie," Priest said and stood. "I'm going to take this phone to the lab. Once they've processed it, we'll have someone return it to you."

She left the interrogation room and met with Oliver on the other side of the glass. He was leaned back in his chair with a big smile.

"Well, she sang like a canary," Oliver said.

"Probably the only good thing she's done in her life," Priest said and crossed her arms. The room felt empty. It was strange interviewing Val without Summers. He'd been with her every step of the way throughout the investigation. Now, he was out of the loop. She didn't like it. "I'm going to call Nate, give him an update." She pointed to the manila envelope on the adjacent chair. "That the warrant?"

"Yep," Oliver said and waved the envelope. "Unfortunately, this'll be the last rubber stamp you'll get from Abrams. I'll explain on the way."

Priest yawned. "Let's go." *Before I pass out.*

CHAPTER THIRTY-THREE

The streets of Downtown Richmond were brightly lit and peppered with snow. Small pockets of slush crystalized in the corners and crevasses of the quiet road. The lack of traffic rewarded her with a quick trip down Broad Street. Every chance she got, Priest flashed her lights to bypass a slow driver or unchanging red light. She needed something to keep her awake. The coffee Jay gave her was wearing off. Coffee could only do so much when she'd barely slept the last two nights.

In the passenger seat, Jay nodded as Oliver explained case details he wasn't supposed to hear. Fortunately, the man had a passion for privacy and discretion and kept secrets better than seasoned officers. He'd make a good confidant, assuming he could stop telling her he loved her. It was freaking her out. That was the last thing she needed right now. She needed a clear head.

"So, to summarize," Priest said. "Judge Abrams is out having a pleasant dinner with colleagues when Dennis arrives. Abrams steps away from the table to help us out. He signs the warrant without reading it, classic rubber stamp move, but after signing it, he glances at it. He reads 'FRTY Import and Export' out loud, gets really pale, and then has a massive heart attack."

"Precisely," Oliver said. "Dennis waited until an ambulance arrived before returning to headquarters. We need a uniform outside his room until we get some answers from him. That was the heart attack of a very scared or guilty man."

"That's a bit of a leap, isn't it?" Priest asked. *Plus, you act like we have an unlimited supply of staff. We're stretched thin as it is.*

"Dennis says he hasn't seen a man that scared since his tour in Afghanistan. Something's up."

Priest frowned and parked in front of the building, ignoring a *No Parking* sign. "If he's involved somehow, I'm taking him down, no matter how much I'll miss his rubber stamping. If he isn't involved, I still think the oversight committee should have a look at him. He clearly knows enough to be frightened to death by whatever this is. Imagine the difference he could have made had he spoken up sooner."

"You're assuming he's going to survive that heart attack," Oliver said. "Something tells me he signed his last warrant."

"I'd rather he survived so we can ask him some questions."

Oliver unbuckled his seat belt. "In any event, let's get in there before our plan goes south." He got out the jeep, laptop bag and tablet in hand. "We need to be in there to deactivate the server's kill switch before backup arrives."

Priest grabbed her firearm and a few backup clips. *I hope I won't need these.* She glanced at Jay and got out of the jeep. "You seem to know a lot more about these people than you've let on. If they're dangerous, we should leave Jay behind."

"If you've ever watched a cop movie, ever, you'll know the person left behind in the car gets captured, killed, or goes in anyway," Oliver said and shrugged.

She wasn't amused. *Except, this isn't a movie.*

"They won't try anything," he reassured her. "That would bring a lot of unwanted attention. Two missing cops, and a famous local author? Come on. And even if they try something, we'll have backup here any minute now."

As much as she wanted to, Priest couldn't disagree. It was silly to think anything would happen to them. The whole world would come crashing down on top of this organization if two investigating detectives disappeared. Why was she worrying?

A hunch. That's why. She trusted her hunches.

"Trust me," Oliver said. He shared a reassuring smile. "Plus, Jay can handle himself. Out of the three of us, he's the only one guaranteed to survive."

We talking about the same guy?

Jay approached, stuffed bag on his back, and handed Priest

the warrant. "Can we strategize inside the building? It's cold." He wrapped his arm around hers.

"My thoughts exactly." Oliver checked his watch. "Let's go." He crossed the street.

She looked at the office building. All the answers were here. Dakota. Carissa. The Bradshaws. The camera in the girl's locker room. Their digital bloodhound followed the trail and lead them here. This was the end of the line. Was she ready for what they would find?

"It'll be fine," Jay said and collected Priest's hand in his. *God, he's warm.* "Let's get what we came for."

2

After flashing her shield and badge to the security camera at the front entrance, the door unlocked. They entered.

It was like any other office building. Plenty of windows looked out to the active city traffic and urban life. The white and gray marble floors had that extra shine from a recent wax job. The tan walls had commercial and abstract paintings on the walls in random places, including gray columns and pillars. And of course, what interior decorator would forget potted plants to give the office a little life? There were pink lilies in a white ceramic vase on the reception desk to their left.

At the desk stood a dark-haired, sun-tanned security officer. His massive shoulders and arms squeezed tight against his black uniform. A large pistol rested on his right hip.

Armed guards. Noted.

In front of him, security footage streamed in a cycle from different floors, stairs, and elevators. His eyes, however, were locked on his late-night visitors.

Priest held her badge and shield in one hand and waved her warrant with the other. "Good evening," she squinted her eyes as she read his name badge, "Mister Richter. I'm Detective Amy Priest, Henrico Police. I have a warrant to search some of the offices in this building. Do you have a late-night janitor available or someone else here to open doors for us?"

Richter grabbed his radio and called up, "Pete, I'm going to need you to come down here. We have visitors." His eyes never left Priest. They were cold. His face was tense.

He's on alert. It's his job.

"On my way," the radio said.

Richter pointed at the warrant. "To which floors are you requesting access?"

"Tenth."

Richter blinked, emotionless. "Are you sure?"

Am I sure? Priest frowned and looked at the warrant. "Yes. Tenth floor."

If he says there's no tenth floor, I will strangle Oliver. I will strangle him dead. I wonder if Jay loves me enough to hide a body and be an alibi.

"Show me."

Priest showed him the warrant.

"If you don't mind, I'll confirm your badge number and identification," Richter said. He extended his hand for her badge. She held it so he could read it but not take possession of it. He wrote down her information and made a phone call.

By the time his help arrived, her information was verified. He hung up the phone and greeted the other security guard, a pale, bald man with a similar build. *You two go to the gym together? Sheesh. These guys make Terry Crews look anorexic.*

"This is Pete," Richter said. "He'll take you where you need to go."

Pete leaned over the counter and peered at Richter's surveillance monitor. "Where are we going?"

"The *tenth* floor." Richter glared at Priest and added, "They have a warrant."

Pete's eyebrows rose. "Ah." He examined his guests, frowned at Jay. "Which elevator?"

Richter's eyes flashed over the unwelcomed guests. "Three."

Pete smirked and turned to Priest, Jay, and Oliver. "Follow me." He strode to the elevator. Before they turned the corner, Priest saw Richter pick up his phone and dial a number.

No doubt he's calling whoever oversees this FRTY office. I should expect what? A lawyer? An angry manager or owner? An armada of armed guards to mow us down? Honestly, I don't know what to expect.

I can't believe both Rogers and Nate went along with this plan. If there isn't a kill switch like Oliver believes, we just put our heads in the lion's mouth for no reason.

She reached for her phone as they got to the elevator and pasted the building's address into a text message. She typed, "ETA on backup," and pressed *send*. The message failed. She had no bars, no signal. The elevator doors closed.

Oh, you have got to be kidding me!

She gave Oliver a look that communicated how frustrated she was with him. He hadn't stopped typing on his tablet since they entered the building. She whispered, "You have a signal on your phone or tablet?" She tried to send a message again. And again, it failed.

Oliver blinked slowly and shifted his eyes from her to Pete. Her to Pete. Her to Pete. Her to Pete. His eyes settled on the back of Pete's head. She followed his gaze and noticed a red tattoo on the base of his skull and upper neck. *A three-headed snake?* She looked back at Oliver, then Jay. Jay and Oliver looked at each other and nodded.

Note to self: Check prison database for any gangs, mobs, cliques, or other criminal organizations associated with snake or dragon tattoos of the three-headed variety. Also check military tattoo database. Is it a coincidence that Brian has a similar tattoo on his chest? Doubt it.

"Interesting tattoo," Priest said and licked her drying lips. "What does it mean?"

The elevator doors opened. Pete turned around, locked eyes, and said, "I've proven my loyalty."

He stared. If he was trying to intimidate her, he failed. She had a taser and wasn't shy about using it. He stepped out of the elevator and stood to the side. All eyes turned to the tenth-floor entry wall.

On the white wall was a large black pyramid with its top section separated, creating a second, smaller pyramid. Inside the main section was a red, three-headed dragon. In the upper, separated section was a red eye with lines like rays. Bold black letters under the triangle read: FRTY I&E, INC.

O-K. That's unsettling. All-seeing eye over a dragon in a pyramid. Odd twist to the image on the back of the dollar bill. Conspiracy theorists would shit their pants if they saw this. But it explains the tattoo, sort of. FRTY employs the building's security.

Likely to preserve their own interests. Anything or anyone that comes out of this building, they know about it.

"Tenth floor," Pete said and pointed with an open hand down the hallway to a reception desk. "Where do we start?"

As Priest opened her mouth to speak, Oliver said, "Server room and any locked offices on this floor." He proceeded off the elevator and down the hallway.

Damn you, Oliver! Not only am I in charge of this search, you're not supposed to charge off ahead like that.

Pete waited next to the elevator for Priest and Jay. "After you."

Nope. The moment I have my back turned to him, we're in trouble. He's twice my size and armed. I can't take him alone. Oliver can't take him. Jay's a pacifist. I can't even imagine what he'd look like in a fight with this guy, but I'm sure it wouldn't look pretty. Guaranteed to survive. What is Oliver smoking?

"You first," she said. "You have the keys. Follow him."

Pete looked at Jay. "Him?"

Are you playing stupid?

"No," Priest said. She almost leaned forward to see where Oliver walked but stopped when she realized the vulnerable position she'd put herself if she did. His fist was the size of her head. One clean shot, and she'd be out of commission. She wasn't sure why he hadn't made a move. "The one that went down that hallway. We'll follow you two."

Pete stood with his arms to his sides, but his feet were positioned in a way that he could engage her at any moment. His right foot pointed towards her. He watched her, stiff as a board, with no emotion.

She shot a glance at her phone. Still no service. *Dammit. To hell with that kill switch. I want to call in backup, but I can't leave Oliver alone up here. What made me think I could trust him instead of my honed detective instincts?*

"After you, Pete," she said in her most authoritative voice. No matter how big he or his fists were, she was still the boss here. Police detective outranked security guard last time she checked.

Pete walked ahead. Oliver waited for them at the end of the entryway, next to the FRTY receptionist desk. While Priest gave Oliver a head shake of disapproval, Pete pointed left towards the far end of the office. "The server room is over there."

"Great, but let's start over there," Oliver said and walked in the opposite direction. His fingers tapped his tablet as he stepped. Priest followed the two, Jay in tow, but stayed at least four meters behind in case Pete tried something.

The floor wasn't empty. Two women and eight men typed in their gray-walled cubicles on the left. One or two office doors were open on the right. A janitor's cart kept one door wedged open. A few eyes looked up from their projects and followed the group.

They're working late. If these people only knew what dark and twisted things were hidden in their servers. Maybe they do.

She checked her phone again. Still no signal. Her text never transmitted. It didn't make any sense. They were no longer in or near the elevator.

"You have a signal?" Priest whispered to Jay. "Your phone?"

Jay checked his phone. "Nope." He swiped his finger a few times. "Not even a local wi-fi network."

Crap. I need to reach out to Nate. Rogers. Jane. Somebody.

"But I do have your police walkie-talkie from the car." Jay reached to his backpack and pulled a walkie out of a mesh side pocket. "I figure police officers should always hold on to these. You never know when you're going to need them." He handed it to her, then pulled out his whistle.

You aren't supposed to take police issued equipment without my permission, but I'll give you a pass. You may have just saved our lives.

She turned on the walkie, confirmed it was on the correct channel, and listened for comm traffic. There was no activity. She double-checked the channel. Nothing. Switched to another police channel. Still nothing. Non-emergency relay channels. Nothing. She switched it back to primary.

Silence? Really? That's impossible.

"Detective Priest to anyone on this channel, can you hear me, over?" Priest called into the walkie. Pete turned around and glared at her before returning his attention to Oliver, who kept pressing for his attention. *Most likely saying something inane.*

"Nothing?" Jay asked. He stepped closer and rubbed her shoulders. His hands felt like hot coals. She felt the transfer of his body heat and couldn't help but feel her tensions easing.

"Nothing," she said. It amazed her how much power his presence had over her. Every touch lit up her entire body, excited her. But that was a distraction. She couldn't be distracted right now.

Something must be interfering with our radio. But they can't be using a jammer. If they were, how was Richter and Pete able to communicate with each other with their radios?

"Unless they jam every signal except a specific frequency or channel," Priest whispered to herself. "Only their walkies."

"Aren't jammers illegal?" Jay asked.

"Yes," Priest said. "How do you know that?"

"Research for a novel." *That's his answer for everything.*

"Here, this door." Oliver pointed at a metal reinforced door. "This is it."

Pete frowned. "Guy, the server room is at the *other* end of the office."

Oliver smiled. "Humor me. And if I'm wrong, I'll arrange a date with my friend here."

You will most certainly not. I will beat this door open with your head before that ever happens.

"No, he won't," Priest said and pointed. "Open, please."

Pete measured Priest top to bottom and reached down. Her hand instantly shot towards her pistol but she relaxed her grip when he collected the keys on his belt, instead of the gun in his holster. He unlocked the reinforced door, opened it, and stood to the side.

There were four long rows of tall, black server racks that stretched to the end of the room. Every rack was packed from top to bottom with servers. A single computer terminal stood in the middle, far end of the room.

"Well, I don't know about you, but this looks an awful lot like a server room to me," Oliver said with a smug smile. "But don't beat yourself up. You're just a security guard. We don't expect you to know anything."

Pete glared at him.

Don't ghoat the man. He's twice your size.

"Check it out," Priest ordered. She wasn't going in until she was sure the door unlocked from the inside. Last thing she wanted was to be locked inside with no means of contacting the outside world.

Oliver went in and whistled. "Nice! This is one of the coolest server rooms I've entered. Literally. Feels like I just walked into Rura Penthe. All we're missing is a shape-shifting hottie and a burly guy with nuts in his knees. Anyone bring a fur coat?"

Priest tensed. *I don't care about the temperature! We're here to find the server that has my sister's rape video and a million other terrible and illegal things and deactivate the kill switch. Then, we're holding tight until Nate and half of Richmond's finest come bursting up the elevator to seize everything.*

"I'm not looking for a weather report," Priest huffed. "Is this the server we're looking for or not?"

"Can't imagine there'd be another here." Oliver pulled out his laptop and cords. "Let me plug in first."

Priest turned to Pete. "While we're waiting, please unlock the other offices. We'll have reinforcements here to check them."

Pete glanced in the server room, frowned, and checked his watch. His entire face wrinkled and furrowed as he grabbed his radio. "Pete to Richter, over." No response. "Pete to Richter, over." Still no response. "It is still active, over." He pressed the call button three times and then listened.

It's odd that his radio isn't working. What's going on?

"Are you listening to me?" Priest asked.

"Yea, sure," Pete said. He marched down the hall towards the elevator, turned the corner, and disappeared.

What the?

"Hey!" Priest yelled. "He's supposed to unlock the offices."

"Perhaps he has to pee," Jay said.

He can hold it!

"Stay here, Jay." She pulled her gun, charged down the hall, shrunk to a squat, and turned the corner. No one was there. The elevator was on its way down. "Crap."

She raced back. "He's in the elevator. Probably alerting his comrade that reinforcements are coming. They might activate the kill switch. Do whatever it is you need to do, now."

"Pssh," Oliver said and waved his hand at her. "I prepared for that. The elevator will have him stuck between the sixth and seventh floor."

"Oh," Priest said, relaxed her grip on her pistol. "And the kill switch?"

"What kill switch?" Oliver smiled. "I've been systematically deactivating their network since I walked in the building. Their wireless networks and communications are jammed. I cut their access to the server. They can't kill nothing but cockroaches."

You jammed their communications. Wait a second!

"Are you why my phone's not getting a signal?" Priest wagged her phone, ready to scold him for not telling her he was going to completely disconnect her from their backup.

"Yes," Oliver said and joined her and Jay. "It occurred to me that, even though the network is deactivated, they could easily call someone in the office to begin the data-purging process. There might be a kill switch that could be activated via text. Or, they could call reinforcements from a different floor, or this floor, to swarm us. I figured, by inhibiting all communications, even radio frequencies, we had a better chance of survival. So, I'm using their wired and wireless networking tech against them to jam all communications and network access."

"All communications *except* for landlines," Jay chimed in.

Oliver tapped his nose. "Right. I have a program in place that repeatedly spams their phone lines with fax attempts but can't do much with their internal lines."

"You should have told me," Priest argued.

"It was a spur of the moment decision," Oliver said. It wasn't. "Besides, we know our backup is coming. What a surprise it'll be for them when our backup shows up and overwhelms them before they can coordinate."

People like you get teams killed. You improvise without telling the team and go outside of the chain of command. You could have at least messaged first telling me your plan. I need to know when backup is coming.

"Do you have a signal, at least?" Priest asked. "I need to know when Nate's here."

An alarm blared, and blue lights flashed.

"Shit." Oliver looked at flashing lights. "I could have sworn I deactivated their fire suppression system. If those sprinklers go off, we'll have large, wet, paperweights for evidence."

"You think they're trying to destroy evidence?" Priest asked.

"My theory." Oliver rushed to his laptop. "But their security system is compromised. They shouldn't be able to remotely activate the sprinklers. Someone or something would have to manually trigger the sprinklers with smoke or a fire."

"Can they trigger them with a fire in another room?" Priest asked.

Oliver thought about it. "I wouldn't think so. In an office building like this, I'd hope a server room with all this electrical equipment would be on a different fire suppression circuit."

"Whatever you say," Priest said. Her attention was on the office staff.

Twelve of the office staff congregated in the hallway in front of the elevator. *They're about to evacuate.* But instead of going down the stairwell, they turned to Priest and Jay. One of the twelve pointed his finger and yelled, "Get them!"

I've got a bad feeling about this.

"That wasn't us!" Jay yelled back.

"Jay." Priest removed her gun from her holster. "Step behind me and get in the server room. We're going to have to barricade ourselves in until reinforcements arrive."

"Don't mind if I do," Jay said. He stepped behind her and reached into his bag. She could only imagine what other trinket he brought with him. *Hopefully its more useful than a whistle.*

The crowd of twelve, in unison, marched forward. They picked up speed with each step.

"Stop right there!" Priest yelled and raised her weapon. They kept forward. "Don't move!" They accelerated.

Dammit. I can't shoot unarmed civilians, disobedient or not. I'd never hear the end of this. I could lose my badge. Then again, they do pose a physical threat.

She stepped back rapidly until the door was to her right. The mob would be on her in eight seconds.

"Here, throw this!" Jay yelled and passed her an object. "I'll shut the door."

She caught it but couldn't believe what was in her hand. "A flash grenade? Are you insane?"

"Yes," Jay said.

Shit. She tossed it. Jay slammed the door shut, cranked the bolt lock, and pressed his body against it with all his strength.

BANG! Bodies crashed against the door, followed by cries of pain.

Priest pressed herself against the door and looked around for something to wedge the door. She grabbed a metal folding chair and forced it under the door handle.

"That'll keep them busy for a few seconds," Jay said.

Priest blinked rapidly at him. "Where the hell did you get a flash grenade?"

"You said come prepared." Jay backed away from the door and put his bag down. He dug intently for something else.

Well, that's a mistake I'll never make again. What's he going to pull out next, a machinegun?

"Where'd you find flash grenades, Jay? They're illegal."

Jay scratched the thin layer of hair he called a beard. "Not those. They're low grade, civilian version. I found them online. Besides, every police officer should carry a flash grenade for riot control."

But you're not a police officer.

"Never *in my life* have I carried a flash grenade," Priest said. "If you have any more, give them to me."

Jay shrugged and handed one over. "You'll need this more than I will."

Oliver chuckled. "Told you he'd be fine."

"Shut up," was her only retort.

The door handle rattled but did not give. Then, one after the other, bodies slammed against the door. Angry voices yelled, coordinated kicks. The metal frame rattled. Priest braced herself. Reinforced or not, it was only a matter of time before that door gave away.

"Anyone have a plan for getting out of here?" Jay asked and pulled out a can of pepper spray.

Pepper spray. Of course. Because every police officer should carry pepper spray. Did someone give him a police manual?

Crap. I did. Three weeks ago. Research for his book, naturally.

"You know how to use that, right?" Priest asked, hesitant. "You're not going to mistakenly blind yourself or me, right?"

"Please." Jay said, followed by a confident smirk. He pointed the spray head in the correct direction and mimed pressing the button. "Ye of little faith."

"Yea, Amy!" Oliver yelled from the computer terminal in the back. "According to your faith, be it done to you."

Jay scratched his brow. "A bit out of context, but I'll allow it."

Those people out there are trying to kill us and you guys are in here making bible references. I'd be pissed if this wasn't somehow keeping me calm. You win points for being cool under pressure.

Wait. *Oliver has a gun. Why is he back there and Jay up here?*

"Get over here, Oliver," Priest ordered. "We need to hold them off. They'll be through that door any second—"

Angry voices on the other side quieted and were replaced by authoritative yells to "get down", "shut up", and "put your hands on your head".

Oh, thank God. It's the cavalry.

"Backup's here." Priest holstered her gun. "Oliver, whatever you're using to jam communications. Deactivate it."

Someone knocked at the door.

"Who is it?" Jay asked.

"Someone not trying to beat down the door," Summers replied. Priest recognized the voice and immediately unlocked the door. Summers opened it. "Is our evidence intact?"

Priest nodded. "I wasn't expecting to be chased by a mob of angry employees, but yeah. It's intact. Whatever is in here is worth getting shot for." She peaked around Summers and was met with angry faces. The office staff were all on their knees, hands behind their heads. Uniformed officers handcuffed them, one by one.

"Looks like you put up quite a fight," Summers said, pointed towards the group. "Half of them are bruised and bleeding."

Flash grenade, twelve. Bad guys, zero.

She smirked. "If I told you, you wouldn't believe it."

"You'll have to tell him later," Oliver said as he approached. "Now that the place is secure, there's a lot for you to see. I mean, a lot."

She didn't want to see any more than what she'd already seen. If there was anything resembling her sister's rape, she couldn't bear it. Her heart could only handle so much.

"I think we've seen enough for today," Priest said. She felt the buzz of adrenaline wear off and exhaustion set in. She sat on the floor, yawned, and rested herself against a server stack. "I'm ready to go home."

"Before you leave," Oliver said. He sat in front of her and crossed his legs. "You need to know what's going on here, what you've stumbled upon."

"So, you're finally giving us straight answers," Priest sassed.

"Some of them. This place has all the answers: why there's been a growing wave of disappearances in the community; why Carissa was raped; why your sister was."

Priest closed her eyes and visualized Dakota, smiling, dancing in the yard on a hot summer day while the sprinklers sprayed. Her bare feet were covered in mud. Her jean shorts were wet and clung to her. Her yellow dandelion tank flared as she spun. She was fifteen and without a care in the world.

There was a point in her life when she wasn't despondent, depressed, and doubting herself. Before she became a moody loner, she was overflowing with joy and spirit. Though quiet and private, she loved to sing and dance, and had a beautiful voice. She secretly wished to be on Broadway. Be a movie star. But the Bradshaws took that away from her, drove her to suicide. If that was, in fact, her true fate. Which was doubtful.

Priest needed to know why. "Tell me everything."

3

Priest, Summers, and Jay huddled over Oliver's shoulder as he interfaced with the server room's main computer terminal. He bypassed the multiple passwords as fast as the prompts appeared on the screen and zoomed through file folders pointing out items of interest.

"You see this folder," Oliver said. "That's their imports." He double-clicked. "It's showing where all of their products are coming in. There's schedules, locations, product." He double-clicked product. "I'm going to need you to brace yourselves, you see. Because their business is a front for the transport of their products. They're import and export consultants that do all the communications and arrangements for hundreds of companies, ships, trucks, ports, and airports. They're connected to the whole global distribution network. They load, unload, and examine containers. They even offer ship and port security." He double-clicked again. "After everything seems kosher with customs officers, they slip their product on the ships."

"What's the product?" Summers asked. "Drugs? Weapons?"

Oliver clicked a file. *Oh my God.* It pulled up the image of a teenage girl. On the bottom right corner was her name, age, weight, height, hair color, eye color, other physical parameters, as well as an eight-digit number. On the top right was the word SOLD in red. Below it, the buyer's name. He clicked another file. Another teenage girl appeared. SOLD. He clicked three more files. Each had an image and details. SOLD. SOLD. SOLD.

"Trafficking," Priest said. She felt lightheaded and wanted to vomit. They were trafficking girls in and out of the country. "They're sex traffickers."

Oliver didn't respond but kept on clicking through the files and folders. He'd moved on to their schedules. The schedules had shipment details, addresses, maps, times, security personnel details, official contacts, and product numbers. He double-clicked the most recent shipment.

"Four girls, on a truck, driven from New Jersey to Alabama, one dropped off to buyer, then they drive to Texas, two dropped off to a single buyer, then a final stop in Las Vegas, the last dropped off to a buyer," Summers read. He bent to a squat like he wanted to sit down, needed to sit down, and then corrected himself.

Oliver continued to click through folders. It was as though he was scanning for something. She wasn't sure what. But she had a feeling he was looking for something specific. He'd moved past product and schedules to contact details. He scrolled past hundreds of folders. Contacts were categorized by members, clients, employees, opponents, officials, and potentials. He double-clicked members and scrolled until he saw the name Kent Bradshaw. He double-clicked it. He highlighted a video titled "Initiation" and stopped.

"That's it," Oliver said. "That's what we need for Carissa." He clicked back and double-clicked Brian Bradshaw's folder. He highlighted the video titled "Initiation". "And that's the video of your sister."

"Initiation?" Priest leaned forward, invading Oliver's space and blinding him with her hair in his face. "That doesn't make sense. I don't understand."

"Can I see the screen, please?" he asked.

"Sorry." She straightened.

Oliver backed out of the folder and clicked around for other members. Each had an initiation video. Finally, he scrolled down to the name Judge Benjamin Abrams and double-clicked. He highlighted the initiation video and double-clicked. The video started.

A little boy, no older than seven-years-old, was playing with a toy when the camera zoomed in on him and then zoomed out. Abrams approached slowly and asked if the boy wanted to play a game. He unzipped his pants.

No, I can't watch this.

"Turn it off," Priest demanded and reached for the spacebar. Oliver closed the video and let out a sigh. Silence lingered in the air for twenty seconds as she convinced her body not to toss her dinner. Then, she rejoined the group. "That explains why Abrams had a heart attack."

"Yea," Jay said, his eyes watery. He blinked rapidly until any sign of vulnerability was gone. "The man molested a child and recorded it. The moment that recording gets out, his life is over. A video like that will get you the needle." He took a long, deep breath.

If you cry, I'll cry. I'm going to need you to hold it together.

"There's no death penalty in the state of Virginia," Oliver clarified. "Worst he'd get is ten to fifteen years. But since this is his initiation, I'm sure there's a lot more on him in this database."

Priest shut her eyes and asked the question everyone else wondered. "Why? Why are they doing this? My sister, Carissa, that, that, that little boy? I don't understand."

Oliver turned from the computer screen and placed his hands on his knees. "Initiation into The Fraternity requires a mutually assured destruction contract. It's the only way to get into the organization. The only way they know you won't turn on them. And only a certain kind of person would agree to do whatever it is they ask of them. You must commit an atrocious and vile act, record verifiable proof of it, collect any evidence, and give it to them. That way, if they even think you're going to cross them or talk, they can destroy you. And probably kill your family. But once you've done your terrible deed, you're in. You've proven your loyalty. And they slap a dragon tattoo on you."

The security guard in the elevator. Brian Bradshaw. How many people out there have those tattoos?

Summers scowled. "Why would anyone want to join them?"

"Money, Nate," Oliver said. "Real money. Crazy, sick money. The Fraternity has a large trafficking network involved in mass kidnappings, slavery, sex trade, pornography, voyeurism, and all sorts of other vile things. They're connected to illegal organ and weapons sales. They're the mothership of big evils, and this is only one of the dragon's heads. Anyone plugged in the organization is living very well for the rest of their lives. And most of it is money off the books, cash. Some of it is official. These members are private shareholders of FRTY I&E. They get a cut of laundered and fronted business profits as well as money under the table based on individual contributions."

He turned around and clicked until he had a spreadsheet on his screen. "This is their estimated annual haul for last year." He pointed at the number at the bottom. "Trillions of dollars. Every one of these members saw dollar signs and sold their souls for a piece of the pie. They don't care who lives or dies."

Money. Priest teared up. *My sister was raped, harassed, humiliated, and driven to suicide so what, Brian Bradshaw could get rich? He's already rich!*

"How does one join?" Nathan asked. "I've never heard of this group, not even whispers. Organizations of this size don't have loose lips, which means they've got to be small or private or discreet enough to stay off the radar, even with a mutually assured destruction agreement. So, how would Brian or Kent Bradshaw know of them?"

Oliver clicked back to the members folders and opened the Bradshaw folders. "This organization is invite only. Members approach you. A potential ally, friend, or," he highlighted a folder and pointed, "a family member. Legacy memberships. That's how money stays in the family. That's how organizations stay secret, secluded. You keep money in the family. You marry your kids within the organization."

He double-clicked Janice Bradshaw's folder and *Details* file.

"Janice Bradshaw, born Janice Whittaker, daughter of Clarence Whittaker. Looks like the name links to his file." He clicked the name. "Clarence Whitaker was one of the upper brass of the organization. Chief Operations Officer of FRTY I&E for thirty years before he died two years ago. Member of the organization for sixty-five years. He was also a child of the dragon. So, that's three or four generations part of The Fraternity family their whole life." He clicked to Robert Bradshaw's file. "Let's see, Robert Bradshaw is also a legacy member. His father, Reginald Bradshaw, was the Chief Exports Officer. It was his job to ensure everything was smoothly smuggled out of the country."

"Like you said, they married Robert and Janice to keep the money in the family," Summers said.

Priest frowned. "I don't understand. If their family is so tied into the business, then why would they need to perform acts of barbarism? Why did Brian have to do what he did to my sister?"

"Rules are rules are rules." Oliver wagged his finger. "This organization is bigger than family, thicker than blood. Trust me. All it takes is one relative grandfathered in without proving him or herself, one entitled wanker not sweating bullets out of fear of retribution, one ethical youth, to throw everything in disarray. No. Mutually assured destruction keeps everyone's mouth shut. And if that isn't enough incentive to be quiet, they'll put a bullet in your head. That's also a part of initiation. They might ask you to kill a traitor. We should run a search of every unsolved murder involving someone with a three-headed dragon tattoo. I'm sure we'll find more than a few who said too much or risked exposing the organization." He paused. "No. I take that back. Chances are they probably cut off or burn the tattoo so it doesn't land on our radar. Still worth a look for accidental deaths."

"Makes sense," Priest agreed. "It's inexcusable, but it makes sense."

In the end, Dakota was just a means to an end. But, we've uncovered something massive. What better way of honoring her memory than exposing a corrupt secret organization and bringing down a large trafficking network?

"So, what do we do now?" she asked. "Who do we take this to?"

DAKOTA

"Ourselves, of course," Summers said. "I'm calling Rogers. We're going through member folders and arresting everyone. Tonight. Tomorrow. The next day. The day after that. I'm not stopping until we've taken them all down. We're going to have to get the state police and FBI involved, as well as the TSA, Port Authority, Border Patrol, Coast Guard, and the CIA. But first, we need to see how deep their reach is in our government agencies. We must hit our local police forces and government officials first. Remove anyone that can or will inhibit our arrests and investigations. Then branch out." He pulled out his phone and left the server room.

Oliver kept typing. "In addition to copying everything on a boatload of hard drives, I'm uploading copies of all member information, videos, transportation routes, and as much of everything else I can to secure servers and preparing self-release directives for a worst-case scenario. It'll all go public."

Go public?!

"No," Priest said. "You can't release those videos to the public. What about Carissa? What about my sister? What about all the other victims? You'll be exposing them in their most vulnerable state to the world. They'll be victimized all over again. We're not doing anything of the sort. Plus, half of that content probably involves minors. You'd be distributing."

"It's a security measure," Oliver said and looked her in the eye. "In case someone tries to shut us down, close the investigation, destroy the evidence, make us disappear. The moment we start kicking down doors, you can swear on it that most of the people on this list aren't going down without a fight. And they won't hesitate for a second to put every last one of us in the grave."

Shit. He's right. This is real. We're about to bring down an international, trillion-dollar trafficking network of thousands of criminals, including the rich connected ones, judges, politicians. Of course, they're going to want us dead or worse. Of course, they're going to try and make us disappear. People have killed for less.

But I'm ready for them. I will personally drag every one of those monsters to prison.

"Fine," Priest said. "But you need to leave my sister and Carissa out of it. The only people who'll see those videos are the judges, prosecutor's offices, and defense attorneys and whoever else we need to put the Bradshaws in prison."

"Whatever you say," Oliver said. At no point had he stopped clicking and typing. He jumped between screens so fast, she wondered how he processed it all.

Priest looked at Jay. He watched quietly. *I wonder how he's handling this. Carissa's rape. The Fraternity. We'll have a long discussion about this later, including establishing boundaries about any future involvement in my cases. I made a mistake bringing him here. He could have been hurt or killed and shouldn't know this much about an ongoing investigation. I'm not going to make the same mistake again.*

"You do realize that everything said here—"

"Is confidential," Jay interrupted. "You know me, Amy. I'm not saying a word—" He paused, blinked rapidly. "What exactly are we talking about? Where are we?" He looked around.

She grinned. *It's refreshing to know I'm finally with someone I can trust.* "Thank you."

"For what?" Jay shrugged. "Shouldn't you be headed home? You have a lot of arrests to tend to tomorrow. Jail isn't going to fill itself."

You're exactly what I need in my life.

"You should come home with me."

Their eyes connected. Jay bit his lower lip. "I want to—"

"On the couch, of course," Priest hurried. They agreed to not sleep over at each other's homes to avoid giving into their desires. But she didn't want to be alone. Not tonight. Not after seeing what happened to her sister and everything she learned about The Fraternity. No. She wanted to go home with Jay, let him hold her while all her emotions finally rose to the surface and were dealt with. She held herself together for four years, focused on beating the streets until she had an opportunity to solve her sister's case. Now, she could finally, properly mourn.

"Snuggle with me on the couch until I start to fall asleep," she said. "Then I'll go to bed and you can stretch out."

In other words, we're going to snuggle until I fall asleep on you. If you try to wake me up, I'll put up a struggle. And you'll have no choice but to stay and hold me and fall asleep with me in your arms.

DAKOTA

"You do have a comfortable couch," Jay said and rubbed his chin. "Okay." He quickly picked up his bag and gave her a wink. "But I call the blue blanket."

That's the best blanket. You fiend.

Summers rushed through the door. "Something's happened and we have to go."

No, Nate! I was about to leave! I need sleep. Priest sighed. "What is it?"

"The word is out that we've hit the hub," Summers said.

"Why would you believe that?" Priest asked.

Summers flipped through his phone, then showed her a video. "Janice, Kent, and Robert Bradshaw are on the move. We had a uniform keeping an eye on them. They hopped in their car about ten minutes ago with luggage. Rushing. They're headed east on sixty-four. Probably headed for the airport. We have a car in pursuit. Two others on intercept."

DAMMIT! She balled her fists and clenched her teeth. She wanted to kick something. Anything. But there were only servers. She couldn't afford to kick one of those. "Who could have?" *Wait.* "If it was Val, I swear to God—" She paced in a mad circle. "What about Brian? Do they have eyes on him?"

"Someone tipped him off that they were looking for him. He just disappeared."

We had a car on him. How could this have happened? She ground her teeth. "How? Where was he?"

"He was at a restaurant." Summers shrugged his shoulders. "It was a standard tail. No one expected him to know he was being tailed. No one felt the need to have an officer any closer than inside a car. One moment, he was sitting at his table. The next, it looked like he went to the bathroom. But, he never came back. Left his car. Friends paid the check. He didn't tell them where he was going. He just up and disappeared. There's an APB out for him. Officials are distributing pictures now and have informed bus stations, train stations, the airport. He shouldn't be able to use public transportation. He won't be able to fly anywhere. But, that's all we know."

Priest growled.

Had I gone after Brian instead of Val, I'd already have him in custody. But if I was there, I never would have been here to strike gold. It figures. We found all the evidence we need to convict the Bradshaws for life, and they slip through our fingers. Why did we hesitate to arrest them? We played it safe, that's why. We were too safe. I should have dragged them out by their ears the moment I had something. But of course, again, had I done anything else, we would have spent days arguing with lawyers and never come close to this evidence gold mine. Here, we got enough to arrest hundreds, thousands of people. Save who knows how many young women. This evidence is bigger than my sister. Bigger than Carissa. Bigger than me.

Even if the Bradshaws get away tonight, this investigation has exposed their entire world. Even if they get away, they have no one to turn to. Everyone in the world will know who and what they are. Everyone in the world is going to know who and what all these people are.

But they're not getting away! Not if I have anything to say about it.

"We've gotta go," Priest said to Summers. "We can catch up with them on ninety-five." She turned to Jay. "Can you find a ride to the station?"

Jay nodded. "I Noah guy."

She blinked. *You would use that lame joke.*

"I'll start the car." Summers rushed through the door.

"I'm driving!" Priest called after him. "Jay, can I borrow your bag?"

"Sure." Jay handed it over. It was heavier than it looked. "Why?"

"I just have a feeling it'll be handy," Priest said and gave Jay a peck on the lips. He smiled. She rushed out of the door.

CHAPTER THIRTY-FOUR

On the way to the jeep, Summers assured Priest that plenty of capable officers could pursue and arrest the Bradshaws. She should go home, get some rest, and prepare for another long day tomorrow. But she wasn't having it. There was no way she would sleep until at least one of the Bradshaw brothers was behind bars. If she couldn't get justice for her sister tonight, the least she could do was get justice for Carissa.

"At least let me drive," Summers insisted. On that, she agreed. She was exhausted. He'd had a few hours of sleep in him and wouldn't drift off or otherwise get them killed.

But there was another reason she was going to let him drive.

Summers was the most mild-mannered man she'd met, and also the most astute and aggressive driver she'd ever seen. The moment seatbelts were buckled, he had her blue lights flashing and siren on. He punched the gas and launched them down the street. She couldn't believe they were already on the interstate within four minutes of leaving the office building. He was testing the limits of her vehicle, shifting from lane to lane and avoiding pedestrian vehicles slowing down to get out of their way. Within another five minutes, they'd caught up with the Bradshaw car and two other patrol cars with their flashers on.

"Dumb move on their part," Priest said. "Where do they expect to go? Anywhere they try to stop, we'll have police cut them off. They can't go to the airport. We'll have people waiting."

Summers shrugged.

"And even if they somehow made it to a private jet, I can't

imagine anyone's going to let them land and not arrest them the moment they touch down. Not after they see what we have on them. The whole world is going to know what they did. The whole world is going to know their names, what they're about. Even places without an extradition treaty won't want to touch them."

Summers nodded.

"Why aren't you saying anything?"

"I'm going eighty-five in a high-speed chase," Summers said. He pulled up next to the Bradshaw's black sedan. So close the passenger side rearview almost scraped against the sedan's. "Not exactly the time to focus on anything else other than the road. How do you feel about me bumping them off the road?"

Captain Rogers will probably kill us for using my personal vehicle in a police chase.

Priest could see Robert Bradshaw, a hard-faced man with salt and pepper hair, behind the wheel. She held her badge and shield with one hand and signaled Robert Bradshaw to pull over with the other. He looked at her, gave her the bird, and punched the accelerator. The sedan raced ahead of them.

"You break it, you buy it?" Priest returned. "I just wish I didn't put the doors on. Would be a lot easier to shoot out their tires."

Then again, it's freezing outside. My hands would shake too much to get a clean shot.

They passed a sign. Richmond International Airport was only a couple miles away. "Well, we need a plan," Summers said. "I don't want to get on the streets. This time of night, with fewer cars on the streets, it's harder to pin them down. And we don't have a lot of backup."

"Don't worry, Nate. I have an idea," Priest said and reached in the backseat for Jay's backpack. "Tell me something Jay, you wouldn't have a baton would you?" She pulled out a steel baton and slid it through the driver's and passenger seats.

Summers frowned at Priest and the baton. "And why is Jay carrying around a baton?"

"Because Nate," Priest smirked. "Every police officer should carry a baton."

He poked his tongue into his cheek, chewed on his response,

and decided there wasn't a need for one. Instead, he pushed the Jeep's engines until they were closer to the Bradshaw sedan.

Priest lowered her window all the way down. "Get me close."

Summers stuck his head forward and checked their proximity. "We *are* close."

"Closer," Priest insisted. "I want to see sparks."

"Fat chance of that happening," Summers said, but he accelerated and pushed the jeep closer to the sedan until they were inches apart. "You said if I break it I buy it."

"Trust me," Priest said and extended her arm out of the car. The wind raced. She worried it might pull the baton away from her. She tightened her grip and swung the baton at the driver side window. It cracked. "Yes!" *One more hit should do it.*

"WAIT!" Priest heard Summers yell. "He has a gun!"

Summers slammed on the brakes a split-second before the first shot fired. The bullet ricocheted off the windshield as Priest was flung forward, hit her head, then fell back and down. Her arm slammed against the car door, sending a shooting pain up her arm. She lost her grip on the baton. It clattered away on the highway.

"Ah! Dammit!" Priest said and cradled her arm. Shooting pain filled her existence as blood trickled down her forehead. She flexed her arm to assess the damage. She was able to bend and turn the arm, so it wasn't broken. She was sure of that. But it felt like the fires of Hell and would probably swell. "They tried to shoot me!"

I almost got shot! I can't believe I almost got shot.

Another shot was fired and ricocheted off the right side of the car.

Jesus!

"They're still shooting!" Priest yelled. "Back us off! Back us off!"

Summers slowed but kept pursuit behind them. He grabbed the radio and called, "Shots fired! We have shots fired! Suspects have fired two rounds at our vehicle. Approaching exit one-ninety-seven on sixty-four east. Suspects may be fleeing to Richmond airport. Roadblock one, prepare for their arrival. Prepare officers at secondary roadblock for arrival. Suspects are armed and dangerous." He put down the radio built into her dash. "You okay?"

No. This feels like murder.

She nodded with gritted teeth. "Yea." Ugh. "Just fell on it. It's pulsing, but, it's one of those things where it hurts like a mother until it slowly eases away. It didn't break. It might be bruised. It might be sprained. But it ain't broke. I'm sure of it."

Her head ached. She rubbed her forehead, felt blood, and opened the glove compartment for napkins. She always stored her leftover napkins from restaurants in there. Then, she wiped her forehead.

"Airport exit roadblock is ready," the radio reported. *"Sixty-four east cut off is ready."*

"I'll give them more distance and wait for them to run into our ambush," Summers said and started to slow.

I will not let them best me. I will not let them almost kill me and then give them space. No! Not this girl.

"No," Priest said. "Just give me a minute. I'm going to shoot out their back window."

Summers' eyes almost popped out of his sockets. "No, you are not. We're not about to have a shoot out on the interstate. We're going to hang tight." He glanced at the car's navigation. "We're a minute away from our first ambush. If they don't get off this exit, we'll have three patrol cars ready in wait to ambush them near the next."

She didn't agree. Couldn't agree. These were the Bradshaws. They were rapists, murderers, and sex traffickers. They had to be stopped *now.* She was tired of waiting.

Priest grabbed her pistol with her left arm and checked the magazine.

"Amy!" Summers yelled. "What did I tell you? We are *not* having a shoot out on the interstate. You're hurt for God's sake. You couldn't shoot your own foot with that arm. We need to hang tight. That's the end of it."

She shot him a cold stare, but that was the end of it. What else could she do? He was driving. But the moment the car stopped: different story.

Priest visualized herself charging out of the vehicle, pistol in her right hand, guided and supported by her left. Pain be damned. She'd approach low on the passenger side. After scanning for any movement from Kent Bradshaw in the back seat, she'd spy through the rear-view mirror and front passenger side for Janice. She didn't know how many guns they had, but knew one was in the front. Who held it now?

Robert fired two shots from the driver's side, but could have handed it off at any moment. Or, they could all be armed. They were fleeing after all.

"They're getting off the interstate, on the airport exit," Summers said into the radio. "All units, prepare to converge. Roadblock one, we are incoming."

"Roger that," the radio responded. *"We're ready for them."*

The Bradshaw sedan accelerated on the exit turn and then slammed hard and fast on its brakes until it came to a complete stop. Red and blue lights suddenly came to life ahead of them. They tried to reverse. Summers hurried and blocked them from the rear. There was no place to go.

"We got em!" Summers cheered and looked at Priest. But she had already opened her door and jumped out. "Amy, wait!"

You're mine! Priest thought as she quickly peeked around her car door and eyed the passenger rearview mirror. She rushed forward, low, gun trained and shifting between the rear seats and passenger side. She couldn't track any movement inside the car.

"Out of the car!" she commanded. Though, she doubted they heard her over the approaching sirens. The cavalry was on the way. Not that they were needed at this point.

Three officers slowly approached from the front. She flashed her shield as a fourth officer, the flank, approached her from the trees. They exchanged a head nod and trained their guns once again on the Bradshaw sedan.

There's no way out of this. The question is: are you going to go out shooting or let your lawyers do the fighting for you? Knowing these people, they'll probably be quick to take plea deals, like Val. Try to bury their Fraternity cohorts for a reduced sentence or protected ward, somewhere the general pop won't make good work of them.

The passenger side door opened first. Janice's bony hands and arms stretched out high. The rear door opened next. Kent slowly stepped out, arms raised. But the driver door didn't open.

"Away from the car and on your knees!" Priest commanded and stepped forward, pistol trained on the car. She wouldn't let her guard down until she had eyes on their gun and saw it land on the ground or in the custody of an officer. She pointed at her eyes and then towards the open passenger door. The closer officer nodded. She crept forward. "Janice Bradshaw, down on the ground! On your knees! Both of you, hands behind your heads!"

Janice scowled but slowly lowered herself to the ground. This was the moment of truth, Priest knew. They'd have eyes on Robert Bradshaw. Would he shoot? Would he end this in a fire fight?

She shot a glance at the three officers approaching from the driver's side. Summers was one of them. They crept forward, stopped, and lowered their weapons. Two of them turned away. Summers closed his eyes and lowered his head. She didn't understand why until she got a good look inside the cabin.

Robert Bradshaw had shot himself in the head.

Oh, God. Priest turned away and took in deep breaths. *Wasn't prepared to see that.* She felt herself becoming queasy. *Not again. Not again, Amy. You are not some first year on the beat rookie. I refuse to get sick. Don't puke. Be strong.*

Her first year on duty, she puked at least ten times after arriving at gruesome crime scenes. The visuals, the smells. It was too much for her to absorb. Her comrades lovingly nicknamed her Amy Upchuck, which inevitably shortened to Upchuck. She suffered that name for the first three years until she gained the respect of her comrades and earned a more flattering nickname, One-Punch. A suspect resisted arrest and grabbed ahold of an officer's gun, but was knocked out by a quick and hard right jab before he had a chance to use it. Still, it took her a while to develop an iron stomach. Some days, that iron needed reinforcement.

Priest took another set of long deep breaths and forced herself to focus on Janice and Kent. They rest on their knees with their hands behind their heads. *Forget about the dead man. Arrest Kent.*

"Can I borrow your handcuffs?" she asked the closest officer, squint, "Officer Kelly." He handed her his handcuffs and flagged another officer forward. They approached Kent Bradshaw.

"Kent Bradshaw, you are under arrest for the rape of Carissa Boisseau," Priest said and knelt behind him. Kent kept his eyes down and didn't say a word.

Silence. Sounds like you've already talked to your lawyers.

"Officer Kelly, please escort Mister Bradshaw to your car," Priest said and turned her attention to Janice Bradshaw. She pulled out her phone and pulled up the information Oliver copied to her from Janice's file. She wagged her phone at Janice as she approached.

"We know what you did, Janice." She hesitated. "I have your file. Your confession. The picture you took with the dead body to prove your loyalty to the Fraternity."

Janice turned away, towards the police cars and flinched at the blinding headlights. She elected instead to close her eyes. Priest leaned in close.

"Thirty years ago, you killed your friend, Madelyn James," Priest said. Janice's head spun back towards Priest, then the phone. *That got her attention.*

"You convinced your friend, Francesca, to have sex with Madelyn's boyfriend, Tom Angelo, at the sorority party. Not that it took much convincing. You led an intoxicated Madelyn up to Francesca's room so that she would walk in on them. Francesca gave her best performance and enjoyed any attempt to spite Madelyn, because you convinced Francesca that Madelyn was stealing from her. Only, it was you who was stealing from her."

Janice opened her mouth to speak, but Priest shushed her. "Oh no, not yet, honey. I haven't read you your rights, yet.

"So, Madelyn walked in on them, had a meltdown and ran out in tears. Ran to you. You convinced her to go for a walk and get some air. There was an artificial waterfall not far from your sorority house where she liked to sit down and think. You said you'd meet her there. Then, you established your alibi. You told your boyfriend you were going to your room to prepare for him, went to the bathroom, turned on the shower, snuck out of your window, which was easy since you were on the ground floor. You found Francesca, hit her over the head with a wrench you borrowed from Tom's job, Quick Stop and Supply, and drowned her. Then, you put the wrench in the back seat of his car, because he never locked his car door, slipped back through your bathroom window, jumped in the shower, cleaned off any trace of Madelyn, and came out to a waiting boyfriend.

"The next day, after the police found her body, you told them Madelyn walked in on Tom and Francesca. You convinced them that Tom was capable of harming Madelyn if he was angry enough. You said Tom knew where Madelyn would go to clear her head if she was upset.

"I must say, you were a clever girl, Janice. Since you put the wrench from his work in his car, the prosecution raised the question of why he took it from his job and if there was any forethought or premeditation to using it as a weapon. I mean, who takes a wrench to meet an angry girlfriend at a waterfall after a fight about infidelity? Tom was charged with first-degree murder and has spent the last thirty years of his life in prison."

She ground her teeth. "You ended two lives that day. Then, decades later, you helped your son, Brian, get away with raping Dakota Priest. You arranged the abortion. You knew Brian did it for the Fraternity!" She balled her fists. "He threatened her. He, he humiliated her until she became so depressed," she teared up, "so, so depressed and scared that she swallowed a bunch of pills, committed suicide."

Breathe, Amy. Breathe. But she couldn't.

She felt hot. Her sweaty hand locked on her gun. Part of her wanted to punch Janice in the face and leave her exactly like her crooked husband: brains decorating the car.

That part of Priest calmed as a cool breeze passed through her chest and rested on her soul. She thought of Jay and Jesus. She blinked back tears and let out a sigh. Her vision sharpened, mind cleared.

Oh God, I came this close. So close to striking her. So close to, to doing something I couldn't take back. Thank you. Thank you for stopping me.

"Lieutenant?" an officer said. He watched her with concern.

"I'm fine." Priest gave the officer a reassuring nod. "Just tired." She returned her attention to Janice, who watched her with wide eyes. "Janice Bradshaw, you are under arrest."

CHAPTER THIRTY-FIVE

Morning came too soon, again. Priest could barely peel herself out of bed. Fortunately, she had an obsequious boyfriend willing to roll off the couch and brew a fresh pot of coffee. He delivered a steaming mug with apple slices, a blueberry bagel and cream cheese. She kissed him and told him he was too good for her.

His response, "You thought that was free? That'll be twelve ninety-nine. And I expect a tip." She laughed. He kissed her, slapped her on the butt, and told her to go to work. He crashed back on the couch.

Thirty minutes later, Priest stepped off the elevator and froze. Phones were ringing off the hook. Support staff scrambled between offices and cubicles. Officers stood beside lines of suspects. She exhaled and slowly backed into the elevator—*Nope, nope, nope*—but Rogers had already seen her and waved her forward. She sighed. The man's office was intentionally across from the elevator. It allowed him to see everyone's comings and goings throughout the day.

She peeked in. He ate his usual sack lunch: a sandwich with sliced ham, turkey, chicken breast, two slices of cheese, and leaf lettuce, an apple, and homemade chicken noodle soup. Her stomach growled. Suddenly, that small coffee and bagel she had wasn't enough.

Lunch for breakfast?

"Pop a squat," Rogers said and motioned her until she took a seat across from him. Was this a congratulatory conversation, or would she be reprimanded for her recklessness last night? She kicked herself after it was all over.

I could have easily been killed. The better move was to pursue patiently while closing all their routes. That was protocol.

He said, "You and Nate did a bang-up job with this investigation. Your approach was careful and subtle." He sipped his orange juice. "I hate seeing detectives blunder through investigations, making more noise than a wild bull in heat."

I, uh, don't want to know how that sounds.

"When you and Nate came to my office with the details of this case, part of me was concerned you were going to lose your shit. But you didn't." *Yes, I did.* "You stuck with the game plan, stayed discreet. Your restraint and focus impressed all of us. I want to apologize for doubting you, even if I didn't show it. I doubted you, and well, you've proven yourself to be a disciplined and competent detective. I won't forget that. You've made a name for yourself here. You've earned a lot of respect."

"Thank you, sir," Priest said, shocked.

It took every bit of me to not beat their faces in with my pistol. And when my restraint wasn't enough, there was Jesus. What a nice inspirational t-shirt.

"Now, before we get on to business, how's your arm?" Rogers pointed.

Priest slowly rotated her arm and suppressed the urge to grimace. The pain pulsed, ached, and then faded. "It aches a little. But, it'll pass."

"Great," he said. "With Janice and Kent Bradshaw in custody, you can take a couple days off and rest." She opened her mouth to protest. "That's an order. Give yourself some time to heal, physically and mentally. Allow yourself some closure and start moving forward."

We only have Janice and Kent. What about Brian? He's the one that raped my sister. How can I rest? How can I, even for a moment, allow myself to relax knowing he's still out there? How can I take a day off until I know he's behind bars?

"What about Brian Bradshaw?"

Rogers swatted her question like a pesky fly. "Everyone in Virginia is looking for him. We've locked his accounts. He can't get a hotel room. He can't rent a car. He can't do anything. I doubt he has enough cash to float for more than a few days. Soon, he won't be able to buy a Slurpee at the corner seven eleven."

Dang it. Now I want a Slurpee.

"There's nowhere for him to go," Rogers continued. "Williamsburg Police searched his apartment and it's under surveillance. Every single member of his family, even his distant cousins, are either being questioned by the police or arrested. We've already got him on Crime Stoppers. Those guys are boss. His face, and what he's done, is everywhere. We'll have him by the end of the week. Don't worry about him."

You're right. Brian fled without his car. Did he steal or borrow someone else's? Where could he go? How long could he stay? I suppose as far as his cash will take him.

Rogers took a big bite of his sandwich, chewed as he thought, then swallowed. "Chances are, law enforcement aren't the only ones looking for him."

I'm sure you're right, but— "What do you know?"

He took another bite. *Or you can eat.* She waited as he chewed methodically and wiped the mustard and mayo from the corners of his mouth. "It's been all over the news that the Bradshaws were at the center of our investigation. So, anyone that's been outed as a rapist, murderer, trafficker, kidnapper, whatever, will be after Brian Bradshaw. In situations like this, if you cause the exposure of a secret organization, your head shows up on a stick in someone's yard."

We can only hope. I'll be dreaming about that tonight.

"We've had time to go through the names on the list. A lot of powerful people are going down. We're talking congressmen, senators, judges, lawyers, three ambassadors, the secretary of transportation, businessmen, celebrities, four national news anchors, dirty cops. Like Paulson." He grumbled something under his breath. "The list goes on." He took another sip of his orange juice. "We hit the motherload. We hit the jackpot. So much so that, honestly, I'm concerned about retaliation."

This was the last thing she expected him to say. She leaned closer and lowered her voice, "Have you been threatened?"

He sipped his orange juice. "I've received a number of phone calls asking how much we have, how much we know, and for a comprehensive list of all involved parties in our investigation. Probably want to know who to silence. I've enjoyed a few aggressive calls strongly urging me to stop what we're doing. That and everyone wants a piece of the collar. Any moment now, the FBI are going to stroll in here and take this away from us. I'm hoping they're part of Oliver's task force, but I don't know. That's why it's all hands on deck out there. I'm getting as much accomplished as I can. With enough people off the street and exposed, any veiled threat made against us will be just that."

"What about Carissa?" Priest asked. "Will she be safe? The last thing I want is for our investigation to put her or one of the other victims in danger."

"She'll be safe. None of the specifics of her case have gone public. Besides, harming her wouldn't benefit anyone. What would be the point? We have all the evidence we need."

I don't know. Her case is the reason we investigated the Bradshaws. What if they off her out of spite? We should watch her for a while. Someone should.

"The new Mayor wants to be involved so he looks like a hero. Remember his campaign about being tough on crime? This is every mayor's wet dream. He's been in office for what, five minutes, and he's already prepared a press conference. He'll start with a speech, introduce me, and then stand next to me as I go over what's been uncovered."

Ugh. The last thing we need is a politician using our hard work to accelerate his career. But I'm not surprised. It happens everywhere, all the time. They give us our props and pat us on the back, but at the end of the day, it's their faces people remember. Their names you hear repeated on the news. They're the ones promoted to higher offices and fatter paychecks. They'll shake our hands in a photo op while their policies stab us in the back.

"Well, better you than me," Priest said. "I hate politics *and* politicians. I don't want to have anything to do with any of it."

Rogers chuckled and patted his arm rest. "Nate said the same thing. I have the feeling you'll be sitting in a chair like mine one day. When that day comes, you won't have a choice." He smiled. "But before that day comes, enjoy being on the field. Solving cases. Bringing justice to the people." He folded his hands and leaned back. "Which brings us to my last assignment for you for a couple days."

"What's that?"

DAKOTA

"Delivering the good news to the Boisseau family," Rogers said. "You made the arrest. We have the evidence we need to convict Kent. We won. Now, for any long-term financial support, which will be calculated in victim settlements, we still have to prove Kent's the father. I'm told the sample you got wasn't conclusive. There wasn't enough baby DNA in her blood."

So far, that was the only setback. Eight weeks was too soon to collect viable fetus DNA in Carissa's blood. Twelve weeks would offer better results.

"We'll try again next week," Priest said. "If she's willing."

"Great. That was all. On your way home, deliver the news to the Boisseaus."

That was her cue. She stood, said, "With pleasure, sir," and headed for the door.

"One more thing," Rogers said and smiled.

She turned around. "Yes?"

"Take Oliver with you," he said. "You would have locked the case either way with the phone video and testimony from DeQuan and the others. But, we owe Oliver for the strongest piece of evidence: the rape video and the Fraternity network. I think it would be great for him to be able to look at least one of the people he's helped in the eye and receive some thanks. He's earned it."

Priest agreed. "Yea. He has."

2

Priest parked in front of the Boisseau residence. The last time she approached the house, it was covered in vandalism and urine. This time: a thin layer of snow. She loved the Winter season. It was cold, wet, and caused her to trip and fall on her face at least once a season. But snow was aesthetically pleasing. She'd taken up photography because of snow.

Twelve years ago, Priest was confident she'd be a professional photographer and have her own studio. Her mom encouraged her and bought a high-quality camera, lens, and tripod as a Christmas present. Priest spent the rest of the month capturing the snow on her leafless trees. She got a ride downtown to her mom's office building, sat in the office next to the window with the tripod aimed at the closest intersection, and practiced short and long exposure shots. Then she went outside, fixed an umbrella and tripod upright, and spent an hour adjusting the shutter speeds and capturing snowflakes as they fell. It was the snowiest winter they'd ever had. And she loved every moment of it. There was something majestic about snow.

She slipped and almost fell forward on her face, but Oliver caught her.

"Thanks," Priest said and righted herself. *Phew. That would have been embarrassing.*

The front door opened. Kate Boisseau stood at the entrance and called out, "I'm so sorry! We put salt down, but it looks like there are a few naked patches."

Yea, yea, yea. Salt stops snow from becoming ice. It won't stop me from busting my face wide open.

Priest carefully stumped forward, making sure she didn't find another naked patch. "Good morning, Misses Boisseau. It's nice to see you again."

"Thank you." Kate glanced at Oliver. "It's nice to see you as well. Though, I wasn't expecting company today, with the snow and everything. Do you have more questions for Carissa?"

"No more questions," Priest said. "I came to inform you that late last night, we arrested Kent Bradshaw."

"I know. It's on the news. There was a police chase."

Right. Of course. "We also arrested his mother, Janice, as a co-conspirator in pressuring a minor into an illegal abortion, among other charges we have on her. We still have officers looking for Brian Bradshaw. It's only a matter of time before we find him. But we've come with answers. Answers as to why they did what they did, and what the next steps are for your family. May we come in?"

"Of course." Kate held the door open. "Please pardon the mess. We weren't expecting visitors."

The house was spotless, minus a few dishes in the sink. *Pardon my mess.* Kate walked to the stairwell, called for Carissa, and guided her guests to the kitchen.

"Would you like something to drink? Coffee? Tea? Water?"

Priest said water, no ice. Oliver asked for a coffee with two hot cocoa packets and whipped cream, if Kate had them. *Really, Oliver? Really?* She did.

"You're not Detective Summers," Kate said as she poured two packets into a coffee mug. She said nothing else but watched him with curious eyes.

"Oh," Priest said, "I'm sorry. You two haven't met, yet. This is Detective Oliver Courier. The one who set up Carissa's secure email account. He works in a joint task force between the FBI and NYPD's cybercrime department and vice squad. He's been instrumental in the investigation. He got us the digital evidence we needed to put the Bradshaws behind bars."

Kate stopped stirring Oliver's drink and approached him. "Thank you. Thank you so much." She blinked back tears and extended her hand. "It's good to meet you. Thank you for everything you've done."

"A pleasure to meet you," Oliver said and shook Kate's hand. He admired the kitchen before adding, "You have a lovely home, Misses Boisseau."

"Thank you," Kate said and returned her attention to his coffee. "If you want, you can take a seat in the family room where it's more comfortable. Carissa should be down any minute now."

"Of course." Priest said, eager to give this woman space. She guided Oliver to the family room and pointed to the chairs she and Summers sat on a month ago, when they were dispatched. They took a seat.

Five minutes later, Carissa casually strolled down the steps and turned into the kitchen. There were whispers. Then she walked into the family room in a pink fleece blanket with sleeves and a glass of orange juice. Her mother followed her, a tray with drinks in her hands.

"I love blankets with sleeves," Oliver said as he accepted his drink. "I have three." He smirked. "Same color, too."

Carissa smiled. It was good to see.

Kate handed Priest her water and set the tray on the coffee table. "So, you said you have answers for us."

Priest took a sip of her water. "We know why Kent did what he did to Carissa. And we know why he chose you."

"Why?" Carissa asked. "Why me?"

The everlasting, burning question.

"Kent's family is part of an international organization, a secret cult, involved in sex trafficking, drugs, weapons, and war proliferation. Kent's parents are shareholders of a front that manages this organization's imports and exports. To become members of this organization, you're required to commit a horrific crime and provide the organization with verifiable evidence. That's why he attacked you and then recorded it—"

"It's called a mutually-assured destruction contract," Oliver said and sipped his coffee.

Priest agreed, "What he said," but hoped this was his last interruption.

"So why me?" Carissa leaned forward. "Of all the people at that school, why me?"

I asked the same thing about my sister.

"He saw you as an easy target," Priest answered.

"An easy target?" Kate asked and glanced at Carissa. "How? She knows martial arts."

Kent didn't know that. If he tried what Brian did with my sister, he'd probably have ended up in the hospital. If only.

Priest aimed her dialogue at Carissa. "You're an incredible athlete, kind of a local celebrity, but that's all most people at the school know of you. You're still new, not very social, and don't have many friends. It was easy for the Bradshaws to establish whatever narrative they wanted. He asked around about you, not just to get a better idea of who you are, but also to determine how and if he could get away with attacking you. When he learned how skittish and reclusive you tend to be, he saw you as the perfect mark. Socially reserved or anxious people are less likely to report a crime or grievance if victimized. They're more inclined to internalize it." She looked Carissa in the eyes. "And you did."

Like my sister.

Carissa thought about that long and hard. No one interrupted the silence. This was her time to process. "What happens now?"

"Testimony and evidence are reviewed by the Prosecutor's Office," Priest said. "They'll have a preliminary court date to determine whether or not Kent gets bail." Fat chance of that, happening. "It might be expected of you to testify against him at the trial. If all goes well, he'll spend his adulthood behind bars. As will the rest of his family."

Except his father. He took a shortcut to Hell.

"And what about the baby?" Carissa asked, forehead molded into a confused frown.

What about the baby?

Priest took a sip of her water. "I don't understand."

"I, I can't afford to take care of the baby," Carissa said. "Not by myself. Not as a student in college. If they're in jail, and their money is connected to a criminal enterprise, it'll all be taken away, and they can't pay child support. So, what happens to my baby? Does it all then fall on me?"

Fair question. "That's your cue, Oliver."

He smiled. "After some digging into the Bradshaw Will and Testament, I discovered your child is due to inherit a percentage of their assets divided almost equally between Brian and Kent Bradshaw's descendants. As the first born, your child would receive a ten percent increase and be responsible for the management of all assets until the others are of age. That means, until either Brian or Kent have another child, your child is the sole heir. Sole heir of what, I don't know. I'll investigate that as we comb through their financials and provide you with whatever information I'm permitted."

Carissa sighed. Priest wasn't sure if it was of relief or regret. "I mean, it's not about the money. I never planned on asking them for money. That was all Val. I don't want them to be involved in any way with the child. I just, it's a heavy burden. And since they're being charged, it only seems fair that I get some compensation or help."

"Of course," Priest said. "I absolutely understand. Virginia has a victim compensation program that will reimburse you for any medical costs, mental health counseling, and loss of wages due to the attack. And we'll be talking with the Prosecutor's Office about the details of further compensation for all the victims once we're able to determine how much of the organization's money is tied to criminal activities. But, trust us, trust me." She looked into Carissa's eyes. "We won't let you be left in the cold on this. We're working the hardest we can to make sure there's justice for what's happened to you."

Carissa nibbled her lower lip. "Okay." She looked to her mom to see if she had any questions. Kate sipped her coffee but offered no additional words. It was now that Priest noticed the darkness under her eyes. She wasn't sleeping. But who could sleep with everything that's happened in the last month?

There was another lingering silence. Oliver finished his coffee. "I should add: your DNA sample didn't prove a viable source. We'll still need to get another sample of the baby's DNA as we get closer to the trial. It's necessary to prove, without a shadow of a doubt, that he's the father, so there can be compensation."

"Okay." Carissa looked approvingly to her mother.

Kate grabbed her phone. "I'll call Amy." She blinked at Priest and amended, "The other Amy. My Amy." She frowned. "Doctor Sanchez."

I knew you weren't talking about me.

"Great." Priest stood. "We'll stay in contact." Everyone else followed her lead. They transitioned the conversation towards the front door.

"Thank you again for everything you've done." Kate half-smiled.

Priest was tired of being thanked. As much as she wanted justice for Carissa, she wanted justice for her sister more. It wasn't something she needed to be thanked for. If anything, she needed to thank Kate. Had they not called, had they not reported the rape, she may have never had an opportunity to investigate the Bradshaws. They never would have called Oliver, who, despite his eccentricities, had his finger on the pulse of the secret cult, The Fraternity. In the end, the investigation proved to be fortuitous for everyone except Carissa and her family.

"Thank you for the coffee; it tasted like friendship," Oliver said and held the screen door for Priest. She followed him. They waved and walked towards Priest's Jeep but stopped when they heard the screen door open.

It was Carissa. "I decided on a name for the baby," she called out.

Already? You're in your what, third month? Kind of early for settling on a name, but okay.

"What's that?" Priest asked.

"Dakota," Carissa said, gave Priest a nod. "I'm naming him or her, Dakota." After dropping that bomb, she shivered, rushed back inside, and closed the door.

DAKOTA

Oh.

Priest opened her mouth to speak but couldn't. She lowered her head, grinned, and returned to her Jeep.

CHAPTER THIRTY-SIX

"Ugh," Carissa groaned as she crawled out of bed and looked down at her abdomen. She was near the end of her second trimester and it showed. It was only a matter of time before the neighbors started asking questions. People at church were already murmuring. So far, she'd been able to conceal the baby bump as she went to her classes. She wore loose shirts and sweats. Sometimes, she even wore her pajamas and slippers.

She looked at the clock. *Shit.* And rushed to class.

College was the best place she'd ever been. In high school, people would have made fun of her pregnancy. Judged her. Everyone would have gossiped about it. Life would have been a nightmare.

There was none of that at college. People went to class, listened to their lectures, took notes, had group conversations on occasions, but outside of that, minded their own business. The few people who did notice were accommodating. In biology, there were three pregnant girls. *Three!* They exchanged information, went maternity shopping, and met regularly for lunch and dinner.

Truly, high school was toxic. College was liberation.

Why can't all school be like college?

Chemistry professor and mother of three, Doctor Charlotte Franks, occasionally gave pregnancy advice. Carissa's favorite suggestion: eating more mangos and peaches during her pregnancy. This was the beginning of her peach addiction.

"Just don't eat too much."

DAKOTA

I eat everything too much. Everything!

"Make sure you drink plenty of water. If you feel hot, drink cooler than room temperature water to balance your temperature."

Until, of course, the baby starts pressing against my bladder and I pee every hour. I pee enough as it is.

The students in her classes varied in age. Half of them were in their twenties. A quarter were recent high school grads. The rest were a sprinkle of students from thirties to their sixties. Most of them had jobs.

Kyle, a lanky, freckled brunet from her chemistry class—*who clearly has the hots for me*—offered to help her get a job during a dreaded group assignment. He was twenty-one, and an associate manager at a King's Port gas station.

"At King's Port, patrons are treated as royalty."

Or at least, that's the slogan. The hardest part of the job, Kyle complained, was living up to such a high standard of service in a world full of demanding, ungrateful people. They honestly thought they were royalty. After complaining about the customers for five minutes, he went back to offering her a job. She didn't care. He had her at "the pay is decent" for a first-time part-timer.

The next step was getting her mother to go along with her having a job. With Dad gone, and the pregnancy, Mom was a bit skittish about Carissa driving around, especially at night, after work, alone. She also depended on Carissa to run errands like trips to the grocery store or getting Sean to or from basketball practice and games.

With the family budget dependent on one income—Mom chose to save Dad's life insurance money, trusts, and savings for Carissa and Sean's tuition—Carissa prepared her argument. She could pay for her own stuff. She'd only work part-time for extra pocket money. The schedule wouldn't interfere with her studies. If she got the basketball game schedule in advance, she could make sure she worked before or after Sean's games started or practice ended.

Mom said, "No, Carissa," every time Carissa mentioned it, which was every day, twice a day, for two weeks, until Sean burst through the door with a new scooter he custom-built from parts in the junkyard. This gave Mom a lot more to worry about than Carissa.

Thanks for saving the day, Sean!

They knew Sean started working on a "secret project" at the beginning of the new year. Mom asked Rebecca about it. She said it was "some kind of engineering project". *So helpful.* She said he'd "been at the junkyard a lot" collecting metal, discarded computers, and car parts. That put Mom at ease. She was happy Sean had a creative and constructive outlet after Dad's passing. Her son riding a metal death machine, however, was the last thing she wanted.

Carissa was a lot less worried and more impressed by what he'd put together. It was clean, shiny, with a small frame. It looked like a motorcycle but could only go about thirty miles per hour.

"Look at this," Sean said pointed at the odometer. There was a touch-screen interface built into the handle bar. "I installed a small computer from the parts of a couple abandoned laptops and used a discarded tablet and two cellphones for the visual, audio, and touch interface. This phone gives me the odometer, speed, fuel level. This one connects via Bluetooth to my phone and gives me directions, voice calls. Everything else goes through the tablet. I have gold wiring throughout the inner workings of the frame. It's sick." He buzzed with excitement. "Programming was the hardest part. But a guy we, err, I know recommended some software. Oh, and check this out."

My little brother is a genius. A genius! Holy cow! What else could there possibly be?

"I've installed four small, refillable nitrous tanks," Sean whispered and revealed a secret compartment. "I can press a valve and kick it up to fifty or sixty if I want." He lowered his voice even more so she could barely hear him. "Maybe faster going downhill, just in case someone tries to run me over." *Why would someone want to do that?*

He smiled. "I also have small smoke grenades I made, and cantrips," he pointed towards the back, at another compartment, "that come out if I press a lever, just in case anyone tries to pursue me. Made them myself."

Well damn. Now I'm worried. Do you plan on joining a

motorcycle gang? Why would you need that?

"If you want, I can hook you up, too," Sean said. He leaned close. She could feel his breath on her cheek. There was a coldness in his eyes. "Just in case, you know, one of the dragons comes around."

Carissa stood there, stunned. The last few months, all she'd heard about on the news was the exposed secret organization. Daily, more members were arrested and charged. Victims were coming forward or set free. Yet, she hadn't heard a thing from the police about the missing Bradshaw. Where was he? Mom refused to mention the Bradshaws. That name was a swear word, taboo, like Voldemort. Carissa didn't asked questions about Brian, settled on the idea and hope that someone got to him before the police and snuffed him out.

"No, I'm fine," Carissa said. She didn't know what else to say. The last thing she wanted was to tell Mom. Mom would freak out if she knew he had nitrous in his scooter and evasive gadgets stored in the back. Who taught him how to make smoke grenades, anyway?

Again, why does he need those? It makes no sense.

"It's safe Mom," Sean assured Mom. *Safe. Hmm.* "It's easier to balance because I have two tires on one hub in the front. One tire in the back. It's like, a manlier tricycle with gadgets." He pointed to it. "It rides nice. I could probably build more and make a fortune off these."

Mom wasn't a materialistic woman, but something clicked when she heard fortune. Sean aspired to be an inventor entrepreneur and she didn't want to get in the way of that. Both she and Dad always thought Sean was destined for something great. He loved constructing models and read anything involving architecture, mechanics, engineering, or computer science. He spent a summer with Uncle Angus as an apprentice working on cars and motorcycles. Who knew what else he could create?

He's going to do a lot more with his life than I ever will.

Mom sighed and caved. "Okay, okay. But always wear a helmet, and pads, and avoid busy streets. I don't care if it takes you an extra twenty minutes to an hour to get somewhere. I want you taking the safest, quietest routes. Follow all the rules on the road to the letter. Let me know where you're going. We'll have to get you a license for this."

Sean smiled. "Of course."

"And if anything happens, if you hit something, ding something, go off the road, scrape your knee, you let me know immediately."

"Scrape my knee?" Sean complained. "I do that like every morning."

Mom stared at him.

"Fine." Sean pouted his lip. "But it'll get redundant after a while."

"You know what I mean," Mom said and gave him a hug. "You two are all I have left. If anything happened to you, I don't know what I'd do."

Lay on the guilt. Lay it on thick. That's how you do it.

"You have Amy."

Mom released the hug. "You're getting awfully mouthy."

"I love you, Mom," Sean returned.

Mom smiled. "That's more like it."

Carissa asked the next important question. "Does this mean I can get that part-time job? You know, since Sean can drive himself?"

Mom sighed. "He can drive himself to and from the Cole's house, a nearby store, and church. I still don't feel comfortable with him going all the way to school, especially in the morning. But yes, we'll give it a trial run." She smiled. "Having a job isn't as fun as you think it is."

But cashing a paycheck is.

She called Kyle and told him the good news. He agreed to set up an interview with the general manager. She cheered and told him thank you repeatedly until he begged her to stop. He was happy to do what he could.

"I like having you around," Kyle said. She could hear the smile in his voice.

That could get complicated. I'm not sure how I feel about him. But I don't care! I might have a job!

2

She got the job. No surprise to her. The general manager and owner, Joe King, said he suspected she'd be gone in several months, without mentioning her pregnancy specifically, but they could use the help while she was able.

Since she was a minor, she'd always have to work with a manager. *Probably Kyle.* She wouldn't sell smokes or alcohol or lottery tickets. *That's a relief.* She'd handle gas and convenient store purchases, help in the attached diner, stock merchandise, and clean.

"Don't worry about dealing with any of the gas pump issues, either. Maybe grab the trash. I wouldn't want you to inhale the fumes—" Joe paused. "It's, uh, a health safety guideline. Nothing to do with, uh."

He rubbed his head.

"You'll start at nine fifty an hour. I give all part-timers a two-week trial run. You work three four-hour shifts the first week. Three four-hour shifts the second week. That's twenty-four hours total. A day's worth of our time. If we like you, you stay. If we don't, you have the opportunity to find something more suited to your talents. Sound good?"

"Yes, sir," Carissa said with a smile. *Yay, money!*

Joe handed her a pile of paperwork. "Great. You're hired. Fill these out. Don't touch anything or talk to any customers until they're completed." He pointed at the multi-purpose printer. "You brought your driver's license and social security card, right?"

"Yep."

"Great. Leave a copy with the paperwork. Give it all to Kyle. He'll sign that we received them, put them in an envelope, and slide it under my door."

He left.

After she filled out the paperwork and handed them to Kyle, he showed her around the store, gave her a brief orientation, told her everyone's job, what they expected from her, and introduced her to the other staff. It was a small staff.

Three full-timers and one part-timer worked the diner throughout the week. Two associate managers and three associates worked the register and maintained the convenience store. That was nine staff. She was now the tenth person, the cushion person as they called her. The extra person they needed during the busy hours. The person they could call in if someone couldn't come.

The staff was evenly half male, half female. The ladies ran the diner. The men ran the convenience store. One of the women commented on how very nineteen fifties the arrangement was. Carissa shrugged. Technically, she worked both sides.

Kyle scheduled Carissa around his work schedule, so she was his help. She kind of felt sorry for him, because she didn't know what she was doing. She kept making mistakes and slowing things down. But that didn't seem to bother him. He'd worked there long enough to know what to do and how to fix things. He just sprung over and told her what to do and the problem was solved.

Every time he looked at her, he lit up. It was a new thing for her. She wasn't used to being looked at that way. It excited her. She felt desired and accepted. Not once did he pry about how or why she was pregnant. He only wondered if she was seeing someone. It was, of course, followed by an immediate *no*. He smiled, happy to hear that, and continued being Mister Fix-it, Mister Smiles.

They had a lot of laughs. If someone approached the counter asking silly questions, they giggled about it. They had nicknames for the regulars. Some positive, others the furthest from nice.

Mom said work was difficult. Somehow, Kyle found a way of making the best of the most stressful days. They'd both been yelled at by stupid guests. One woman mistakenly put diesel gas in her car and was furious that the gas wasn't labelled well enough to tell the difference. It didn't matter that regular pumps had a single pump, while diesel pumps had two: one labeled *diesel* with the color, green, and the other labeled regular, premium, and super with a different color, red. After the woman left, Carissa wanted to cry. She couldn't help herself. But Kyle wouldn't have that. He cracked jokes about the woman until Carissa did cry, but not tears of sorrow.

That night, he walked her to her car. She looked up at him, her eyes big. He looked down at her. His eyes locked on her. They shared a kiss. She couldn't remember the last time she'd been kissed. It was soft, gentle, and a little wet. He wrapped his arms around her and pulled her in. Her whole body and mind screamed with excitement. She couldn't believe it was really happening. Finally, it was really happening.

And then, she had flashes. Flashes of when she was kissed. Flashes of when she did have a man's hands on her. This time she wanted them. But last time, that last time a boy had his damned hands on her, her whole being was in terror and torment. The last time she was touched and kissed, it wasn't to give, but to take.

She wanted to cry. She felt overwhelmed by the conflict inside of her. She wanted to be kissed. She wanted to be touched. She wanted to be physically loved. Her whole body came to life for it. But she also wanted to scream.

Kyle let go and looked at her. There was a look of satisfaction, then of worry.

"Are you okay?"

Carissa nodded and teared up. "Yea. I'm fine." She smiled. It was a forced smile. She hoped it would convince him. She hoped he wouldn't regret kissing her. She hugged him, squeezed, concealing her mixed emotions. It was good to be held and to hold someone. The physical connection. It put her at ease.

"Okay," Kyle said and held her. She slowly released the hug and looked up at him. He kissed her again on the lips, and then on the cheek. She smiled, blushed.

"I don't want things to get complicated," he said.

Things are already complicated.

"Life is complicated," Carissa said. *I would know.*

Kyle smiled. "True." He kissed her again.

Don't stop kissing me. Never stop.

There was a whistle. Kyle and Carissa froze and looked in the direction of the whistle. It was Margaret, head of the dining staff, and the oldest employee. There was a line of three people at the register.

"Oh shit," Kyle said. "I have to go." He kissed her one more time and bolted for the store. Margaret gave Kyle a few choice words. They went inside while she scolded him.

They're such a fun group. It's not the most glamourous job, like working in Mom's office, but I love this place.

Carissa opened her car door and sat her purse in the passenger seat. She noticed a naked picture of herself, spread eagle, on the foot mat on the passenger side. Her heart sank. She checked the back seat and looked desperately around the parking lot, trembling.

Oh my God! Someone was in my car! And they have pictures of me. Pictures of me from that night. I don't understand. How? It's all over. The Bradshaws are in jail about to go to trial. Who could have done this? Why?

Instinct told her to look at the passenger window. She left the windows cracked so the car wouldn't be stuffy. *Whoever slipped this in my car is going to pay. I'm calling the cops.*

She dug in her purse for her phone, retrieved it, and leaned over to examine the picture more closely. A message in red ink was on the naked picture: "I bet they don't know they hired a fucking whore. A dead whore."

Oh no, no, no, no!

Carissa, pale as death, looked around to see if anyone was nearby, lurking in the bushes, watching her from the street, following her. That's when she saw a large hooded figure in her passenger side rearview mirror, standing from a crouched position. She quickly reached out and slammed her car door shut, locked it.

The hooded figure ran around her car, yanked at the door handle, and pounded on the door. "Open up!"

Fat chance of that happening!

She shoved her keys into the ignition and turned. The car came to life. She glanced in the direction of the hooded figure, ready to reverse, and saw him swing a baseball bat. She leaned to the passenger seat and shielded her face as her driver's side window burst into a thousand pieces. Glass sprayed all over the front of the cabin.

The hooded figure reached in, unlocked the door, and opened it. In seconds, one hand took hold of her hair while another claimed her arm. He yanked her out of the car and let her tumble on the cement parking lot. She controlled her fall the best she could to land on her back, instead of her stomach, and shielded the womb she worried would be under attack.

Carissa screamed for help as the hooded figure stood over her. But her cry was answered by no one. She looked around. Anyone that could help was inside the gas station. She turned to the hooded figure, saw the baseball bat next to his feet, and reached for it. He kicked her leg with full force. The pain made her woozy, nearly knocked her unconscious. She cried out in pain and sobbed.

"Stupid whore!" the hooded figure yelled and kicked her again. Her leg throbbed. "You ruined everything! My money's gone. My family's in jail. *My dad's dead!* I've got nowhere to go."

She recognized his voice and took a hard look at his face. It was Brian Bradshaw. She gasped.

For months, he'd been on the run, hiding in a hole somewhere while his face and a reward for information leading to his arrest were advertised. The first few weeks, a police car was stationed outside Carissa's house and followed her to college just in case he came back in town to cause trouble. But as time passed, most believed he'd escaped their search radius before the police locked his accounts, deactivated his passport, and distributed his picture. Apparently, he didn't get as far as they thought.

Brian picked up his baseball bat. "You shoulda got that abortion and shut your stupid whore mouth. Now you're gonna die." He tightened his grip on the bat and raised it to hit her. His rage-filled eyes narrowed and focused on hers. She could feel hate radiate from him like a thick fog. It pressed down on her. It was overwhelming, suffocating.

Carissa raised her hands to shield herself and screamed, "Please don't do this! It wasn't my fault! I didn't do anything!"

God help me!

An arrow shot into Brian's chest. He froze, eyes widened, and looked down at the arrow. Another arrow shot through his right arm. He screamed in pain and loosened his grip on the bat. It fell on the cement and clattered behind him. He turned to run away when another arrow struck his right thigh. He cried out, "Ah!" and fell to the cement clutching his leg. One more arrow shot into Brian's left ankle.

Loud voices followed behind his cries as people exited the gas station and ran towards Carissa and Brian. Carissa turned her head and saw someone with a black quiver on his back dart through the bushes.

What the heck? Was that Sean? She heard a buzz from a

motorcycle. *No, a scooter.*

Kyle bolted around the approaching crowd to her side. "Are you okay?"

She righted herself. Her eyes fixed on the bushes. *I can't believe this.*

"Carissa!" Kyle hollered in her ear. "Are you hurt?"

I heard you the first time! She blinked back her tears and pointed at Brian. "He tried to kill me. He's trying to kill me!"

"That guy?" Kyle looked at Brian, mystified. "You must be confused. He's the one that got shot." He turned to where Carissa was looking. "Where's the weirdo that shot him? I'm calling the police." He pulled out his phone.

"NO!" Carissa yelled and slapped the phone out of his hand. "That's Brian Bradshaw! He's the one that tried to kill me."

Kyle glared and picked up his phone. "Obviously, you hit your head. He's the one that just took some arrows for you. He just saved your life."

Are you kidding me right now?!

"Shut up and listen, you idiot!" she yelled, fists balled. She pointed at Brian. "I know what my attacker looks like. That's Brian Bradshaw. He was there when I was *raped!* He bust out my window with a bat, and, and, almost killed me. The person who shot him—" She pointed back to where the person stood. "That person saved my life."

"Rape?" Kyle frowned and looked at Brian. "Really?"

Does it look like I'm joking, you stupid fool?!

"Yes, really!" She yanked the phone out of his hand. "I'm calling the cops. But not on the shooter." She dialed Priest's number, which was burned into her brain after her house was vandalized. "On Brian. Make sure he doesn't go anywhere."

Carissa and Kyle watched Brian. He grunted with agony at his wounds and fumed. Two people ran off to their cars, while three pedestrians and Margaret stood over Brian with their phones. They took pictures and recorded video.

Welcome to the modern world, where he's likely to bleed out before the ambulance gets called. No great loss. But hey, at least we'll have it on video. I'll watch it every night before I go to bed and sleep like a baby.

3

Priest was out of town and pissed about it. "It figures that sorry sack of shh—crap would show up the day Nate and I are in DC. I'm calling Captain Rogers right now."

Police arrived within minutes. An ambulance soon afterward. They lifted Brian on a stretcher, into the ambulance, and drove off with a police escort while uniformed officers questioned Carissa, Kyle, Margaret, and the other witnesses.

"You're telling me you were saved by a person with a bow and arrow?" the officer asked for the third time. "Like that guy on television. Was he wearing leather, too?"

What did I just tell you? Carissa rolled her eyes. "I know it sounds crazy. I'm just telling you what happened. Brian got shot. I turned to see who shot him. Then, the guy ran off."

The officer examined her, looked at Kyle who confirm what she said, and then took some notes. "Did you recognize anything else about the person? Did you get a glimpse of his face? Could you tell his age? Height? Weight?"

"I didn't get much of a look before the person ran off," she lied. "I was a bit overwhelmed by almost being murdered by a psychopath."

"Okay," the officer took more notes. "We might need you to come down to the station and provide us with a description of your hero. Work with the sketch artist. Until then, if you can think of anything else, here's my card." He handed her his business card. "Thank you for your time, Miss. You're free to go."

The officer joined the rest of the officers. Seconds later, they all looked in her direction, then back at him.

Great. Just great.

Kyle ran his hand through his hair and looked around the parking lot. "When you said your life was complicated, I thought it was getting knocked up at seventeen."

She glared at him.

"Don't look at me like that, Cari. I didn't mean it in a bad way. It's not every day a person is saved by a vigilante." *We're calling Sean a vigilante now?* "I just, I'm just saying your life is a lot more complicated than I thought."

So what? My life is more complicated than you thought. Do you want a prize for figuring that out? You want a gold star?

"My mom's here," Carissa said as she saw Mom's car pull into the parking lot. "I'll talk to you later." She walked away.

Mom sprung out of her car and raced towards Carissa. She screamed, "Oh my God!" as she closed the distance. She was a total wreck. Her makeup ran down her face from tears that continued to stream. She wrapped her arms around Carissa and squeezed. "You're okay. You're okay." She kissed Carissa on the forehead and cheeks, and hugged her again. Then she examined her.

I'm anything but okay.

"I nearly lost my mind," Mom continued. "I can't lose you. I can't lose you, too."

Since the attack and during her questioning, Carissa felt numb and irritable. But Mom's presence unlocked a raging storm of emotions that burst to the surface. She settled into Mom's embrace and sobbed.

"He, he, he tried to kill me, Mom," Carissa cried. "I thought I was going to die."

She cried for the next ten minutes. Mom held her the entire time. When the tow truck left with Carissa's car, Mom drove her to the hospital for a quick examination, then home.

4

When they made it home, Mom ordered Chinese—two large shrimp fried rice, one General Tso's chicken, one Hunan beef, one sweet and sour chicken, and six eggrolls—and suggested Carissa take a warm bath to relax until the food arrived. Carissa found no reason to disagree.

She dragged herself upstairs and past Sean's room. She stopped—*It was him at the gas station. I know that was him. It had to be*—took three steps back, and knocked.

Sean opened his door dressed in grey sweat pants and a white tank, his hair disheveled. He looked like he'd just crawled out of bed. Carissa hugged him and inhaled the strong smell of gasoline on his shirt. She teared up, squeezed him, and started to cry.

"Thank you."

"Uh," responded and hugged her back.

"Thank you so much, thank you," Carissa continued, sobbing

more and more. She thanked him until he was embarrassed.

He stood stiff, frozen, until she let go. Then, he grabbed her a box of tissues from his computer table and handed them to her. She wiped her face and blew her nose.

"How did you know?" Sean asked minutes later, after she'd calmed down.

She snorted. "Well, for one, I saw you. And two, you smell like you just robbed a gas station and rolled around in the fuel on your way out."

He sniffed himself. "I had to put some gas in my scooter to get back."

"I heard your scooter drive off. It has a very distinct sound, especially since you made those ridiculous modifications."

He slapped himself in the forehead and then chastised himself. "I knew I should have installed that engine silencer. I know what I'm doing tomorrow."

"You don't have your license," she said. "You could get yourself killed out there or arrested."

Sean tensed. "Did you tell Mom? Does anyone else know?"

"Of course, not," she said. "If I told Mom, she'd freak. For good reason, mind you. Don't you know how much trouble you could get into if you're caught?"

"Well, I did what I needed to do."

Did what you needed to do? "And what exactly was that?" *Save me?*

He let out a long sigh and pointed to the loft. "You should sit down for this."

Okay... She followed him to the loft and sat on the couch. He sat beside her.

"Months ago, Dad asked me if I'd had any unusual dreams," Sean said. Carissa frowned. "Apparently, our family has a history of being in greater touch with the spiritual plane. He says our ancestors used to be sought after as seers, communicators with spirits, and were treated as nobility, second only to royalty."

Carissa rolled her eyes. "Grandma used to tell me the same thing, among other things. We were the secret guard of the royal family. We transformed into mythological werecats. The woman's losing it. Wouldn't surprise me if she said we used to sprout wings and fly."

Sean stared at her. "Dad dreamt of a large, three-headed dragon that devoured little girls and young women."

Get outta here. Her mouth dropped open as she remembered everything Priest and Oliver told her about The Fraternity. Further details were released in a special on primetime news. "No."

"Yes," Sean said. He lowered his head and folded his hands. "On the way to the movie theater, Dad told me he dreamt we were all on a boat in the sea. A storm came and a large wave ripped the boat in half. Dad was swept up in the storm. You were separated from me and Mom on the other half of the boat. And a dragon swooped down from the sky to take you."

Oh my God! You have got to be kidding me, Carissa wanted to say. But Sean's face was beet red. He rapidly blinked away tears and barely held it together. "What else? What else did he say? What happened?"

Sean raised his head to the ceiling, breathed, and closed his eyes. "He said I shot an arrow that slayed the dragon. And when it fell in the water, the storm passed and both halves of the boat met land." He paused and looked at her. "On the beach, a little girl waited for us. She was standing next to a crystal door framed in gold. And when you touched her, the door and the girl disappeared, and your belly expanded."

A little girl!? I'm going to have a little girl?

He closed his eyes again. "That's when the accident happened." He squeezed his fists together and pressed them against his thighs. "His last words were to protect you."

She reached around his shoulder and hugged him. But she was mystified. In all the time she'd spent with Dad, he'd never shown this side of himself. In all her life, not once did he have a spiritual or prophetic conversation with her. Why?

"You slayed the dragon." The hug became a squeeze. "Dad would be proud."

Sean shook his head. "I was sleep." He looked at her. His eyes red and tear-filled. "I was sound asleep. And then, suddenly, I woke up panicked and terrified." He exhaled. "I've never felt so terrified in my life. Even during the crash." He breathed again. "I felt this urgency to go to you and there was this heat, this fire deep down inside of me. I went out the window, got on my scooter, and fired it up to max speed, with the nitrous."

He mimicked driving his scooter with his hands up on the handles. "I didn't get a single red light. I didn't have a single car in my lane in front of me. I had a direct, unhindered, straight path to you. And I got there just in time, just as he raised his bat to hit you."

He lowered his hands. "For a moment, all I could see was the bright lights from the gas station, but then my eyes sharpened on him. And I swear I could see crosshairs on him." He swallowed hard and mimicked holding a bow and arrow. "I shot him right where I needed to. Right at the crosshairs." He fired fake arrows. "Thwip. Thwip. Thwip. Thwip. And then, the panic and terror faded. That heat inside of me cooled and fizzled away. And there I was, completely at peace, standing there in the cold looking at you. When the others approached, I panicked and ran."

This is crazy. This is all so crazy.

He looked her directly in the eye. "I didn't slay the dragon. The Holy Spirit did."

CHAPTER THIRTY-SEVEN

Carissa woke up, turned on the television, and flipped through the channels to the local news. The headline of the day: BRIAN BRADSHAW BEHIND BARS.

Charlie Gay reported, "—manhunt for Brian Bradshaw ended last night with the attempted murder of a local resident. Witnesses at the King's Port gas station say he attacked a pregnant teenager with a baseball bat. She was not injured and is expected to testify against both him and his brother, Kent Bradshaw, next week.

"But this story takes a turn into the strange. Apparently, a mysterious man with a bow and arrow saved the pregnant teen and put Brian Bradshaw in the hospital. We have Joanne live at the scene with the boyfriend of the victim. Go ahead Joanne."

Wait! What? I have a boyfriend?

Charlie Gay's muscular face and salt and pepper hair disappeared, replaced by a thin woman in her mid-twenties. *She looks like she hasn't eaten a full meal in years.* Beside her stood Kyle dressed in a red polo and khakis. His dark hair, normally a shaggy mess—*just the way I like it*—was combed back with a shine. He'd also recently shaved.

He cleaned himself up for the interview? He took the time to shave, and comb back and gel his hair.

"Last night, you were here during the attack," Joanne said. "Tell us your firsthand account of what happened."

The camera zoomed in on Kyle. "I was busy at my register taking care of our customers, because, you know, our customers always come first here at King's Port. And as one of my customers was leaving, she screamed for all of us to come outside. She said someone was being attacked. So, I jumped over the counter." The camera zoomed out as he mimicked his maneuver. "I ran out the front door. That's when we saw an arrow go into Brian Bradshaw's arm. Another one went into his leg. He was trying to get away when he was shot again. I ran forward to get a look at the shooter."

Joanne smirked. "It was very brave of you to put yourself in danger like that."

"That's me," Kyle smiled back, blushed. *Oh, good grief.*

"Tell us," Joanne said. "What did you see?"

"A skinny short guy, or maybe a flat-chested girl. He had short hair, wavy hair. Hard to tell in the dark. Anyway, I tried to catch up with him, but I noticed Carissa's car. Carissa's my girlfriend." *Oh my God!* Joanne glanced at the camera. "Her window was broken. So, I had to make sure she was okay, first."

You just said my name, you dickwad! Now everyone knows it's me!

She changed the channel to another news station and saw the same headline. Changed it again, different but similar headline. Brian's manhunt had become national news. Naturally, his capture would be also. *Son of a—. Kyle's interview is going to end up on national television.*

"Mom!" she yelled and crawled out of bed. She nearly toppled to the floor but caught herself on the end of the bed. Her feet were numb.

Dang it! I can't even walk now? Tears ran down her face. *I'm six months in. How am I supposed to get through the next three?*

She flexed her legs and wiggled toes until she could comfortably feel her feet and put weight on them. *Let's try this again, shall we?* She stood and treaded carefully down the stairs. Mom was in her office focused on a manuscript.

"Mom, have you seen the news?"

The woman had the nerve to chuckle. "Oh yea. I saw it. Watched two of your boyfriend's interviews."

Two!? Two interviews? How many interviews has he had?

"He is *not* my boyfriend."

She chuckled more. "You tell him that?"

"Mom!" Carissa complained. "How can you laugh at a time like this? He just said my name on *live* television. Everyone knows now. They know why Brian attacked me. They know Kent is being arrested for rape. They know that I'm his victim. The entire world is going to know that I'm carrying his rape baby."

Mom sighed, took off her glasses, and looked Carissa straight in the eye. All humor removed from her face. "Don't you ever call her that again. Ever."

"Sorry, I just—" Carissa stopped. "I thought my identity was supposed to be protected. Would be protected. I thought I would have this kid and be able to move on without my life becoming a public spectacle of pity and shame and God knows what else. Now, we have that idiot on the news telling the whole world my name."

Mom smirked and took a sip of her tea.

I fail to see the humor in this.

"Seriously?" Carissa complained. "It's not funny."

Mom put down the tea, stood, and wrapped her arms around Carissa. "My baby." She held Carissa and rubbed her back. "Yes, it is." She smirked. "With all that mousse in his mound of hair, he looks like he has a greased beaver trapped on his head."

Carissa blinked and recalled the image of Kyle on the news. It was true.

"I don't know who gave him the idea to comb his hair that way," Mom continued, "but it is a borderline mullet."

Whether she wanted to or not, Carissa smirked. *My mom is a savage.*

"Half of them probably didn't hear what he said, because they were too busy looking at his head," Mom said. "But even if they all heard him. Even if they all know who you are. It doesn't matter." She looked Carissa in the eye. "It doesn't matter what anyone else says or thinks. What matters most is that you're safe, and the baby's safe, and I love you."

"I love you, too, Mom." They hugged.

Mom let go and smiled, "Now, get cleaned up and ready to go."

"Go where?" *This is Saturday. I've got nothing to do and a whole lot of time to do it.*

"Shopping," Mom said with a coy expression and sat at her

desk. "With Jay."

"Wait. What?" *What do you mean shopping with Jay?* "Why?"

Mom sipped her tea. "He offered to take you shopping. He said he wants to help you get supplies for the baby."

How the hell does he know about the baby on the way? Oh. Of course. The news. Everyone and their great grandmother knows about my pregnancy now.

"When did this happen?"

"He called this morning," Mom said and smirked. "Right after the morning news." *That's still not funny.* "He said he wanted to help out our family, and that he owed you one."

Owes me one? I have no idea what he's talking about. Unless, perhaps, he's trying to make amends. We've barely spoken since I screamed at him months ago.

"You have any idea what he's talking about?" Mom asked.

Maybe.

Carissa shrugged. "I've helped out around the church, tutored a few times with the girls." The Cole sisters and Fiona. "I don't see him much, except when he's wandering the halls of the church and his occasional talks on stage with Pastor Brown."

Mom saw through her. "Right. Now, I'll be straight with you. I know you have a crush on him. You're a minor; he's an adult man. He's also the boyfriend of the detective on your case. So, remember what I've said to you about spending time with older guys." She smirked. "Especially handsome ones."

Carissa glared. *Ugh. We're having this conversation about him? All you're doing is reminding me of the fact that he* rejected *me.*

"Don't worry about it," Carissa said and felt a swell of new tears demanding release. *Stupid hormones.* "He's not interested in me." She tried her best not to sound bitter but did. "He's too infatuated with his detective."

Mom immediately understood. "I see." She sipped her tea. "Well, he'll be here in an hour. So, I'd get a move on it if I were you."

"An hour?" *I can't get ready in an hour! Especially if I'm going out with Jay. I need to wash my hair, spend at least thirty minutes on makeup, and what about my outfit? I didn't prepare anything.*

Mom read her mind. "Just take a shower and throw your hair

in a ponytail. This isn't a date."

And there won't ever be a date with me looking like a heathen! Why didn't you wake me?

"Move, Carissa. Shoo!"

Carissa stormed off. *How could you do this to me? There's not enough time!*

2

An hour later, Jay was at the door in a white dress shirt and black slacks. Carissa wore a yellow sundress and white sandals. It occurred to Carissa that she'd not seen him dress otherwise. Not one time had she seen him wear a pair of jeans, shorts, or tees or polos. Just business casual. He wore comfort shoes, but only because he was on his feet all the time. She'd also rarely seen him sitting down, except at church services, or when she accidentally walked in on him in his office restroom.

He should have locked the door. How was I supposed to know?

"Are you prepared, are you excited, for a shopping *extravaganza* with yours truly?" Jay announced with a dramatic voice that echoed down the hall and across the front lawn.

You know. I could just shut this door in your face and go back to sleep. You have way too much energy right now. Tone it down. I need some coffee to catch up before I'm ready for anything.

"Sure," Carissa shrugged and forced a grin. She looked back at Mom who greeted Jay with a smile and hello.

Jay waved. "Always a pleasure to see you, Misses Boisseau. I'm so excited about tomorrow. I can barely contain myself."

Carissa's eyes narrowed. "What's happening tomorrow?"

There was a thick silence as Mom and Jay exchanged looks. Jay shot her a confused frown. "You didn't tell her?"

Mom looked guilty. "Figured I'd let you two talk first before I told her the good news."

Good news?

"Ooo, double entendre!" Jay raised his hand for a high five. Mom slapped his hand. "Good news, indeed."

What is going on?

"Mom?" Carissa crossed her arms.

He checked his phone. "Well, time and tide wait for no man. Or woman. We better get a move if we're going to make a dent in the hit list."

"Hit list?"

"Oh yea," Jay said. "We're going to assassinate some sales today. Amy happens to be a talented shopper. She put together an extensive shopping itinerary. A very, very extensive one. Because she's awesome."

Carissa glared at Mom. *You hear that, Mom. She's awesome.*

"Well," Mom smiled and waved, "you two have fun." She shut the door.

The hell? I tell you he's infatuated with another woman and you send me out to spend a day with him while he sings her praises? I thought we were on the same team!

"Ready to go?" Jay asked. He pointed at his silver Trinity Echo, a two-doored, electric hatchback with solar panels built into the roof, hood, and trunk top. This was the first time she'd seen his car.

That car is so you.

"Sure," she said and followed him to his car. *But I have no idea how you plan on fitting anything in that.*

3

When Jay passed her the list, she expected to see a few items: a car seat, baby crib, and stroller. When she read the list, she cried until they made it to the store, where Priest waited for them with a moving truck.

First on the list was baby and toddler clothes: onesies, shirts, pants, pajamas, jackets, hats, mittens, socks and shoes. Handwritten on the list, in barely intelligible handwriting, was a baby *Star Trek* uniform, TNG era. *That has to be Jay.*

There was a preordered baby crib waiting for them, as well as a pack-in play, blankets, sheets, and form-fitted, suffocation-free pillows designed specifically for infants. Priest had also preordered a pink car seat with red strawberries all over it.

Why has everyone assumed this baby is going to be a girl?

They bought her a diaper subscription worth a thousand dollars, which allowed her to pick up diapers, or have them delivered, as needed as the baby grew. They bought a portable changing table, bag, baby bathtub, soap, and all the other cleaning and grooming essentials.

And the list went on and on. Baby swings. Stroller. Breast pump. Et cetera. Et cetera. Everything a mother would need.

Seven thousand dollars and four crying spells later, Jay insisted they have an ice cream break, hoping it would stop her from crying.

"I'm sorry," Carissa said and wiped her face with a tissue. "I just, I can't believe you're doing all of this. Both of you. You went through all this trouble and bought me all this stuff. And, I didn't do anything. I haven't done anything for you. And I can't pay you back." She sniffed. "And I don't deserve any of this. I just don't understand. Why are you doing this?"

Jay smiled and handed her two more tissues. "What you have said, that feeling you have right now, the feeling of gratitude and appreciation and thankfulness. That is how I feel about Yeshua. He came so that we could be reconciled with God, because we could not do it on our own. Now, we are not only elevated to God's kingdom, but given an inheritance in the holy places.

"What you are feeling right now, the appreciation and joy and relief, it is but a sample of how salvation tastes. These are only temporary things, material things, that we have given you. There is something greater for you on the horizon."

Carissa listened.

"I want you to know something about me." He hesitated. "Earlier in my life, I had enough to get by, and I had more than I needed, but not as much as a lot of others. And I made some poor choices, choices which led to some very low moments where I barely had anything of my own. But, because of God's grace, I was blessed with more than I could ever imagine. I didn't deserve it. I still don't deserve it. And surely, as long as I live, I can't imagine doing anything that can ever pay Him back, as much as I want to. But that is God's grace." He smiled. "That's God's grace bestowed upon me. That's God's grace bestowed upon you, now, through me. I have been given many things so that I can give many things.

"This is why you have received what you have received today. Because God is good, and his grace has no bounds."

Wow. How do I respond to that? I've heard this before. I heard Gabby say it; Rebecca say it. I've heard the sermons at church. I'm grateful for everything they've said and done, but I don't know

DAKOTA

what he expects of me.

"I'm not sure what to say," Carissa said.

Jay looked at Priest. She rubbed his shoulder and smiled but remained silent.

"Well, you've come to church regularly for several months. We haven't had the time to talk about what you believe, where you stand in your journey toward salvation. Have you accepted Yeshua as your personal Lord and Savior?"

Uh. "I'm not really sure what that means for me."

"It means, the moment you accept Yeshua, wholeheartedly, you are free from the eternal cost and bondage of sin, and upon the gift of the Holy Spirit, about which we have taught you, you will have God with you, within you, guiding you towards betterness for the rest of your life. Your old life will be behind you. Your new life will have begun. You will gradually embody love, joy, peace, patience, kindness, goodness, faithfulness, gentleness, and self-control."

I feel so silly. All this time, they've all been so nice to me. And this is why. This is clearly why. Gabby, Rebecca, Hannah, well, sometimes Hannah, Fiona, and even Sean. He's become this whole other person. A better person. I want that. I want the joy that they have. The peace that they have. I want to have the kindness they have.

"Okay," Carissa said. "Let's do it."

Priest laughed, but Jay watched her intently. She'd never seen that kind of expression on someone's face before. It was as though he was looking straight through her.

"Now, answer me honestly: do you believe in God? Do you believe in Yeshua?"

Do I? Of course, I do, don't I?

"I, I believe someone has had an influence over my friends. I mean, I, I've seen stuff. I've experienced stuff. And, I."

She sighed—*I need to not sound like an idiot*—and put her words together.

"Gabby met me on the bus before things went bad. Had I accepted her invitation to the church party on Halloween." She looked at Priest. "A lot of things would have been different. But I didn't go. And, I was attacked instead. And, I, I felt terrible. The absolute worse I've ever felt in my whole life. And I didn't trust

Val. I didn't want to talk to my other friends. But, here came Gabby again, just being loving and friendly." She looked away.

"I had a difficult choice to make. And, I felt this war inside of me. One part of me wanted it all to be over and was willing to do anything to end it. But, the other side of me, it insisted that I had to go through with it." She closed her eyes. "And I wanted to go through with it, but I also wanted to be done with it all. Just erase it from my mind and life. I was so close to giving up, even if I didn't want to. And then, here comes Gabby again. She spoke to me and convinced me to go through with it. And her and her sisters supported me through this whole thing.

"The others turned their backs on me and stuck with Val. I lost fraudulent friends but made new ones. New ones that were fun, kind, sweet. They wanted to help people and have clean fun. I feel like a better person around them. And when I felt threatened, I was able to reach out to Detectives Priest and Summers." She smiled at Priest. "They supported me in a way I didn't know police did. I mean, Detective Summers painted my house."

Priest grinned. "That he did."

"The Cole family supported me and my family after my dad died. My dad, who was a very distant man, also, to my surprise, happened to be a spiritual man who saw more of what was happening than he'd ever let on. He had a dream about the dragon. I wish he'd told me. But now I understand. This is all part of something bigger, ya know. A bigger plan.

"God sent you to meet me at the coffee shop. He sent Gabby to sit next to me on the bus. And even though I rejected her, I sent Sean to that party and he met Rebecca, and eventually, from dating her he became a Christian. And, God sent Gabby again to support me and swayed me against doing something I would have regretted for the rest of my life. I mean, had I gotten rid of the baby, I never would have called Detectives Priest and Summers. They wouldn't have investigated the Bradshaws. Meaning, they'd still be free, their organization would still be doing awful things, and all those girls who have been rescued would still be victimized.

"And after all that, God then sent someone to save me from Brian when he tried to kill me."

She closed her eyes, breathed and exhaled, and embraced calm. "Yea. I believe. I believe in God. I believe in Yeshua. It all makes sense. This whole time, he's been trying to protect me, redirect me, and bring me to him. He kept calling out to me to come to church through you and the Coles. It all makes sense now."

Priest smiled. "Well, would you like to be baptized with me and your mom, tomorrow?"

So that's what he was so excited about tomorrow. Why didn't she tell me?

"Yea." Carissa smiled. "Let's do it."

CHAPTER THIRTY-EIGHT

Sunday morning, in front of hundreds of people, Carissa stood in a white baptism gown and publicly professed her faith in Yeshua HaMashiach, Jesus the Messiah. Standing in the pool beside her, Gabby took hold of her and said, "Carissa Asami Boisseau, I baptize you in the name of the Father, the Son, and the Holy Spirit." She carefully lowered Carissa in the water, completely submerged, and then raised her. The assembly roared with cheers and applause.

A thought came to her: *The old is dead. The new is born.*

Carissa and Gabby stepped out of the water and were met with fluffy white robes. They watched and waited as Mom stepped into the pool with Sean and stood in the center. After Kate Boisseau professed her faith in Yeshua HaMashiach, Sean said, "Kate Avana Boisseau, I baptize you in the name of the Father, Son, and Holy Spirit." He lowered her into the water, completely submerged, and then raised her. Again, the congregation burst to life with cheers and applause. Sean and Mom stepped out of the water and joined Carissa and Gabby, who fitted them with white robes.

Afterward, Priest and Jay entered the pool. Priest tearfully professed her faith in Yeshua HaMashiach. Afterward, Jay said, "Amy Marie Priest, I baptize you in the name of the Father, Son, and Holy Spirit," and carefully lowered her into the water, completely submerged, and then raised her. For the third time, the crowd roared and cheered and applauded as another child of God was amongst them in the assembly. The two stepped out of the water and were outfitted with fluffy white robes.

"And the angels rejoice," Jay whispered.

They all waited as three more believers were baptized after them. Each time, the hall rumbled as the body of Christ cheered and roared and applauded enthusiastically and joyfully. And when everyone was baptized, the whole assembly prayed, and praised, and dispersed.

CHAPTER THIRTY-NINE

Monday morning, Carissa wrestled with her closet for an hour. It shouldn't be this difficult to choose a dress. It's not like this is a special occasion.

Not special, no, but it was important to choose how she dressed. It was a ridiculous concept that any jury would measure Kent's guilt and her testimony based on how she dressed, especially considering the mountain of evidence the prosecutors had at their disposal. Yet, the Prosecutor, Kayla Sharpe, insisted on certain criteria.

No casual attire. "After all, you are in a court of law."

Don't wear red. Period.

No dresses above the knee. Nothing strapless. No high heels. Don't reveal too much skin or wear too much makeup. "Look as professional as possible, as if you're going in for an interview. But don't dress like your mother. It's best to wear something modern, so it looks like what you'd normally wear. Authenticity is important."

A common assumption people made about rape victims was their provocativeness. Their sexiness. What was she wearing? Was it provocative? How was she behaving? Was she advertising? Did she give him reason to believe she was the kind of girl interest in casual sex? Was she the kind of girl that was into casual sex? In short order, was she a slut or whore? As if that was an excuse. As if rape was acceptable if a person dressed or looked or thought a certain way.

Rape was rape, no matter how she was dressed. If it wasn't

consensual, it was rape. No other criteria need be applied.

Not that she disagreed with sage wisdom to dress modestly.

Grandma Cowden once said, "You can be 'open for business', but only take one customer at a time. Don't show anything you don't want people to see. Don't advertise anything you're not willing to sell." And she firmly amended, "And by that, I mean, conceal your lady parts and don't give anyone any ideas that they're getting sex unless you want to have sex. Don't even think about having sex before you have a wedding ring on that finger."

Then she went on and on about getting knocked up and carrying around a baby while the men lived their lives. Not that she was speaking from experience. Every child grandma ever had, she had with grandpa. Her sister on the other hand.

Goodness. Do I want to get started on Great Aunt Margorie's life?

Carissa sighed and made her final decision: a shoulder-less, pastel green blouse and black, knee-length, pencil skirt.

Shoes? Eyeroll. Basic as basic could get. Black suede wedge pumps.

I wonder if it's going to be cold in the court room.

She grabbed a black, shawl-collared cardigan and rushed downstairs. They were only fifteen minutes late. It was a solid record for her. She was impressed.

Mom was not and said she'd have to speed to make up lost time. "I hope I don't get pulled over."

Oh you know, because I'm in such a rush to go to court, look that smug, piece of crap jerk face in the face and cry my eyes out reliving the worst day of my life to a bunch of strangers who probably couldn't give a crap and are too busy filling out their grocery lists in their heads between witnesses. Just give him the chair. We have the evidence. We have him on video putting a drug in my drink, joking about it, and raping me an hour later. Do we really need me on the stand torturing myself? No.

Sharpe said something about the sixth amendment and confronting accusers. "Also, you're the plaintiff, but have been absent the entire case. The defense has argued this point every day of this case, because they know you don't want to face him. We need you on the stand telling your story. The jury needs to see you protesting what's happened to you."

The evidence alone is damning. Ugh. Whatever. I'll look him straight in the eye and tell him he's garbage.

Sharpe said to address the prosecutor, defense attorney, jury, judge, bailiff, and any other courtroom attendees and workers, but not to look at the accused unless asked to identify her attacker.

I didn't want to look at him anyway. I'll just take a seat, wait to be called, say what needs to be said, and wait to be dismissed. Assuming, I get there before they send the police to find me.

They managed to slip in the courtroom and take their seats one minute before the presiding judge, the Honorable Isaac Abramson, walked in.

2

Defense attorney, Lorenzo Santoro, had the greatest head of hair she'd ever seen. Who ever heard of a lawyer with a ponytail? She hadn't. But it was rich, thick, shiny, and long. He also had the build of an athlete and a strong, tense face. His full lips pursed between each question or statement. *And his eyes!* His eyes looked more gold than brown. She wondered if he modeled full-time and practiced law during his spare time.

But because he was sitting next to Kent, she hoped he accidentally found his way off a cliff.

Sharpe followed Carissa's glare and whispered, "He has an eight-year-old daughter from his first ex-wife." She took a sip of her coffee. "I've been in his shoes. This is not an easy case for anyone sitting at the defendant's table."

Yea. I can only imagine.

"You ready?" Sharpe asked.

No. Never. "Sure."

"Your Honor," Sharpe said and stood. "I'd like to call Carissa Boisseau to the stand."

Kent leant forward, past Santoro, to scold her with his eyes.

Him. Her eyes narrowed. *It's all your fault, you know. You saw me. You asked around about me. You invited me to the party. You got me drunk. You drugged me. You raped me. You impregnated me. You recorded and mocked me and left me naked and alone. You convinced Val to say bad things about me. You threatened me and tried to get me to have an abortion. You, or someone you know, trashed my house. It's all your fault. Don't you dare look at me like I'm the bad one here.*

She stared at him longer than she'd intended, receiving an elbow nudge from Sharpe before standing from her chair. The eyes of every juror were on her, measuring. She swallowed hard and walked slowly towards the stand. She'd never been in a court room in her life. Now she was about to take the stand in a rape case. So why did she feel like the guilty one? Why did she feel like, if she said the wrong thing or made the wrong move, suddenly everything would come crashing down on top of her head? Why did she feel like if she said the wrong thing, hesitated at the wrong moment, stumbled on any word, it would be used against her and a rapist would go free?

How could he? They have video of him raping me. They have video of him saying terrible things. They show him putting a tranquilizer in my drink for God's sake. How could he go free? Why am I even here? Why do they need me to say a word when the video speaks for itself? The evidence speaks for itself. They even had Val on the stand yesterday spilling her guts to be removed from any blame as an accomplice. What else did they need?

Her eyes teared up. She wanted to cry. That was the last thing she needed. That was the one thing Sharpe said she had to have complete control over: when she chose to cry. She was allowed to cry. She was expected to cry. She needed to cry. But she had to cry at the right time. The jurors needed tears. She just had to cry when sympathy was necessary. Not before she made it on the stand.

Why was she coaching me like I'd said anything but the truth?

Perhaps because, in the court of law, it was about what could be proven, not the truth.

You have your proof. I don't want to be here!

Deep breaths, Carissa. Deep, deep breaths.

What felt like a cool breeze blew through her chest and settled on her heart. Suddenly, there was calm. She couldn't explain why but felt at peace. Her tears took a vacation. Her mood lightened. She gasped.

It's going to be okay. Everything was going to be okay.

At the stand, the bailiff approached her and motioned for her to put her left hand on the bible. She did so.

"Please raise your right hand," the bailiff requested. She raised her hand. "Do you solemnly swear that you will tell the truth, the whole truth, and nothing but the truth, so help you God?"

"Yes."

"Please, take a seat."

She sat.

Sharpe measured Carissa, then said, "For the past few days, our defense has asked: Where is the plaintiff? I want to say, as a woman, it is hard to stand and look your attacker in the eye. It is hard to go over, again, and again, and again, how you were brutalized. How you were touched without consent and violated. It is a challenge not to feel intimidated, threatened, scared, and even feel partly guilty, blaming yourself for something that was done to you. The worst part is living that moment again and again. Because that's what happens every time you tell someone about it. Every time you talk about it to your family, friends, police officers, lawyers, jurors. Every single time you talk about it, you relive it. I've spared my client the struggle of living what we saw in that video, again, until now. Because now, it is so important that you hear from her, what happened. It's important that you see a person, flesh and blood. Not a person in a video. Here she is, a young pregnant teenager, scared about the rest of her life, in the same room with the young man that had his way with her."

Sharpe paused, took a deep breath, and looked at Carissa. "Okay, Carissa. From the beginning. Tell us what happened."

Carissa took a deep breath and exhaled. *You got this.* She made eye contact with Sharpe, the twelve jurors, various others in the courtroom, and told her story.

3

Two days later, Carissa was back in the courtroom. The jury spent thirty minutes deliberating the case before they walked in, single file, and took their seats. The courtroom was still, quiet as they waited for the foreman to deliver the verdict.

It was a unanimous guilty verdict to every charge pointed against Kent Bradshaw. *Yes!* Half of the courtroom cheered and clapped their hands. The judge smacked his gavel several times and told the courtroom to quiet down. This was a court of law not a football game.

Court was adjourned until sentencing the following day.

The following day, Kent Bradshaw was sentenced to twenty-five years without parole.

EPILOGUE

It was Summer, on a Saturday. The sun beamed in Carissa's eyes as she lay on the beach. She felt like a beached whale: couldn't move and was thirsty as life. But not being in school, in class, in a courtroom, or hounded by the thirsty media, felt like a small slice of heaven. She soaked in the rays, belly covered, and smiled.

She was free. At least for now, she was truly free.

In two weeks, responsibility would consume her life. She still had no idea how to be a mother. There were brief opportunities to babysit her cousins when she was younger. The age difference wasn't so great that she'd seen them as babies and not been one still herself.

Women in her church small group encouraged her to babysit. As much as she liked the idea of watching her own child, other people's children were of no interest to her.

Your children are precious, but not enough for me to willingly let them try my nerves.

Her pregnant friends from college were both three years older than her. They'd recently had their babies and encouraged her to hang with them. We could be a newborn trifecta, they said. The idea: their babies would grow together and be friends. Now this, she could go along with. She'd watch them like a hawk and learn from all their successes and failures. The babies would be old enough that the girls knew what they were talking about from experience when hers was around.

She smiled. *Dakota.* She still couldn't believe she was having a little girl. *Better believe it. I already feel like I'm going to pop.*

"I think I stepped on a jellyfish," a girl said as she walked by.

She leaned forward and shielded her eyes to see who it was. That was when she felt a popping sensation and sudden increase in pressure in her lower abdomen. She looked down as her bathing suit darkened and leaked water.

Did I just piss myself, again? AGAIN! This is getting embarrassing. She groaned and tried not to cry but could feel the tears swelling. *I didn't even feel the urge. It just came. Now I have to stroll out of here sly as a thief in the night to not look like an idiot.*

She grabbed her towel and wrapped herself. *At least I have a towel to hide the damage.*

"Going back inside?" Mom asked, leaned back in her chair under a large umbrella. Her attention shifted from a new science fiction novel about an extradimensional temple that existed on a plane between life and death. "Are you overheating?"

Should I tell her? Carissa wondered as she turned to her right. She shifted her weight on all fours and steadied herself slowly on her two feet. She was pleased with herself for sticking to a strict squats regiment. It allowed her to support herself. Who thought standing would be so taxing?

Mom's eyes shifted down to the sand. She saw a small patch of wet sand. She smiled, "It's okay, Carissa. There's so much pressure on your bladder with the baby. I peed myself at least five times while I was carrying you."

Lovely. We're the pee-pee family. The family of women who piss themselves. How encouraging!

She felt more pressure and clutched her belly. She grimaced.

Mom watched her, blinked rapidly, and shot out of her chair. "Okay, well, I know that expression," she said, materializing beside Carissa like a freaking magician.

I wish you moved this fast when I asked you to order Chinese yesterday. I dang near starved. She had to wait a whole ten minutes. *It felt like a lifetime.*

"I don't know." Carissa felt another pang of pressure in her pelvis. "There was this pop, and then the pee." She rubbed her back. "My lower back feels like, uh, Shiatzu." Mom smirked. "I just started feeling pressure down here. Is this what I think it is?"

Mom smiled, "Well, I don't want to assume, but that might be amniotic fluid running down your leg, and it looks like you're feeling contractions. This might be it, kiddo." Her eyes widened. "I can't believe this. I'm going to be a grandmother at forty."

Carissa frowned. "A little less about you, and a little more about me, right now, Mom? It could pop out at any moment."

"There are worse places to have a child, Carissa," Mom said. She waved at Sean and Rebecca and hurriedly urged them over.

The two rushed.

"You're having her now?!" Rebecca asked, panic in her tone. "I thought you had a week or two."

Yea, well, I'm sorry the person coming out of my vagina isn't adhering to the schedule.

"So, did I," Carissa pointed at her abdomen. She felt another wave of pressure and grimaced. "Can we go?"

"Absolutely," Mom said. "Sean, take care of our stuff. Bring it inside. We're going to the hospital."

Sean frowned. "I can't come?"

Mom glared. "Of course, after you collect our things. Oh, and tell Gabby and Hannah we're off to the hospital." She put her arm under Carissa's and supported her weight as they rushed to the car. "Becca, could you grab her flip-flops?"

Rebecca waved the flip-flops as she rushed in front of them. "Already got them. Do you want me to get a head start and start the car or are we taking an ambulance?"

"I'll drive," Mom said. "The hospital's right there. We could walk there under different circumstances. But please, get it started."

Rebecca handed her the flip-flops in exchange for the keys in Mom's purse, then ran ahead.

"Are you ready?" Mom asked, this time with a serious face. "How do you feel?"

I'm not ready for this, but it's a bit late to have a change of heart, isn't it?

"Scared, but okay." Carissa sought comfort in Mom's eyes and found love. Everything was going to be alright.

AUTHOR'S NOTE

First and foremost, all glory goes to the Most High God, my Heavenly Father, Yahweh, Adonai Elohim, who has honored and blessed me with the talents I used to write this novel. I wouldn't have written or finished this without Him. My best words came from Him. He is my guide, my life, my everything.

I wrote this novel, before continuing my sci-fi series, due to a calling. The story came to me and wouldn't leave me alone in a way only writers understand. There was a sense of urgency.

DAKOTA's purpose is to bring notice to things that should not be and inspire hope, ponder meaning, and offer possibilities after pain, tragedy, and suffering. I have a deep love and respect for women and hope nothing portrayed in this novel suggests otherwise.

I don't make characters perfect. They have flaws, fears, and can be casually cruel, rotten to their core. Some are portrayed as such but will mature into impressive people. One such character is Valerie Caulfield. I look forward to writing her in the future as someone who went through a complicated growth period and blossomed. Thus, is the human condition.

Special thanks to Anna Read. I appreciate your willingness to read my work, as well as your continued moral support.

Thank you, Jackie, for your friendship and companionship. Thank you, Twitter writing community, for your support and advice.

I wish you the best, Readers. Thank you for your time.

www.ingramcontent.com/pod-product-compliance
Lightning Source LLC
Chambersburg PA
CBHW030612100526
44584CB00036B/930